AWARD WINNING SOUTHERN RECIPES

A collection of favorite recipes
presented by
The Junior League of Pine Bluff, Inc.
Pine Bluff, Arkansas

IN ASSOCIATION WITH
AUGUST HOUSE PUBLISHERS, INC.
Little Rock, Arkansas

First Edition	July, 1976	10,000 copies
Second Edition	January, 1977	10,000 copies
Third Edition	January, 1978	20,000 copies
Fourth Edition	November, 1980	20,000 copies
Fifth Edition	March, 1982	30,000 copies
Sixth Edition	May, 1985	20,000 copies
Seventh Edition	October, 1990	15,000 copies
Eighth Edition	April, 1994	15,000 copies

The purpose of the Junior League is exclusively educational and charitable and is to promote voluntarism; to develop the potential of its members for voluntary participation in community affairs; and to demonstrate the effectiveness of trained volunteers. The proceeds from the sale of Southern Accent *will be used for community projects approved or sponsored by the Junior League of Pine Bluff.*

ISBN 0-87483-376-0

Published by
August House Publishers, Inc.
201 E. Markham Street
Little Rock, Arkansas 72201
800-284-8784

Acknowledgements

To all who spent their time in any way toward the assembly and completion of Southern Accent, we say a big southern thank you.

Committee

Mrs. Walter M. Simpson

Mrs. J. Wayne Buckley

Ms. Bess McFadden Sanders

Mrs. Kenneth Baim

Mrs. Ronald D. Blankenship

Mrs. Ted Drake

Mrs. Martin G. Gilbert

Mrs. Dan Harrelson

Mrs. Royce O. Johnson, Jr.

Mrs. Richard Milwee

Mrs. Robert Nixon, sustaining advisor

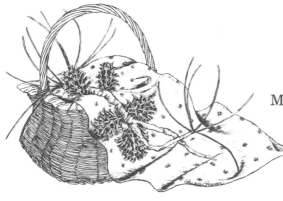

Mrs. Henry W. Gregory, Jr.
Twig Drawings

Larry Jernigan
Photography

Mrs. Steve Allison
Mrs. Michael Neuner
Cover Design

CONTENTS

Southern Accent recipes are presented to you after careful testing and evaluation.

Trade names of products are used only when necessary.

PINE BLUFF

Pine Bluff and Jefferson County's first residents were various Indian tribes who inhabited the lower Mississippi Valley. Among these tribes were the Quapaw, whose famous chief Saracen made his home here and wove his life into the region's history. Early records list many other illustrious names as visitors to the area. DeSoto, LaSalle and DeTonti are thought to have traversed these lands in their explorations of the New World.

Due to an Arkansas River flood in 1819, an early settler named Joseph Bonne set out in search of higher ground. After eight days of canoeing, he found a high bluff with towering pine trees on the west banks of the river. Here Bonne started his settlement which later was to become Pine Bluff and the seat of justice of Jefferson County.

The pine forested hills to the west and north of Pine Bluff drop suddenly away on the southern slope to form the gateway to the delta. These rich alluvial plains formed by the Mississippi and Arkansas River Valleys provide the finest type of soils for the support of a large and varied agricultural system.

In the years since its humble beginning, Pine Bluff and its trade area have progressed from a strictly agricultural economy to one balanced between agriculture and industry. As the first port city on the Arkansas River navigation channel, Pine Bluff has indeed become a tower of golden opportunity and a living reminder of its eighteenth century American heritage.

It is through these lines that we are proud to share with you the ideas and recipes that grace our tables and exemplify Pine Bluff's tradition of warm, southern hospitality.

A LITE ACCENT

Medical research shows that healthy eating plays a large part in creating a healthy lifestyle. Getting started on the path to healthy eating need not be difficult. We hope the following information will allow you to accomplish positive lifestyle changes.

FATS

When frying or sautéeing, use nonstick sprays in place of vegetable oil. (Olive oil, butter and vegetable flavors are available)

Season vegetables with lemon juice or herbs instead of butter or high calorie sauces.

Cut calories by using lite mayonnaise and diet dressings.

Substitute tofu for sour cream in cooked recipes. Replace sour cream with yogurt in non-cooked recipes.

DAIRY

Look for low-fat versions of cottage cheese, cream cheese, yogurt, buttermilk, butter, and margarine in most supermarkets.

Use 2% or ½% milk in place of whole milk.

Reduce fat content in recipes by using part skim or low-fat cheeses.

Replace one whole egg with ¼ cup egg substitute.

BREADS/CEREALS

Serve whole-grain products. (Breads, pasta, crackers, flour and cereals)

Select cereals with less than 2 grams of fat and/or 8 grams of sugar per serving.

Combine half white flour and half whole-grain flour for pastry recipes.

MEATS/PROTEINS

Substitute ground turkey or chicken for ground beef when possible.

Chill all broths and stocks before using; when cold, skim off fat.

Always select lean cuts of meat: tenderloin, loin chops, ground round and round steak. Broil, grill and roast if possible.

MENUS

HUNT BREAKFAST

Bloody Bulls

Basted Doves
with
Hot Pepper Jelly

Creamed Eggs

Mushroom Casserole

Sally Lunn Bread

Pumpkin Bread

Steamed Ginger Pudding
with
Lemon Sauce

For a wonderful Hunt Table—use your (or borrow a pair of) stuffed pheasants . . . Stand them on a bed of two limbs and mosses (alive and dry) either in a fighting position or standing guard over your Basted Doves. Also, try using pottery, stoneware, pewter, or china with hunt motifs for your table appointments.

ELEGANT SEATED DINNER

Easy & Elegant Artichoke Soup
Broiled Pompano with Chives
Champagne Ice Sorbet
Quail Pontalba
Carrot Souffle
Coral Cauliflower
Johnita's Rolls
Fresh Mushroom Salad
Marquise de Chocolat

For a successful dinner party, make sure you hire extra help—otherwise you will spend your entire evening working and not enjoying your guests.

Don't be afraid to have a dinner for twelve just because you have only eight place settings of any one china, silver or crystal pattern. There is no reason not to have two or more patterns on a table.

Experiment! Find out what looks good. In fact, one of the most beautiful tables I have ever seen was a table for twelve with twelve different floral patterns. Be brave and daring—your guests will be delighted!

AFTERNOON TEA

(High Tea!)

Café Brulot   *Hot Tea*

Hot Mulled Wine

Apricot Bars

Ribbon Cakes

Junior Sesame Club Cookies

Cheese Finger Souffles

Sandwich Loaf

Adriennes Delight

Clam-filled Cream Puffs

Cucumber Tea Sandwiches

This is the time to get out your grandmother's lace doilies and linens and finally use the sterling tea strainer that your great-aunt gave you as a wedding present. As far as decorations for afternoon tea . . . Too Much Is Never Enough!

DESSERT PARTY

Papa Perdue's Favorite Angel Pie

*French Baked Custard
with Caramel*

Grand Marnier Sponge Cake

Pecan Slices

Spiced Nuts

*Old Fashioned Custard Ice Cream
with*

Coffee Walnut Sauce   *or*   *Hot Fudge Sauce*

A dessert party is a good time to show off your creative abilities. Emphasize each item on your menu by using exciting serving pieces, silver baskets or porcelain pieces. Stagger the heights of each offering using cake stands and plateaus.

Decorate the serving table with sugar-frosted fruits and greenery. (Dip the fruit in egg whites first and then coat with granulated sugar.) For an extra touch, tuck fresh flowers (perhaps orchids!) into your fruit arrangement.

BRUNCH AND MORE

Sauteed Chicken Livers
Ham Rolls
French Egg Casserole
Cheese Fritters
Baked Bananas
Little Hot Biscuits
Fresh Apple Muffins
Fig Preserves
Apricot Fried Pies
Apple Dumplings

Milk Punch   *Tomato Juice Cocktail*

Brunch is a good time to get away from traditional flower arrangements. Try showing off your collections of whatever items you might collect, such as—paperweights, enamelled boxes, birds, toy soldiers, or antique dolls.

You can arrange your items along your serving table with flowers. A note of caution: If you perchance collect antique jewelry or diamonds—be sure you know and trust all of your guests!

BUFFET SUPPER

Picatta Slices of Pork Tenderloin
Seafood Newburg
Brown Rice
Broccoli Timbales
Stuffed Tomatoes with Hot Vegetables
Congealed Asparagus Salad
French Bread
Aunt Lucy's Fresh Coconut Cake

For convenience sake, one can take your folded napkins, place the flatware inside and roll the napkin. Tie them with an attractive ribbon and slide a short-stemmed fresh flower in the bow.

For decorations, try using pots of flowering plants in pretty jardenieres or wrapped in exquisite fabric tied with the same ribbons as those around the napkins, for a coordinated casual look.

CHILDREN'S TEA PARTY

Instant Spiced Tea
Punch Slush
Gumdrop Cookies
Peanut Butter Sticks
Mother's Famous "Little Fellows"
Potato Chip Cookies
Cinnamon Bars

Use your demi-tasse cups for the children. This is a good time for the little ones to learn to use and begin to appreciate fine china.

Make a centerpiece from an assortment of stuffed animals or antique toys.

COCKTAIL PARTY

Breaded Veal Cutlets
(cut into "fingers" to dip with)
Blender Hollandaise Sauce
Eggplant Caviar or Caviar Pie
Chicken Bits
Asparagus Goodies
Hot Cheese Balls
Terrine of Chicken Livers
Toasted Cheese Rounds
Stuffed Cucumbers
Coffee

Lemon Bars Deluxe   *Forgotten Cookies*
Millionaires

Cocktail parties can be a wonderful way to entertain or a great disaster. Make sure if you are inviting guests for cocktail food at dinner time to be certain your menu is heavy enough to suffice as an evening meal and finish it off with coffee and sweets. Don't expect your guests to jockey for position at the table. Supply them with plates, let them make their choices and move on to visit. (This also saves rug spots.)

LADIES LUNCHEON

Hot Madrilene
Chicken Mousse
Ginger Cheese Salad Bowl
Quick Herb Rolls
Peaches Royale

For some reason it seems that Ladies' Luncheons tend to occur in numbers exceeding the capacity of most family dining tables. Don't feel that everyone needs to be in the same room—spread your guests around your home with tables of four draped with two squares of coordinating prints and centered with small arrangements of bright spring flowers.

One can have the plates already arranged and placed on the table while your guests sip their soup that you have served from a tureen into coffee cups as they enter your home.

SUMMER SUPPER

Cream of Avocado Soup
Picnic Cornish Hen
Horseradish Mold
Creole Zucchini
Elizabeth Young Bread   Poached Pears with Custard Sauce

A Summer Supper is a perfect time to put away the family silver and bring out all of your collections of pottery, crockery, baskets, copper and depression glass.

Keep your flowers simple—daisies are perfect.

For a tablecloth, try using grandmother's quilts or even natural canvas, with your food being the brightest colors on the table.

HOLIDAY DINNER

(As guests arrive)
Vodka Wassail Bowl
Mushrooms Tapenade
Braunschweiger Pate

Coquilles St. Jacques
Hot Kettle Soup
Crown of Pork with Plum Sauce
Brandied Cranberries
Scalloped Asparagus and Artichokes
Potatoes in Orange Shells
Pickled Squash
Cucumber Cream Salad
Ethiopian Honey Bread
Miss Bess's Eggnog Pudding Dessert
Buche de Noel

Kahlua   *Creme de Menthe*

Divinity

For a festive touch add plenty of candles placed on flat mirrors with holly and fresh flowers. Salt makes a good snowy look. When adding garnish to food remember that small flowers can be very elegant and during the holidays evergreens with desserts are appropriate.

THE DEXTER HARDING RESTORATION
Pine Street and Freeway
This small house is actually the original three rooms of the old Dexter Harding home that was located on the south bank of Harding Lake about East 11th Avenue and Texas Street. Harding, as a veteran of the War of 1812, received a land grant of 160 acres from the United States government. This grant was located in the central states and Harding exchanged it for 160 acres on the southern border of the little town of Pine Bluff. He moved here in the spring of 1850 and built the small house. As a Bicentennial project, the Jefferson County History Commission, using materials from the old house as much as possible, completed the restoration in 1974. The Commission now operates the house as a tourist center and mini-museum.

HOT ARTICHOKE SPREAD

1 (14 oz.) can artichoke hearts,
  drained and chopped
1 cup Hellmann's Mayonnaise

1 cup Parmesan cheese
Garlic powder to taste

Mix all ingredients and put into ramekin. Heat at 350° for 20 minutes or until mixture bubbles. Serve with Waverly Crackers for spreading or Doritoes for dipping!
Serves 6.

Mrs. Robert Deal

Delicious!

CURRY VEGETABLE DIP

1 cup mayonnaise
2 Tbsp. Durkee's
1 tsp. celery seed
½ tsp. Worcestershire sauce
Dash of Tabasco

¼ garlic clove, crushed
1 Tbsp. horseradish
1 tsp. curry powder
1 tsp. seasoning salt

Combine all ingredients. Use with an array of raw vegetables (celery, carrots, turnips, cucumber, cauliflower or zucchini). This keeps well in the refrigerator and is easily doubled.
Yields 1 cup.

Mrs. John E. Caruthers, Sr.

GUACAMOLE

2 large avocados, mashed
3 Tbsp. lemon juice
1 small onion, chopped fine
1 small green chili
1 tomato, peeled, seeded
  and chopped

1 tsp. Worcestershire sauce
Dash cayenne
½ tsp. coriander
Salt to taste
1 garlic clove, crushed
3 Tbsp. mayonnaise

Mix all ingredients together, but do not blend. Serve with chips or raw vegetables.

Mrs. M. Stanley Cook, Jr.

Let carrots come to room temperature before trying to slice lengthwise. When plunged in water and refrigerated, crispness returns.

Mrs. Mark A. Shelton, III

CHIPPED BEEF DIP

1 (8 oz.) pkg. cream cheese,
  softened
1 (3 oz.) pkg. chipped beef,
  chopped
2 tsp. horseradish

Dash of Worcestershire sauce
2 drops Tabasco
½ cup mayonnaise
½ cup pecans
1 tsp. grated onion

To cream cheese add the remaining ingredients. Serve with chips.
Yields 2 cups.

Mrs. Don Callaway
Columbus, Mississippi

HOT CHIPPED BEEF

2 (8 oz.) pkgs. cream cheese
4 Tbsp. milk
6 oz. chipped beef, chopped
1 cup sour cream
½ cup chopped green pepper

2 Tbsp. onion flakes
½ tsp. pepper
½ tsp. garlic salt
1 cup chopped pecans, sautéed
  in 4 Tbsp. butter

Soften cream cheese and mix with all ingredients except pecans. Put in ramekin, top with pecans and bake at 350° for 20 minutes. Spread on crackers.
Serves 12.

Mrs. Royce O. Johnson

ASPARAGUS GOODIES

½ cup butter
4 oz. blue cheese
14 slices bread,
  (thin sliced)

1 (14½ oz.) can asparagus
  spears
Butter
Parmesan cheese

Cream together butter and blue cheese. Remove crust from bread and roll each slice flat with a rolling pin. Spread cheese mixture on bread. Drain asparagus on paper towels. Then place 1 spear of asparagus on the bread and roll up in jelly roll fashion. Place on cookie sheet, side by side, seam down. Drizzle with melted butter and sprinkle generously with Parmesan cheese. Bake at 350°, 15 to 20 minutes or until browned and crisp. Cut in thirds and serve hot.

These can be made the day before and refrigerated, but wait until baking time to put on the butter and Parmesan cheese.
Yields 42.

Mrs. Robert Alexander
Columbia, South Carolina

ARTICHOKE HORS D'OEUVRES

1 (14 oz.) can artichoke hearts,
  drained and minced
1 cup Progresso Bread Crumbs
2 Tbsp. olive oil
Juice of ½ lemon

2 Tbsp. Parmesan cheese
2 eggs
2 garlic cloves, crushed
Extra bread crumbs and
  Parmesan cheese

Combine all ingredients except extra bread crumbs and Parmesan cheese and roll into 1 inch balls. Roll in remaining bread crumbs and Parmesan cheese. Freeze if you wish. Preheat oven to 350° and bake for 15 minutes or until warm all through.

Mrs. Jonathan Pardee
Atlanta, Georgia

STUFFED CUCUMBERS

2 medium cucumbers
2 (3 oz.) pkgs. cream cheese,
  softened
2 Tbsp. onion, finely minced

2 Tbsp. green pepper, finely minced
Paprika to taste
Worcestershire sauce to taste
½ cup pecans, finely chopped

Peel cucumbers. Cut in half *across* the cucumber. (This makes for easier handling.) Scoop out inside with apple corer and salt the cavity. Mix remaining ingredients and *tightly* stuff into the cucumbers. Wrap with foil and refrigerate overnight. Slice when ready to serve.

Mrs. Walter C. Eden

ANTIPASTO

1 pt. jar Giardiniera, well
  drained (this is a mixture
  of pickled vegetables)
12 oz. artichoke hearts in oil,
  undrained
1 (8 oz.) can whole button
  mushrooms, well drained

2 (8 oz.) cans tomato sauce
1 (7½ oz.) can water-pack
  tuna, well drained
4 Tbsp. white wine vinegar
1 (8 oz.) can pitted ripe
  olives, drained and halved

Combine all ingredients, mixing well. Place in a covered dish; refrigerate at least 24 hours. Mix well once or twice while it marinates. (This will keep indefinitely.) Serve with small slices of pumpernickel and rye bread. *Serves 14-20.*

Mrs. John G. Lile

Enticing "quickie" to precede Italian or Spanish entrée!

MUSHROOMS TAPENADE

4 Tbsp. capers
6 anchovy filets, drained
1 cup olive oil, good quality
¼ cup lemon juice

Freshly ground black pepper
1 lb. small fresh mushrooms
1 hard boiled egg (optional)
Romaine lettuce (optional)

Rinse 2 tablespoons of capers and dry on paper towels. Mash along with anchovies in a bowl. Put in blender, add oil, lemon juice and pepper; blend. Allow sauce to stand, covered, 4 hours. Remove stems and clean mushrooms with damp paper towel. Pour sauce over mushrooms and let stand a few hours. Drain and serve from bowl with remaining rinsed capers sprinkled over.

May also be served as a first course on individual salad plates by placing several mushrooms on bed of Romaine lettuce. Pour over additional tablespoon of sauce. Sprinkle with capers.

Or for a lovely salad; slice mushrooms and break Romaine lettuce into bite size pieces, toss with sauce and garnish each salad with finely chopped egg.
Serves 6.

Mrs. R. Teryl Brooks, Jr.

GRILLED MUSHROOMS
STUFFED WITH MINCED CLAMS

4½ oz. cream cheese
1 (7 oz.) can minced clams,
  drained
1 small onion, minced
Salt to taste

Freshly ground black pepper
1 egg, beaten
60 medium mushroom caps
½ cup bread crumbs
¾ cup butter

Mix clams, onion, salt and lots of pepper with softened cream cheese. Add enough of the egg to give a semi-firm texture. Pile mixture into mushrooms, sprinkle with bread crumbs and dot with ½ cup of the butter. Heat remaining ¼ cup butter in a shallow oven-proof pan, arrange the mushrooms in the pan and simmer over medium heat for about 4 minutes. Run mushrooms under broiler, at a 4 inch distance, and grill until puffed and golden. Serve immediately!
Yields 60.

Mrs. Robert Nixon

STUFFED FRESH MUSHROOMS

1 lb. fresh mushrooms
Lemon
1 (8 oz.) pkg. cream cheese

Minced onion
Chopped chives
Salt

Remove stems from mushrooms and wipe mushroom caps with damp cloth. Rub caps with lemon juice. Chop stems into softened cream cheese seasoned with minced onion, chopped chives and salt. Fill mushroom caps with mixture. Serve cold.
Serves 10.

Mrs. Royce O. Johnson, Jr.

PICKLED MUSHROOMS

3 (8 oz.) cans button mushrooms
1¼ cups Progresso Wine Vinegar
2 pkgs. Good Seasons Italian
    Dressing Mix
4 tsp. chopped green onion

2½ tsp. dehydrated
    parsley flakes
1 tsp. Worcestershire sauce
Dash Tabasco

Drain mushrooms. Combine the remaining ingredients in a bowl and let sit about 15 minutes until the parsley and green onions soften. Add mushrooms and marinate overnight. This will last for several weeks in the refrigerator if tightly covered.

Mrs. Donald W. Stone

EGGPLANT CAVIAR

1 medium eggplant
1 large onion, chopped
1 green pepper, chopped
2 large garlic cloves,
    crushed
½ cup olive oil
2 tomatoes

2 tsp. salt
1 tsp. pepper
¼ tsp. cayenne pepper
¼ tsp. Worcestershire sauce
1 tsp. Accent
2 Tbsp. dry white wine

Punch several holes in eggplant and place in a shallow pan with a small amount of water. Bake at 400° until soft (about 1 hour). Sauté onion, green pepper, and garlic in olive oil until tender (but not brown). Peel and chop eggplant and tomatoes. Add to sautéed mixture. Add salt, pepper, cayenne pepper, Worcestershire sauce and Accent. Add wine. Mix everything thoroughly and continue to cook gently until the mixture is fairly thick. Cool, then place in refrigerator. Serve chilled with rye crackers.

Mrs. Carter Stovall
Stovall, Mississippi

HOT PEANUTS

2 Tbsp. crushed red pepper
3 Tbsp. olive oil
4 garlic cloves
1 (12 oz.) can cocktail peanuts

1 (12 oz.) can Spanish peanuts
1 tsp. salt
1 tsp. chili powder

Heat red pepper in oil for 1 minute. Crush garlic and add to oil. Add peanuts. Cook over medium heat for 5 minutes. Remove from heat; add salt and chili powder. Drain on paper towels.

Mrs. J. William Sanders

PEANUT BUTTER STICKS

6 slices of thin sliced white
  bread, crust removed
½ cup smooth peanut butter

¼ cup cooking oil
2/3 cup graham cracker crumbs

Cut each slice of bread into 5 sticks. Place sticks on cookie sheet and toast in oven at 250° for 30 minutes or until browned. Mix peanut butter and Wesson Oil in top of double boiler. Dip each stick into the peanut butter mixture and coat with graham cracker crumbs. Let cool completely and store in tins.
Yields 30.

Mrs. Sidney Mann

Excellent for brunch!

CHEESE STRAWS

3½ cups flour
Pinch of salt
2-3 tsp. cayenne pepper

1½ cups margarine, cold
1 lb. Cracker Barrel
  Sharp Cheese, grated fine

Sift together dry ingredients in a large bowl. Dice margarine and work into flour mixture with hands until consistency of coarse meal. Add cheese and work (again with hands) until all cheese is well blended. Form into 4 balls. Roll out each ball, ⅛ inch thick, on a floured board. Cut into straws (½ x 4 inches) using a 4 inch french fry cutter. Place, not touching each other, on an ungreased cookie sheet. Bake at 375° for 10 minutes. Watch, for they burn easily. Store in tins when *completely* cool.
Yields 300 straws.

Mrs. William Ursery

CHEESE FINGER SOUFFLES

3 loaves day old bread	Melted margarine
2 eggs	3 (8 oz.) cans Parmesan
1½ cups milk	cheese

Remove crust from bread. Combine eggs with milk. Put melted margarine into 1 bowl, cheese in another. Dip one slice bread in egg mixture and place it between 2 slices of *dry* bread. Cut into 4 pieces. Dip each piece in margarine, then in cheese, leaving bottom side clean. Place this uncheesed side *down* on cookie sheet. Bake 350° for 10 minutes. Allow at least 3 for each person.
Yields about 80.

Mrs. Joe Campbell
Mena, Arkansas

Excellent with a salad luncheon.

TOASTED CHEESE ROUNDS

¾ cup Hellmann's Mayonnaise	Dash Worcestershire sauce
½ cup onion, finely chopped	Dash salt and pepper
1/3 cup Parmesan cheese	Rye bread rounds

Mix all ingredients except rye bread rounds. Spread mixture on rye rounds and place under broiler until bubbling. Serve hot.
Yields 36.

Mrs. W. E. Ayres

ONION ROUNDS

1 loaf white bread	Tabasco to taste
1 (8 oz.) pkg. cream cheese	2 onions, finely
1 (4 oz.) pkg. blue cheese	minced
1 cup Hellmann's Mayonnaise	

Cut bread with 1 inch round cutter. Soften cream cheese and mix with blue cheese, ¼ cup mayonnaise and Tabasco. Spread mixture on rounds of bread. Sprinkle onions on top of mixture. Top with mayonnaise. Bake at 400° for 15 minutes or until brown and puffy. Serve hot.
Yields 60.

Mrs. James S. Rogers

LITTLE PIZZAS

6 English muffins
10 oz. Kraft Cheddar Cheese
1 cup chopped green onion
   tops
1 cup Hellmann's Mayonnaise

½ tsp. salt
½ tsp. curry powder
1 (2¼ oz.) can pitted
   chopped ripe olives

Toast muffins which have been sliced in halves. Grate cheese; mix with remaining ingredients. Spread each half with mixture and cut into 4 pieces. Broil until cheese melts. Can be frozen.
Yields 48.

Mrs. Ed McCain
Memphis, Tennessee

SALAMI PUFF

1 (8 oz.) pkg. Pillsbury Crescent
   Rolls (8)

1 (12 oz.) salami

Unroll dough and pinch holes together. Wrap dough completely around salami and seal all edges. Bake puff at 400° until well browned. Serve hot. Serve with mustard for dipping.

Mrs. Herb Krauss
Roslyn, New York

HOT CHEESE BALLS

1 cup grated American cheese
6 drops Worcestershire sauce
½ cup bread crumbs (not
   commercial)

1 egg, well beaten
Dash cayenne pepper
½ tsp. salt
Rolled cracker crumbs

Mix all ingredients except cracker crumbs. Shape into balls the size of a walnut. Roll balls into cracker crumbs. Fry in deep hot fat. Serve immediately.

Mrs. E. T. Phillips

CHILI DIP

1 (6 oz.) roll jalapeno
   cheese

8 oz. Velveeta Cheese
1 (15 oz.) can chili without beans

Melt cheese in double boiler. Add chili. Serve hot with Fritoes.
Serves 6.

Mrs. Lloyd Sivils

MEXICAN CHEESE DIP

4 Tbsp. margarine, melted
4 Tbsp. flour
1 heaping tsp. dry mustard
1 tsp. chili powder
1 tsp. cumin
1 tsp. pepper juice from
    jalapeno pepper

1 Tbsp. ketchup
2 cups milk
½ jalapeno pepper, chopped
8 oz. American cheese
1 garlic clove, crushed

On low heat stir margarine and flour together. Remove from heat and add mustard, chili powder, cumin, pepper juice and ketchup. Return to heat and add milk, jalapeno pepper, cheese and garlic. Cook over low heat until thick.
Yields 2½ cups.

Mrs. Don Moore
Wabbaseka, Arkansas

CHEESE AND BACON SPREAD

1 lb. Hoffman's Super Sharp
    Soft Cheddar Cheese
16 slices crisp bacon,
    crumbled
1 tsp. salt

12 green onions, chopped
    (include tops)
1 cup slivered almonds,
    toasted
2 cups mayonnaise

Grate cheese. Mix all ingredients in order given. Serve on Ritz Crackers or Sesame Melba Rounds. Keeps for days.

Mrs. J. Wayne Buckley

Also good cooked in scrambled eggs.

SAM CHEESMAN CHEESE BALL

8 oz. blue cheese
1 (8 oz.) jar Cheez Whiz
8 oz. sharp Cheddar cheese,
    grated
1 (8 oz.) pkg. cream cheese
8 oz. Velveeta Cheese
½ cup parsley flakes

3 Tbsp. Worcestershire sauce
3 Tbsp. chili powder
2 tsp. garlic powder
1 cup chopped pecans
2-3 tsp. cayenne pepper
1 tsp. onion flakes

In a large mixing bowl let cheeses stand until room temperature. Add remaining ingredients. Mix well. Shape cheese as desired and roll in parsley flakes, chili powder or both.
Yields 4 medium balls.

Dr. Sam Cheesman

AUNT RUTH'S CHEESE BALL

2 (8 oz.) pkgs. cream cheese
½ lb. Roquefort or blue
    cheese

3 Tbsp. dried or frozen chives
2 garlic cloves
1 cup chopped pecans

Mix softened cheeses and chives. Place in bowl and add the uncut garlic cloves. Cover and leave in refrigerator overnight or longer. Two hours before serving, remove garlic, shape into ball and roll in chopped pecans. Keep in refrigerator until ready to serve.
Serves 10-12.

Mrs. C. D. Allison, Jr.

SHRIMP AND CHEESE BALL

2 (8 oz.) pkgs. cream cheese
4 oz. sharp cheese, grated
2 Tbsp. Worcestershire sauce
1 tsp. garlic salt

1 Tbsp. Durkee's Salad
    Dressing
1 Tbsp. lemon juice
1 (4½ oz.) can flaked shrimp

Have ingredients at room temperature; mix. Add cream if necessary to blend well. Form into a ball and chill overnight. Serve with crackers.

Mrs. Travis Creed

ADRIENNE'S DELIGHT

4 (3 oz.) pkgs. cream cheese
½ cup butter
½ cup sour cream
½ cup sugar
1 Tbsp. gelatin
¼ cup cold water

½ cup white raisins
1 cup slivered almonds,
    toasted
Grated rind of two lemons
Saltine crackers

Let cream cheese, butter and sour cream come to room temperature. Cream well and add sugar. Soften gelatin in cold water, dissolve over hot water and add to cream cheese mixture. Then add raisins, almonds and lemon rind. Put in a quart mold, refrigerate. When firm, unmold and serve with saltine crackers. (This can be frozen after unmolding.)

Can be used as a dessert tray; unmold and serve with assorted fruits and crackers. Or without the gelatin, spread mixture on dark bread for tea sandwiches.

Mrs. Thermon Smith
Little Rock, Arkansas

Great for an afternoon sherry party!

GINA'S CREPES FOR STUFFING

You can cook the crepes in a small flat griddle such as the Danes use with six or seven round depressions or any crepe pan.

6 Tbsp. flour
2 eggs
½ cup milk
6 Tbsp. cold water
Pinch of salt
1½ Tbsp. unsalted butter,
    melted and cooled
1 Tbsp. fresh parsley,
    chopped

1 Tbsp. fresh chives (frozen
    or freeze dried)
1 Tbsp. fresh tarragon or
    ½ Tbsp. dried tarragon
1 Tbsp. fresh chervil or
    ½ Tbsp. dried chervil
3 Tbsp. melted, clarified
    butter or oleo

Mix the flour and eggs. Mix milk, water and salt together and gradually stir in. Slowly add the melted unsalted butter. This may be slightly lumpy. Now stir in the herbs. Heat the griddle until a drop of water just sizzles, brush it with the clarified butter and drop just enough batter into the depressions to fill them. Cook one side and then the other. Stack them off when done. They may be filled with liver paté or various other items. Tri-corner them with toothpicks.

Dr. James T. Rhyne

COCKTAIL MEATBALLS

Meatballs:
4 lbs. ground beef
4 cups bread crumbs
¼ cup chopped onion
½ tsp. dry mustard
3 tsp. salt

¼ tsp. pepper
2 eggs, beaten
2/3 cup milk
¼ cup lard or drippings

Sauce:
1 cup brown sugar
2 tsp. ginger
1 tsp. salt
¼ cup cornstarch

2 cups pineapple juice
1 cup vinegar
¼ cup soy sauce

Mix beef, crumbs, onion, mustard, salt, pepper, eggs and milk. Form into balls. Brown in lard and drain on paper towels. Pour off drippings. In same skillet mix sugar, ginger, salt and cornstarch. Add pineapple juice, vinegar and soy sauce. Cook and stew until thick. Put sauce in chafing dish and add meatballs. Serve hot with toothpicks.
Yields 150.

Mrs. Lloyd Tanner

SWEET AND SOUR RIBS

¼ cup peanut oil
2-3 lbs. country style ribs
    (Have butcher cut into thirds
    and trim excess fat.)
½ medium onion, chopped
½ medium green pepper,
    chopped
1 cup unsweetened pineapple
    juice
¾ cup cider vinegar

¾ cup water
2 Tbsp. ketchup
1 Tbsp. soy sauce
¼ tsp. Worcestershire sauce
½ tsp. ginger
1 medium garlic clove, crushed
½ cup brown sugar,
    firmly packed
2 Tbsp. cornstarch

Heat peanut oil in skillet, brown ribs well. Drain. Blend in blender other ingredients until onion and green pepper are no longer in chunks. Add to drained ribs; bring to boil and simmer over *low* heat until sauce has almost disappeared, stirring occasionally to prevent ribs burning—about 3 hours. *Serves 8.*

Mrs. Harry A. Metcalf

CHICKEN BITS

Chicken wing joints
Butter, melted

Progresso Bread Crumbs

Dip the chicken pieces in the melted butter and then drop them into a medium sized baggie containing bread crumbs. Place on foil lined cookie sheet. Bake at 350° for 1 hour, turning once after 30 minutes. Serve hot.

Mrs. Floyd Bridger, Jr.
Jonesboro, Arkansas

BRAUNSCHWEIGER PATE

1 lb. Braunschweiger sausage
2 pkgs. Frito Green Onion Dip
    Mix
1 tsp. sugar
2 tsp. water

1 Tbsp. garlic spread
2 (3 oz.) pkgs. cream cheese
1 Tbsp. milk
⅛ tsp. hot pepper sauce

Mash sausage. Combine dip mix, sugar and water. Add to sausage and blend thoroughly. Form mixture into an igloo shape. Place on serving plate and chill. Melt garlic spread. Whip softened cream cheese with milk and hot pepper sauce. Blend in melted garlic spread. Spread cheese mixture over sausage. Chill. Serve with crackers or Melba rounds. *Serves 10.*

Mrs. Hollis L. Hughes

LIVER MOUSSE

1 Tbsp. gelatin
2 (10½ oz.) cans consommé
2 (3 oz.) pkg. cream cheese,
  softened

1 (8 oz.) pkg. Braunschweiger
Juice of ½ lemon
Scraped onion

Soak gelatin in one can cold consommé. Add this to the other can of heated consommé. Mix with cream cheese, Braunschweiger, lemon juice and onion. Pour into ring mold. Refrigerate until set. Serve with Melba toast, wheat thins, etc.

Mrs. James S. Rogers

CHICKEN LIVER MOLD

½ cup butter
1 lb. chicken livers
1 large onion, chopped

Salt and pepper
2 Tbsp. Worcestershire sauce
6 hard boiled eggs, chopped

Put butter, livers and ¼ cup onion in a saucepan. Cook slowly, covered, until livers are no longer pink. Remove from heat, salt and pepper to taste and add Worcestershire sauce. Add hard boiled eggs and the rest of the onion. Mash with potato masher until well mixed. Put in mold and chill until set. Serve with crackers.

Mrs. Dick Falk
Jonesboro, Arkansas

TERRINE OF CHICKEN LIVERS

1 lb. chicken livers
2 Tbsp. butter
3 eggs
2 Tbsp. whipping cream
2 Tbsp. milk
½ tsp. salt
¼ tsp. freshly ground pepper

3-4 drops Tabasco
½-1 tsp. Worcestershire sauce
1 tsp. prepared wine mustard
1 tsp. savory
6 sprigs parsley, chopped
6 spring onions, chopped
½ cup chopped mushrooms

Remove any connective tissue from chicken livers and blanch for five minutes. Force through a sieve or food mill. Melt butter (do not burn). Cool. Beat eggs with cream and milk. Add butter gradually, beating all the time. Add salt, pepper, Tabasco, Worcestershire, mustard and savory. Stir in the chicken livers and work with fork until as smooth as possible. The smoother the better, but it does take a while. Add parsley, onions and mushrooms. Pack lightly, but firmly enough to hold together, into a buttered terrine or casserole. Cover tightly. Place in pan containing ½ inch hot water. Bake at 350° for 20 minutes or until firm. Cool and refrigerate. Unmold and serve.

Mrs. Sanborn Wilkins

SMOKED CATFISH PATE

2 cups smoked catfish meat, flaked
2 (8 oz.) pkgs. cream cheese, softened
2 dashes Worcestershire sauce
1 egg sized onion, grated
½ tsp. Accent
¼ tsp. smoke salt
2 dashes Tabasco
Chopped pecans

Mix all ingredients except pecans and form 2 logs in plastic wrap. Chill. Then roll in chopped pecans.

Look for smoked catfish at specialty shops. Or, if you have a smoker, you can smoke your own whole catfish.
Serves 12.

Jack Slenker
Memphis, Tennessee

CAVIAR PIE

6 hard-boiled eggs
Sour cream or mayonnaise
1 (8 oz.) pkg. cream cheese
1 small onion, minced
7 oz. caviar
Thin lemon slices

Chop eggs, reserving one yolk for decoration. Mix eggs with enough sour cream to have an egg salad mixture. Spread this on the bottom of a pie plate. Soften cream cheese and add enough sour cream to make it spreadable. Spread this on top of egg mixture. Sprinkle onion over cream cheese. Spread caviar over onion. Decorate top by sprinkling the yolk (which has been pressed through a sieve) over the caviar, and adding lemon slices. Chill. Serve with pumpernickel bread.

Mrs. Herb Krauss
Roslyn, New York

CLAM DIP

2 (3 oz.) pkgs. cream cheese
1 (7½ oz.) can minced clams, drained
1 Tbsp. lemon juice
1 tsp. Worcestershire sauce
½ tsp. salt
¼ tsp. Accent
⅛ tsp. pepper
⅛ tsp. onion salt

Let cream cheese soften at room temperature. Mix all ingredients. If too thick add ½ cup sour cream or a few drops of milk. Serve with Fritoes or crackers.
Serves 8-10.

Mrs. Harry L. Ryburn

CLAM FILLED CREAM PUFFS

Miniature Cream Puffs:
1 cup water   *1 cup flour*
½ cup butter   *4 eggs*

Pour water into a saucepan, add butter and bring to a boil. Reduce heat; add flour (all at once), stirring rapidly. Cook and stir until mixture thickens and leaves sides of pan, about 1 minute. Remove from heat. Add eggs, one at a time, beating thoroughly after each addition. Beat until mixture looks satiny and breaks off when spoon is raised. Drop by teaspoonfuls onto an ungreased cookie sheet. Bake at 425° for about 20-25 minutes. Cool.

Clam Filling:
2 (7½ oz.) cans minced clams,   *1 cup Parmesan cheese,*
  drained   *grated*
1 lb. cooked ham, chopped   *1/3 cup finely chopped onion*
1 cup sour cream   *2 tsp. anchovy paste*
1 cup mayonnaise   *½ tsp. pepper*

Combine all ingredients and set aside. Split puffs in seam and fill with clam filling. Refrigerate until serving time. Heat in 350° oven until warm. *Yields 90.*

Mrs. E. L. Hutchison

HOT CRAB CANAPE PIE

1 lb. lump crabmeat   *½ tsp. Accent*
1 Tbsp. horseradish   *Dash Tabasco*
½ (2¼ oz.) bottle capers,   *2 cups Hellmann's Mayonnaise*
  drained   *¾ cup grated sharp cheese*
1 tsp. grated lemon rind

Mix together all ingredients except cheese. Add more seasonings if you desire (grated onion, Worcestershire sauce, garlic, herbs or whatever your "taste" desires). Put into a 10 inch pyrex pie plate. Spread out and cover top with cheese. Heat at 350° about 20-25 minutes or until mixture bubbles. Run under broiler for a *few* minutes until cheese is lightly browned. Place pie plate in center of tray encircled with crackers. *Serves 10.*

Mrs. H. Moody Caruthers

Popcorn will pop better if you leave it in the freezer for a full 24 hours before using.

CRABMEAT CANAPES

½ cup butter
1 (5 oz.) jar Cheez Whiz
½ tsp. garlic salt

½ tsp. seasoned salt
1 (6½ oz.) can crabmeat
6 English muffins

Soften butter and cheese at room temperature. Blend cheese, butter and salts. Add crabmeat to mixture. Cut muffins in half. Spread mixture on muffins. Freeze until ready to use. When ready, thaw for 10 minutes. Slice into eighths. Place on cookie sheet and broil for 2 minutes or until bubbly or bake at 400° for 12 minutes.
Yields 96.

Mrs. Jack A. McNulty

SEAFOOD SPREAD

1 (8 oz.) pkg. cream cheese
Juice of one lemon
1 lb. boiled shrimp, coarsely
    ground
1 lb. crabmeat

5 green onions, minced
Mayonnaise
Hot sauce
Worcestershire sauce
Salt and pepper

Soften cream cheese with lemon juice. Add shrimp, crabmeat and green onions to cream cheese mixture. Add enough mayonnaise to give a consistency for spreading on crackers. Season with hot sauce, Worcestershire sauce, salt and pepper. Better if made 8 hours ahead of time.
Serves 15.

Mrs. Lewis Crow
Little Rock, Arkansas

MARINATED SHRIMP, MUSHROOMS, ARTICHOKES

3 pkgs. Good Seasons Salad
    Dressing Mix (1 Blue Cheese,
    1 Italian and 1 Cheese
    Garlic)
1 (2¼ oz.) bottle capers, drained
2-3 onions, thinly sliced
    and ringed

2-3 lbs. fresh shrimp,
    cooked and peeled
2 (4 oz.) cans whole button
    mushrooms, drained
2 (14 oz.) cans tiny artichoke
    hearts, drained
½-1 tsp. salt

Prepare salad dressings according to package directions, omitting the water and replacing with vinegar. (Slightly less oil may be used.) Put dressings and remaining ingredients in a deep bowl and marinate overnight. Stir occasionally, very carefully to avoid breaking artichoke hearts.
Serves 20.

Mrs. Dan Harrelson

SHRIMP MOLD

1 lb. cooked shrimp, cut into
   tiny pieces (save a few
   whole shrimp for decoration)
1 (8 oz.) pkg. cream cheese,
   softened
3 Tbsp. mayonnaise
3 dashes Tabasco

1 tsp. Worcestershire sauce
A few capers plus some
   of the juice
1 Tbsp. Heinz India Relish
Salt to taste
Parsley for decoration
Crackers or Melba toast

Mix all ingredients except parsley and crackers. (May season to taste with other seasonings such as scraped onion, lemon juice, Accent and Beau Monde seasoning.) Pile mixture into oiled mold or one lined with plastic wrap. Chill in refrigerator until serving time. Unmold, decorate with whole shrimp and surround with parsley. Serve with assorted crackers or Melba toast.
Serves 12-15.

Mrs. C. J. Maupin

FIRESIDE SHRIMP DIP

½ lb. sharp Cheddar cheese
1 (4½ oz.) can shrimp
1 small onion

1 cup mayonnaise
1 tsp. Worcestershire sauce

Grate first three ingredients. Then mix with mayonnaise and Worcestershire sauce. Serve as spread on crackers or as dip with Fritoes.
Serves 6.

Mrs. Paul Lewey

MINI QUICHES

2 (8 oz.) pkgs. refrigerated
   butterflake rolls (12)
24 large shrimp, boiled
1 egg, beaten
½ cup half and half cream

1 Tbsp. brandy
½ tsp. salt
Dash pepper
1½ oz. Gruyere or
   Swiss cheese

Grease 2 muffin pans (1¾ inch for 24). Separate each roll in half; press into muffin pans to make shell. Place one shrimp into each shell. Combine egg, cream, brandy, salt and pepper. Divide evenly among shells, using about 2 teaspoons for each. Slice cheese into 24 small triangles and place one atop each appetizer. Bake at 375° for 10-12 minutes or until golden.
Yields 24.

Can be cooled, wrapped in foil and frozen. When ready to serve, place frozen quiches on a baking sheet in 375° oven for 10-12 minutes.

Mrs. Robert H. Holmes

CINDI'S SHRIMP DIP

1 (8 oz.) pkg. cream cheese
1 (10 oz.) can Rotel Tomatoes
   and Green Chilies

Garlic salt to taste
Ground cominos to taste
1 (4½ oz.) can shrimp, drained

Soften cream cheese. Start with half the can of Rotel, and mix it into cheese with mixer. Add more to taste. Add garlic salt, cominos and shrimp. Refrigerate until chilled. Serve with Doritoes. Can omit shrimp.
Serves 6.

Mrs. Richard M. Perdue

NANCY'S OYSTER DIP

1 medium onion, chopped
2 cups celery, chopped
1 bunch parsley, chopped
Tops of a few green onions,
   chopped
2 Tbsp. butter

½ tsp. red pepper
¼ tsp. dry mustard
2 pts. oysters
1 egg, slightly beaten
1 cup seasoned bread crumbs

Sauté onion, celery, parsley and green onions in butter. Add red pepper and dry mustard. Drain oysters on paper towels and mince. Add oysters to sautéed mixture. Cook until oysters curl. Add egg and bread crumbs; mix well. Put into casserole and bake at 350° for 10 minutes. Put in chafing dish and serve with Melba rounds.
Serves 8.

Mrs. Don Callaway
Columbus, Mississippi

SMOKED OYSTER ROLL

2 (8 oz.) pkgs. cream cheese
3 Tbsp. mayonnaise
2 tsp. Worcestershire sauce
Tabasco to taste

1 Tbsp. grated onion
½ tsp. salt
Garlic salt (optional)
2 (3¾ oz.) cans smoked oysters

Let cream cheese soften; add mayonnaise and seasonings. Mix well. Spread mixture about ½ inch thick on aluminum foil. Mash oysters with fork. Spread oysters on top of cheese mixture. Let chill in refrigerator. Take out and roll, as for a jelly roll, using a knife to start it. Refrigerate 24 hours. Set out 15-20 minutes before serving. Serve on Melba toast or crackers.
Serves 12-14.

Mrs. Charles Scarbrough

BEVERAGES

TOMATO JUICE COCKTAIL

1 (46 oz.) can tomato juice
Juice of 6 limes
2 tsp. salt

8 dashes Tabasco
2 tsp. ground cumin
Lime slices

Mix all ingredients except lime slices. Put mixture in a pitcher and float the lime slices. Guests can serve this over ice or add vodka.

Mrs. J. Wayne Buckley

BLOODY BULL

1½ (10½ oz.) cans consommé
24 oz. tomato juice
3 Tbsp. lemon juice
2 Tbsp. Worcestershire
  sauce

1 tsp. celery salt
1 tsp. garlic salt
2 tsp. salt
Tabasco to taste
9 oz. vodka

Mix all ingredients and serve over ice.
Yields 6 drinks.

Mrs. Richard Milwee

MARTHA ROWLAND'S PEACH FUZZ

3 ripe, soft peaches, seeded
  but not peeled
1 (6 oz.) can pink lemonade

6 oz. vodka
Ice cubes to fill
  blender

Put the first three ingredients in the blender. Add ice cubes to the liquid mark. Be sure ice cubes are cracked before adding to blender. (One whack with the back of a small kitchen spoon is sufficient.) Blend until ice is crushed. Can be served immediately, but is better when put in freezer in a plastic container for three or four hours before serving. Can be made three or four days in advance and stored in freezer. Just before serving, put into a mixing bowl and stir with a wooden spoon. Serve with a short straw. This is not just a ladies' drink.
Yields 6 servings.

Mrs. Robert S. Cherry

MILK PUNCH

1 cup cold milk
¾ oz. créme de cocoa

1½ oz. bourbon

Stir or shake with ice.
Yields 1 drink.

Mrs. James F. Clark
El Dorado, Arkansas

VODKA MINT

1 (6 oz.) can frozen limeade
6 oz. vodka
17 mint leaves

Lime slices to garnish
Mint leaves to garnish

Put limeade, vodka and 17 mint leaves in blender and fill with crushed ice.
Blend at highest speed. Put in stemmed glasses and top each glass with a
thin slice of lime and two mint leaves.

Mrs. Don Huge
Houston, Texas

Great summer drink. This is good before lunch.

BRANDY JULEP

1 tsp. sugar
1 Tbsp. water
12 sprigs mint
4 oz. brandy

Fresh pineapple or other fresh
  fruit
½ oz. light rum

In an old fashion glass, dissolve sugar with water and add 6 sprigs of
mint. Muddle and pack with crushed ice. Stir and add brandy. Decorate
with a piece of pineapple or other fresh fruit and remaining mint leaves.
Add rum. Place in freezer for about ½ hour to frost glass.
Yields 1 drink.

Mrs. Robert H. Holmes

FROZEN DAIQUIRIS

½ (6 oz.) can frozen
  limeade

2 cans rum
Maraschino cherries

Blend limeade and rum in blender filled with crushed ice. Pile into glasses
and top with maraschino cherry.

Dick Falk
Jonesboro, Arkansas

CAJUN COFFEE

3 cups strong black coffee
6 Tbsp. molasses
1 cup whipping cream

Grated nutmeg
Dark rum, optional

Mix coffee and molasses, stirring to dissolve. Heat to very hot, but not boiling. Divide mixture among 6 cups or heat-proof glasses. Whip cream and top each cup with a swirl. Sprinkle with nutmeg. Sip coffee mixture through the cream. Do not stir coffee and cream together before drinking.

If desired, 1 tablespoon dark rum can be placed in each cup before filling with hot coffee mixture. To make coffee quickly, use 2 tablespoons freeze-dried coffee mix with 3 cups boiling water.
Serves 6.

Mrs. John Garrison

CAFE BRULOT

30 whole cloves
2 sticks cinnamon
35 lumps sugar
½ lemon, sliced thin

½ orange, sliced thin
1 cup brandy
1 qt. strong drip coffee

Combine spices, sugar, lemon and orange slices in a *warm* chafing dish. Warm the brandy and add to spices. Heat, then flame brandy stirring constantly until sugar melts. Add coffee slowly, continuing to stir until flame dies out. Serve in brulot or demi-tasse cups.
Serves 12.

Mrs. R. Teryl Brooks, Jr.

SPANISH COFFEE

1 tsp. nutmeg
1 scant tsp. brown sugar
¾ oz. brandy
¾ oz. triple sec

¾ oz. Tia Maria
6 oz. hot coffee
Whipping cream, whipped

Dampen rim of an 8 ounce stemmed glass and dip it into a mixture of nutmeg and brown sugar. In glass pour brandy, triple sec, Tia Maria and fill with coffee. Top with whipped cream.
Yields 1 drink.

Michael Small
Memphis, Tennessee

COFFEE PUNCH

½ of 2 oz. jar instant coffee
  (more if desired stronger)
1 cup sugar
2 cups hot water

4 qts. milk
1 gal. carton vanilla ice cream
1 gal. carton chocolate ice cream

Blend first three ingredients and cool. Soften ice cream slightly before adding to mixture.
Serves 45.

Mrs. W. L. McColgan

SCRATCH EGGNOG

12 eggs, separated
1 pt. whipping cream
¾ cup sugar
Bourbon to taste

Vanilla ice cream,
  optional
Nutmeg

Beat egg whites. Whip cream. Fold egg whites and cream together. Beat egg yolks, gradually adding sugar. Add bourbon to egg yolks and sugar mixture. Combine all. Vanilla ice cream may be added if desired. Sprinkle nutmeg on top.
Serves 15.

Mrs. Talbot Benton

CREME de MENTHE

½ gal. vanilla ice cream
2 oz. creme de menthe

1 oz. white creme de cocoa
1 oz. triple sec

Put all ingredients in blender and blend. Serve in stemmed glasses.
Serves 4-6.

Mrs. Lunsford W. Bridges

KAHLUA

4 cups sugar
4 cups water
1 (2 oz.) bottle instant
  coffee

1 fifth bourbon or vodka
  (100 proof)
1 vanilla bean, split

Boil sugar and water for 5 minutes. Slowly add instant coffee. Bring to a good boil, then cool. Add bourbon or vodka. Put mixture into ½ gallon jug with bean. Age 3 weeks. Remove bean from bottle.

Mrs. W. B. Banker
New Orleans, Louisiana

HOT CHOCOLATE MIX

1 (8 qt. size) instant non-fat
   dry milk
1 (2 lb.) can Quik

1 (1 lb.) bottle Coffee-mate
   Creamer
2 cups powdered sugar

Mix ingredients and store in refrigerator. When ready to serve, place 3
heaping tablespoons of mix in cup. Pour boiling water over and stir.
Yield 5 qts.

Mrs. Bryan Harris
Crossett, Arkansas

INSTANT SPICED TEA

2 (9 oz.) jars Tang
1 (3 oz.) pkg. Twist
   Lemonade Mix
1¼ cups sugar

¾ cup instant tea
1 tsp. cinnamon
1 tsp. ground cloves
1 tsp. nutmeg

Mix all ingredients. Put in covered container. Use 2 to 3 teaspoons per cup
with boiling water.

Mrs. Jack Cockrum

MEXICAN PUNCH

2 cups sugar
2½ qts. brewed tea
2 cups pineapple juice

2 cups orange juice
1 cup lemon juice

Add sugar to hot tea. Stir until dissolved. Add juices. Serve cold.

Mrs. W. O. Pearcy, Jr.

PUNCH SLUSH

2 cups sugar
4 cups water
1 (12 oz.) can frozen
   lemonade
1 (12 oz.) can frozen
   orange juice

20 oz. pineapple juice
3 mashed bananas (blender
   or potato masher)
4 qts. 7-Up
2 tsp. lemon juice

Boil sugar in water until dissolved. Cool and add the next 4 ingredients.
Mix well and freeze in 2 containers. Thaw 2 hours before using. In punch
bowl pour 7-Up and lemon juice over frozen mixture to serve.

Mrs. Leonard Dunn

Great for children's parties!

HOT MULLED WINE

1½ cups boiling water
½ cup sugar
½ lemon, sliced
½ orange, sliced
3 sticks cinnamon

3 whole cloves
1 fifth burgundy
½ cup brandy, optional
Cinnamon sticks
Nutmeg

Combine boiling water, sugar, lemon, orange, cinnamon and cloves. Stir until sugar dissolves. Add burgundy and brandy. Do not boil. Strain. Serve hot in a mug with cinnamon stick as stirrer and with a sprinkling of nutmeg on top. The longer you simmer this, the better it is.
Serves 5.

Mrs. Robert H. Holmes

SANGRIA

1 lemon
1 lime
1 orange
¼ cup sugar
4 oz. dark rum or brandy

1 bottle red wine
2 Tbsp. lemon juice
1 qt. sparkling water
  (optional)

Slice lemon, lime and orange very thin and cover with sugar and rum. Allow to sit at least 1 hour at room temperature. Add wine and lemon juice. Refrigerate several hours. Serve over ice. If you want a wine punch, add sparkling water when ready to serve. For a white sangria, use a white wine such as sauterne and white fruits such as grapes, pears and peaches.

Mrs. Clarence Roberts, III

VODKA WASSAIL BOWL

Whole cloves
3 large oranges
1 gal. apple juice
½ cup lemon juice

10 (2") cinnamon sticks
2 cups vodka
1 cup brandy

Preheat oven to 350°. Insert cloves ½ inch apart in unpeeled oranges. Place oranges in shallow pan and bake uncovered for 30 minutes.

Heat apple juice in large kettle until bubbles form around edge. Add lemon juice, cinnamon sticks and baked oranges. Heat 30 minutes, covered, over low heat. Remove from heat and add vodka and brandy. Pour into punch bowl and serve warm.
Yields 36 (4 oz.) servings.

Mrs. Clyde Tracy

JEFFERSON COUNTY PUNCH

2½ lbs. sugar
2 qts. water
2 qts. lemon juice

3 fifths gold label rum
5 fifths sauterne wine
1 pt. Apple Jack Brandy

Make a simple syrup by boiling together the sugar and water for 1-2 minutes and then chill. Add lemon juice, rum, sauterne and brandy. Fill 12 quart containers or 3 gallon containers full.

12 qts. champagne   24 qts. club soda

To each of the 12 quart containers add 1 quart champagne and 2 quarts club soda. Temper punch bowl; add *dry* ice. Pour punch over this. This will keep the punch cold and make it smoke.
Serves 100.

Mrs. Louise Scott May

OPA'S PUNCH

1 bottle claret wine
2 bottles dry white wine
1 (20 oz.) can pineapple
   tidbits with juice

1 (2 oz.) jar maraschino
   cherries without juice
1 bottle champagne

Mix all ingredients together except champagne which is added just before serving. May also add 1 fifth of vodka. Serve in punch bowl over ice.

Mrs. Thomas F. Stobaugh

Ice Molds: Freeze water or fruit juice, and fruit in a large bowl or ring mold. Unmold and float in punch bowl.

PAMPLEMOUSSE PUNCH

1 block of ice
1 qt. grapefruit juice,
   unsweetened
1 qt. cranberry juice,
   unsweetened

1 fifth gin or vodka
   or whiskey
1 qt. lemon or lime
   flavored carbonated soda
Candied orange peel sticks

Float a block of ice in a holiday punch bowl. Add juices. Add gin (or vodka or whiskey). Mix carbonated soda in last. Pour into stemmed wine glasses, garnish each with a stick of candied orange peel.
Serves 30.

Mrs. Martin G. Gilbert

DAIQUIRI PUNCH

2 qts. lemon juice
4 qts. lime juice
4 qts. orange juice

1 lb. powdered sugar
4 qts. club soda
2½ fifths light rum

Mix fruit juices and sugar. Refrigerate several hours. Add soda and rum. Pour over ice in bowl.
Serves 75.

Mrs. Dottie Levi

CHAMPAGNE PUNCH

1½ qts. sauterne
2 qts. champagne

1 qt. club soda

Pour all ingredients over ice in bowl and mix. Serve immediately.

Mrs. Dottie Levi

SORBET (CHAMPAGNE ICE)

½ cup sugar
1 cup water
Grated rind of ½ lemon

Juice of lemon
2 cups champagne or
  medium dry white wine

Make the sorbet one day before it is to be served. Bring sugar and water to a boil and allow to cool thoroughly. Add the grated lemon rind, the lemon juice and the wine. Pour mixture into a bowl and put in freezer. Stir a few times after it has begun to freeze. Remove from freezer 10 to 15 minutes before serving. May be served in parfait glasses or unmolded whole and surrounded with fruits. May also be flavored with other fruit juices, and served as a dessert. The French serve this between entrées to "cleanse the palate."

Mrs. Edward E. Brown

CRANBERRY ICE

1 qt. cranberries
2 cups water

Juice of 1 1/3 lemons
2 cups sugar

Cook cranberries in 1 cup of water until all pop. Stir in another cup of water and run through sieve; mash. Add lemon juice and sugar. Freeze in freezer, stirring occasionally, so air will make mixture light.

Mrs. Richard Smart

Excellent served with Thanksgiving or Christmas dinner.

JEFFERSON COUNTY COURTHOUSE

The first permanent brick courthouse was built in 1840, but in 1856 it was torn down and the inner core of the present courthouse was built by George E. Keeler. Subsequently, the structure was remodeled many times. The cupola was shot off by Confederate cannon fire during the Battle of Pine Bluff on October 25, 1863. The roof was repaired and in 1870 another cupola was added. In 1890 a major remodeling was done, with the clock and bell tower added. In 1906 an addition was made on the rear which cost $200,000 and in 1936 two fireproof vaults were constructed in wings on the east and the west. During the fire that destroyed the courthouse on April 28, 1976, these vaults saved the invaluable county records, which date back to the county's formation on January 1, 1830.

EGGS SARDOU

Hollandaise Sauce:
4 egg yolks
1 Tbsp. water
1 cup butter

Juice of 1 lemon
Salt
Cayenne pepper

In top of double boiler combine egg yolks and water. Fluff the yolks and cook over hot but not boiling water until thick, being careful not to scramble. Add the butter (room temperature), 1 tablespoon at a time, allowing the sauce to thicken after each addition. Add lemon juice, salt (to taste), and a dash of cayenne pepper. Remove pan from over hot water and set aside until ready to use.

1 pkg. frozen creamed
  spinach
4 Tbsp. butter

6 artichoke bottoms
6 poached eggs
Paprika

Prepare spinach by package directions; drain. Melt 4 tablespoons butter in a 10-12 inch skillet. Add the artichoke bottoms, concave side down, and baste with hot butter. Sprinkle with a little salt, reduce heat to low, cover and cook until heated through without browning.

Assemble by placing a generous tablespoon of spinach on each plate. Add an artichoke bottom, concave side up, and top with 1 egg. Cover with the Hollandaise Sauce, sprinkle with paprika and serve at once.
Allow 2 per person.

Dr. Sam C. Harris

POACHED EGGS BEARNAISE

1 lb. fresh mushrooms, minced
3 Tbsp. minced green onions
3 Tbsp. butter
1½ Tbsp. flour
¼ cup port wine
Dash pepper

½ tsp. salt
½ cup whipping cream
8 baked patty shells
8 poached eggs
2 cups Bearnaise Sauce
  (See Index)

Dry mushrooms. Sauté with onions in butter until tender, about 8 minutes. Stir in flour; cook 2 minutes. Add wine, seasonings and 2/3 of the cream. Simmer 3 minutes, adding more cream if mixture becomes too thick.

Before serving, reheat mushrooms, patty shells and eggs. Place 3 tablespoons of the mushroom mixture into each shell. Place egg over mixture and coat with Bernaise Sauce.
Serves 8.

Mrs. Lunsford W. Bridges

CREAMED EGGS

10 Tbsp. butter
½ cup flour
1½ cups milk
1½ cups half and half cream
1 tsp. salt
¼ tsp. pepper

Dash tarragon, cayenne pepper
½ lb. fresh mushrooms
6-8 hard-boiled eggs
¼ cup sherry
8 crisp toast triangles or cups
Paprika

Melt 8 tablespoons butter in a double boiler, stir in flour. Add combined milk and cream slowly, allowing sauce to thicken (medium thick). Add seasonings.

Sauté mushrooms in 2 tablespoons butter until tender. Add sherry; simmer 1 minute. Stir into white sauce along with chopped egg whites. Adjust seasonings and pour over toast. Crumble yolks of eggs and sprinkle over top. Add a shake of paprika.
Serves 6-8.

For Creamed Ham: Add 3 cups chopped ham, ¼ cup finely chopped green onions, sautéed, and a dash of Worcestershire sauce to white sauce. Leave off tarragon and yolks of eggs.

Mrs. Walter M. Simpson

Serve for Easter Brunch!

SHRIMP AND CRAB SCRAMBLED EGGS

1 (7½ oz.) can king crab meat
1 (4½ oz.) can shrimp
3 Tbsp. sherry
10 Tbsp. butter or oleo
2 Tbsp. flour
¾ cup milk

1 Tbsp. chives
1 tsp. seasoning salt
1 tsp. salt
⅛ tsp. pepper
Few drops Tabasco
12 eggs

Drain and flake crab. Drain shrimp and combine with crab and sherry; set aside. Melt 6 tablespoons butter in saucepan and remove from heat. Stir in flour until smooth and slowly add milk. Bring to a boil, stirring *constantly.* Reduce heat, simmer 1 minute. Stir in chives and shrimp mixture. This can be prepared the day before and refrigerated.

When ready to serve, combine eggs, seasoning salt, salt, pepper and Tabasco. Beat with rotary beater. In large skillet melt 4 tablespoons butter, pour in eggs (low heat) and cook until partially done. Add seafood mixture and cook to desired doneness. Sprinkle with chives.
Serves 8.

Mrs. Robert Ellzey
El Dorado, Arkansas

SPANISH SCRAMBLE

½ medium onion, chopped
½ medium green pepper,
  chopped
1 Tbsp. butter

1 (10 oz.) can Rotel Tomatoes
  and Green Chillies
6-8 eggs, beaten

Simmer onion, green pepper and Rotel ingredients in butter until vegetables are tender and sauce is thick. Add eggs and cook until set.

Mrs. C. J. Giroir, Jr.
Little Rock, Arkansas

EGG AND CHEESE SPECIALTY

10 slices day-old bread
½ cup grated Cheddar cheese
6 or 7 eggs
2 2/3 cups milk (or part cream)
¼ tsp. cornstarch

¼-½ cup cooking sherry
¼ tsp. almond extract
3-4 Tbsp. butter, melted
½ cup slivered almonds

Trim bread and cube. Layer bread and cheese in a 2-quart casserole. Beat eggs, milk, cornstarch, sherry and almond flavoring together in blender. Pour over bread and cheese; pour melted butter over this. Refrigerate overnight or at least 8 hours before baking. When ready to bake, sprinkle almonds on top of casserole. Cook 1 hour at 325° or until brown on top. Serves 12.

A Man's Variation: Add chipped beef, cubed ham or crisp bacon. Leave out almond flavoring and almonds when adding meat and top with more grated cheese.

Mrs. Cal P. Hollis

Be sure and put a pan of water underneath an egg casserole while baking.

FRENCH EGG CASSEROLE

¼ cup butter
¼ cup flour
1 cup non-dairy creamer
2 cups boiling water
¾ tsp. salt
Pinch cayenne pepper
⅛ tsp. white pepper
½ lb. Gruyére cheese,
   grated

1 Tbsp. prepared mustard
2 egg yolks, beaten
2 Tbsp. water
½ cup butter
4 large onions, thinly sliced
¼ lb. fresh mushrooms,
   thinly sliced
12 hard-boiled eggs
Paprika

In heavy saucepan, melt ¼ cup butter over low heat until frothy. Blend in flour with wire whip and cook, while stirring, for 1 minute. (Do not allow to brown.) Add the creamer, then boiling water all at once, beating with wire whip to blend. Increase heat to moderately high. Cook until sauce comes to a boil and thickens, stirring constantly. Fold in seasonings, cheese and mustard. Continue stirring and cook *only* until cheese melts. Remove from fire; add egg yolks which have been beaten with 2 tablespoons water. Return to fire and heat until *just* heated through. Do not boil!

Melt ½ cup butter in a skillet. Sauté onions until tender. Remove onions, toss in mushrooms and sauté until tender. Mix onions and mushrooms and place in a shallow 2-quart casserole. Blend in 1 cup of preceding sauce. Cut each egg into 4 slices and layer over vegetables. Top with remaining sauce, sprinkle with paprika. Cook in 350° oven for 15 minutes, then brown *briefly* under broiler.
Serves 8.

Mrs. John E. Caruthers, Sr.

Absolutely delicious!

EGGS WITH SOUR CREAM

½ cup breadcrumbs
4 hard-boiled eggs, sliced
½ lb. fresh mushrooms
2 slices bacon, fried
2 Tbsp. butter

1 cup sour cream
¼ tsp. salt
¼ tsp. paprika
½ cup grated sharp
   Cheddar cheese

Sprinkle breadcrumbs in a small (6x6 inch) buttered casserole. Place sliced eggs on the crumbs. Sauté the mushrooms in butter until tender. Stir in rest of ingredients, except cheese, and pour over eggs. Sprinkle cheese on top. Bake at 375° for 15-20 minutes. Do not double this recipe.
Serves 4.

Mrs. Meryl Brand
Little Rock, Arkansas

SCOTCH EGGS

2 tsp. flour
Salt and pepper
Paprika
3 hard-boiled eggs
1 drop hot sauce

½ lb. sausage (mild or hot)
1 beaten egg
Breadcrumbs
Vegetable oil for frying

Season flour with salt, pepper and paprika. Roll the shelled eggs in flour mixture. Add a drop of hot sauce to the sausage, divide into 3 equal parts, and cover each egg. (Do this as evenly as possible to keep the eggs in good shape.) Brush each with beaten egg, toss gently in breadcrumbs and fry in ⅛ inch oil.

As the sausage is raw, it is essential that the frying not be hurried and the grease not too hot. When eggs are golden brown, remove from fat, drain, cool and cut in half.
Serves 3.

Mrs. John Dolby

EGGS RIO GRANDE

6 slices bacon
2 Tbsp. bacon drippings
1 medium onion, chopped
1 (8 oz.) can tomato sauce
½ tsp. salt

¼ tsp. pepper
1 tsp. chili powder
8 eggs
1 cup grated sharp
Cheddar cheese

Sauté bacon until crisp; drain and crumble. Pour off all but 2 tablespoons drippings. Add chopped onion and sauté until soft. Stir in tomato sauce, salt, pepper and chili powder; simmer 15 minutes and stir in bacon bits. Butter 4 individual baking dishes and pour in sauce. Break 2 eggs into each dish and cover with cheese. Bake in 350° oven for 15 minutes.
Serves 4.

Mrs. J. Wayne Buckley

SHIRRED EGGS

2 eggs
Salt
Pepper

1 ample Tbsp. butter
4 Tbsp. half and half cream

Break eggs in an individual (buttered and preheated) ramekin, sprinkle with salt and pepper. Dot butter on top, cover with cream and bake at 350° for 12 minutes.
Serves 1.

Mrs. J. Wayne Buckley

PICKLED EGGS

1 doz. eggs	20 whole cloves
1 cup white vinegar	1 tsp. salt
½ cup water	1 tsp. pepper
1 medium onion, coarsely	1 tsp. dry mustard
chopped	1 tsp. pickling spice
1 clove garlic	

Hard boil eggs, plunge them in cold water, remove shells and place in a sterilized jar. Heat vinegar and water. Add seasonings and pour the mixture over the eggs. Allow eggs to stand for at least 1 week. Refrigerate after opening.

John B. Osier

CURRIED STUFFED EGGS

6 hard-boiled eggs, shelled	Curry powder to taste
¼ cup ham, finely chopped	Salt and pepper to taste
1 tsp. grated onion	Mayonnaise to blend

Cut eggs in half, lengthwise. Remove yolks and force through a fine sieve. Add ham, onion, curry powder, salt and pepper. Blend with enough mayonnaise to bind. Stuff egg whites.

Mrs. James O. Bain

STUFFED EGGS

As this recipe is strictly by taste, you must gauge your own measurements by number of eggs you use.

Hard-boiled eggs	Finely minced sweet pickle
Hellmann's Mayonnaise	(optional)
Prepared mustard	Salt
Onion salt	White pepper
Sweet pickle juice	Paprika or olive slices

Boil the eggs, rinse with cold water and shell while warm. Halve lengthwise. Spoon out yolk and mash. Add enough mayonnaise to get a thick creamy consistency, along with a small amount of mustard. Add pickle juice, sweet pickle and seasonings. Taste and adjust ingredients. Cream well and stuff egg whites. Garnish with olive slice or paprika. Cover and refrigerate until ready to use.

Mrs. Walter C. Eden

BASIC OMELETTE

2 eggs
Pinch of salt
⅛ tsp. pepper

1 Tbsp. water
1 Tbsp. butter

Break eggs into a bowl; add salt, pepper and water. Beat lightly with a fork until whites and yolks are thoroughly incorporated. Place omelette pan on moderate heat until hot, then add butter. (It should sizzle but not brown.) Pour in egg mixture and stir rapidly with a fork until outside of omelette begins to set. (Keep tines of fork flat on bottom of pan while stirring.)

Lift the edges of the omelette carefully and tilt pan to let the uncooked part run under the set part. When the omelette is set, but not dry, place filling on the half of the omelette that is on the side opposite the handle of the pan. Tilt the pan away from you and slide a spatula under the unfilled side, carefully turning it over the filled side.

Tip a warmed plate up to the pan and invert the pan over the plate so that the omelette will slide easily onto the plate.
Serves 1.

Mrs. Ben Quinn, Jr.

Variations:
Add ½ cup grated Cheddar cheese and 1/3 cup finely chopped onion to the basic omelette before cooking.

Mix 3 tablespoons sour cream with 1 tablespoon snipped chives. Heat in double boiler until just lukewarm. Fill basic omelette before folding.

Omelette Tips:
1. *If the unfilled side of the omelette tries to stick when you turn it over the filling, slide a small pat of butter in front of the spatula.*
2. *An omelette will not wait. A piece of butter drawn over the top will make it glossy.*
3. *Clean omelette pan with salt.*

RANCHERO OMELETTE

½ cup onion, chopped
¼ cup green pepper, chopped
2 tomatoes, chopped

1 Tbsp. butter
Hot sauce to taste

Sauté onion, pepper and tomatoes in butter until tender and juice of tomatoes has cooked down. Add hot sauce and fill basic omelette before folding.

Mrs. Thomas F. Stobaugh

MUSHROOM AND HAM OMELETTE

½ cup sliced fresh mushrooms
½ cup finely chopped ham
½ cup chopped green pepper

1 Tbsp. butter
½ cup grated Swiss cheese

Sauté mushrooms, ham and peppers in melted butter. Fill basic omelette with mixture and sprinkle with cheese before folding.

Mrs. Ben Quinn, Jr.

GOURMET OMELETTE

½ Tbsp. butter
2 strips bacon, diced
4 green onions, chopped
1 medium potato, diced
1 tomato, chopped

1 Tbsp. parsley, chopped
2 Tbsp. fresh mushrooms,
  chopped
Salt and pepper

Melt butter in pan and add rest of ingredients. Cover and cook slowly 7-8 minutes or until vegetables are tender. Remove cover and cook until slightly browned. Fills 2 basic omelettes.
Serves 2.

Mrs. Harry A. Metcalf

SAUCY OVEN OMELETTE

Omelette:
6 eggs, separated
6 Tbsp. milk, heated
¾ tsp. salt

1½ Tbsp. butter
¾ cup grated Swiss cheese

Beat egg yolks, add milk and salt. Fold in stiffly beaten egg whites. Melt butter in 10-inch pan on surface burner; brown slightly. Pour in egg mixture and bake in 325° oven for 20 minutes. Top with cheese and return to oven for 3 minutes. Top with sauce before serving.

Sauce:
1 (4 oz.) can mushrooms,
  drained (or fresh)
4 chopped green onions

1 tsp. sherry
1 Tbsp. butter

Sauté mushrooms and onions in butter until tender. Add sherry and simmer about 1 minute. Pour over omelette and serve immediately.
Serves 6.

Mrs. Lunsford W. Bridges

Beautiful prepared in a Swedish glass frying pan.

SPANISH PUFFY OMELETTE

Sauce:

1/3 cup chopped onions	1 (16 oz.) can tomatoes
¼ cup chopped celery	½ cup water
¼ cup chopped green pepper	1/3 tsp. pepper
4 Tbsp. vegetable oil	¾ tsp. salt

In heavy skillet sauté onion, celery and green pepper in oil until soft but not brown. Add tomatoes, water and seasonings. Cook for 20-25 minutes, remove from fire. Reheat before pouring over the omelette.

Omelette:

6 eggs, separated	½ tsp. salt
6 Tbsp. hot water	1½ Tbsp. vegetable oil
Dash pepper	½ cup grated Cheddar cheese

Beat egg whites until stiff; set aside. Beat egg yolks until thick and lemon colored. Beat hot water into egg yolks along with salt and pepper and fold in egg whites. Heat heavy iron skillet, grease bottom and sides with oil. Pour in egg mixture and cook over low heat until omelette is puffy and a light brown underneath. Cook in a 350° oven for 10-15 minutes or until top is dry. Run a spatula around edge of omelette to remove from skillet. Turn into a warm platter and fold. Serve with sauce. Top with grated cheese. *Serves 3.*

Mrs. Rufus A. Martin

CHEESE GRITS CASSEROLE

3½-4 cups water	½ roll smokelle cheese
1 cup grits	½ roll bacon or garlic cheese
1 tsp. salt	2 eggs
1 tsp. Worcestershire sauce	Milk
½ cup oleo	1 cup grated sharp cheese

Bring water to a boil; add grits and salt and cook until thick. Add Worcestershire, oleo, smokelle and bacon cheese to the hot grits. Stir to slightly melt cheeses. Break the eggs into a measuring cup and lightly beat. Fill the cup with enough milk to make 1 cup; add to grits mixture. Bake 1 hour at 325°. About 5 minutes before removing from oven, sprinkle sharp cheese over top. Return to oven until cheese melts. *Serves 8.*

Mrs. Walter Trulock, Jr.

FRIED GRITS

3 cups water   ½ tsp. salt
1½ cups grits   White soda crackers

Bring water to a boil over high heat; add grits and salt. Lower heat, stir constantly about 5 minutes or until fairly dry. Pour into a rectangular dish and chill overnight.

Mash crackers into fine crumbs. Slice grits ¼ inch thick and roll in crumbs. Fry in heavy skillet in ¼ inch hot butter or vegetable oil about 7 minutes, turning once. Drain on paper towel. Serve with syrup or sprinkle with cinnamon sugar.
Serves 4.

Mrs. Armistead C. Freeman

CHEESE FRITTERS

2 eggs   1 tsp. baking powder
2/3 cup milk   1 cup flour
Dash salt   ½ cup grated American
1 tsp. melted butter   cheese

Beat eggs slightly, add milk, salt and butter. Sift baking powder with flour and add to egg mixture. Beat until smooth, add cheese. Drop by teaspoonfuls into deep hot fat (380°) and cook 3-5 minutes.
Yields about 15.

Mrs. E. T. Phillips

FRIED CHEESE PATTIES

1 (16 oz.) carton creamed   1 tsp. salt
  cottage cheese   2 Tbsp. sugar
2 eggs   ¼ cup butter
1 cup flour   1 (8 oz.) carton sour cream

In large bowl mix cheese, eggs, flour, salt and sugar. (Mixture will be thick.) Melt butter in 12-inch skillet over medium heat. Drop five ½ cup mounds of cheese mixture in hot butter. Using a pancake turner, shape each mound into a 3 inch round patty. Fry 8-10 minutes until lightly browned, turning once. Remove patties to a warm platter and keep warm. Repeat with remaining mixture to make 10 patties. To serve dot with sour cream and sprinkle with sugar.

Mrs. Ronald D. Blankenship

TOMATO RAREBIT

2 Tbsp. butter
2 Tbsp. flour
½ cup milk
2 cups finely grated American
    cheese
2 eggs, beaten
1 cup tomato juice

Pinch soda
Salt
Pinch dry mustard
Pinch cayenne pepper
Crisp buttered toast
¼ cup finely grated
    green onions (optional)

Melt butter, stir in flour and slowly add milk. Add cheese, heating slowly until melted. Stir in beaten eggs and cook until set. Heat tomato juice with seasonings and just before serving combine with cheese mixture. Serve on toast. Top with chopped green onions.
Serves 6.

Mrs. Rufus A. Martin

SUPPER RAREBIT

½ cup beer
1 tsp. Worcestershire sauce
½ tsp. paprika
1 tsp. dry mustard

Dash cayenne pepper
1 lb. Cheddar cheese
1 egg, beaten
English muffins or toast

In a double boiler over hot but not boiling water, combine beer, Worcestershire, paprika, mustard and cayenne. When mixture is hot, add shredded cheese. Cook until cheese is melted, stirring constantly.

Add a small amount (about 3 tablespoons) of hot mixture to beaten egg to warm it. Add egg mixture to double boiler, stirring until smooth and hot. Pour over muffins, sprinkle with paprika and serve immediately. A thick slice of tomato, crisp bacon or slices of ham make delicious garnishes.
Serves 4.

Mrs. Orlando Carmichael
Little Rock, Arkansas

1861 "English Cookery" refers to Welsh Rarebit as simply cheese melted on pieces of toast with no mention of today's version. The current preferred spelling is "Rabbit".

OLD ENGLISH SOUFFLE

4 Tbsp. butter
4 Tbsp. flour
1½ cups warm milk
1 tsp. salt
Dash cayenne pepper

Dash Worcestershire sauce
Dash garlic salt
½ lb. sharp hoop cheese,
    grated
6 eggs, separated

In top of double boiler, melt butter. Add flour, stirring until smooth. Slowly stir in warmed milk, salt, pepper, garlic salt and Worcestershire. Cook, while stirring, until smooth and thick. Add cheese; stir until melted and sauce is smooth. Remove from heat and allow to cool slightly.

Beat egg yolks with a fork until light in color. Stir a little of the cheese sauce into the yolks. This warms the yolks. Slowly add the yolk mixture to the cheese sauce in the double boiler, stirring constantly.

Put egg whites into a large mixing bowl; beat until stiff. Pour cheese sauce onto egg whites, *folding mixture together carefully.* Pour into an ungreased 2-quart casserole or soufflé dish to within ¼ inch of the top. Bake 1 hour and 15 minutes at 300°.
Serves 6-8.

Mrs. Odus H. LeMay

CHEESE SOUFFLE FOR FOUR

1 cup half and half cream
2 Tbsp. butter
2 Tbsp. flour

½ lb. Old English Cheese
3 eggs
¼ tsp. cream of tartar

Melt butter, stir in flour and slowly add cream until thick. Add diced cheese, allow to melt and take off stove. Cool slightly and beat in 1 egg at a time. Add tartar. Place in pyrex bowl in pan of water and bake at 450° for 50 minutes. The secret of this dish is to be sure and beat it enough. If you make ahead, beat it thoroughly again before cooking.

Mrs. Alfine Jones (Hortense)
Cateress

Soufflé tips:
1. *Do not open oven while cooking.*
2. *Cool cheese sauce before adding eggs.*
3. *To form "top hat" use a teaspoon to draw a line 1 inch from the edge of the soufflé before cooking.*
4. *Must serve immediately.*
5. *One extra egg white will make soufflé hold shape better.*
6. *When adding the egg whites to the soufflé mixture use and up and down chopping movement rather than circular.*

SHRIMP SAUCE FOR CHEESE SOUFFLE

1/3 cup half and half cream
1 can cream of shrimp soup
⅛ tsp. pepper
1 (4½ oz.) can large shrimp

2 Tbsp. dry white wine
1 Tbsp. fresh parsley
chopped or 1 tsp. dried

Slowly stir cream into soup. Drain shrimp and add to soup along with rest of ingredients; heat. Serve over a cheese soufflé.
Serves 4.

Mrs. Frank Surface
Jacksonville, Florida

RED APPLE INN CREAM CHEESE SOUFFLE

4 eggs, separated
Pinch salt
1 Tbsp. flour
1 cup sour cream

2 (3 oz.) pkg. cream cheese,
softened
¼ cup honey

Beat egg yolks until thick and creamy. Add flour and salt. Combine sour cream and cream cheese, blending until smooth. Add to egg yolks and beat with an electric beater until smooth. Add honey gradually.

Beat egg whites until stiff, but not dry, and fold in yolk mixture. Spoon soufflé into a 1½ quart soufflé dish. Place in a pan of water and bake in 300° oven for 1 hour.
Serves 4.

Mrs. M. J. Probst

For a change, oil then dust soufflé dish with Parmesan cheese instead of flour.

CRAZY SOUFFLE

¾ cup of a solid (any
cheese, cooked vegetable,
chopped left-over fowl, meat,
or seafood, fresh or canned,
shredded, chopped or minced)

1 can condensed cream soup
5 egg yolks
6 egg whites

Heat soup and solid together. Whisk in the egg yolks, one at a time. Cool. *Stiffly beat* the egg whites and fold into soup mixture. Pour in a buttered 1½ quart soufflé dish or 4 individual dishes. Bake 40 minutes (20 minutes if using individual dishes) at 325-350°.
Serves 4.

Mrs. William H. Roberts

Cream of Asparagus Soup and Muenster cheese—Fantastic!

EASY BLENDER CHEESE SOUFFLE

1½ cups milk
2 Tbsp. butter
7 pieces crustless bread
½ tsp. salt
⅛ tsp. pepper

⅛ tsp. dry mustard
6 oz. sharp Cheddar cheese
4 egg yolks
4 egg whites

Heat milk just to boiling and pour into blender. Quickly add butter, bread (torn into bits), salt, pepper and mustard. Blend until thickened and add diced cheese. Beat egg yolks just to lemon color; pour *slowly* into blender while blender is on. Pour mixture into large bowl and *gently* fold in stiffly beaten egg whites. Pour into a well-greased 8 inch soufflé dish. Bake 50 minutes or until set. Serve with the mushroom sauce.
Serves 5.

Mushroom Sauce:
½ lb. fresh mushrooms, sliced
2 Tbsp. butter
1 can undiluted cream of
  mushroom soup

¼ cup half and half
  cream

Sauté mushrooms in butter until limp; add soup. Slowly add the cream, stirring with a wire whisk until smooth. When hot, pour over the soufflé and serve immediately.

Mrs. Willard R. Burks

CHEESE AND SAUSAGE SOUFFLE

8 slices white bread
1 lb. hot sausage

1 lb. sharp Cheddar cheese,
  grated

Remove crust from bread and butter each side. Break up into small pieces and cover bottom of a 3-quart soufflé dish. Crumble and cook sausage until done. Drain. Make 2 layers each of sausage and cheese on top of bread.

Soufflé Mixture:
6 eggs
3 cups milk
4 dashes Tabasco
¼ tsp. paprika

2 tsp. Worcestershire sauce
2 tsp. dry mustard
¼ tsp. salt
Dash garlic salt

Mix soufflé ingredients with electric mixer for 5 minutes and pour over layers of bread, sausage and cheese. Refrigerate at least 4 hours. (This can be made a day ahead.) Cook for 2 hours at 300°. Soufflé is done when it pulls away from sides of pan.
Serves 8.

Mrs. Larry Stone

CREPES FROMAGE

4 oz. Swiss cheese
4 oz. sharp Cheddar cheese
4 Tbsp. Parmesan cheese
2 Tbsp. chopped parsley (fresh)
1 Tbsp. chopped chives
  (freeze dried)

1 tsp. Worcestershire sauce
⅛ tsp. freshly ground pepper
12 (6 inch) crepes
4 Tbsp. Parmesan cheese
2 Tbsp. butter

Grate cheeses and mix in seasonings. Put a full tablespoon on each crepe; roll up tightly and place on buttered baking dish. Crumble 4 tablespoons Parmesan cheese and 2 tablespoons butter together, sprinkle on top. Cook at 400° about 10 minutes.
Serves 6.

Mrs. Harold Blach, Jr.
Birmingham, Alabama

Use a thin white sauce for soups, a medium white sauce for scalloped dishes and cheese sauces, and a thick sauce as a base for croquettes and soufflés.

MUSHROOM SOUFFLE CREPES

40 large mushrooms
1 small onion, minced
6 Tbsp. butter
2 Tbsp. flour
1 cup chicken broth
4 eggs, separated

½ tsp. salt
¼ cup Parmesan cheese
16 crepes (no sugar or
  vanilla in batter)
Hollandaise Sauce

Wash, dry and detach stems of mushrooms. Chop stems and 8 whole mushrooms. Sauté with onion in 4 tablespoons butter. In another pan, melt 2 tablespoons butter; stir in flour and slowly add chicken broth, stirring until smooth and thick. Add the sautéed mushrooms, cool. Beat egg yolks and blend into creamed mixture. Season with salt. Fold in stiffly beaten egg whites.

On 2 greased baking sheets lay 16 crepes out flat. Place 2 uncooked mushroom caps and a mound of soufflé mixture on each crepe. Sprinkle with Parmesan cheese. Run the baking sheets into a 350° oven until soufflés are toasted brown, approximately 15-18 minutes. As soon as you take from oven, fold each crepe over and press lightly into a taco shape. Serve hot with Hollandaise Sauce. (See Index)
Serves 6-8.

Mrs. John G. Lile

QUICHE LORRAINE

1 (10 inch) pie shell
8-10 slices bacon, fried
   crisp and crumbled
5 eggs, beaten
2½ cups half and half cream
2 Tbsp. butter, melted

2½ tsp. minced onion
1½ tsp. salt
1¾ tsp. Worcestershire sauce
¼ tsp. nutmeg
1 lb. Swiss cheese, grated
3 Tbsp. Parmesan cheese

Bake pie shell 10-12 minutes at 400°. Cool before filling. Scatter bacon over bottom of pie shell. Combine remaining ingredients (except for Parmesan cheese). Pour over bacon and sprinkle with Parmesan cheese. Place pie on cookie sheet and bake at 375° for 15 minutes. Reduce oven temperature to 350° and bake another 30 minutes or until custard is firm.

Mrs. Ferd M. Bellingrath

Can be made ahead and kept in refrigerator overnight. When doing so, substitute ¾ cup ham for bacon.

QUICHE BRETAGNE

1 (9 inch) unbaked pastry shell
½ cup mayonnaise
2 Tbsp. flour
2 eggs, beaten
½ cup white wine
1 2/3 cups (7½ oz. can) crabmeat,
   drained and flaked

1 (8 oz.) pkg. Swiss cheese
1/3 cup cooked shrimp
1/3 cup sliced green onion
Salt and pepper to taste

Mix mayonnaise, flour, eggs and wine until well blended. Stir in remaining ingredients and pour into the pastry shell. Bake at 350° for 35-40 minutes.
Serves 6.

Quiche Tips:
1. *When filling a pie with a custard, prebake pie shell 10-12 minutes at 400°. Cool before filling.*
2. *Quiche is done when puffed up into a dome and slightly brown. Remove from oven and cool on a cookie sheet. The puff will subside, but don't be alarmed; this is not a soufflé!*
3. *The correct temperature to eat a quiche is pleasantly warm.*
4. *True quiche is strictly custard and cheese. Quiche Lorraine is made with added meats, seafoods, etc.*

CHEESE AND PARSLEY PIE

Pastry for 2 (8-inch) pies
1 onion, thinly sliced
2 Tbsp. butter
4 Tbsp. chopped parsley
1 cup Gruyere or Swiss
   cheese, cubed

¼ cup Parmesan cheese
4 eggs, slightly beaten
1½ cups milk
¼ tsp. nutmeg
½ tsp. salt
¼ tsp. white pepper

Bake pie shells in 450° oven for 5 minutes. Sauté onion in butter until tender. Sprinkle onion, parsley and cheeses over pie shells. Combine eggs, milk, nutmeg, salt and pepper. Strain over the onion-cheese mixture. Bake at 450° for 15 minutes. Reduce oven temperature to 350° and bake about 10 minutes longer or until knife inserted in center comes out clean.
Serves 6-8.

Mrs. E. W. Freeman, III

Serve hot or cold, as a main course, or cooked in small patty shells for appetizers.

CRAB AND MUSHROOM QUICHE

Pastry for a 10 inch pie shell
1 (4 oz.) can sliced mushrooms
1 tsp. butter
1 (7½ oz.) can white lump crab
   meat
1 1/3 cups finely diced Gruyére or
   Swiss cheese (about 1/3 lb.)

¾ cup sour cream
¼ cup mayonnaise
½ tsp. salt
1 tsp. flour
Half and half cream
3 eggs, slightly beaten
½ tsp. hot pepper sauce

Roll pastry dough between 2 sheets wax paper and fit into a 10 inch pie pan. Bake in 450° oven for 10 minutes. (It will be partially baked.)

Drain mushrooms, reserving liquid, and sauté in butter for 2 minutes. Scatter in pie shell. Remove any membrane from crab meat, then scatter crab and cheese over mushrooms. Mix sour cream and mayonnaise with reserved mushroom liquid in a large measuring cup. Stir in salt and flour and add enough cream to make 2 cups. Blend in eggs and hot pepper sauce. Pour into pie shell. Bake at 350° for 55 minutes or until set. Let stand 15 minutes before cutting.
Serves 6.

Mrs. Clendine Washington
Cateress

BAKED MANICOTTI WITH CHEESE FILLING

Sauce:

1½ cups finely chopped onion	2 Tbsp. chopped parsley
1 clove garlic, crushed	1 Tbsp. salt
1/3 cup olive or salad oil	1 Tbsp. sugar
1 (2 lb. 3 oz.) can Italian	1 tsp. dried oregano
tomatoes, undrained	1 tsp. dried basil
1 (6 oz.) can tomato paste	¼ tsp. pepper

In quart-size Dutch oven, sauté onion and garlic in hot oil for 5 minutes. Mix in rest of ingredients and 1½ cups water, mashing tomatoes with fork. Bring to a boil and reduce heat. Simmer mixture, covered, stirring occasionally, for 1 hour.

Filling:

2 lbs. Ricotta cheese	1 tsp. salt
1 (8 oz.) pkg. Mozzarella	¼ tsp. pepper
cheese, diced	1 Tbsp. chopped parsley
1/3 cup grated Parmesan	¼ cup grated Parmesan
cheese	cheese
2 eggs	

In large bowl, combine Ricotta, Mozzarella, 1/3 cup Parmesan, eggs, salt, pepper and parsley. Beat with wooden spoon to blend well. Spread about ¼ cup filling down the center of each manicotti and roll up.

Spoon 1½ cups sauce into each of the two 12x8x2 baking dishes. Place 8 rolled manicotti, seam side down, in single layer; top with five more manicotti. Cover with 1 cup sauce, sprinkle with Parmesan. Bake 350° uncovered ½ hour or until bubbly.

Fix packaged manicotti according to directions on box, or I suggest you make your own. (See recipe below.)
Serves 12.

Mrs. Robert Nixon

MANICOTTI

6 eggs, room temperature	¼ tsp. salt
1½ cups flour	1½ cups water

In medium bowl, combine eggs, flour, salt and 1½ cups water. With electric mixer, beat until just smooth. Let stand ½ hour or longer. Slowly heat an 8 inch skillet. Pour in 3 tablespoons batter, rotating the skillet quickly to spread batter evenly over bottom. (Lightly oil skillet before cooking each manicotti.) Cook over medium heat until top is dry, but bottom is not brown. Turn out on a wire rack to cool. Continue cooking until all the batter is used. As the manicotti cool, stack them with waxed paper between them.
Makes 12.

Mrs. Robert Nixon

MUENSTER CHEESE LASAGNA

2 Tbsp. oleo
1 (4 oz.) can sliced mushrooms
 drained (reserve liquid)
½ cup chopped onion

9 lasagna noodles,
 cooked and drained
8 oz. Muenster cheese, grated
Chopped parsley

Cream sauce:
Reserved mushroom liquid
Milk
6 Tbsp. oleo

6 Tbsp. flour
2 tsp. salt

To make sauce: Pour reserved mushroom liquid into measuring cup and add milk to make 3 cups. Set aside. In saucepan, melt oleo and blend in flour and salt. Cook until bubbly. Gradually stir in liquid and cook, stirring, until sauce is thick and smooth. Makes 3 cups. Set aside.

To make lasagna: Melt oleo in skillet and sauté mushrooms and onions until tender. Grease 12x8x2 inch glass baking dish. Layer sauce, noodles, cheese and mushroom-onion mixture three times, starting and ending with cream sauce. Bake in preheated 350° oven about 45 minutes. Garnish with parsley.
Serves 4.

Mrs. Richard Milwee

A good "meatless" meal or side dish with veal.

ROLLED ENCHILADAS

1 pkg. (12) fresh or frozen tortillas

Cooking oil

Sauce:
2½ Tbsp. fat or oil
2½ Tbsp. chopped onion
1¾ tsp. flour
½ tsp. Tabasco

1¼ tsp. salt
1¼ tsp. garlic salt
2¼ tsp. chili powder
1 (1 lb. 4 oz.) can tomatoes

Filling:
2¼ cups grated sharp cheese
1½ cups chopped onion

¾ tsp. salt

To make the sauce, brown the onion and flour in fat, then add other sauce ingredients. Simmer for 15 minutes.

Combine cheese, onion, and salt for the filling.

Fry each tortilla in hot cooking oil just until soft. Remove from pan and place small amount of filling on it and roll it up. Place in baking dish. When all are done, cover with sauce. Bake at 350° for 15 minutes or until cheese has melted.
Serves 4-5.

Mrs. Charlie F. Pope

ENCHILADAS WITH SOUR CREAM

2 Tbsp. vegetable oil
1 large onion, chopped (1 cup)
1 large clove of garlic, minced
1 (1 lb. 12 oz.) can whole peeled
   tomatoes
1 tsp. salt
1 tsp. oregano
½ tsp. basil

½ tsp. ground cumin
1 (4 oz.) can whole green chilies
1 doz. corn tortillas (fresh,
   frozen or canned)
¼ cup vegetable oil
3 cups coarsely grated
   Monterey Jack or Cheddar cheese
1 (8 oz.) container sour cream

In a medium saucepan, heat 2 tablespoons of oil; add onion and garlic; cook gently until tender; add undrained tomatoes, salt, oregano, basil and cumin. Simmer 20 minutes.

Have the sauce extremely hot, remove from heat. One at a time, dip each tortilla into the additional ¼ cup oil (heated quite hot), then into hot sauce. Then place the tortilla on waxed paper and top it with a chili strip and ¼ cup cheese, then roll it up.

Placed stuffed tortillas as they are rolled, seam side down, in a single layer in a 3 quart oblong glass baking dish (13½x9x2) or similar utensil.

Stir sour cream into remaining sauce; pour over tortillas. Bake in a preheated 325° oven until bubbly, 20-30 minutes. Serve at once.
Serves 6.

Mrs. Martin G. Gilbert

BAKED CHILIES

4 (4 oz.) cans peeled green
   chilies
1 cup grated sharp
   Cheddar cheese

2 cups milk
1 egg
½ cup flour
Dash of salt

Split and remove seeds from chilies; rinse and drain well. Fill chilies with cheese and roll. Place in a greased 1½-quart oblong dish. Blend together the milk, egg, flour and salt. Stir until smooth. Pour the batter over the chilies. Bake uncovered in a 350° oven for 30-35 minutes until thick like custard.
Serves 6.

Mrs. Elton Lyle
Hot Springs, Arkansas

Great with a steak or a Mexican dinner!

THE HUDSON - GRACE - PEARSON HOUSE
716 West Barraque Street
The original portion of this house was built by William E. Woodruff about 1830. The property was then purchased by Marion E. Hudson in 1860, and the house was expanded and remodeled. Hudson died and the house was sold in 1868 to W. Porter Grace, who married Hudson's widow, Emily, a few days later. Grace apparently remodeled the house and made additions to give it its present appearance. The architecture is Second Empire Victorian, which Grace had seen in New Orleans. The house was restored by Ben Pearson in 1968 and is on the National Register of Historic Places.

TIPS FOR BAKING YEAST BREADS

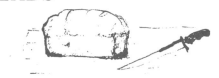

Kneading: Dough should be kneaded on a board that is lightly sprinkled with flour. Rub a little flour on your hand. Form the dough into a round ball. Fold it toward you. Using heels of hand, push dough away with a rolling motion. Turn dough one-quarter turn around. Repeat until dough is smooth and elastic, about 8-10 minutes.

Greasing the bowl: Rub the bowl with a thin film of butter, margarine or oil and turn the dough in it so it is greased on all sides. This prevents a crust from forming during rising.

Rising: Doughs that rise in the conventional way need an even temperature of about 80°-85° F. Doughs that rise by the Cool Rise Method need a refrigerator temperature of 38°-41° F.

Bread that doesn't rise: When bread dough refuses to rise after a considerable time span, the yeast has probably been killed by combining it with liquid that was too hot. The best solution is to dissolve 1 package of active dry yeast and 1 teaspoon sugar in ½ cup warm water (110°). Mix in ½ cup all-purpose flour. Let stand in warm place for 10 minutes, or until spongy. Beat this mixture into the unrisen dough. Then knead in enough additional flour for correct consistency. Proceed as usual by placing the dough in a warm spot to rise.

Testing for Double in Bulk: Press the tips of two fingers lightly and quickly into the dough. If the dent stays, it is double.

Punching down: Push your fist into the center of the dough. Pull the edges of the dough to the center and turn dough out onto lightly floured surface.

No time to finish: Let the dough rise once, punch it down and refrigerate it, covered with plastic wrap. Later, either the same day or the following one, remove pan from refrigerator and let the dough rise in a warm place until doubled in size. Shape, let rise, and bake.

Baking: Always *pre-heat* the oven to whatever temperature is designated.

Testing for Doneness: When baking time is up, remove loaf from pan and tap the bottom or sides. It is done if it sounds hollow.

Cooling: As soon as the bread is baked, remove from pans to a wire cooling rack. When cool, package in plastic bags and tie securely.

Freezing: Breads freeze beautifully when packaged air-tight in plastic freezing bags or wrapped in foil. To reheat, let thaw completely at room temperature, wrap in foil, and heat in a 350° F oven 20-30 minutes. It is wise to leave bread unfrosted if you plan to freeze them. Frost just before using.

FRENCH BREAD

2 cups warm water (105° - 115°)
1 pkg. dry yeast
3 Tbsp. shortening
1 Tbsp. salt

6-6½ cups sifted flour
Cornmeal
1 egg white
2 Tbsp. water

Pour 2 cups warm water into large mixing bowl; sprinkle in yeast; stir to dissolve. Add shortening, salt, and 4 cups flour. Beat until smooth. Add enough remaining flour to form a stiff dough, mixing in with hands, if necessary. Turn out onto floured board. Knead about 5 minutes or until dough is smooth and elastic. Put dough into large greased bowl; turn over to bring greased side up; cover with damp towel. Let rise in warm place (85°) free from draft, about 1½ hours or until doubled in bulk. Punch dough; let rise about 30 minutes or until almost double. Punch dough down; turn out onto board; knead to distribute air bubbles; divide in half. Shape into 2 long loaves, tapering ends with hands. Place on cookie sheet which has been greased and sprinkled with cornmeal. Make several gashes in each loaf about ¼ inch deep. Do not cover; let rise about 1 hour or until doubled in bulk. Heat oven to 400°. Place shallow pan of boiling water on bottom of oven. (This will help to create steam for crispy crust.) Beat egg white slightly with water; brush on loaves. Bake 20 minutes; brush again; bake 20 minutes longer or until glazed and brown. Cool on wire rack.
Yields 2 loaves.

Mrs. Ted Drake

LOAF BREAD

1 pkg. dry yeast
2 Tbsp. warm water
½ tsp. sugar
¾ cup milk
3 Tbsp. shortening
1/3 cup cornmeal
1/3 cup quick oats

½ cup Kellogg Special K
3 Tbsp. honey
¼ cup brown sugar
1 egg, beaten
1 tsp. salt
3 cups flour, unsifted

Dissolve yeast in warm water; add sugar. Scald milk, add shortening, then allow to cool. Add milk mixture to yeast mixture. Stir in remaining ingredients except flour. Stir in 1½ cups flour, then remainder, leaving ½ cup to sprinkle on board. Turn dough out on board and knead in flour, 8-10 minutes. Shape in ball in bowl. Grease top. Let rise until doubled in bulk. Make into loaf and grease. Put in greased loaf pan; let rise until doubled. Bake at 350° for 1 hour or until done.
Yields 1 loaf.

Mrs. Robert Smith

ELIZABETH YOUNG'S HOMEMADE BREAD

2½ cups lukewarm water
2 Tbsp. sugar
1 pkg. dry yeast (2 may be
   used on a cold day)
½ cup sugar

1½ tsp. salt
2½ Tbsp. bacon fat, melted
   (or any other drippings)
6 cups unsifted flour
Butter or margarine

Stir 2 tablespoons sugar and yeast into water. Let mixture sit 5-15 minutes. Add ½ cup sugar, salt and bacon fat. Stir in flour, cup by cup, until too thick to stir, then work in by hand. Turn onto floured board; add more flour if necessary and knead at least 10 minutes. Place in large greased bowl and brush top with melted butter or margarine. Cover and let rise in warm place (76° to 85°) until doubled (about 1½ hours).

Gently divide into 2 equal portions. *Do not knead*. Mold into 2 loaves. Place into greased loaf pans (9¼x5¼x2¾ inches). Brush entire top surface of loaves with melted margarine. Cover pans with light cloth and let rise (about 1½ hours). Bake at 375° for 15 minutes, lower temperature to 275° and bake 15-20 minutes. Test loaf for doneness by trying to slip out of pan easily. If it doesn't, return to oven for 5-10 minutes.

Remove from oven. Brush margarine on tops of loaves while still in pan. Lift loaves gently out of pan. Let cool on wire rack. For softer crust, brush sides of loaves with butter while hot. Leave loaves uncovered while cooling.
Yields 2 loaves.

Mrs. Gordon E. Young
Mrs. C. D. Allison, Jr.

EASY NO-KNEAD BREAD

1 cup milk
3 Tbsp. sugar
1 Tbsp. salt
1½ Tbsp. shortening

1 cup warm water
2 pkgs. dry yeast
4½ cups flour, unsifted

Scald milk, sugar, salt and shortening. Dissolve yeast in warm water, then mix with cooled milk mixture. Add flour and stir until well mixed. Cover and let rise in warm place until tripled in size, about 45 minutes. After rising, stir dough about half a minute. Place dough in greased 1½-quart casserole.

Cover and let rise until doubled, about 1 hour. Bake at 400° for 25-30 minutes or until done. Turn out on wire rack and brush with margarine.
Yields 1 loaf.

Mrs. C. B. Hall
Wynne, Arkansas

RUSSIAN BLACK BREAD

4 cups unsifted rye flour
3 cups unsifted white flour
1 tsp. sugar
2 tsp. salt
2 cups whole bran cereal
2 Tbsp. caraway seed,
  crushed
2 tsp. instant coffee
2 tsp. onion powder
½ tsp. fennel seed,
  crushed

2 pkgs. dry yeast
2½ cups water
¼ cup vinegar
¼ cup dark molasses
1 square (1 oz.) unsweetened
  chocolate
¼ cup margarine
1 tsp. cornstarch
½ cup cold water

Combine rye and white flour. In a large bowl, thoroughly mix 2 1/3 cups flour mixture, sugar, salt, cereal, caraway seed, instant coffee, onion powder, fennel seed and dry yeast. Combine 2½ cups water, vinegar, molasses, chocolate and margarine in a saucepan. Heat over low heat until liquids are very warm (120°-130° F). Margarine and chocolate do not need to melt. Gradually add to dry ingredients and beat 2 minutes at medium speed of electric mixer. Beat at high speed 2 minutes, scraping bowl occasionally. Stir in enough additional flour mixture to make a soft dough. Turn out onto lightly floured board. Cover; let rest 15 minutes. Then knead until smooth and elastic, 10-15 minutes (dough may be sticky). Place in greased bowl, turning to grease top. Cover; let rise in warm place, free from draft, until doubled in bulk, about 1 hour. Punch dough down; turn onto lightly floured board. Divide in half. Shape each half into a ball in the center of a greased 8-inch round cake pan. Cover; let rise in a warm place until doubled in bulk, about 1 hour. Bake at 350° for 45-50 minutes, or until done.

Meanwhile, combine cornstarch and cold water. Cook over medium heat, stirring constantly, until mixture starts to boil; continue to cook, stirring constantly, 1 minute. As soon as bread is baked, brush cornstarch mixture over top of loaves. Return bread to oven and bake 2-3 minutes longer and glaze is set. Remove from pans and cool on wire racks.
Yields 2 loaves.

Mrs. Martin G. Gilbert

SALLY LUNN BREAD

¾ cup warm water (110°)
3 pkgs. dry yeast
1/3 cup sugar
2½ cups of lukewarm milk
2¼ tsp. salt

1/3 cup oil or melted
   shortening
3 eggs, lightly beaten
16 drops yellow food coloring
8 cups sifted flour

Measure water into your largest mixing bowl and add sugar and yeast, stirring until dissolved. Let sit a few minutes until light and bubbly, then stir in the lukewarm milk, salt, oil, food coloring and eggs. Gradually add 8 cups of flour. With a wooden spoon beat until smooth (about 100 strokes). Cover and let rise until very light (about 1 hour). Beat down and pour into 3 greased loaf pans or 1 Bundt-type pan and 1 loaf pan. Let rise until within 1 inch of the top of pans (about 45 minutes). Bake at 350° for 45-50 minutes. *Yields 3 loaves or 1 loaf pan plus 1 Bundt-type pan.*

Mrs. John G. Lile

This makes a rich, yellow bread traditional in the Colonial period of America. Very good for cold turkey sandwiches, as toast, and lovely on your Thanksgiving and Christmas tables.

SWEDISH RYE BREAD

2 pkgs. dry yeast
½ cup warm water
2 cups sifted rye flour
¾ cup dark molasses

1/3 cup shortening
2 Tbsp. salt
2 cups boiling water
6 cups sifted enriched flour

Soften yeast in warm water. Combine rye flour, molasses, shortening and salt. Add boiling water and blend well. Cool to lukewarm. Add softened yeast. Gradually stir in enriched flour to make soft dough. Mix well. Turn out on well-floured surface. Cover and let rest 10 minutes. Knead until dough is smooth and satiny, about 10 minutes. Place in lightly greased bowl, turning once to grease entire surface. Cover, let rise in warm place until doubled, about 1½-2 hours.

Punch down, cover, and let rise again until almost double, about 30 minutes. Turn out on lightly floured surface and divide into 4 equal parts. Form in balls. Cover and let rest 15 minutes. Shape into 4 loaves and place on 2 greased baking sheets. Cover, let rise until almost double again, about 1 hour. Brush loaves with slightly beaten egg yolk. Bake at 350° for 35 minutes. The dough can also be formed into loaves and baked in loaf pans. *Yields 4 loaves.*

Mrs. James S. Rogers

WHOLE WHEAT BREAD

2 pkgs. dry yeast
¾ cup brown sugar
3 cups warm water
4 cups all-purpose flour

4 tsp. salt
1 cup hot water
½ cup margarine, melted
8 cups whole wheat flour

Dissolve yeast and ¼ cup of brown sugar in ½ cup of warm water. Add remaining 2½ cups warm water, sugar, all-purpose flour and salt. Beat until smooth. Cover and let rise until doubled in bulk. Punch down. Mix in hot water, margarine and whole wheat. Turn out on floured surface and knead 8-10 minutes or until smooth and elastic. Place in greased bowl, turning to greased side up. Cover, let rise until doubled in bulk. Punch down and shape into 3 loaves to fit 9x5x3 inch pans. Cover, let rise until doubled. Bake at 375° for 30-35 minutes.
Yields 3 loaves.

Mrs. Joe Campbell
Mena, Arkansas

EGG BRAID

½ cup warm water (105°-115°)
2 pkgs. dry yeast
1¾ cups warm milk
2 Tbsp. sugar
1 Tbsp. salt

3 Tbsp. margarine
3 eggs
6¾-7¼ cups unsifted flour
Peanut oil or cooking oil

Measure warm water into large warm bowl. Sprinkle in yeast; stir until dissolved. Add warm milk, sugar, salt, margarine, 3 egg yolks and 2 egg whites. (Reserve remaining egg white for brushing braid.) Add 2 cups flour. Beat with rotary beater until smooth (about 1 minute). Add 1 cup flour. Beat vigorously with a wooden spoon until smooth (about 150 strokes). Add enough additional flour to make a soft dough. Turn out onto lightly floured board and knead until smooth and elastic, about 8-10 minutes. Cover; let rest 20 minutes. Divide dough in half. Divide one half of the dough into 5 equal pieces. Roll each piece into an 18-inch roll. On a greased baking sheet braid 3 of the rolls together. Twist together remaining two rolls and place on top braid. Pinch ends to seal and tuck under braid. Repeat with remaining half of dough. Brush braids with oil. Cover with plastic wrap. Refrigerate 2-24 hours.

When ready to bake, remove from refrigerator. Uncover dough carefully. Brush braid with slightly beaten egg white. Let stand uncovered 10 minutes at room temperature. Puncture any gas bubbles. Bake at 375° for 25-30 minutes, or until done. Turn out on wire racks and brush with melted margarine.
Yields 2 braids.

Mrs. Martin G. Gilbert

BRAIDED ONION BREAD

6-6½ cups unsifted flour
1 pkg. dry yeast
1 envelope onion soup mix
2 Tbsp. sugar
2 tsp. salt
¼ tsp. baking soda

1 cup water
2 Tbsp. butter or margarine
1 cup sour cream
3 eggs, beaten
Sesame seeds

In a large bowl combine 2 cups flour, yeast, soup mix, sugar, salt and baking soda. In small saucepan heat 1 cup water, butter, and sour cream until very warm (120°-130° F). Butter does not need to melt. With electric mixer at medium speed, add sour cream mixture to flour mixture; beat 2 minutes. Add all but 2 tablespoons of the beaten eggs and enough additional flour (about 4 cups) to make soft dough. Place dough on lightly floured surface and knead until smooth, about 5 minutes. Place in large greased bowl, turning once to grease surface. Cover with towel; let rise in warm place (80°-85° F) 1½ hours or until doubled.

Punch dough down; turn onto floured surface; cover with bowl and let rest 10 minutes. Divide dough into 6 equal parts. With the palms of your hands, roll 3 of the parts into 15-inch strips. Braid the 3 strips together, sealing ends. Repeat with remaining 3 parts of dough. Place braids on greased cookie sheet; cover and let rise in warm place until doubled. Brush braids with remaining 2 tablespoons beaten egg; sprinkle with sesame seeds. Bake at 350° for 40-45 minutes or until golden and firm. Cool on racks. *Yields 2 braids.*

Mrs. James H. McKenzie
Prescott, Arkansas

ARMENIAN THIN BREAD

1 cup warm water
1 pkg. dry yeast
¼ cup butter, melted

1½ tsp. salt
1 tsp. sugar
3¼ - 3¾ cups unsifted flour

Measure warm water in large bowl, sprinkle in yeast, stirring until dissolved. Add cooled butter, salt, sugar and 2 cups flour. Beat until smooth. Add enough additional flour to make a stiff dough. Turn out onto lightly floured board. Knead until smooth and elastic, 8-10 minutes. Place in greased bowl, turning to greased side up. Cover and let rise in warm place until doubled. Punch dough down, divide into 4 equal parts; roll and stretch each piece into a rectangle 10x14 inches. Place each on an ungreased baking sheet. Bake at 350° for 15-20 minutes. *Yields 4 sheets.*

Mrs. Ronald D. Blankenship

For a real change, serve this with spaghetti, soup or salads.

ETHIOPIAN HONEY BREAD

1 pkg. dry yeast
¼ cup warm water
1 Tbsp. coriander
½ tsp. cinnamon
1 cup lukewarm milk
6 Tbsp. melted butter

1 egg
½ cup honey
¼ tsp. cloves
1½ tsp. salt
4-4½ cups unsifted flour

Sprinkle yeast on warm water and let stand until bubbly. Combine rest of ingredients with yeast mixture and beat until blended. Shape into a ball and place in buttered bowl, turning to buttered side up. Cover and let rise in warm place until doubled in bulk. Punch down, then knead on board 1-2 minutes. Place in buttered 9-inch round dish, 3 inches deep. Cover and let rise 1 hour. Bake at 350° for 1 hour or until tests done.
Yields 1 loaf.

Mrs. Joe Campbell
Mena, Arkansas

OATMEAL BREAD

2 cups quick cooking rolled oats
2 tsp. salt
2 cups boiling water
2 Tbsp. oil
1 pkg. dry yeast
2 Tbsp. dark brown sugar,
firmly packed

¾ cup lukewarm water
1 cup instant non-fat dry
milk powder
4-4½ cups unsifted flour

Put oats in a large mixing bowl. Add salt to boiling water and stir into oats. Add oil and stir until smooth; cool to lukewarm. Dissolve yeast and sugar in lukewarm water. Combine oat mixture and yeast mixture. Add milk powder and 4 cups of flour; mix thoroughly. Cover. Let rise until doubled in bulk, about 1½ hours. Punch down and place on lightly floured board to knead. If dough is sticky, add a little more flour. Shape into 2 loaves and place in 2 medium-sized greased loaf pans. Let rise in warm place until doubled in bulk. Bake at 375° for 35-45 minutes or until done.
Yields 2 loaves.

Mrs. John Garrison

Bread bakes uneven—Caused by using old dark pans, too much dough in pan, crowding the oven shelf or cooking at too high a temperature.

SOURDOUGH STARTER

3½ cups unsifted strong,
bread-type flour
1 Tbsp. sugar

1 pkg. dry yeast
2 cups warm water

Combine flour, sugar, and yeast in large bowl. Gradually add warm water to dry ingredients and beat until smooth. Cover with plastic wrap; let stand in warm place for 2 days.

To use in a recipe: Measure out amount called for in recipe and use as directed.

To replenish starter: To remaining starter add 1½ cups strong bread-type flour and one cup warm water. Beat until smooth. Store covered in warm place. Stir before using. If not used in one week, remove 1½ cups starter and follow directions for replenishing.

Mrs. Robert Smith

SOURDOUGH BREAD

1½ cups sourdough starter
¾ cup milk
3 Tbsp. sugar
1 tsp. salt

2 Tbsp. margarine
½ cup warm water (105°-115° F)
1 pkg. dry yeast
5-6 cups unsifted flour

Prepare sourdough starter at least two days in advance. Scald milk; stir in sugar, salt, and margarine; cool to lukewarm. Measure warm water into large warm bowl. Sprinkle in yeast; stir until dissolved. Add lukewarm milk mixture, starter, and 2½ cups flour; beat until smooth. Stir in enough additional flour to make a stiff dough. Turn out onto lightly floured board; knead until smooth and elastic, about 8-10 minutes. Place in greased bowl turning to grease top. Cover; let rise in warm place until doubled in bulk, about 1 hour. Punch dough down; divide into three equal pieces. Form each piece into a smooth round ball or a 14-inch tapered roll. Place on greased baking sheets. With sharp knife make several cuts in crisscross fashion on tops of round loaves, or make several diagonal cuts on tops of long loaves. Cover, let rise in warm place free from draft, until doubled in bulk, about 1 hour. Bake at 400° for 25 minutes. Cool on wire racks.
Yields 3 loaves.

Mrs. Robert Smith

BRIOCHE

½ cup milk
½ cup butter or oleo
1/3 cup sugar
½ tsp. salt
¼ cup warm water
1 pkg. dry yeast

1 egg yolk, beaten
3 whole eggs, beaten
3¼ cups sifted flour
1 egg white beaten with
   1 Tbsp. sugar

Scald milk; cool to lukewarm. Cream thoroughly the butter, sugar and salt. Measure warm water into a bowl sprinkling yeast over it; stir until dissolved. Stir in the lukewarm milk and creamed mixture. Add egg yolk, whole eggs and flour. Beat for 10 minutes. Cover. Let rise in warm place, free from draft, about 2 hours, or until more than doubled in bulk. Stir down and beat well. Cover tightly and chill overnight. Stir down and turn out soft dough onto floured board. Divide into 2 pieces, one about ¾ and the other about ¼ of the amount. To make 3 dozen small rolls, divide the larger amount of dough into 36 balls and place into well-greased muffin tins. Make an indentation deep in the center of each ball and dampen slightly with cool water. Divide the remaining dough into 36 tiny balls and press one into each indentation. Cover and let rise in a warm place, free from draft, about 1 hour, or until more than doubled in bulk. Brush with egg white and sugar mixture. Bake at 375° for 15 minutes or until golden brown.
Yields 3 dozen rolls.

1975 Charity Ball Royal Supper

REFRIGERATOR ROLLS

1 qt. milk
1 cup melted shortening
1 cup sugar
1 tsp. salt
2 pkgs. dry yeast

½ cup warm water
1 tsp. soda
1 tsp. baking powder
9 cups flour

Combine milk, shortening, sugar and salt. Bring to boil. Let cool. Add yeast softened in warm water. Sift together soda, baking powder, and flour. Add to milk mixture and mix well. Cover and let rise at room temperature until doubled in bulk. Punch down and refrigerate 3 hours to 10 days (covered tightly). To use, roll out dough ¼-inch thick and cut with a 2½-inch biscuit cutter. Dip in melted butter and crease roll with dull knife to make Parkerhouse rolls. Let rise 1½ - 2 hours. Bake at 400° for 10-15 minutes.
Yields 12 dozen.

Mrs. Ronald H. Jeter

Made up rolls can be frozen before baking. Remove from freezer 2-3 hours before baking.

JOHNITA'S ROLLS

1 cup milk
½ cup sugar
½ cup shortening
1 tsp. salt

1 pkg. dry yeast
¼ cup warm water
3-3½ cups sifted flour

Scald milk. Add sugar, shortening and salt. Let cool. Add yeast dissolved in warm water. Add flour—don't get dough too stiff. Turn dough into greased bowl; grease top of dough then cover with cloth. Let rise at least 2 hours. Turn out on lightly floured board. Roll out dough about ¼ - inch thick. Cut into rounds with a biscuit cutter. Crease each round with knife and fold over. Warm stick of oleo on cookie sheet in oven; dip rolls in oleo. Let rise uncovered for 2 hours. Bake at 400° about 10-15 minutes. Yields 4-5 dozen.

Mrs. W. R. Jones

ONE BOWL HARD ROLLS

4½-5½ cups unsifted flour
2 Tbsp. sugar
2 tsp. salt
1 pkg. dry yeast
3 Tbsp. softened margarine
1½ cups very hot tap water

1 egg white (at room
  temperature)
Cornmeal
½ cup water
1 tsp. cornstarch

In a large bowl thoroughly mix 1 1/3 cups flour, sugar, salt and dry yeast. Add softened margarine. Gradually add very hot tap water to dry ingredients and beat 2 minutes at medium speed of electric mixer, scraping bowl occasionally. Add egg white and 1 cup flour, or enough flour to make a thick batter. Beat at high speed 2 minutes, scraping bowl occasionally. Stir in enough additional flour to make a soft dough. Turn out onto lightly floured board; knead until smooth and elastic, about 8-10 minutes. Place in greased bowl, turning to grease top. Cover; let rise in warm place free from draft, until doubled in bulk, about 45 minutes.

Punch dough down; turn out onto lightly floured board. Cover; let rest 10 minutes. Divide in half. Form each half into a 9-inch roll. Cut into nine 1 inch pieces. Form into smooth balls. Place about 3 inches apart on greased baking sheets which have been sprinkled with cornmeal. Cover; let rise in warm place until doubled in bulk, about 45 minutes. Slowly blend remaining ½ cup water into cornstarch. Bring mixture to a boil. Cool slightly. When ready to bake, brush each roll with cornstarch glaze. Slit tops with a sharp knife crisscross fashion. If desired, sprinkle with sesame or poppy seeds. Bake at 450° about 15 minutes or until done. Cool on wire rack.
Yields 18 rolls.

Mrs. Martin G. Gilbert

QUICK HERB ROLLS

½ cup butter (not oleo)
1½ tsp. parsley flakes
½ tsp. dill weed
1 Tbsp. onion flakes

2 Tbsp. Parmesan cheese
1 (10 or 11 oz.) can refrigerator
   biscuits, (buttermilk variety)

Melt butter in 9-inch pan. Mix herbs and cheese together and stir into butter. Let stand 15-30 minutes. Cut biscuits into halves or fourths and swish around in herb-butter to coat all sides. Bake at 425° for 12-15 minutes. This may be prepared several hours ahead and refrigerated. *Serves 4.*

Mrs. Sam Boellner
Little Rock, Arkansas

RYE BREAD STICKS WITH CARAWAY SEEDS

1¼ cups warm water
1 pkg. dry yeast
3 Tbsp. sugar
½ tsp. salt
1 Tbsp. caraway seeds
3 Tbsp. margarine, softened

2 cups unsifted rye flour
1½ - 2½ cups unsifted
   white flour
Melted margarine
Caraway seeds

Measure warm water into large warm bowl, sprinkle in yeast, stir until dissolved. Add sugar, salt, 1 tablespoon caraway seed, and softened margarine. Stir in rye flour and beat until smooth. Add enough white flour to make a stiff dough. Turn out onto lightly floured board and knead until smooth and elastic, about 8-10 minutes. Place in greased bowl, turning to grease top; cover and let rise in warm place until doubled in bulk, about 1 hour. Punch dough down; divide in half. Cut each half into 12 equal pieces. Roll each piece into a rope about 6 inches long. Place on greased baking sheet about 2 inches apart. Cover; let rise in warm place until doubled in bulk, about 30 minutes. Brush lightly with melted margarine and sprinkle with caraway seeds. Bake at 400° for 15-20 minutes, or until done. Cool on wire racks.
Yields 24 sticks.

Mrs. C. Frank Williamson

CHEESY ONION BURGER BUNS

5¾ - 6¾ cups unsifted flour
3 Tbsp. sugar
1½ tsp. salt
2 pkgs. dry yeast
2 Tbsp. softened margarine

2 cups very hot tap water
1½ cups grated sharp
    Cheddar cheese
¼ cup finely chopped onion

In a large bowl thoroughly mix 2 cups flour, sugar, salt and dry yeast. Add softened margarine. Gradually add very hot tap water to dry ingredients and beat 2 minutes at medium speed of electric mixer, scraping bowl occasionally. Add 1 cup flour, or enough flour to make a thick batter. Beat at high speed 2 minutes, scraping bowl occasionally. Stir in cheese, onion and enough additional flour to make a soft dough. Turn out onto lightly floured board; knead until smooth and elastic, about 8-10 minutes. Place in greased bowl, turning to grease top. Cover; let rise in warm place free from draft, until doubled in bulk, about 1 hour.

Punch dough down; turn out onto lightly floured board. Divide dough into 20 equal pieces. Form each piece into a smooth ball. Place balls 2 inches apart on greased baking sheets. Cover. Let rise in a warm place until doubled in bulk, about 45 minutes. Bake at 400° for 15-20 minutes or until done. Remove from oven, place on wire racks and brush with butter or margarine.
Yields 20 buns.

Mrs. Martin G. Gilbert

These are especially good for ham or corned beef sandwiches.

PRETZELS

1 pkg. dry yeast
1¼ cups warm water
1 Tbsp. sugar
1 Tbsp. salt

4 cups unsifted flour
Egg white
Coarse salt

Dissolve yeast in warm water. Add sugar, salt and 4 cups flour. Mix well. Shape pieces of dough into large fat pretzels on cookie sheet. Thin beaten egg white with 1 teaspoon water and brush each pretzel. Sprinkle with coarse salt. Bake at 450° until golden brown, about 12-15 minutes.

Laurie Baim

Making these will entertain your children for hours — so easy!

CHERRY-GO-ROUND

3½-4½ cups unsifted flour
½ cup sugar
1 tsp. salt
1 pkg. dry yeast
1 cup milk
¼ cup water
½ cup margarine
1 egg (at room temperature)

½ cup unsifted flour
½ cup chopped pecans
½ cup firmly packed light
 brown sugar
1 (1 lb.) can pitted red sour
 cherries, well-drained
Powdered sugar frosting

In a large bowl thoroughly mix 1¼ cups flour, sugar, salt and undissolved dry yeast. Combine milk, water and margarine in a saucepan. Heat over low heat until liquids are warm. Gradually add to dry ingredients and beat 2 minutes at medium speed of electric mixer, scraping bowl occasionally. Add egg and ¾ cup flour, or enough flour to make a thick batter. Beat at high speed 2 minutes, scraping bowl occasionally. Stir in enough additional flour to make a stiff batter. Cover bowl tightly with aluminum foil. Refrigerate dough at least 2 hours. (Dough may be kept in refrigerator 3 days.)

When ready to shape dough, combine ½ cup flour, pecans and brown sugar. Turn dough out onto lightly floured board and divide in half. Roll ½ of the dough to a 14x7 inch rectangle. Spread with ¾ cup cherries. Sprinkle with ½ the brown sugar mixture. Roll up from long side as for jelly roll. Seal edges. Place sealed edge down, in circle, on greased baking sheet. Seal ends together firmly. Cut slits two-thirds through ring at 1-inch intervals; turn each section on its side. Repeat with remaining dough, cherries and brown sugar mixture. Cover; let rise in warm place until doubled, about 1 hour. Bake at 375° for 20-25 minutes, or until done. Remove from baking sheets and cool on wire racks. Frost while warm with powdered sugar frosting.
Yields 2 coffee cakes.

Mrs. Martin G. Gilbert

EXTRA-QUICK COFFEE CAKE

1 cup sugar
1 Tbsp. cinnamon

2 cans refrigerator biscuits
½ cup melted butter or oleo

Combine sugar and cinnamon and mix well. Separate biscuits and dip each in butter and roll in cinnamon sugar. Stand on edge in a circle in tube or Bundt pan. Pour remaining butter and sugar over top. Bake at 350° approximately 45 minutes (depends on size of biscuits used). Serve by breaking off in individual pieces.
Yields 1 cake.

Mrs. Dean Copeland
Atlanta, Georgia

BEIGNETS
(NEW ORLEANS DOUGHNUTS)

½ cup boiling water
2 Tbsp. shortening
¼ cup sugar
½ tsp. salt
½ cup evaporated milk

½ pkg. dry yeast
¼ cup warm water
1 egg, beaten
3¾ cups sifted flour
Powdered sugar

Pour boiling water over shortening, sugar and salt. Add milk and let stand until warm. Dissolve yeast in warm water and add to milk mixture along with beaten egg. Stir in 2 cups flour and beat. Add enough flour to make a soft dough. Cover with waxed paper and a cloth. Chill until ready to use. Roll dough to a ¼ inch thickness— do not let dough rise before frying. Cut into squares and fry a few at a time in deep fat (360°). Brown on one side, turn and brown on other. Drain on absorbent paper. Sprinkle with powdered sugar.
Yields 2½ dozen.

Mrs. Joe Richardson
Leawood, Kansas

APRICOT CRUNCH COFFEE CAKE

Topping:
¼ cup flour
¼ cup sugar

1 Tbsp. cinnamon
2 Tbsp. butter

Crumble ingredients then spread in bottom of a Bundt pan which has been coated with vegetable spray.

Cake:
½ cup butter
1 (8 oz.) pkg. cream cheese,
  softened
1¼ cups sugar
1 tsp. vanilla
2 eggs
2 cups flour

1 tsp. baking powder
½ tsp. soda
¼ tsp. salt
½ cup milk
1 (12 oz.) jar apricot
  preserves

Beat butter, cream cheese and sugar until fluffy. Beat in vanilla and eggs. Add sifted dry ingredients alternately with milk, beating until smooth. Pour half of batter into pan. Spread preserves on batter being careful not to touch sides of pan with preserves. (This will prevent cake from sticking in pan.) Add remaining batter. Bake at 350° for 50-60 minutes or until done.
Serves 16.

Mrs. Kenneth Baim

DANISH PUFF

Crust:
1 cup flour, sifted
½ cup margarine
2 Tbsp. water

Mix ingredients as you would a pie crust. Divide dough into two parts. Make two 12x2½ inch strips by pressing out dough on ungreased cookie sheet.

Paste:
1 cup water
½ cup margarine
1 tsp. almond extract
1 cup flour
3 eggs

Boil water, margarine and extract. Remove from heat and quickly add flour. Beat in eggs, one at a time, until well blended. Spread paste on dough. Bake at 350° for 1 hour. Let cool.

Frosting:
1½ cups powdered sugar
¼ cup margarine
¼ tsp. almond extract
2 tsp. vanilla extract

Mix ingredients well, then frost puff. Sprinkle with chopped nuts if desired.

Mrs. Joe Campbell
Mena, Arkansas

PISTACHIO NUT COFFEE CAKE

1 box yellow cake mix
1 (3 oz.) pkg. Pistachio Nut
   Pudding Mix
½ cup cooking oil
4 eggs
1 (8 oz.) carton sour cream
½ cup sugar
1 Tbsp. cinnamon

Cream cake mix, pudding mix, oil and eggs. Mix in sour cream. Mix sugar and cinnamon in a small bowl and set aside. Pour half of cake mixture into lightly greased Bundt cake pan. Sprinkle half of sugar and cinnamon mixture into center and swirl around. Pour remaining cake mixture into pan and sprinkle top with rest of sugar and cinnamon. Bake at 350° for 1 hour.
Serves 18 to 20.

Mrs. C. Fletcher Welch, Jr.

SOUR CREAM COFFEE CAKE

1 cup sugar
½ cup butter or oleo
2 cups flour, sifted
¼ tsp. nutmeg

½ tsp. cinnamon
1 (8 oz.) carton sour cream
1 tsp. soda

Combine sugar, butter and flour; crumble like pie dough. Set aside half of this mixture for topping. To other half add nutmeg, cinnamon and sour cream to which soda has been added. Mix well. Pour into a greased 8x8 inch pan. Sprinkle reserved crumb mixture on top. Bake at 350° for 45 minutes.
Yields 1 coffee cake.

Mrs. Maury Goodloe

LITTLE HOT BISCUITS

3 cups flour
2 tsp. baking powder
1 tsp. salt

½ cup plus 3 Tbsp. shortening
1½ cups milk
½ tsp. lemon juice

Sift flour, baking powder and salt. Cut in shortening. Slowly add milk and lemon juice until a soft dough has formed. Roll out on a floured board to a ½ inch thickness. Fold in half and roll twice. Cut with a small cutter and place in greased pan. Bake at 400° until brown.
Serves 8.

Mrs. Leland Harris
Wynne, Arkansas

To make biscuits from a ready-bought mix extra good, use light cream instead of water for the liquid.

SOURDOUGH BISCUITS

1 cup flour
¼ tsp. soda
¼ tsp. salt

2 tsp. baking powder
4 Tbsp. shortening
1 cup sourdough starter (See Index)

Sift together flour, soda, salt and baking powder. Cut in shortening. Add 1 cup sourdough starter. Mix quickly and until dough follows fork around bowl. Turn out on lightly floured wax paper or board. Pat or roll to desired thickness (usually about ½ inch). Dip cutter into flour, cut biscuits, and place on ungreased baking tin. Brush lightly with margarine or fat. Best to let biscuits rest for about 30 minutes. Bake at 450° for 12-15 minutes or until lightly browned.

Mrs. Robert Smith

FOOLPROOF POPOVERS

1 cup milk
1 cup unsifted flour

2 eggs
½ tsp. salt

Combine ingredients in bowl. Stir with a spoon until flour is moist—it will be lumpy. Pour into a cold, greased iron popover pan with 11 cups. Fill each cup about half full. For larger popovers, use 6 custard cups. Place in a cold oven; set the temperature at 450° and the timer for 30 minutes. Do not open the oven door during this time. Serve hot.
Yields 11 popovers.

Mrs. Currin Nichol, Jr.

RAISIN BRAN MUFFINS

1 (10 oz.) box raisin bran
5 cups unsifted flour
3 cups sugar
5 tsp. soda

2 tsp. salt
1 qt. buttermilk
1 cup vegetable oil
4 eggs

Combine all ingredients in a large bowl and mix well. Fill greased muffin tins 2/3 full. Bake at 400° for 15-20 minutes. Mixture may be stored in refrigerator for 6 weeks or all muffins may be baked and frozen.
Yields 5 dozen.

Mrs. Stuart Tribble
Grady, Arkansas

COLLEGE INN BLUEBERRY MUFFINS

3 cups sifted flour
4 tsp. baking powder
½ cup sugar
½ tsp. salt
1 cup blueberries, frozen
   or canned, well drained

2 eggs, beaten
¼ cup liquid shortening
1 cup milk

Sift dry ingredients together and mix in the blueberries. Mix eggs, shortening and milk; combine with dry ingredients. Stir gently just to dampen dry ingredients. Fill greased muffin tins 2/3 full. These are better if baked in regular size muffin tins, not the small ones. Bake at 400° for 20 minutes.
Yields 15-20 muffins.

Mrs. John G. Lile

These are the old fashioned kind, not too sweet.

FRESH APPLE MUFFINS

½ cup all-purpose flour
¾ cup whole wheat flour
2 tsp. baking powder
½ tsp. salt
½ tsp. cinnamon
¼ cup melted butter or oleo

½ cup sugar (brown or
    white or 3 Tbsp. honey)
1/3 cup milk
1 egg, lightly beaten
1 cup shredded unpeeled
apple

Sift dry ingredients. Add butter, sugar, milk, egg and apple. Stir just to moisten (batter should look lumpy). Fill greased muffin tins about 2/3 full. Bake at 350° for 30 minutes or until done.
Yields 10-11 muffins.

Mrs. Joe Campbell
Mena, Arkansas

QUICK MUFFINS

½ cup milk
¼ cup mayonnaise

1 cup self-rising flour, unsifted

Stir together all ingredients. Pour into well greased muffin tins, filling cups about 2/3 full. Bake at 450° for 20 minutes or until golden.
Yields 6.

Mrs. Ralph McNair
Meridian, Mississippi

Muffins—The name means "little muffs" to warm the fingers.

FRENCH PUFFS

1/3 cup butter
½ cup sugar
1½ cups flour
1½ tsp. baking powder
½ tsp. salt
¼ tsp. nutmeg

1 egg
½ cup milk
6 Tbsp. melted butter
½ cup sugar
1 tsp. cinnamon

Cream butter and sugar. Sift together flour, baking powder, salt and nutmeg. Add the egg to the creamed mixture. Add the dry ingredients alternately with the milk, mixing thoroughly after each addition. Place a teaspoonful of the dough in lightly greased small muffin tins. Bake at 350° for 20 minutes. Cool slightly. Roll muffins in melted butter, then in ½ cup sugar to which cinnamon has been added. These may be made in advance, then rewarmed.
Yields 4 dozen.

Mrs. Louis L. Ramsay, Jr.

YORKSHIRE PUDDING

1 cup flour (unsifted)   2 eggs
1 cup milk   Salt and pepper

Cook a tender roast such as rolled rib, rump or standing rib as usual in a shallow, open pan. Thirty minutes before it is done, remove it from the oven and increase the heat to 450°.

While the oven is heating, quickly prepare the Yorkshire pudding ingredients. Sprinkle the salt and pepper into the beef drippings around the roast. Mix other ingredients together at medium speed for 4-5 minutes, scraping the bowl often. The mixture must be smooth.

Pour the batter into the seasoned drippings around the roast. Place in the oven for about 20 minutes; it should rise and be full of large air-filled humps.

Make gravy in the pan after removing the meat and the Yorkshire pudding.
Serves 4-6.

Mrs. John Dolby

WELSH CAKES

4 cups flour   ½ tsp. nutmeg
1 tsp. baking powder   ½ tsp. cinnamon
Pinch of salt   1 egg, beaten
1¼ cups butter or oleo   3 Tbsp. milk
¾ cup sugar   Granulated sugar
1½ cups mixed currants
    and sultanas

Sift together flour, baking powder, and salt; rub in the butter. Add sugar, fruits, and spices. Mix in egg and milk. (This should be the consistency of short crust pastry.) Turn onto lightly floured board. Roll out and cut into rounds about 3 inches across and ½ inch thick. These are cooked on a "bakestone", heavy skillet or griddle, which is lightly wiped with oil or shortening. Cook over medium heat, never hot, for about 3 minutes on each side. If they brown too quickly, lower heat so the inside will have time to cook thoroughly. These little cakes have a slightly sandy texture. While hot, sprinkle with granulated sugar.
Yields 20.

Mrs. Jess Reeves

These are easy, but different. They are only slightly sweet and are especially good with tea or coffee.

ORANGE BREAD

4 California oranges   1 cup sugar
1 cup water

Peel oranges. Set aside pulp for another use. Remove most of white part
from rind. Grind rind twice. This should make 1½ cups. Put rind in a 2-
quart pan and cover well with water. Boil until tender, 20-30 minutes.
Drain rind and discard water. Mix 1 cup water and 1 cup sugar in saucepan and bring to a boil. Add rind and continue cooking until liquid is
absorbed. Set aside to cool.

3½ cups sifted flour   3 tsp. baking powder
1 cup sugar   ¼ tsp. salt
1 Tbsp. butter, melted   1 cup milk
1 egg   1 cup nuts, finely chopped

Keep out small amount of flour to dredge nuts. Combine remaining flour
with orange rind and other ingredients; mix well. Grease 6 soup cans well,
placing a piece of brown paper in the bottom. Fill cans half-full. Bake at
350° for 35 minutes or until done. Let set a minute then remove from cans.
Cool.
Yields 6 loaves.

Mrs. Henry F. Trotter, Jr.

Sliced and spread with cream cheese, these are so good for a coffee or tea.

WHOLE WHEAT BANANA NUT BREAD

2 cups whole wheat flour,   ½ cup chopped pecans
    unsifted   4 eggs
1 cup all-purpose flour, unsifted   5 or 6 bananas
1 cup unprocessed bran   1/3 cup shortening
    or wheat germ   ½ cup butter or oleo
1 tsp. cream of tartar   2 cups sugar
¾ tsp. salt
2 tsp. baking soda

Thoroughly combine both flours, bran, cream of tartar, salt, soda, and
pecans in a large mixing bowl. Put eggs, bananas, shortening, oleo, and
sugar into blender. Blend until very smooth and creamy. Pour liquid
mixture over dry mixture and stir just until moistened. Pour into 2 greased
and floured loaf pans. Bake at 350° for about 1 hour or until tested done.
Turn out on rack to cool. If desired, 4 cups all-purpose flour, sifted, can be
substituted for the combination of flours. This bread freezes well.
Yields 2 loaves.

Mrs. John G. Lile

BANANA NUT BREAD

½ cup butter
1½ cups sugar
2 eggs
1½ cups flour, sifted
½ tsp. salt

1 tsp. soda in ½ cup
   buttermilk
1 cup mashed bananas
½ cup chopped nuts

In a bowl cream butter and sugar. Add eggs, flour and salt. Mix. Add buttermilk mixture and beat. Mix in bananas and nuts. Pour into a greased and floured loaf pan. Bake at 350° for 1 hour or until done. *Yields 1 loaf.*

Mrs. Del Brannon

DATE AND NUT BREAD

1½ cups dates, chopped
2 cups boiling water
2 tsp. soda
½ cup shortening
2 cups sugar

2 eggs, beaten
1 cup nuts, chopped fine
1 tsp. vanilla
4 cups sifted flour

Combine dates, boiling water and soda. Let cool. Add other ingredients and mix well. Grease and flour 5 (16 oz.) cans. Fill half-full. Bake at 350° for 1 hour or until done. Keeps for weeks in the refrigerator and freezes beautifully.
Yields 5 loaves.

Mrs. Joe Campbell
Mena, Arkansas

RAISIN BREAD

2 cups water
2 cups raisins
2 tsp. soda
2 cups sugar
½ cup shortening

2 eggs
4 cups sifted flour
1 cup raisin juice, cooled
1 cup chopped nuts

Boil together water and raisins for 2½ minutes. Cool, then stir in soda to water-raisin mixture. Let set a few minutes. Strain raisins, reserving 1 cup of juice. Cream sugar and shortening. Add eggs, flour, raisins, raisin juice and nuts. Mix well. Pour into 3 greased and floured 1 pound coffee cans, filling only half full. Bake at 350° for 45 minutes or until done. Cool upside down on a rack. Baked bread keeps for weeks in the refrigerator or freezes beautifully.
Yields 3 loaves.

Mrs. David R Perdue

BOSTON BROWN BREAD

3 cups flour
4 tsp. soda
3 tsp. salt
2 cups wheat germ

2 cups graham cracker crumbs
4 eggs, lightly beaten
2/3 cup vegetable oil
2 cups light corn syrup
4 cups buttermilk

Sift together flour, soda and salt. Add wheat germ and graham cracker crumbs. In a separate bowl mix eggs, oil, corn syrup and buttermilk; add to dry ingredients. Mix to blend with a wooden spoon. Grease 4 (1-pound) coffee cans with vegetable oil. Fill cans one-half full then place on baking sheet. Bake at 350° for 1 hour or until done. Cool on rack 10 minutes, run knife around sides of cans and turn out bread. Keep refrigerated after cooling.
Yields 4 loaves.

Mrs. Walter M. Simpson

Spread with cream cheese and serve cold, lavish with orange marmalade or butter and toast — good so many ways!

ZUCCHINI BREAD

3 eggs, well beaten
1 cup vegetable oil
2 cups sugar
2 cups zucchini, peeled
  and grated
1 Tbsp. vanilla

3 cups flour
1 tsp. salt
¼ tsp. baking powder
1 tsp. soda
¾ tsp. nutmeg
1 Tbsp. cinnamon

Mix together eggs, oil, sugar, zucchini and vanilla. Sift together flour, salt, baking powder, soda, nutmeg, and cinnamon; add to first mixture. Pour into 2 greased and floured loaf pans. Bake at 350° for 1 hour or until done.
Yields 2 loaves.

Mrs. Marvin Gresham

LEMON BREAD

3 Tbsp. shortening
3 Tbsp. butter
1 cup sugar
1 lemon rind, grated
2 eggs
1½ cups flour

1 tsp. baking powder
½ cup milk
½ cup chopped nuts
¼ cup sugar
Juice of 1 lemon

Cream shortening, butter, 1 cup sugar and rind. Add eggs; mix in well. Sift flour and baking powder. Alternately add flour and milk to creamed mixture. Mix well and fold in nuts. Bake at 350° for 45 minutes or until done. Mix remaining sugar and lemon juice. Pour over hot bread and pierce with fork. Let stand 5 minutes before removing from pan.
Yields 1 loaf.

Mrs. Joe Campbell
Mena, Arkansas

APRICOT BREAD

3 cups flour
1½ tsp. salt
1½ tsp. soda
1½ tsp. cinnamon
2½ cups sugar

¾ cups vegetable oil
4 eggs
1 cup pecans, chopped
1½ cups cooked apricots,
    mashed

Sift flour, salt, soda and cinnamon together. Add sugar, eggs and oil, mixing well. Add nuts and mashed apricots; mix thoroughly. Pour into 2 greased and floured loaf pans. Bake at 300° for 1½ hours or until done. Turn out onto wire rack and cool.
Yields 2 loaves.

Mrs. Joe Bond
Warren, Arkansas

PUMPKIN BREAD

3 cups sugar
1 cup vegetable oil
4 eggs
½ cup water
3½ cups flour

2 tsp. soda
4 tsp. cinnamon
1½ tsp. salt
2 cups pumpkin
1 cup chopped pecans

Reserve 2 tablespoons flour to dredge pecans. Mix sugar and oil. Add eggs one at a time, beating after each addition. Add water. Sift flour, soda, cinnamon and salt; add to mixture. Beat in pumpkin. Add nuts and mix well. Pour in 4 (1-pound) coffee cans, filling only half full. Bake at 350° for 1 hour. Cool slightly in cans; turn out on rack to finish cooling. Flavor is best if baked day before using. This keeps for weeks in refrigerator or freezes beautifully.
Yields 4 loaves.

Mrs. John D. Tharp

CORN BREAD

4 Tbsp. bacon drippings
1½ cups white cornmeal
3 Tbsp. flour
1 tsp. salt

1 tsp. soda
2 cups fresh buttermilk
1 egg

Melt bacon drippings in a 9-inch iron skillet until very hot. During this time, sift dry ingredients into bowl. Add buttermilk and egg; beat until batter is smooth. Add one-half of drippings to batter and stir well. Pour batter into skillet and bake at 450° for 20-25 minutes.
Serves 6.

Mrs. Dan Harrelson

JALAPENO CORN BREAD

1½ cups yellow cornmeal
3 tsp. baking powder
½ tsp. salt
2 eggs
1 cup sour cream
1 cup Cheddar
  cheese, grated

1 (8¾ oz.) can cream style
  corn
¼-½ cups chopped Jalapeno
  peppers
½ cup shortening or bacon
  drippings

Melt bacon drippings in a 9-inch iron skillet until very hot. During this time, sift dry ingredients in bowl. Add remaining ingredients, plus hot drippings, and mix well. Pour batter into skillet and bake at 450° for 20-25 minutes. Muffin tins may be used, filling half full, and baked 15-20 minutes.
Serves 6.

Mrs. Royce O. Johnson, Jr.

CORN BREAD DRESSING

1 pan corn bread
  (See Index)
6 slices white bread,
  broken up
1 section (¼ lb.) crumbled
  saltine crackers
2 onions, chopped

5-6 ribs celery, chopped
½ cup butter or oleo
4 eggs, well beaten
Salt and pepper to taste
Chestnuts (or water chestnuts)
2 or more cans Swanson's
  Chichen Broth (or fresh)

Crumble corn bread and white bread and mix with crackers. Sauté vegetables in butter; add to bread mixture and mix well. Add enough broth to moisten well. Add eggs, salt and pepper along with fresh chestnuts (or sliced water chestnuts). Pour into 9x13 inch pan. Bake at 350°-375° for about 1 hour or until firm. Top with giblet gravy!

Mrs. Talbot Benton

DROP CORN BREAD

1 cup white cornmeal
1 tsp. salt
3 tsp. baking powder

¾ cup boiling water
2 eggs
2/3 cup shortening

Mix dry ingredients. Gradually add boiling water and mix to a paste. Add eggs and beat well. Add more water if needed. Heat 2/3 cup of shortening or oil in an iron skillet until sizzling, but not smoking hot. Drop meal a teaspoon at a time into oil and cook until golden brown.

Mrs. Alex Rowell

HUSHPUPPIES

¾ cup white cornmeal
¼ cup flour
¾ tsp. salt
1 tsp. baking powder

1 tsp. sugar
1 small onion, chopped
1 egg, slightly beaten
Buttermilk

Mix all ingredients except buttermilk. Gradually add buttermilk until consistency desired. Drop by teaspoons into hot deep fat and fry until golden brown.
Yields 1 dozen.

Mrs. J. Gordon Reese

CHEESE HUSH PUPPIES

1 cup flour
1 cup yellow cornmeal
3 tsp. baking powder
1 tsp. salt
1 Tbsp. sugar

1 egg, slightly beaten
¾ cup milk
1 medium onion, chopped
½ lb. grated Cheddar cheese

Mix dry ingredients together. Add egg, milk, onion and cheese. Form into small mounds. Drop in hot fat and cook until golden.
Serves 10-12.

Donnie Mead

One tablespoon of lemon juice or vinegar plus enough sweet milk to make one cup can be substituted for one cup sour milk or buttermilk.

HOTEL ROANOKE SPOON BREAD

1½ cups white cornmeal
1 1/3 tsp. salt
1 tsp. sugar
1½ cups boiling water

¼ cup butter, melted
5 eggs
2 cups milk
1 Tbsp. baking powder

Mix cornmeal, salt and sugar. Scald with boiling water. Add melted butter. Beat eggs in separate bowl, add milk. Combine two mixtures, stirring in baking powder. Pour into greased baking dish. Bake at 350° for 30-40 minutes.
Serves 6-8.

Mrs. Sanborn Wilkins

BUTTERMILK SILVER DOLLAR PANCAKES

½ tsp. soda
1½ cups buttermilk
1 cup flour
½ tsp. salt

1 tsp. baking powder
1 Tbsp. sugar
1 egg, beaten
2 Tbsp. shortening, melted

Mix soda in a little warm water. Then stir into buttermilk (mixture will foam); set aside. Mix dry ingredients. Add buttermilk mixture to dry ingredients and stir well by hand. Add well-beaten egg and melted shortening. Batter should be rather thin for light pancakes; if too thick add more buttermilk. Bake on hot griddle and serve immediately.

Mrs. Ferd M. Bellingrath

APPLE FLAPS

1½ cups flour
2 Tbsp. sugar
1 Tbsp. baking powder
¼ tsp. salt

2 eggs, beaten
¾ cup milk
2 Tbsp. melted butter
1 cup applesauce

Sift together the flour, sugar, baking powder and salt. Combine eggs, milk, butter and applesauce; add to dry ingredients and stir until moistened. Use 2 tablespoons of batter per pancake.
Yields 20 pancakes.

Mrs. Henry F. Trotter, Jr.

INSTANT PANCAKE MIX

Mix:
4 cups flour
3 Tbsp. plus 1 tsp. baking
   powder

2 tsp. salt
2 Tbsp. sugar
1 1/3 cups non-fat dry milk

Mix ingredients thoroughly. Store in airtight container in cool, dry place. This makes about 6 cups mix. When ready to prepare pancakes, combine the following for 14-16 small pancakes.

Pancakes:
1 1/3 cups Mix
1 egg, beaten
1 scant cup water

4 tsp. shortening or bacon
   drippings

Heat griddle moderately hot; grease lightly. Pour batter in small circles. Bake until top side is full of air bubbles, underside is golden. Turn only once. Regrease griddle between batches.

Mrs. Richard Milwee

WAFFLES

2 cups flour
1 Tbsp. baking powder
1 tsp. salt
1 Tbsp. cornmeal

2 eggs, separated
1½ milk
6 Tbsp. vegetable oil

Sift the dry ingredients together. Beat egg yolks slightly; add milk alternately with dry ingredients. Add oil and mix well. In another bowl, beat egg whites until they hold a peak. Fold into batter. Bake on greased, hot waffle iron.
Serves 4.

Mrs. Frank Gilbert
Prescott, Arkansas

BASIC CREPE BATTER

2 cups flour
1 tsp. salt

4 eggs
2½ cups milk

Combine flour and salt. Combine slightly beaten eggs and 1½ cups of the milk with dry ingredients. Beat with a rotary beater until smooth. Add remaining milk, beating steadily until smooth. (If any lumps, strain batter.) Let stand 2 hours at room temperature before using.

To Prepare: Brush pan lightly with cooking oil. Add 1½ tablespoons of batter, more or less. Tilt pan until bottom is covered. Cook about ½ minute, turn with spatula, cook ½ minute. Remove from pan and repeat. Brush pan lightly with cooking oil between every two crepes. If making ahead of time, wrap in plastic or foil. These will freeze well. To use after freezing, defrost at room temperature. Roll crepe loosely around filling.
Yields 40, 5 inch crepes.

Mrs. John G. Lile

For a dessert crepe add 1 tablespoon sugar and 1 teaspoon vanilla.

TRINITY EPISCOPAL CHURCH

700 Block of West Third Avenue

Trinity Episcopal Church is of Medieval Revival architecture and is the oldest Episcopal church building in use in Arkansas. The cornerstone was laid on December 27, 1866, and the first services were held in the church on Christmas Day 1870. The building is well preserved and maintained; it was placed on the National Register of Historic Places in 1974.

ARTICHOKE OYSTER SOUP

½ cup butter
1½ cups chopped green onions,
    including 2 onion tops
2 garlic cloves, minced
3 Tbsp. flour
3 (14 oz.) cans artichoke
    hearts, drained and rinsed

6 cups chicken stock
½ tsp. crushed red pepper
¼ tsp. anise seed
1 tsp. salt
1 qt. oysters, cut in
    half if large

Melt butter in a large heavy pot, add onions and garlic and sauté for 3-5 minutes. Add flour and cook 5 minutes stirring constantly. Stir in quartered artichokes; add stock and seasonings and cook 20 minutes. Add oysters and their liquor and simmer 10 minutes. *Do not boil* and *do not overcook.* This soup is most delicious if made the day before serving, allowing flavors to blend. If you want to drink the soup from mugs, purée in blender and top with a lemon slice.
Serves 12-14.

Mrs. R. Teryl Brooks, Jr.

CREAM OF ARTICHOKE MUSHROOM SOUP

1 pkg. frozen artichoke
    hearts
1 chicken bouillon cube
3 Tbsp. butter
½ cup fresh mushrooms,
    finely sliced

2 Tbsp. onion, finely chopped
1 Tbsp. flour
2½ cups milk
½ tsp. salt
Dash cayenne pepper

Cook artichokes according to package directions. Drain; reserve any cooking liquid. Add enough hot water to reserved liquid to measure ½ cup. Dissolve bouillon cube in this liquid. Finely dice artichoke hearts—reserve one for garnish. Heat butter in saucepan until bubbly. Cook onions and mushrooms in butter stirring until tender. Stir in flour. Cook over low heat, stirring constantly, until mixture is bubbly and light brown, about 2 minutes. Remove from heat, gradually stir in bouillon, artichoke liquid, and milk. Heat 5-10 minutes until mixture thickens. Add salt, cayenne and artichokes. Cook over low heat stirring occasionally, 5-10 minutes.
Serves 4.

Mrs. Ronald D. Blankenship

EASY AND ELEGANT ARTICHOKE SOUP

½ cup green onions with
   tops, chopped
½ cup celery, finely chopped
6 Tbsp. butter
6 Tbsp. flour
6 cups chicken broth

¼ cup lemon juice
1 bay leaf
1 tsp. salt
⅛ tsp. red pepper
¼ tsp. thyme
3 (14 oz.) cans artichokes

In large saucepan, sauté onions and celery in butter until soft. Add flour. Cook one minute stirring constantly. Add broth and lemon juice stirring until well blended. Add bay leaf, then seasonings a little at a time. Separate drained artichoke bottoms from leaves. Add bottoms to soup, cover. Simmer 20 minutes. Purée in blender. Add artichoke leaves and stir until blended through soup. May be prepared a few hours ahead to this point. Heat and serve. Garnish with slice of lemon and finely chopped parsley.
Serves 8.

Mrs. J. Wayne Buckley

Wonderful first course!

CREAM OF AVOCADO SOUP

1 large avocado
1 cup chicken broth
1 cup whipping cream

2 tsp. lemon juice
Salt and pepper to taste
Red caviar

Peel avocado and blend. Mix with broth. Stir over low heat until smooth. Add cream, lemon juice, salt and pepper. Stir well, cool. Chill in refrigerator. Serve sprinkled with caviar. May substitute fresh dill or julienned cucumber for caviar.
Serves 4.

Dr. James T. Rhyne

CREAM OF CORN SOUP

1 cup fresh corn
2 cups water
1 small onion, cut up
1 Tbsp. butter

1 Tbsp. flour
2 cups milk
Salt and pepper to taste

Boil corn, water and onion for 30 minutes. Strain and discard corn and onion. Add rest of ingredients to liquid and mix well. Simmer, stirring constantly, for 10 minutes. For a party, top with a spoonful of whipped cream and a sprig of parsley.
Yields 3 cups.

Mrs. Virgil L. Payne

This makes a delicious meal with chicken sandwiches and tomato salad.

BEAN SOUP

1 lb. Great Northern beans	1½ tsp. salt
¼ lb. lima beans	¼ tsp. pepper
1 ham hock	1 (16 oz.) can stewed tomatoes
1 beef knuckle bone	¼ cup onions, chopped
1 medium onion, chopped	¼ cup celery, chopped
2 cloves garlic, minced	1 Tbsp. Pickapeppa Sauce
2 stalks celery, whole	Green onions to garnish

Wash both beans. Cover with water (2 inches over) bring to boil. Let stand off heat, 30 minutes. (Beans can be soaked overnight.) In another large pot place bone, ham hock, medium onion, celery stalks, garlic, salt and pepper. Cover with water. Boil 30 minutes. Remove celery stalks. Combine beans and bones. Cover with water; cover pan and boil slowly 1 hour. Add remaining ingredients. May need to add more salt. Cook until Great Northern beans are soft. Lima beans will cook to pieces to thicken soup. Garnish with green onion.
Serves 8.

Mrs. Milton Hughes

If a soup is too salty, add a few slices of raw potato. Boil a few minutes and if still over-salty, repeat the process with fresh potato slices.

ENGLISH CHEDDAR CHOWDER

2 cups salted water	4 cups boiling milk
1/3 cup carrots, finely chopped	4 cups boiling chicken stock
1/3 cup celery, finely chopped	1 lb. sharp Cheddar cheese,
1/3 cup onions, finely chopped	grated
1 medium onion, finely	1 Tbsp. prepared mustard
chopped	Salt to taste
½ cup butter	White pepper to taste
¾ cup flour	Cayenne pepper to taste

In large pan bring water to boil. Add carrots, celery and 1/3 cup onions. Boil for 5 minutes. Set aside. In skillet sauté medium onion in butter for 1 minute or until wilted. Blend in flour. Slowly add milk and chicken stock whisking constantly until smooth. Add cheese and vegetables with liquid. Whisk. Add remaining ingredients, whisking constantly until cheese is melted. Bring to boil and serve.
Serves 10-12.

Mrs. Martin G. Gilbert

This makes a great meal with Sausage Tarts and Curried Fruit. (See Index)

CAULIFLOWER SOUP

2 Tbsp. shortening
½ cup onions, chopped
1 cup celery, chopped
1 small carrot
1 head firm white cauliflower
  (about 1 qt. cut up)
2 Tbsp. parsley, chopped
2 qts. chicken broth
1 Tbsp. salt

½ tsp. peppercorns, ½ bay
  leaf, 1 tsp. tarragon tied
  in a cheesecloth bag
4 Tbsp. butter
6 Tbsp. flour
2 cups milk
1 cup half and half cream
1 cup sour cream at
  room temperature

If you make your own chicken broth, put leaves, hard white core and stalks from cauliflower in to cook with soup bones. This gives the broth a more cauliflower flavor.

In large pot, melt shortening, add onions; stir constantly over medium heat until onions start to turn yellow. Continue stirring, add carrot and celery and cook 2 minutes. Add cauliflower and 1 tablespoon parsley. Cover pot and turn heat very low, stirring occasionally to keep it from sticking. After 15 minutes, add chicken broth, salt and cheesecloth bag of herbs. Bring to a boil over medium heat. Reduce heat and let simmer.

In a small pan, melt butter. Mix flour into milk with wire whip and slowly, using wire whip, add to butter. Cook to medium consistency. Remove from heat; dilute with half and half and pour into simmering soup. Stir gently with wooden spoon and simmer for 15-20 minutes. Just before serving, place sour cream in a soup tureen and mix in remaining parsley. Put 2 or 3 ladles hot soup in tureen and stir into sour cream. Remove cheesecloth bag from soup and pour all of soup into tureen. Serve immediately.
Serves 8.

Mrs. John E. Caruthers, Sr.

CLAM CHOWDER

6 slices bacon
⅛ tsp. white pepper
½ cup water
1/3 cup onions, chopped
1 cup potatoes, diced

¼ tsp. salt
1 (7½ oz.) can of clams
1½ cups milk
1½ cups evaporated milk
Parsley

Chop bacon, fry until crisp. Remove bacon from skillet. Drain on paper towel. Add pepper, water, onion, potatoes and salt to grease in skillet. Cook for 10 minutes then add both milks and clams. Cook 10 more minutes or until potatoes are tender. Add bacon and sprinkle with parsley. Serve hot.
Serves 4.

Mrs. James S. Rogers

Served at 1975 Charity Ball Royal Supper.

CHICKEN BROTH

¼ cup butter
6-7 ribs celery, chopped
2 fresh tomatoes, peeled
  and chopped
2-3 green onions (white part
  only), chopped

6 (10¾ oz.) cans Campbell's
  Chicken Broth
Salt, pepper, Worcestershire
  sauce to taste

Sauté vegetables in butter until soft. Add broth and simmer 45 minutes. Strain. Season to taste if needed. Serve hot in cups. This keeps in refrigerator for a week.
Yields 7 cups.

Mrs. Charles Slater

SHORTCUT DUCK GUMBO

2 ducks
2 bay leaves
2 cloves garlic, minced
4-5 ribs celery, chopped
1½ (12 oz.) pkgs. frozen
  chopped onions, or 2
  large onions, chopped
1 bell pepper, chopped
1 (1¼ lbs.) pkg. frozen okra
1 (¾ oz.) pkg. brown gravy mix

3 Tbsp. oil
1 (1 lb.) can whole tomatoes
1 tsp. cracked black pepper
3 Tbsp. parsley flakes
½ - 1 tsp. Tabasco sauce
1 Tbsp. Worcestershire sauce
Juice of ½ lemon
3 Tbsp. gumbo filé
Salt to taste
Rice, cooked

Boil ducks and bay leaves in water to cover. Remove ducks when tender; pull meat from bones and chop. Add garlic, celery, onion, bell pepper and okra to broth. In another pan make roux of gravy mix and oil. Add tomatoes and pepper to roux, then mix with broth. Add parsley and duck. Simmer 2½ - 3 hours, stirring often. Add Tabasco, Worcestershire sauce, lemon juice, salt and filé. Serve over rice. Ham hock, shrimp or oysters may be added for variety.
Serves 8-10.

Mrs. Johnny Keesee
Clarksdale, Mississippi

Filé is the powdered sassafras leaf. It is used as a thickening agent. Filé is never put in until just a minute before serving, whereas okra is cooked with the gumbo. Filé is added after the gumbo is removed from the heat. Never add filé while gumbo is cooking because boiling after the filé is added tends to make the gumbo stringy and unfit for use.

SMOKED DUCK AND OYSTER GUMBO

3 ducks, wild
½ cup butter
½ cup flour
1 medium green pepper,
    chopped
1 large onion, chopped
1 large clove garlic, minced
¼ cup fresh parsley, chopped

1 (10 oz.) pkg. frozen cut
    okra, or ½ lb. fresh, cut
1 (16 oz.) can tomatoes, or
    4-6 fresh tomatoes
Salt, pepper, paprika and
    red pepper to taste
1 pt. fresh oysters
Rice, cooked

Smoke the ducks, away from the flame, on a charcoal smoker with hickory chips on the charcoal for flavor. Keep smoker closed throughout cooking period, about 4 hours. Next stew the ducks in a covered dutch oven, in water halfway up the depth of the ducks, for 2-3 hours or until meat almost falls away from bones. Debone and cut meat into bite-sized chunks. (Use as much meat as possible, but take care to remove any shot!) Strain and reserve duck broth.

Melt butter in a large iron skillet; add flour and brown until roux is dark golden. Add green pepper and onion, continuing to brown slowly; add garlic toward the end. Pour reserved broth into a large dutch oven and whisk in roux mixture. Add duck meat and cook, covered, over low temperature for 30 minutes. Stir in parsley, okra, tomatoes and seasonings. Cook slowly until okra is tender. Can be chilled at this point. When ready to serve, heat to boiling and add oysters (which you have picked over carefully), cooking until *just* done. Check seasonings and ladle large amount of gumbo over rice in large soup bowls.
Serves 8.

Mrs. John G. Lile

CHICKEN GUMBO

1 fryer, boiled
¼ lb. bacon, diced
¼ cup onion, chopped
¼ cup green pepper, diced
1 cup celery, diced
3 sprigs parsley, finely
    chopped

1 cup tomatoes, fresh
    or canned
4 cups chicken stock
Salt and pepper
½-1 tsp. thyme
1 cup cooked rice
2 cups okra, sliced

Debone chicken and cut into medium sized chunks. Sauté bacon in soup pot. Add onion, green pepper, celery, and sauté. Add parsley, tomatoes, stock and seasonings. Slowly simmer until vegetables are soft. Add chicken, okra and rice; cook for 10 more minutes.
Serves 6.

Mrs. Martin G. Gilbert

GUMBO

6 Tbsp. bacon grease
¼ cup flour
1 onion, chopped
1 lb. okra, sliced
1 cup tomatoes, chopped
5 cups water
2 tsp. parsley, chopped
1 clove garlic, crushed
1 bay leaf
Pinch of thyme

2 tsp. Worcestershire sauce
½ tsp. hot sauce
1 lb. shrimp, peeled
  and deveined
2 (7½ oz.) cans crabmeat
1 pt. oysters and juice
Juice of ¼ lemon
Salt and pepper to taste
Cooked rice

Heat bacon grease; add flour and brown. Add onion and cook until transparent. Add okra; stir and cook until like a paste. Add tomatoes, water, parsley, garlic, bay leaf, thyme, Worcestershire sauce and hot sauce. Cook for 15 minutes. Add remaining ingredients, except rice. Cook 30 minutes. Serve over cooked rice.
Serves 6-8.

Mrs. Phillip Strickland

To make a roux: A roux is a mixture of oil and flour. The oil is heated and flour is added. You stir the roux constantly until the desired browness is reached. You must have a heavy pot for making a roux. A light weight pot will cause the roux to brown too fast and burn easily.

JANIE'S FAVORITE

2 (10¾ oz.) cans cream of
  celery soup
1 (10¾ oz.) can chicken broth

2 Tbsp. lemon juice
Salt, Accent, and red
  pepper to taste

Mix with wire whisk. Heat and serve.
Serves 4.

Mrs. J. Wayne Buckley

HOT KETTLE SOUP

1 (46 oz.) can V-8 juice
2 (10½ oz.) cans beef broth
5 Tbsp. lemon juice

5 Tbsp. Worcestershire sauce
1½ tsp. salt
½ tsp. Tabasco

Mix all ingredients together. Heat and serve in mugs.
Serves 12.

Mrs. Harry A. Metcalf
Mrs. M. Maury Goodloe

GAZPACHO

1 cup onions, chopped
3 cups cucumber, peeled
  and chopped
2 cups green pepper, chopped
6 cups canned Italian
  tomatoes
2 cups consommé
½ cup lemon juice
1½ cups V-8 juice
1 cup Snap-E-Tom

½ cup olive oil
2½ tsp. salt
¼ tsp. pepper
½ tsp. tarragon
¼ tsp. sweet basil
¼ tsp. marjoram
1 clove garlic, minced
¼ tsp. thyme
¼ tsp. oregano
½ tsp. parsley

Combine all ingredients in a large bowl. Blend in blender 1 cup at a time until of pouring consistency. Stir well and chill.
Serves 12.

Mrs. Thomas F. Stobaugh

SPANISH WHITE GAZPACHO

3 medium cucumbers,
  peeled and sliced
1 clove garlic, minced
3 cups chicken broth,
  fresh or canned
3 cups sour cream
3 Tbsp. white vinegar
2 tsp. salt
Ground pepper to taste

4 medium tomatoes, peeled
  and diced
½ cup parsley, snipped
½ cup green onions and
  tops, sliced
½ cup almonds, chopped
  and toasted
2 medium cucumbers,
  peeled and sliced

Blend 3 cucumbers, garlic and a little broth in blender until smooth. In large bowl, combine cucumber mixture with remaining broth. Blend sour cream and 1 cup of the cucumber-broth mixture together; then blend with rest of cucumber-broth mixture. Add vinegar, salt and pepper. Cover and chill until serving time.

Place each remaining ingredient in small serving bowls on a large tray. Ladle soup into pre-chilled bowls or cups, ¾ full. Pass garnishes and let guests choose their own. Serve with crusty French bread for a cool summertime treat.
Yields 2½ quarts.

Mrs. Howard Stern

HOT MADRILENE

¼ cup butter
¼ cup onion, chopped
2 (18 oz.) cans tomato juice
2 (10½ oz.) cans beef broth

2 Tbsp. parsley
1 bay leaf
Parmesan cheese

Melt butter, add onion, and cook until tender. Add tomato juice, broth, parsley and bay leaf. Heat to boiling, reduce heat and simmer 5 minutes. Remove bay leaf. Top with cheese and serve.
Serves 6.

Mrs. John Bohnert

QUICK MUSHROOM SOUP

1 small onion, chopped
1 (4 oz.) can mushroom
  pieces and stems, drained
4 Tbsp. butter
2 soup cans of milk

2 (10¾ oz.) cans cream of
  mushroom soup
Salt, white pepper, and
  Accent to taste

Sauté onion and mushrooms in butter until soft. Add other ingredients. Stir with wire whisk until hot.
Serves 4.

Mrs. J. Wayne Buckley

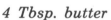

CREAM OF MUSHROOM SOUP

4 Tbsp. butter
2 tsp. onion, chopped
1 lb. fresh mushrooms, sliced
1 qt. chicken stock, or
  3 cans chicken broth

2 Tbsp. flour
1 tsp. salt
1 cup half and half cream
2 Tbsp. dry sherry (optional)
½ cup whipping cream, whipped

Sauté onion in 2 Tbsp. butter in deep skillet or Dutch oven. Add mushrooms and sauté 3 minutes. Add stock, cover and simmer 15 minutes. Melt 2 tablespoons butter in another skillet. Add flour and salt; cook until bubbly. Using wire whisk, add half and half to make white sauce. Continue to whisk and add 2 cups mushroom mixture. Pour all back into skillet or Dutch oven. Add sherry. Strain if desired. Serve with dollop of cream.
Serves 6.

Mrs. Willard R. Burks

CREAM OF ONION SOUP

1½ cups butter
4 cups onions, thinly sliced
1 cup flour
5 tsp. instant chicken
  bouillon
9 tsp. instant beef bouillon

12 cups boiling water
½ tsp. cayenne pepper
1½ Tbsp. salt
1 egg yolk, beaten
2 Tbsp. whipping cream
Fresh Parmesan cheese, grated

Melt butter, add onions and reduce heat to low. Cook until onions are soft but not brown, about 45 minutes. Add flour and cook 5-10 minutes. Dissolve chicken and beef bouillon in the boiling water. Add this to onions. Add pepper and salt. Bring to boil, reduce heat and simmer 15 minutes. Mix egg yolk and cream. Add a little soup to egg mixture then return to soup. Stir to blend. Pour into mugs and top with cheese.
Serves 8.

Mrs. Dan Harrelson

FRENCH ONION SOUP

5 cups thinly sliced yellow
  onions (1½ lbs.)
3 Tbsp. butter
1 Tbsp. vegetable oil
1 tsp. salt
¼ tsp. sugar
3 Tbsp. flour
3 (10¾ oz.) cans beef
  bouillon

3 cups boiling water
½ cup dry white wine
Salt and pepper to taste
2 oz. Swiss cheese, slivered
16 (½-1 inch) French bread
  slices
½ cup grated Parmesan cheese
1 Tbsp. melted butter

Cook onions slowly with butter and oil in heavy, covered 4 quart saucepan for 15 minutes. Stir in salt and sugar. Cook uncovered over moderate heat 35-40 minutes, stirring often until onions are a deep golden brown. Sprinkle with flour; stir 3 minutes. Remove from heat; add boiling bouillon and water to onion mixture, blend well. Add wine and seasonings; simmer partially covered, 35 minutes. While soup is simmering, place 1 layer of French bread slices on cookie sheet and bake at 325° for 30 minutes or until they are dried and golden brown.

Bring soup to boil; pour into oven-proof tureen. Stir in Swiss cheese; float toast rounds on top. Cover toast with Parmesan cheese and sprinkle with melted butter. Bake at 325° for 20 minutes. Broil 2 minutes.
Serves 6-8.

Mrs. James S. Rogers

OYSTER BISQUE

3 Tbsp. butter
4 green onions, chopped
Garlic sliver, minced
1 Tbsp. celery leaves, chopped
1 Tbsp. parsley, chopped
1-1½ pts. oysters, drained
1½ cups milk

½ cup whipping cream
½ tsp. salt
½ tsp. Accent
Ground pepper to taste
¼ cup dry white wine
2 egg yolks, beaten

Sauté onions and garlic in butter until brown. Add celery leaves and parsley. Cook and stir 1 minute. Add other ingredients *except* wine and egg yolks. When milk is hot and oysters float, add wine. Pour a small amount of bisque over egg yolks and mix. Then slowly pour yolks into hot bisque. Heat slowly until hot but not boiling.
Serves 4.

Mrs. Harry A. Metcalf

COUNTRY STYLE PEA SOUP

1 lb. split peas
2 qts. hot water
1 (2 lb.) ham hock or bones
1 clove garlic, chopped

1 medium onion, chopped
1 stalk celery, chopped
1 tsp. salt
⅛ tsp. pepper

Combine all ingredients. Heat to boiling, reduce heat and simmer 1 hour and 15 minutes or until peas are very soft. Put through coarse strainer. Reheat and serve.
Serves 8.

Mrs. Jay Dickey, Sr.

POTATO SOUP

½ cup butter
2 medium onions, chopped
4 or 5 medium potatoes, peeled (cut in small quarters)
5 cups water
½ cup beef consommé

1 cup chicken broth
2½ cups milk
1½ cups half and half cream
Salt
White pepper

Sauté onions in butter until limp. Cook potatoes in water until 1½ cups of water remain and potatoes are tender, about 45 minutes. Add onions, consommé, broth, milk and cream. Stir well. Season to taste with salt and white pepper.
Serves 6-8.

Mrs. Louis L. Ramsay

VICHYSSOISE

2 cups finely diced
  raw potatoes
4 Tbsp. butter
6 leeks, chopped
3 cups chicken bouillon
1 tsp. salt

½ tsp. freshly ground
  black pepper
Dash nutmeg
1½-2 cups whipping cream
Chives, chopped

Cook potatoes in salted water to cover until tender. Melt butter in skillet and add leeks. Cook leeks gently, tossing them lightly for a few minutes. Add bouillon and bring to boil. Lower heat and simmer leeks until tender. Add potatoes to leek mixture; season to taste with salt, pepper and nutmeg. Put this mixture in blender (you will need to blend it in 2 lots), and blend for 1 minute until smooth. Chill. When ready to serve, mix in cream. Garnish with chives.
Serves 4.

Mrs. E. Russell Lambert, Jr.

SHRIMP SOUP

1 (10¾ oz.) can shrimp soup
1 (8 oz.) carton sour cream
2 medium tomatoes, peeled
  and chopped

Red pepper, chives and salt
  to taste

Blend. Chill and serve. This is a great summer soup. Serve with cucumber or asparagus sandwiches.
Serves 2.

Mrs. Henry F. Trotter, Jr.

SUMMER SQUASH SOUP

2 medium yellow squash
2 small zucchini
1½ cups celery leaves
3 Tbsp. butter
4 cups chicken stock

Salt and pepper to taste
Celery salt
2 Tbsp. parsley, finely
  chopped

Without peeling, chop squash and zucchini into small pieces. In a covered pan cook squash, zucchini and celery leaves with butter over very low heat until tender (about 20 minutes). Purée mixture in blender, adding 1 cup of stock. Mix purée with rest of stock. Correct seasoning with salt, pepper and celery salt. Bring back to boil. Serve hot or cold garnished with parsley.
Serves 6.

Mrs. Harold Blach, Jr.
Birmingham, Alabama

100

GRANDMOTHER HOWELL'S CREAM OF TOMATO SOUP

1 (1 lb.) can tomatoes
1 onion, chopped
½ tomato can of water
¼ tsp. soda

3 cups milk
1 Tbsp. butter
Salt and pepper to taste

Cook tomatoes, onions and water slowly until cooked down. Push mixture through strainer or use blender. Add soda to tomatoes. Heat milk in double boiler until very hot and remove from fire. When tomatoes and milk are *same* temperature, add tomatoes to milk slowly, beating constantly. (Milk and tomatoes must be the same temperature or mixture will curdle.) Add butter, salt and pepper. Keep warm over hot water in double boiler.

This is a very delicate, buttery tasting soup. Goes great with homemade Melba toast, stuffed mushrooms and cheese straws. For an extra touch add raw peeled shrimp before serving and let cook until done. Top with chives and a dollop of sour cream.
Serves 4.

Mrs. Jack P. Smith

TORTILLA SOUP

1 medium onion, chopped
2 green chilies from (4 oz.) can, chopped
3 cloves garlic, chopped
2 Tbsp. vegetable oil
1 (10¾ oz.) can condensed beef bouillon
3 (10¾ oz.) cans condensed chicken broth
6 cups water
2 tsp. ground cumin

2 tsp. chili powder
1 tsp. salt
¼ tsp. pepper
4 tsp. Worcestershire sauce
2 Tbsp. soy sauce
5 tortillas, canned or frozen, cut in ½ inch strips
1 cup Cheddar cheese, shredded
6 strips bacon, fried
Avocado for garnish

Sauté onion, chilies and garlic in oil until soft. Add beef and chicken bouillon, water, cumin, chili powder, salt, pepper, Worcestershire sauce, and soy sauce. Bring soup to boiling; lower heat and simmer, covered, for 1 hour. Before serving, add tortillas and simmer 10 minutes longer. In each soup bowl, place 3 tablespoons cheese and 1 piece bacon, crumbled. Cover with soup. Pass bowl of cubed avocado for garnish.
Serves 6.

Mrs. C. D. Allison, Jr.

This is a hearty soup. Serve with fruit salad and dessert.

VEGETABLE SOUP

3 lbs. lean, boneless stew
   meat, cut in small pieces
1 medium soup bone
1 Tbsp. salt
2 (1 lb.) cans tomatoes
1 large onion, chopped finely
5 ribs celery, chopped finely
¼ small head cabbage,
   chopped
2 large carrots, sliced finely
Dash cayenne

Black pepper to taste
1 tsp. thyme
3 bay leaves
¼ lb. spaghetti, broken
   into small pieces
1 (1 lb.) can cut green
   beans, drained
¾ cup okra, fresh or
   frozen, sliced
1 large white potato,
   cubed

Into a large heavy stewing pot place a gallon of cold water, stew meat and soup bone. Add salt. Boil, skimming frequently until contents are clear, about 1 hour. Continue a gentle boil and add tomatoes, onion, celery, cabbage, carrots and seasonings. Cover and gently boil until vegetables and meat are tender. Add remaining ingredients and cook until potatoes are tender. You may need to add more water as soup is cooking. Serves 6-8.

Mrs. Clyde Tracy

The beauty of a vegetable soup is to adjust the vegetables and the thickness to your family's liking!

EASY CHICKEN VEGETABLE SOUP

1 (2½ lb.) chicken
1 medium onion, chopped
2-3 ribs celery, chopped
3 carrots, scraped and
   sliced thin

1 large potato, diced
1 (8¼ oz.) can lima beans
2 (1 lb.) cans tomatoes
Salt and pepper to taste

Cut chicken up, cover with water, add onion and celery. Bring to boil then simmer until meat is tender. De-bone chicken. Return chicken to broth and add remaining ingredients. Bring to boil; reduce heat and simmer about 1 hour 30 minutes until vegetables are tender. You may need to add more water to soup while cooking. Serves 4.

Mrs. H. T. Plummer
Forrest City, Arkansas

Once a soup begins boiling, important to continue "roll" until done.

SANDWICHES

SANDWICH LOAF

1 unsliced loaf sandwich bread
1/4 cup butter, softened

1/4 cup margarine, softened
2 (8 oz.) pkgs. cream cheese
1/2 cup whipping cream

Shrimp Filling:
1 boiled egg, chopped
1 1/3 cups finely chopped shrimp
1/4 cup chopped celery

2 Tbsp. lemon juice
1/4 tsp. salt
Dash pepper
1/4 cup mayonnaise

Cheese-Pecan Filling:
1 (3 oz.) pkg. cream cheese
1 cup chopped toasted pecans

3/4 cup crushed pineapple, well-drained

Chicken-Bacon Filling:
8 slices crisp bacon, crumbled
1 cup cooked chopped chicken

1/2 cup mayonnaise
1 Tbsp. chopped pimiento
1/4 tsp. salt
1/8 tsp. pepper

Mix each filling separately and reserve at room temperature. The more finely ingredients for filling are chopped, the more easily the loaf will slice when served.

Using an electric knife, trim crust from sandwich loaf and cut into 4 lengthwise slices. Cream butter and margarine together and spread 1 side of each slice. Place one slice, buttered side up, on a serving plate. Spread evenly with one of the fillings. Continue with other bread slices and fillings. Spread butter-margarine mixture over whole loaf; *chill thoroughly*. Then frost entire loaf with cream cheese and cream mixture. Decorate and chill at least 3 hours before serving. When making several, refrigerate on cookie sheets and use two egg-turners to remove to serving platter.
Serves 12-14.

Mrs. Joe Holmes

To decorate Sandwich Loaf: Boil 2 eggs, peel and dye them with Easter egg dye. Thinly slice the eggs; use for flowers with green peppers as stems.

103

PIMIENTO CHEESE

Rat cheese or mild Cheddar
American cheese
Celery, finely chopped
French's Seasoning Salt

Pimiento
Mayonnaise
Miracle Whip

Grind in food grinder equal portions of rat cheese or Cheddar with American cheese. Add celery, salt and pimiento. Add equal portions of mayonnaise and Miracle Whip. Make any desired amount.

Mrs. Haywood Wright

JALAPENO PIMIENTO CHEESE

1 (8 oz.) wedge Mellow Kraft
  Cheese
1 (10 oz.) stick sharp or
  extra sharp cheese
1 (7 oz.) jar pimientos
Hellmann's Mayonnaise to
  taste

2 Tbsp. mustard
2 tsp. Worcestershire sauce
1 tsp. onion, grated
¼ tsp. sugar
1½-3 hot pickled jalapenos,
  seeded and finely grated

Grate cheese on finest grater. Stir all ingredients together and refrigerate. This is great as a sandwich spread or a dip.
Yields 3 cups.

Mrs. James S. Rogers

GRILLED CHEESE SANDWICH

2 slices bread
Butter
1 slice American cheese

Mustard
1 thin slice white onion

Spread butter on outside of 2 slices of bread. Inside place 1 slice cheese. Spread mustard on 1 slice, add onion and put sandwich together. Grill in iron skillet on each side.
Serves 1.

Lara F. Hutt, III

If you make up sandwiches ahead of time, be sure to spread bread lightly with soft butter before filling sandwiches. The butter will prevent the filling from seeping through and making the bread soggy.

CUCUMBER TEA SANDWICHES

Cucumbers, thinly sliced
Onions, thinly sliced
Vinegar
Salt and pepper
2 Tbsp. homemade mayonnaise

1 (3 oz.) pkg. cream cheese
2-3 tsp. reserved vinegar mixture
Bread slices, crusts removed
Hellmann's Mayonnaise

Soak cucumbers and onions overnight in vinegar, salt and pepper. Soften cream cheese and mix with homemade mayonnaise. Add 2-3 teaspoons vinegar mixture. Spread bread with Hellmann's mayonnaise. Spread cream cheese mixture over mayonnaise. Put a slice of cucumber on 4 corners of 1 slice of bread. Add 2 slivers of onion on top of each 2 pieces of cucumber. Sprinkle on dash of salt and cover with other piece of bread. Cover with a damp tea towel until ready to serve. Cut into quarters.

Mrs. T. P. Devlin
Batesville, Arkansas

CUCUMBER SANDWICHES

3 cucumbers
½ onion
4 (8 oz.) pkgs. cream cheese

1 cup Miracle Whip
Salt and pepper to taste
4 loaves thin sliced bread

Peel cucumbers. Grate cucumbers and onion over a colander so juice can drain off. Combine with cream cheese, Miracle Whip and seasonings. Remove crusts from bread and spread with cucumber mixture. Put top on bread. Place sandwiches on baking sheet with wax paper between each layer. Place wax paper on top and cover with a damp cloth. Refrigerate until ready to serve.
Yields 4 dozen sandwiches.

Mrs. C. D. Allison, Jr.

WINDSOR SANDWICH

3 slices bread
Sharp Cheddar cheese, grated
Mayonnaise

Turkey breast, thinly sliced
¼ cup pineapple tidbits
Chutney

Sprinkle cheese on one slice of bread. Toast all 3 pieces of bread until cheese melts. Spread mayonnaise on one piece of bread. Put turkey on top of mayonnaise. Put pineapple on top of turkey. Spread mayonnaise on back of bread with cheese. Put mayonnaise side down on pineapple. Spread chutney on last piece of bread and put on top of cheese. Cut in half to serve.
Serves 1.

HAM SALAD SANDWICH

2 cups cooked ham, ground
1 medium sweet pickle,
  chopped
½-1 tsp. sweet pickle juice
3 green onions, chopped

2-3 hard boiled eggs, chopped
1 Tbsp. Durkee's Sauce
1/3 - ½ cup Miracle Whip
Black pepper to taste

Mix all ingredients together and serve on rye, whole wheat or white bread.
This will double or triple. Do not freeze.
Yield 2½ cups.

Mrs. Mark A. Shelton, III

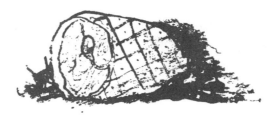

HAM SANDWICHES

½ cup margarine, softened
3 Tbsp. poppy seeds
3 tsp. horseradish mustard
1 tsp. onion, grated

12 buns
Baked ham slices
12 slices Monterey Jack
  or Swiss cheese

Mix margarine, poppy seeds, mustard and onion. Spread on buns. Add
ham and cheese to buns. Wrap *tightly* in foil. Freeze if desired. Heat at
350° for 30 minutes.
Serves 12.

Mrs. Johnny Keesee
Clarksdale, Mississippi

HAM-O-RAMA

8 English muffins
1 (8 oz.) pkg. cream cheese
½ cup butter
½ cup Parmesan cheese, grated
1 tsp. paprika

½ tsp. oregano
½ tsp. garlic powder
Boiled ham, sliced
2 medium tomatoes, sliced

Halve English muffins. Mix cream cheese, butter, Parmesan cheese, and
seasonings. Spread 2/3 of mixture on muffins. Top with ham and tomatoes.
Spoon remaining cheese mixture on centers of tomatoes. Place on baking
sheet. Broil 3 inches from heat for 4 minutes or until cheese bubbles and
browns.
Serves 8.

RICH BOYS (POBOY'S WEALTHY COUSIN)

Individual French loaves, 1
  per person
Mayonnaise
Mustard
¼ lb. meat per person, may
  use thin sliced corned beef,
  pastrami, ham, bologna, etc.
Tomatoes, sliced

Swiss cheese, 1 thin slice
  per person
Lettuce, torn in small pieces
Green onions, sliced
Dill pickles, sliced
  lengthwise
Oregano
Italian dressing

Cut French loaves in half and pull out some of the bread. Spread loaves with mayonnaise and mustard. Layer on meat, tomatoes, cheese, lettuce, onions and pickles. Sprinkle a pinch of oregano over lettuce and drizzle on a little Italian dressing. Put top on sandwich and bake according to French loaf directions. Serve with potato chips and cold beer for a delicious after tennis supper.

Mrs. R. Teryl Brooks, Jr.

GENUINE IMITATION REAL PIT BARBEQUE

1 5-6 lb. pork roast—cheapest
  cut is perfect
3 parts Kraft Hickory
  Flavored Barbecue Sauce

1 part Kraft Hot Barbecue
Sauce

Wrap roast in foil, place in skillet and bake at 225° at least 12 hours. Drain off fat. Shred pork removing any fat. Combine sauces. Mix meat with enough sauce to moisten. Refrigerate or freeze. Reheat meat before serving. Serve on warm buns with slaw and extra sauce.
Serves 10-12.

Mrs. C. D. Allison, Jr.

Serves a crowd cheaply!

OYSTER LOAF

1 small loaf French bread,
  Pepperidge Farm or Riesling
Hellmann's Mayonnaise or
  creole tartar sauce
Louisiana Hot Sauce

12 oysters, fried
Tomatoes, thinly sliced
Lettuce, shredded
Salt and pepper to taste

Bake French bread slightly underdone. Cool slightly and slice in half lengthwise. Spread each half liberally with mayonnaise or tartar sauce. Cover bottom half with fried oysters (See Index). Sprinkle with Louisiana Hot Sauce. Cover with tomatoes, lettuce and seasonings. Top with other half of bread. Serve with cold beer.
Serves 2.

HOT LUNCHEON SANDWICH

16 slices sandwich bread,
   remove crusts
8 slices boiled ham, chicken,
   or turkey
8 slices sharp cheese
6 eggs
3 cups milk

½ tsp. dry mustard (for ham);
   use pimiento for chicken
   or turkey
½ tsp. salt
2 cups cornflakes, crushed
½ cup butter, melted

Butter bread and place 8 slices on bottom of greased (13x9½) baking pan. Top each slice with meat, cheese and remaining bread. Mix eggs, milk and seasonings. Beat and pour over sandwiches. Refrigerate overnight. Sprinkle sandwiches with cornflakes mixed with melted butter. Bake at 350° for 45 minutes. Let stand 5 minutes before cutting.
Serves 8.

Mrs. Ross Sanders

SLOPPY JOES

3 lbs. ground meat
1 large onion, chopped
1 (12 oz.) jar chili sauce
1 (14 oz.) bottle ketchup

4 Tbsp. flour
2 Tbsp. sugar
2 Tbsp. dry mustard
2 Tbsp. vinegar

Brown meat, add onion and cook until onion is clear. Add chili sauce and ketchup. Mix flour, sugar, mustard, and vinegar with "rinsings" from chili sauce and ketchup bottles. Stir well. Add to rest and cook until meat is done. If there is too much grease you can add ½ cup corn flakes. Serve on buns with slaw.
Serves 15.

Scout Recipe

BARBEQUED HAMBURGERS

1 lb. ground beef
1 medium onion, chopped
½ cup ketchup
2 Tbsp. vinegar
1 Tbsp. chili powder

1 Tbsp. Worcestershire sauce
¼ cup water
1 cup corn or bran flakes
Salt and pepper to taste
6 hamburger buns

Brown meat and onions in a skillet. Mix ketchup, vinegar, chili powder, Worcestershire sauce and water; add to meat and onion mixture. Add flakes and seasonings. Put in top of a double boiler and steam 1 hour. Toast buns. Place 2 spoons mixture on each bun and serve open faced.
Serves 6.

Mrs. Claire McClain
Little Rock, Arkansas

JUMBO PIZZA SANDWICH

1 loaf French bread
1/3 cup chopped ripe olives
¼ tsp. pepper
1 tsp. salt
½ tsp. oregano
2 Tbsp. green onion tops,
   finely chopped

1 lb. ground beef, uncooked
1/3 cup Parmesan cheese, grated
1 (6 oz.) can tomato paste
14 thin slices tomato, peeled
8 (1 oz.) slices sharp cheese

Cut bread in half horizontally. Combine olives, seasonings, onions, beef, Parmesan cheese and tomato paste. Spread meat mixture equally over cut sides of bread. Place tomato slices over meat. Place on cookie sheet and cook at 400° for 15 minutes. Cover tomato slices with triangular slices of cheese. Return to oven for 5 minutes.
Serves 4-6.

Mrs. Randy McNulty

BUZZ BURGERS

1½ lbs. ground chuck
4 (1 oz.) slices American
   cheese
4 regular hamburger buns
Mayonnaise
3 Tbsp. butter

1 cup ketchup
2 Tbsp. white vinegar
4 tsp. Liquid Smoke
½ tsp. Tabasco
2 Tbsp. Worcestershire sauce
6 Tbsp. dark brown sugar

Divide meat into 4 equal parts and form into patties ¾ inch thick and 3½ to 4 inches in diameter. Keep in refrigerator until ready to use. In a saucepan melt butter and add ketchup, vinegar, Liquid Smoke, Tabasco, Worcestershire and brown sugar. Over low heat let this bubble for a few minutes. Remove from heat. This sauce is for basting the patties.

Allow charcoal to burn down until coals are gray or to a cooking temperature of 250°. Generously baste patties and place basted side down on the grill; baste top and cook for 4 minutes. Turn 2 times at 4 minute intervals, generously basting both sides each turn. Baste top, turn and top with cheese; cook until cheese melts. Remove and serve on warmed (browned) buns, spread with mayonnaise. This should produce medium rare, juicy burgers; adjust cooking time to grill heat.
Serves 4.

Royce O. Johnson, Jr.

FRENCH DIP SANDWICHES

Roast beef—sirloin tip, pikes
  peak, rump or brisket
4 Tbsp. butter
½ medium onion, sliced

2 Tbsp. beef broth crystals
1 cup water
French bread loaf

Brown roast in small amount of hot fat in skillet on top of stove. Be sure to cook long enough to get lots of dark drippings. Remove roast to an open roasting pan. Using the braising method, cook roast in oven to medium rare stage.

While roast is cooking, make broth. Add 1 cup of water to skillet drippings. Boil and scrape skillet bottom. Add butter, onion and beef crystals. Simmer until onions are done. May need to add a little more water. When roasting is completed add roasting pan drippings to broth base in skillet.

After meat is thoroughly cooled, slice it thinly and pile on a split, buttered and toasted loaf of French bread. Slice loaf into individual serving size sandwiches. Serve with separate cups of steaming hot broth.

Mrs. Jack Gentle

To keep leftover beef rare when reheating, wrap lettuce leaves around beef before placing in oven.

STEAK SANDWICH WITH CHEF'S SAUCE

½ cup butter
3 Tbsp. steak sauce
2 Tbsp. green onions, sliced
1½ Tbsp. Worcestershire
  sauce
¼ tsp. salt

Instant meat tenderizer
1 lb. (¼" thick) round steak,
  cut in 6 pieces
Pepper
6 slices (1" thick) French
  bread, toasted

Melt butter, add steak sauce, onion, Worcestershire sauce, and salt. Heat. Sprinkle steak with tenderizer according to label directions. Grease skillet lightly. Grill steak 2-3 minutes per side. Sprinkle with pepper. To serve dip bread quickly in hot sauce. Top with steak. Spoon on remaining sauce. *Serves 4-6.*

Mrs. Jack Gasche
Dallas, Texas

"DuBocage"
HOME OF
JUDGE JOSEPH BOCAGE
Being Restored by
THE OPTIMIST CLUB OF PINE BLUFF

DU BOCAGE
1115 West Fourth Avenue
Judge J. W. Bocage, one of Pine Bluff's more noted early settlers, built this Greek Revival style home in 1866. His granddaughter, Mrs. H. A. Knorr, gave it to the city; it has been restored and furnished by the Pine Bluff Optimist Club, which also maintains it as a contribution to the community. Du Bocage was the first structure in Pine Bluff placed on the National Register of Historic Places.

ARTICHOKES STUFFED WITH SHRIMP MAYONNAISE

6 medium artichokes
1¼ lb. raw small shrimp
8 Tbsp. lemon juice
½ tsp. tarragon
¼ tsp. ground black pepper

1 cup mayonnaise, homemade
   or Hellmann's
8¾ tsp. salt
Vinegar

Wash each artichoke, remove stems and cut ¾ inch off the top of the center cone of leaves. Trim off the sharp tips of the remaining leaves with scissors. Carefully remove choke by spreading out the center leaves, pulling out the center cone of leaves in one piece and scraping away the fuzzy choke with a spoon. Drop each artichoke into a basin of cold water containing 1 tablespoon vinegar per quart of water to prevent discoloration.

To cook, drop the prepared artichokes into a large kettle of boiling water containing 1 quart water, 1 teaspoon salt and 1 teaspoon lemon juice per artichoke. Boil 30 minutes. Remove artichoke and drain upside down in colander.

To cook shrimp, drop in 1 quart boiling water seasoned with 2 teaspoons salt, and 1 tablespoon lemon juice. Simmer covered, 3-5 minutes until shrimp have turned pink. Reserve ½ cup of the shrimp water. Drain, peel and clean shrimp. Reserve 18 shrimp for garnish. Place remaining shrimp in a blender with reserved liquid, 5 tablespoons lemon juice, ¾ teaspoon salt, the pepper, tarragon and mayonnaise. Blend until smooth. Chill. (Mixture thickens when chilled.) Fill center of artichokes with shrimp mayonnaise and garnish tops with whole shrimp. Serve as first course or for luncheon with finger sandwiches. Dip tips of leaves in shrimp mayonnaise and eat heart with salad fork.
Serves 6.

Mrs. R. Teryl Brooks, Jr.

GRAND STRAND SHRIMP SALAD

2 lbs. shrimp, cooked and
   cleaned
1 cup water chestnuts, sliced
¼ cup green onions, minced
1 cup mayonnaise
¼ cup celery, minced

2 tsp. curry powder
2 Tbsp. soy sauce
Slivered or chopped almonds,
   toasted
Lettuce cups

Combine first 7 ingredients. Pile in lettuce cups and sprinkle with toasted almonds.
Serves 4.

Mrs. Sanborn Wilkins

TUNA LOAF

2 (9¼ oz.) cans tuna,
   water packed, drained
4 hard-boiled eggs, chopped
1 cup celery, chopped
1 (8 oz.) can peas, drained
1 (4 oz.) can pimiento, chopped
1 (2¼ oz.) can ripe olives,
   chopped

2 cups mayonnaise
2 Tbsp. Durkees Sauce
2 Tbsp. lemon juice
2 Tbsp. unflavored gelatin
½ cup cold water
½ cup hot water

Break tuna into small bits. Add next 8 ingredients. Soften gelatin in cold water, add hot water and add to other mixture. Pour into loaf pan or individual molds and chill.
Serves 10-12.

Mrs. Parker Tucker
Miss Mary Crawford

TUNA TOMATO MOLD

1 (8 oz.) pkg. cream cheese
1 cup Miracle Whip Salad
   Dressing
2 Tbsp. unflavored gelatin
½ cup water

1 (10¾ oz.) can tomato soup
1½ cups chopped onion, celery
   and green pepper, combined
1 (9¼ oz.) can tuna

Combine cream cheese and salad dressing. Soften gelatin in water. Heat soup and add dissolved gelatin. Add cream cheese mixture. Mix with beater. Add remaining ingredients. Stir. Chill until firm.
Serves 8-10.

Mrs. J. W. Kennedy

TUNA SALAD WITH CHINESE NOODLES

1 (9¼ oz.) can tuna
2 Tbsp. pimiento
3 Tbsp. olives, chopped
3 Tbsp. green pepper, chopped
½ cup onion, chopped
1 tsp. vinegar

½ cup salad dressing or
   mayonnaise
Dash of Worcestershire sauce
1 (3 oz.) can Chinese noodles
Cherry tomatoes to garnish

Lightly mix all ingredients except noodles and tomatoes. Pile on top of Chinese noodles and garnish with tomatoes.
Serves 4.

Mrs. Joe Campbell
Mena, Arkansas

COBB SALAD

½ head lettuce
½ bunch watercress
1 small bunch chicory
  (optional)
½ head romaine
2 medium tomatoes, peeled
2 breasts of boiled roasting
  chicken

6 strips crisp bacon
1 avocado
3 hard-boiled eggs
2 Tbsp. chopped chives
½ cup Roquefort cheese,
  finely grated
1 cup Old Fashioned French
  Dressing (See Index)

Cut *very* finely lettuce, watercress, chicory and romaine. Toss and arrange a salad bowl. Cut tomatoes in half, remove seeds, dice finely and arrange in a strip across the salad. Dice breasts of chicken and arrange over top of chopped greens. Chop bacon finely and sprinkle over the salad. Cut avocado in small pieces and arrange around the edge of the salad. Decorate the salad by sprinkling over the top the chopped eggs, chopped chives and grated cheese. Just before serving (at the table), mix the salad thoroughly with the French dressing.
Serves 4-5.

Mrs. Jerome Lambert

CHICKEN CRANBERRY MOLD

2 Tbsp. unflavored gelatin
¾ cup cold water
1 Tbsp. soy sauce
1 cup mayonnaise
1½ cups cooked chicken, diced

½ cup celery, diced
¼ cup pecans, chopped
1 (8¼ oz.) can crushed pineapple
1 (16 oz.) can cranberry sauce
2 Tbsp. lemon juice

Soften 1 tablespoon gelatin in cold water. Heat over low heat, stirring constantly until dissolved. Remove from heat. Stir in soy sauce. Cool. Blend in mayonnaise. Add chicken, celery and nuts. Mix well and pour into a 6 cup mold. Chill until top is sticky firm.

While gelatin layer firms, drain pineapple. Add water to syrup to make ½ cup. Soften remaining tablespoon of gelatin in liquid. Heat over low heat, stirring until gelatin is dissolved. Break up cranberry sauce with fork. Stir in pineapple and lemon juice. Blend in hot gelatin mixture. Chill until syrupy. Spoon cranberry mixture over chicken layer. Chill until set.
Serves 8-10.

Mrs. Paul Lewey

CHICKEN MOUSSE

1 hen
2 Tbsp. unflavored gelatin
¼ cup cold water
6 boiled eggs, chopped

1 (2 oz.) jar stuffed olives
1 cup salad dressing
1 (6½ oz.) jar Durkees Sauce
1 cup hot chicken broth

Cook hen; debone and chop in small pieces. Save broth. Soften gelatin in cold water. Combine all ingredients except gelatin and broth in mixing bowl. Dissolve gelatin in hot broth and pour over other ingredients. Mix well and pour into oiled mold or Bundt pan. Slices of mousse can be topped with a dressing of ½ cup salad dressing, ½ cup Durkees and a dash of paprika. Serves 8.

Mrs. C. D. Allison, Jr.

CHICKEN SALAD WITH ALMONDS

4 cups cooked chicken,
  finely diced
2 cups celery, thinly sliced
1-2 Tbsp. onion, minced
1 Tbsp. lemon juice

¾ cup mayonnaise
¼ cup whipping cream
Salt and pepper
¼ - ½ cup almonds, toasted

Toss chicken and celery together. Mix onion, lemon juice, mayonnaise and cream. Add to chicken and toss until chicken and celery are coated. Season with salt and pepper and stir in almonds. Chill. Serves 5.

Mrs. George B. Talbot

PEACHES WITH CURRIED CHICKEN SALAD

¼ cup sour cream
¼ cup mayonnaise
½ tsp. curry powder
2½ cups diced chicken
½ cup chopped chutney
½ cup toasted coconut chips
1½ cups seedless green grapes

¼ cup sliced green onions
1 cup sliced celery
¼ cup blanched, salted
  almonds
1 (16 oz.) can cling peach
  halves, drained

Combine sour cream, mayonnaise and curry powder. Toss with remaining ingredients, except peaches. Mound on peach halves and serve on lettuce beds. Serves 8-10.

Mrs. Jerome Lambert

MARINATED ASPARAGUS

2 (14½ oz.) cans asparagus
1 green pepper, chopped
1 small bunch green onions
  and tops, chopped
1 stalk celery, finely
  chopped

½ cup wine vinegar
½ cup sugar
¾ cup vegetable oil
½ garlic clove
¼ tsp. paprika

Drain asparagus. Combine remaining ingredients and pour over asparagus. Marinate 4-5 hours before serving.
Serves 6.

Mrs. Lula Brown
Cateress

CONGEALED ASPARAGUS SALAD

1 Tbsp. unflavored gelatin
¼ cup water
½ tsp. salt
2/3 cup sugar
½ cup boiling water
½ cup white vinegar
1 cup pecans, chopped

1 (15 oz.) can Green Giant
  Asparagus, drained
2 whole pimientos,
  chopped
1 cup celery, finely chopped
1 Tbsp. onion, chopped

Soak gelatin in ¼ cup water. Add salt, sugar, boiling water and vinegar. Cook on low heat, stirring, until gelatin is dissolved. Add remaining ingredients. Pour into a 6 cup mold. Congeal. Serve on lettuce; top with mayonnaise mixed with celery seed.
Serves 9.

Mrs. Wilton Steed

AVOCADO AND MUSHROOM SALAD

1/3 cup olive oil
1 Tbsp. dry white wine
1 Tbsp. parsley, chopped
  (fresh)
1 clove garlic, crushed
1 tsp. salt

Pepper
Juice of 1 lemon
2 avocados, peeled and sliced
½ lb. fresh mushrooms,
  sliced

Combine the first 7 ingredients to make a dressing. Pour over mushrooms and avocados and marinate 1 hour.
Serves 4.

Rochelle Feritti
La Jolla, California

ARTICHOKE AND OLIVE SALAD

1 pkg. Italian Salad Dressing Mix	1 can seedless ripe olives
1 bay leaf	1 (14 oz.) can artichokes
2 Tbsp. chopped pimiento	1 cup thinly sliced fresh mushrooms

Prepare dressing mix as directed on package; add bay leaf. Pour over pimientos, olives, halved artichokes and mushrooms. Marinate 3 hours in refrigerator, stirring occasionally. Drain and save marinade.

3 Tbsp. unflavored gelatin	¼ cup vinegar
1½ cups cold water	½ cup lemon juice
2¼ cups boiling water	1 Tbsp. grated onion and juice
½ cup sugar	2 Tbsp. Worcestershire sauce
1½ tsp. salt	

Sprinkle gelatin over cold water to soften; add boiling water and stir until gelatin is dissolved. Add remaining ingredients and drained marinated vegetables, mixing well. Pour into large greased mold.

½ cup mayonnaise	¼ cup reserved marinade

Mix mayonnaise and marinade together and serve with salad. This can be garnished with small Belgium carrots, fresh mushrooms and broccoli flowers which have all been marinated in reserved marinade.
Serves 14-16.

Mrs. Sam C. Harris

MARINATED BEAN SALAD

2 (16 oz.) cans French style green beans	1 large green pepper, chopped
1 (16 oz.) can baby lima beans	1 cup sugar
1 (16 oz.) can tiny green peas	1 cup salad oil
1 (4 oz.) jar pimiento, chopped	1 cup vinegar
4 ribs celery, chopped	Salt and pepper to taste
1 large purple onion, chopped	6 or 7 cloves of garlic

Drain all vegetables. Combine first 7 ingredients. Sprinkle mixture with sugar. Add oil and vinegar. Stir well and add salt and pepper to taste. Insert tooth picks into 6 or 7 cloves of garlic and put into salad. Cover; refrigerate overnight. Remove garlic cloves; stir and serve.
Serves 12.

Mrs. Ben Quinn, Jr.

FRESH BROCCOLI-CAULIFLOWER SALAD

1 medium onion, chopped
1 bunch fresh broccoli,
  chopped
1 head fresh cauliflower,
  chopped

1 cup mayonnaise
1 Tbsp. sugar
1 Tbsp. vinegar
Salt to taste

Chop vegetables in ½ inch pieces. May want to chop onion a little smaller. Add remaining ingredients and refrigerate. Very good with ham or any grilled meat. Can be used as a salad or vegetable dish.
Serves 6-8.

Mrs. Oscar Matlock, Jr.
St. Louis, Missouri

CUCUMBER-ONION FILLING FOR TOMATOES

1 cup cucumbers
¾ cup onion

Kraft's French Dressing
Salt and pepper

Finely chop cucumbers and onion. Combine with enough French dressing to coat it all thoroughly without drowning it. Add salt and pepper to taste. Chill. Serve inside peeled cored tomatoes. Top with mayonnaise (preferably the tart home-made variety).
Yields 1¾ cups.

Mrs. M. J. Keesee
Helena, Arkansas

A good way to prepare the tomatoes is to peel and core them, then salt the inside, and place them upside down on a plate until ready to serve.

CUCUMBER CREAM SALAD

1 (3 oz.) pkg. lemon gelatin
1 tsp. salt
1 cup boiling water
1 Tbsp. vinegar
1 tsp. grated onion

¼ cup mayonnaise
1 (8 oz.) carton sour cream
1 cup cucumbers, finely
  chopped and drained

Dissolve gelatin and salt in boiling water. Add vinegar and onion. Refrigerate until syrupy. Beat in remaining ingredients. Pour into 6 individual molds. Refrigerate until firm. Unmold on greens and top with mayonnaise.
Serves 6.

Mrs. Bob Parker
Memphis, Tennessee

CORN SALAD

1 (12 oz.) can shoepeg corn
4 green onions, sliced
1/4 to 1/3 cup green pepper, diced
1/4 tsp. salt

Pepper to taste
1½ tsp. mayonnaise, or enough to bind
1 tomato, diced

Drain corn. Add all ingredients except tomato. Let stand in refrigerator for at least an hour. When ready to serve, add tomato and toss gently. Multiply ingredients for a party and serve in large lettuce leaves. Serves 4.

Mrs. Bo Keeler
Clarksdale, Mississippi

COTTAGE CHEESE RING MOLD

1 lb. cottage cheese, thoroughly mashed
½ medium green pepper, finely chopped
2 Tbsp. pimiento, chopped
1 Tbsp. onion, minced

1½ Tbsp. gelatin, softened in 1/3 cup water
1 tsp. Worcestershire sauce
1 cup mayonnaise
Salt to taste

Mix cottage cheese, green pepper, pimiento and onion. Soak gelatin in water 5 minutes. Melt gelatin over boiling water; add Worcestershire sauce, mayonnaise and salt. Combine cottage cheese mixture with gelatin mixture. Mold in a 4 cup ring mold. Unmold and garnish serving tray with tomatoes, cucumbers and other vegetables. Serves 6-8.

Mrs. Henry W. Gregory

COLE SLAW

½ small cabbage, cored and cut in eighths
¼ medium onion, quartered

¼ green pepper, quartered
1 small carrot, sliced

Fill blender ¾ full with above. Add cold water to cover. Chop for 5 seconds. Drain immediately in colander. You may need to repeat this procedure to chop all ingredients.

Dressing:
¼ cup sour cream
¼ cup mayonnaise
1 Tbsp. lemon juice

½ tsp. salt
⅛ tsp. ground pepper

Stir by hand. Mix with chopped vegetables. Chill before serving. Serves 6.

Mrs. Art Pansze
Horatio, Arkansas

GREEK SALAD

1 (9 oz.) pkg. frozen cut green beans
1 (9 oz.) pkg. frozen artichoke hearts
1 (4 oz.) can sliced mushrooms, drained

1 (6-8 oz.) bottle stuffed olives, sliced
2 small onions, sliced in rings

Dressing:
1 clove garlic (or powder to taste)
1 tsp. salt
¼ tsp. pepper

1/3 cup wine vinegar (garlic or plain)
¾ cup olive oil

Cook green beans and artichoke hearts according to package directions; drain and let cool. Combine all vegetables. Combine all ingredients for the dressing and mix well. (Can use blender.) Pour dressing over vegetables and marinate for at least 6 hours.
Serves 6-8.

Mrs. T. E. Watts
Camden, Arkansas

ENGLISH PEA SALAD

1 (17 oz.) can LeSueur English Peas
1 (8½ oz.) can artichoke hearts
3-4 ribs celery, chopped

Cherry tomatoes
1 pkg. Good Seasons Italian Dressing, mixed according to pkg. directions

Drain peas and artichoke hearts. Cut artichokes into quarters. Marinate peas, artichoke hearts and celery in salad dressing overnight. Before serving add tomatoes.
Serves 6-8.

Mrs. Paul Lewey

HORSERADISH MOLD

1 (3 oz.) pkg. lemon gelatin
1½ cups boiling water
1 Tbsp. gelatin
1 cup mayonnaise

1 (5 oz.) bottle horseradish plus 2 Tbsp.
1 (8 oz.) carton sour cream

Dissolve lemon gelatin in boiling water. Add gelatin. Stir in remaining ingredients and pour into oiled individual molds or a large ring mold.
Serves 6-8.

Mrs. Jack Turner, Jr.
Jonesboro, Arkansas

Great with beef or pork.

POTATO SALAD

10 medium sized potatoes
5 hard-boiled eggs, diced
1 cup sweet pickle relish
1 large onion, chopped
1 tsp. salt

½ tsp. pepper
1½ cups salad dressing
1 tsp. vinegar
½ tsp. mustard
½ tsp. sugar

Boil potatoes with jackets on until tender. Let cool; peel and cube. Add eggs, pickle relish, onion, salt and pepper. Mix lightly. In a separate bowl, combine salad dressing, vinegar, mustard, and sugar. Mix well; add to potato mixture and stir together, being careful not to mash potatoes. Refrigerate. This is better if made several hours ahead or overnight before serving.
Serves 10-12.

Mrs. T. C. Masters
Mena, Arkansas

HOT POTATO SALAD WITH BACON

4 lbs. potatoes
6-8 slices bacon, diced
1 large onion, diced
½ cup white vinegar
1 (15¾ oz.) can chicken broth

½ tsp. pepper
2 tsp. sugar
2 egg yolks
Salt
Chives, optional

Boil potatoes in skins until tender. Cool; peel and cut into ¼ inch slices. Cook bacon until crisp. Add onion and cook until transparent. Stir in vinegar, broth, pepper, and sugar. Beat egg yolks and stir quickly into mixture. Cook over low heat, stirring, until very hot but do not boil. Pour mixture over potato slices and toss gently. Chives may be added for color.
Serves 8-12.

Mrs. Robert H. Holmes

RICE SALAD

2 (6 oz.) pkgs. chicken
 flavored rice
2 (6 oz.) jars marinated
 artichoke hearts, drained,
 sliced; reserve liquid
8 green onions, sliced,
 with tops

16 stuffed olives, sliced
¾ cup green pepper, chopped
2/3 cup mayonnaise
1 tsp. curry powder

Cook rice according to instructions, *omitting butter.* Cool and add other solid ingredients. Mix liquid from artichokes, curry powder and mayonnaise; toss well with rice mixture. Serve well chilled.
Serves 10-12.

Mrs. Walter Thompson
Clarksdale, Mississippi

122

ORANGE AND ONION SALAD

2 Tbsp. red wine vinegar
1 tsp. Dijon Mustard
½ tsp. salt
Pinch cayenne pepper
1 Tbsp. honey
6 Tbsp. oil

1½ tsp. poppy seeds
½ small red onion
1 (11 oz.) can mandarin
 oranges
1 small head lettuce

Combine first 7 ingredients for dressing. Shake well. Peel and slice onion into very thin rings. Place oranges, onion and torn lettuce in salad bowl. Before serving toss with dressing. For a delicious variety substitute fresh orange sections for mandarin oranges.
Serves 4.

Mrs. Keith Harrelson
Germantown, Tennessee

24 HOUR GREEN VEGETABLE SALAD

6 cups lettuce, chopped
Salt, pepper and sugar
6 hard-boiled eggs, sliced
1 (10 oz.) pkg. frozen peas,
 thawed
1 lb. bacon, cooked, drained
 and crumbled

2 cups grated Swiss cheese
1 cup mayonnaise or salad
 dressing
¼ cup green onions, sliced
 with tops
Paprika

Place 3 cups lettuce in bottom of a 2-quart glass or crystal bowl. Sprinkle with salt, pepper and a little sugar. Layer eggs over lettuce in bowl. Sprinkle with more salt. Layer in order peas, remaining lettuce, bacon and cheese. Spread mayonnaise over top, like icing a cake, sealing to edge of bowl. Cover tightly and chill 24-48 hours. Garnish with green onion and paprika. Toss well before serving. For variety Cheddar cheese can be substituted for Swiss cheese; also, celery and bell pepper may be added.
Serves 12.

Mrs. Charles E. Hunter

Great for company since you prepare this ahead of time.

123

FRESH MUSHROOM SALAD

Mixture of romaine lettuce
   and fresh spinach
½ lb. fresh mushrooms,
   cleaned and sliced

1 (8 oz.) bottle Wish-bone
   Italian Dressing
2 tsp. Dijon Mustard
1 tsp. sugar

Wash salad greens; chill and break into bite size pieces. Add sliced mushrooms and toss the salad with the dressing which has been well blended with mustard and sugar.

Mrs. George B. Talbot, Jr.

WILTED LETTUCE

1 slice bacon
1 Tbsp. vinegar
1 tsp. brown sugar

Salt and pepper to taste
1 cup leaf lettuce
1 green onion, chopped

Chop bacon and brown unil crisp. Add vinegar, brown sugar, salt and pepper to hot bacon grease. Pour immediately over lettuce and onion. Toss and serve.
Serves 1.

Mrs. W. H. Fox

GINGER CHEESE SALAD BOWL

1 cup salad oil
2½ Tbsp. fresh lemon juice
2½ Tbsp. dry sherry
1 Tbsp. ground ginger
1 Tbsp. white wine vinegar
½ tsp. salt
1 tsp. sugar
¼ tsp. black pepper
8 cups torn salad greens (use
   romaine—no head lettuce)

2 (3 oz.) pkgs. cream cheese
2½ Tbsp. fresh orange
   rind, grated
1½ cups seedless green grapes
2/3 cup almonds, lightly
   toasted
2 Tbsp. green onions
   with tops, finely
   sliced (optional)

Shake together or beat with fork the first 8 ingredients to make the dressing. Place salad greens in a large salad bowl. Ahead of time, cut cream cheese into thin rectangles and press both sides into grated orange rind, then cut the rectangles into 3/8 inch cubes. Chill. At serving time, place the cream cheese cubes, grapes, and almonds on lettuce and toss with dressing.
Serves 8.

Mrs. John G. Lile

Served at 1975 Charity Ball Royal Supper.

SPINACH SALAD SUPREME

4 slices crisp bacon, drained
1 Tbsp. bacon drippings
4 Tbsp. olive or vegetable oil
3 Tbsp. red wine vinegar
1 lb. raw spinach, washed
    and well drained

2 hard-boiled eggs, peeled
    and sliced
6 green onions, sliced
Freshly ground black pepper
Salt to taste

Fry and crumble bacon; drain on absorbent paper. In small bowl combine bacon drippings, oil and wine vinegar. Mix well and set aside. Place spinach, eggs, onion and bacon in salad bowl. Add seasonings. Toss *gently* with dressing.
Serves 4-6.

Mrs. Dan Harrelson

LINDA'S GREEN SALAD AND DRESSING

2 large garlic cloves
1 tsp. salt
5 flat filets of anchovies
¼ cup vinegar
¼ cup olive oil

2 shakes Worcestershire sauce
1 or 2 cans artichoke hearts
2 avocados, sliced
2 heads of lettuce, torn
    in bite size pieces

In a wooden salad bowl, mash garlic very, very well. Add salt and anchovies. Mash, mash, *mush*. Stir in oil and vinegar a little at a time, then Worcestershire sauce. Marinate artichoke hearts in dressing for 6 hours. Before serving, peel and slice avocados. Combine all ingredients and toss gently.
Serves 8.

Mrs. Lloyd Tanner

TOMATO SALAD

5 medium sized ripe tomatoes,
    sliced ¼ inch thick
¼ cup olive oil
¼ cup vegetable oil
1 Tbsp. wine vinegar
1 Tbsp. fresh lemon juice

1 clove garlic, crushed
1 Tbsp. dried basil
1 tsp. salt
Freshly ground black pepper
1 bunch green onions, chopped
1 Tbsp. parsley

Arrange tomato slices overlapping on platter. Mix oil, vinegar, lemon juice, garlic, basil, salt and pepper. Spoon over tomatoes. Combine green onions and parsley. Sprinkle over salad. May be made ahead and refrigerated.
Serves 4-6.

Mrs. C. S. McNew, III

CHEESE-TOMATO ASPIC PLATTER

Cheese-Olive Layer:

1 Tbsp. unflavored gelatin	¾ cup salad dressing
1 cup milk	2 Tbsp. freshly squeezed
½ tsp. salt	lemon juice
2 tsp. instant minced onion	1 tsp. Worcestershire sauce
2 (3 oz.) pkgs. cream cheese	1 cup stuffed olives, sliced

Sprinkle gelatin over milk in saucepan. Place over low heat and stir constantly until gelatin dissolves. Remove from heat and stir in salt and onion. Soften cream cheese in medium sized bowl. Gradually blend in salad dressing until smooth. Stir in lemon juice and Worcestershire sauce. Gradually stir gelatin mixture into salad dressing mixture; beat, if necessary, until smooth. Chill, stirring occasionally, until mixture mounds slightly. Fold in sliced olives and turn into 9x5x3 inch loaf pan or 2-quart mold. Chill until almost firm.

Tomato Aspic Layer:

3 Tbsp. unflavored gelatin	¼ tsp. Tabasco
2 cups cold water, divided	1 Tbsp. freshly squeezed
3 (8 oz.) cans tomato sauce	lemon juice
1 Tbsp. Worcestershire sauce	Shrimp, olives, salad greens

Sprinkle gelatin over 1½ cups cold water in sauce pan. Place over low heat and stir constantly until gelatin dissolves. Remove from heat; stir in remaining ½ cup cold water, tomato sauce, Worcestershire sauce, Tabasco and lemon juice. Cool to room temperature. Pour over Cheese-Olive layer. Chill until firm. Unmold and, if desired, serve with French dressing-marinated shrimp. Garnish with sliced olives and additional shrimp. Serve with salad greens.
Serves 8.

Mrs. Royce O. Johnson, Jr.

TACO SALAD

1 lb. ground beef	½ (10 oz.) can Rotel Tomatoes
1 (1¼ oz.) pkg. Taco Seasoning	and Green Chilies
½ lb. American cheese	½ (8 oz.) can tomato sauce

Brown ground beef until crumbly. Drain off fat. Add taco seasoning. Melt cheese with tomatoes. Mix all ingredients together. Serve over chopped lettuce, tomatoes and crushed Fritos.
Serves 4.

Mrs. Jack Cockrum

AVOCADO MOLD

1 (3 oz.) pkg. lime gelatin
1 cup hot water
½ tsp. unflavored gelatin
   softened in 2 Tbsp. water
1 (8½ oz.) can crushed
   pineapple, drained
1 Tbsp. lemon juice

½ cup mayonnaise
Pinch of salt
1 or 2 avocados cut in bite-
   size pieces or smaller
½ cup nuts, chopped
1 cup whipping cream,
   whipped

Dissolve lime gelatin in hot water. Add softened gelatin and dissolve. Add drained pineapple juice, lemon juice and mayonnaise. Blend well. Chill in freezer until almost firm. Put in mixing bowl and beat with electric mixer until fluffy. Fold in pineapple, avocado, and nuts. Fold in whipped cream. Pour in mold and refrigerate. Serve with a fruit salad dressing. *Serves 12-14.*

Mrs. Hubert Eisenkramer

APRICOT CREAM CHEESE SALAD

1 (16 oz.) can peeled
   apricots
1 (3 oz.) pkg. lemon gelatin
1½ tsp. unflavored gelatin

½ cup whipping cream, whipped
1 (3 oz.) pkg. cream cheese,
   softened
1½ tsp. unflavored gelatin

Drain juice from apricots and reserve. Mash apricots through sieve. To half of apricot juice, add enough water to make 2 cups. Bring to boil; add lemon gelatin. Next add 1½ teaspoons gelatin softened in ¼ cup tap water. Add apricot pulp and let stand in refrigerator until partially set, about 1½ hours. Whip cream and add cream cheese. To cream mixture add 1½ teaspoons gelatin soaked in ¼ cup water and dissolved in remaining hot apricot juice. Allow to cool.

To mold, pour ½ apricot mixture in a 4 cup mold. Let harden. Pour cheese mixture over apricot layer. Let harden. Add remaining apricot mixture. Chill until set.
Serves 6.

Mrs. Thomas F. Stobaugh

CRANBERRY SALAD

1 (16 oz.) can whole
   cranberry sauce
3 bananas, mashed
1 cup pecans, chopped

1 (15¼ oz.) can crushed
   pineapple
1 (9 oz.) carton Cool Whip

Mix all ingredients together and freeze in cupcake molds.
Yields 20 molds.

Jefferson Preparatory School

BLUEBERRY SALAD

2 (3 oz.) pkgs. black cherry
  gelatin
2 cups hot water
1 (8¼ oz.) can crushed
  pineapple
1 (16 oz.) can blueberries,
  partially drained

1 (8 oz.) pkg. cream cheese
½ cup sour cream
½ cup sugar
¾ cup chopped nuts

Add hot water to gelatin to dissolve and add pineapple and blueberries.
Pour into 2-quart rectangular casserole dish and chill until set. Combine
cream cheese, sour cream, sugar and nuts and spread over firm gelatin
mixture.
Serves 8-10.

Mrs. Travis Creed

BETTER DAY CRANBERRY SALAD

1 lb. cranberries, ground
1 (15¼ oz.) can crushed
  pineapple, drained
¾ to 1 cup sugar

1 pt. whipping cream,
  whipped
½ lb. miniature marshmallows
1 cup nuts, chopped

Mix cranberries, pineapple and sugar. Let stand 2 hours. Mix whipped
cream and marshmallows. Let these stand 2 hours. Combine above
mixtures. Add nuts. Let set 1 hour or more. This keeps a week in
refrigerator.
Serves 14-16.

Mrs. Walter A. Simpson

This is a delicious substitute for ambrosia.

CRANBERRY ORANGE SALAD

1 lb. cranberries, ground
2 oranges, ground
¾ cup pecans, chopped
4 ribs celery, diced
1 (8¼ oz.) can crushed
  pineapple

1 (6 oz.) pkg. cherry gelatin
4 cups hot water
1 cup sugar
1 tsp. salt
1 Tbsp. unflavored gelatin
½ cup cold water

Combine first 5 ingredients. Set aside. Dissolve cherry gelatin in hot
water. Add sugar and salt. Dissolve unflavored gelatin in cold water. Stir
into cherry gelatin. Add first 5 ingredients and pour into 2 large molds or
20 to 25 individual molds. Chill until firm. This is very good served with
Argyle Dressing (See Index).
Serves 20.

FROZEN FRUIT SALAD

1 (1 lb.) can Royal Ann
   cherries, drained
1 (8¼ oz.) can crushed
   pineapple
3 cups marshmallows,
   finely cut

1 pkg. slivered alm
Juice of ½ lemon
¼ cup mayonnais
1 cup whipping c
Pinch of salt

Mix first 5 ingredients with mayonnaise. Add whipped cream and salt.
Place in 9x9 inch pan and freeze.
Serves 6-8.

Mrs. R. Chester List

FRUIT SALAD

2 Tbsp. flour
1 cup sugar
2 eggs, well beaten
Juice of 2 lemons
½ cup pineapple juice
3 bananas, sliced

1 cup pecans, chopped
3 medium apples, peeled
   and cut in pieces
3 stalks celery, chopped
1 (8¼ oz.) can pineapple
   chunks, drained

Cook first 5 ingredients until thick and clear. Chill and pour over
remaining ingredients.
Serves 8.

Mrs. J. Thomas Sullivant

GRAPEFRUIT SALAD

3 fresh grapefruits
3 cups pineapple juice
3 Tbsp. unflavored gelatin

1 scant cup sugar
1 (8½ oz.) can crushed
   pineapple

Peel and section grapefruit. Heat pineapple juice. Add gelatin, then sugar.
Add grapefruit and pineapple. Pour into mold and congeal. Add topping
when ready to serve.

Topping:
4 egg yolks
4 Tbsp. vinegar
1 Tbsp. sugar
1 tsp. salt
¾ tsp. dry mustard

1 Tbsp. butter
Red pepper to taste
12 marshmallows
1 cup whipping cream,
   whipped

Cook in double boiler until thick.
Serves 14-16.

Mrs. James Mays
Tuscumbia, Alabama

ᴸE SALAD WITH SOUR CREAM AND CHEESE

2 (3 oz.) pkg. lime gelatin
1 cup boiling water
1 (15¼ oz.) crushed pineapple
2 cups sour cream

1 (2 oz.) bottle maraschino
cherries, chopped
1 cup pecans, chopped
1 cup Cheddar cheese, grated

Mix gelatin and water; stir until dissolved. Add pineapple, including juice. Chill slightly. Add sour cream, cherries, nuts and cheese. Put in molds and chill.
Serves 12.

Mrs. Walter C. Eden

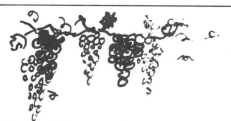

Snow Frosted Grapes: Snip grapes into little bunches. With a pastry brush, coat the grapes with light corn syrup. Dip each bunch in granulated sugar, turning to coat all sides. Allow to dry on a rack over waxed paper. Use to garnish turkey, salads or desserts.

Mrs. Andrew Payne

LAYERED PINEAPPLE-CRANBERRY SALAD

1 (6 oz.) pkg. orange gelatin
1¾ cups boiling water
1 (8½ oz.) can crushed
pineapple
2 Tbsp. lemon juice
½ cup celery, finely chopped
½ cup dark seedless raisins

1 (1 lb.) can whole cranberry
sauce
2 Tbsp. cider vinegar
1 tsp. grated orange peel
½ tsp. grated onion
¼ tsp. salt

Dissolve gelatin in boiling water; divide into 2 equal portions. Chill in refrigerator, stirring occasionally, until slightly thickened. Mix the undrained pineapple, lemon juice, and celery into one portion of gelatin. Turn into 1½-quart mold which has been rinsed with cold water. Chill until set but not firm. Stir remaining ingredients into other portion of gelatin. Chill until set, but not firm. Spoon cranberry mixture evenly over pineapple layer in mold. (Both layers should be of almost same consistency to avoid separation of layers when unmolded.) Chill until firm. Unmold and garnish with crisp lettuce. Add mayonnaise.
Serves 8.

Mrs. John E. Caruthers, Sr.

MINT PINEAPPLE SALAD

1 (20 oz.) can crushed
   pineapple
1 Tbsp. unflavored gelatin
Dash salt

1 (10 oz.) jar mint apple
   jelly (Reeses)
1 cup whipping cream
1 Tbsp. sugar

Drain pineapple. Dissolve gelatin in juice. Add salt and jelly. Heat until melted. Add pineapple and chill until soupy. Whip cream with sugar and fold into gelatin mixture. Freeze. Let stand at room temperature for 10 minutes before serving.
Serves 8.

Mrs. Dick Falk
Jonesboro, Arkansas

Very good with lamb.

CONGEALED PINEAPPLE SALAD

2 Tbsp. unflavored gelatin
1 cup water
1 (15¼ oz.) can crushed
   pineapple, drained

Juice of 1 lemon
1 cup sugar
1 cup Cheddar cheese, grated
1 cup whipping cream, whipped

Soften gelatin in water. Drain pineapple and reserve juice. Boil 1 cup pineapple juice with lemon juice and sugar for 5 minutes. Dissolve softened gelatin in hot juices. When mixture begins to cool add pineapple and cheese. Fold in whipped cream. Mold in 2-quart dish.
Serves 10-12.

Mrs. Dan Proctor
Wynne, Arkansas

RASPBERRY SALAD

1 (15 oz.) can blueberries
1 (15¼ oz.) can crushed
   pineapple
1 (6 oz.) pkg. raspberry gelatin
1 cup boiling water

¼ cup warm water
1 Tbsp. unflavored gelatin
1 cup pecans, chopped
1 cup whipping cream, whipped

Drain fruit juices. Mix raspberry gelatin and boiling water. Sprinkle unflavored gelatin over ¼ cup warm water; soften and pour into raspberry gelatin mixture. Add fruit juices and congeal slightly. Add fruit, pecans and whipped cream. Pour into large ring mold and congeal.
Serves 14-16.

Mrs. William B. Benton
Helena, Arkansas

SALAD DRESSINGS

ARGYLE SALAD DRESSING

3 eggs, slightly beaten
3 Tbsp. lemon juice
½ tsp. salt
1 Tbsp. sugar

1 cup whipping cream,
whipped
2 cups marshmallows, cut up
1 cup nuts, finely chopped

Put first 4 ingredients in double boiler. Cook until thick, stirring constantly. Cool and add remaining ingredients. Let stand 2 or 3 hours. Dressing will be very thick. Serve over canned or fresh fruit.

Mrs. Harold Seabrook

AVOCADO SALAD DRESSING

1 egg
½ cup salad oil
¾ tsp. dry mustard
¼ tsp. Tabasco Sauce
1/3 cup lemon juice
1 Tbsp. Worcestershire sauce
½ tsp. salt

2 ripe avocadoes, peeled
and diced
4 green onions, chopped
1 small garlic clove
4 flat anchovy fillets,
drained
½ cup mayonnaise

Blend all ingredients in blender until smooth and creamy. Chill 2 hours. Serve with tossed green salad or tomato salad. This will hold for weeks in the refrigerator.

Mrs. Harry A. Metcalf

BUTTERMILK SALAD DRESSING

2 cups mayonnaise
2 scant cups buttermilk
2½ Tbsp. parsley flakes
1 Tbsp. coarse ground pepper

1 Tbsp. minced onion flakes
½ Tbsp. garlic powder
1 scant Tbsp. salt
½ Tbsp. Accent

Combine all ingredients and mix until creamy. Refrigerate in well sealed jar. This stays fresh for several weeks.
Yields 1 quart.

Mrs. Ralph Sisk

This also makes an excellent dip for raw vegetables.

BALTIC SALAD SAUCE

½ small onion, chopped
⅝ cup tarragon vinegar
A few tarragon leaves
1 Tbsp. Dijon Mustard
½ tsp. Worcestershire sauce
Dash of Tabasco
1 large garlic clove
Freshly ground pepper

1 egg
2/3 cup olive oil
1 beef bouillon cube
3 Tbsp. boiling water
1 1/3 cups vegetable oil,
   corn or safflower
1-2 tsp. salt
2 tsp. dill weed

Place onion, vinegar, tarragon leaves, mustard, Worcestershire sauce, Tabasco, garlic, pepper and egg in blender and blend well. Very slowly add the olive oil. Add the bouillon cube that has been dissolved in the boiling water. Blend in quickly. Blend in the vegetable oil in a gradual stream. Add salt. (It should be a bit salty because saltiness is dissipated over the salad greens.) Add dill. Dressing may be refrigerated but is best and more flavorful if not very cold when served. Mix this dressing with shrimp, mussels (packed in water), crabmeat and fresh sliced mushrooms. This is then served over lettuce.
Yields 3 cups.

Paul Bash
Jacques and Suzannes
Little Rock, Arkansas

BLUE CHEESE DRESSING

2 cups mayonnaise
½ cup chopped parsley
2 Tbsp. lemon juice

4 oz. blue cheese
½ large onion, minced
1 (8 oz.) carton sour cream

Mix all ingredients with spoon. Refrigerate.

Mrs. James S. Rogers

CRUMBLED DANISH BLUE CHEESE DRESSING

¾ cup wine vinegar
1 Tbsp. salt
4 heaping tsp. sugar
½ tsp. Tabasco sauce

1½ tsp. lemon juice
1 cup salad oil
½ lb. Danish blue cheese

Mix all ingredients except oil and cheese, until sugar and salt dissolve. Blend in oil using a spoon or whisk, not a mixer or blender. Crumble the cheese with a fork and fold in. Before using dressing, stir gently. Toss with washed and dried salad greens, preferably romaine.

Mrs. Edward E. Brown

POPPY SEED DRESSING

½ cup sugar
1 tsp. dry mustard
1 tsp. paprika
¼ tsp. salt
1/3 cup honey
1 tsp. onion, minced

6 Tbsp. tarragon vinegar
3 Tbsp. lemon juice
1 cup salad oil
2 tsp. poppy seeds soaked
  2 hours in water

Mix first 4 ingredients. Add honey, onion, lemon juice and vinegar. Add oil slowly, mixing all the while. Add poppy seeds slowly, continuing to beat slowly.
Yields 2 cups.

Mrs. Kelly H. Powell

Dip fresh fruits (bananas, avocados, apples, etc.) in lemon juice to keep them from turning brown. They will stay pretty for hours.

OLD FASHIONED FRENCH DRESSING

1 cup water
1 cup red wine vinegar
1 tsp. sugar
Juice of ½ lemon
2½ Tbsp. salt
1 Tbsp. ground black pepper

1 Tbsp. Worcestershire sauce
1 tsp. English Mustard
1 clove garlic, minced
1 cup olive oil
3 cups salad oil

Blend together all ingredients except oils. Add oils, mix well again. Chill and shake before serving. Keeps well in refrigerator.
Yields 6 cups.

Mrs. Jerome Lambert

FRENCH DRESSING

1 tsp. paprika
1 tsp. salt
1 tsp. sugar
1 tsp. Colman's Mustard

¼ cup tarragon vinegar
1 cup oil
Blue cheese (optional)

Blend first 5 ingredients. Add oil. Blend thoroughly. Stir in blue cheese. Store in covered jar in refrigerator. Remove 30 minutes before serving. Keeps for several days.
Yields 1½ cups.

T. Walker Lewis, Jr.

OLD SAN FRANCISCO DRESSING

1 tsp. salt
1 tsp. paprika
½ cup sugar
1 cup ketchup

1 cup oil
¼ cup vinegar
Juice of 1 lemon
1/3 cup grated onion

Mix salt, paprika and sugar in a quart jar. Add ketchup, mix well. Add oil, vinegar and lemon juice. Shake well. Add onion and shake again. Yields 3 cups.

Mrs. Rick Beard

FRUIT SALAD DRESSING

2 egg yolks
2 Tbsp. sugar
¼ tsp. salt
4 Tbsp. lemon juice

1 tsp. prepared mustard
1 cup whipping cream,
    whipped
1 tsp. grated lemon rind

Combine egg yolks, sugar and salt. Beat until light. Add lemon juice and mustard. Beat again. Cook over hot water until thick, stirring often. When thick add lemon rind and whipped cream. Let stand in refrigerator to mellow. Delicious served over pears stuffed with cream cheese and pecans. Serves 6-8.

Mrs. James O. Bain

MELON BALL OR FRUIT SALAD DRESSING

1 (10 oz.) jar currant
    preserves
Juice of 2 lemons
1 Tbsp. vinegar

⅛ tsp. salt
½-1 cup salad oil, according
    to consistency wanted

Combine all ingredients and beat well. Refrigerate overnight.

Mrs. Guy C. Billups
Greenwood, Mississippi

GREEN GODDESS DRESSING

1 cup mayonnaise
1 clove garlic, minced
¼ cup chives or green onions,
    minced
¼ cup parsley, minced
1 Tbsp. lemon juice

1 Tbsp. tarragon vinegar
½ tsp. salt
½ tsp. pepper
½ cup sour cream
3 anchovy fillets,
    minced (optional)

Combine all ingredients. Store in refrigerator. Yields 2 cups.

Mrs. Raymond A. Irwin, Jr.

135

HONEY DRESSING

2/3 cup sugar
1 tsp. dry mustard
1 tsp. paprika
¼ tsp. salt
1 tsp. celery seed

½ cup honey
5 Tbsp. vinegar
1 Tbsp. lemon juice
1 tsp. onion juice
1 cup salad oil

Mix dry ingredients. Add honey, vinegar, lemon juice and onion juice. Add oil *slowly*, beating with electric mixer. Very good served over grapefruit, orange and avocado slices.
Yields 2¼ cups.

Mrs. J. T. Slack
Arkadelphia, Arkansas

LYN'S DRESSING

1/3 cup vinegar
1 clove garlic
2/3 cup salad oil
1 tsp. salt

1 Tbsp. tarragon
½ Tbsp. cracked
 black pepper

Mix all ingredients. Store in refrigerator. Shake well before serving.
Yields 1 cup.

Mrs. Ted Drake

TOMATO MARINADE

1/3 cup vinegar
2/3 cup olive oil
1/3 cup ketchup
⅛ tsp. dry mustard

⅛ tsp. paprika
1 clove garlic
Salt and pepper to taste

Combine all ingredients. Slice tomatoes in a glass dish. Marinate 2 hours. Do not marinate too long or tomatoes will become mushy.
Yields 1 1/3 cups.

Mrs. Jerry McClain
Houston, Texas

AUNT MILDRED'S MARINADE

½ cup vinegar
1½ cups olive oil
4 tsp. salt

4 tsp. dry mustard
Pepper to taste
Dash sugar

Blend all ingredients. Slice cucumbers, red onions, tomatoes and bell peppers. Pour marinade over vegetables and let marinate several hours before serving.
Yields 2 cups.

Mrs. James S. Rogers

MAYONNAISE

1 egg
⅛ tsp. cayenne pepper
⅛ tsp. paprika
½ tsp. dry mustard

1 tsp. sugar
2 Tbsp. lemon juice
1 tsp. onion salt
1 cup salad oil

Put all ingredients except oil in blender. Cover and blend a few seconds on medium speed. Add oil gradually. Blend until oil has been mixed in thoroughly. Stop blender; stir mixture with rubber spatula then blend a few seconds longer. Store in refrigerator. This can be doubled.
Yields 1½ cups.

Mrs. A. P. White

ROSA'S SALAD DRESSING

6 Tbsp. cider vinegar
3 Tbsp. sugar
½ tsp. salt
½ tsp. dry mustard

Dash red pepper
½ cup butter, melted
6 egg yolks
½ cup whipping cream, whipped

In a small pan combine first 5 ingredients. Stir to dissolve mustard then put on the fire and boil a few minutes. Put egg yolks in top of double boiler. Add vinegar mixture and butter alternately, beating after each addition. Cook over low heat not letting the water touch the bottom of the pan. Cook until thick, beating constantly. Chill thoroughly or overnight. (It will become very stiff.

When ready to serve, whip cream, then whip salad dressing. Combine the two and beat until just blended. The stiff mayonnaise will keep in the refrigerator several days.
Serves 18-20.

Mrs. Robert S. Cherry

RUSSIAN DRESSING

¾ cup mayonnaise
6 Tbsp. chili sauce
3 Tbsp. chopped pimientoes
1 Tbsp. capers
1 Tbsp. tarragon vinegar

12 sprigs chives or green
   onions, chopped
3 Tbsp. whipping cream,
   whipped

Mix all ingredients in the order listed. Toss with a mixture of fresh salad greens.

Mrs. James F. Clark
El Dorado, Arkansas

Great for a shrimp dip—not runny.

SHIRL'S SALAD DRESSING AND MARINADE

2 cloves of garlic
1 tsp. salt
1 tsp. whole black
  peppercorns
½ tsp. leaf oregano

¾ cup vinegar
2 Tbsp. dry white wine
2 Tbsp. lemon juice
2½ cups light salad oil
½ cup olive oil

Place garlic cloves, salt, peppercorns and oregano in blender and blend together. Add vinegar, white wine and lemon juice and blend well. Combine the oils and add slowly to the mixture in the blender until smoothly combined. Place this in a quart jar and keep in refrigerator. This dressing is particularly delicious on mixed, crispy greens, especially lettuce.

For an added treat, marinate crabmeat in part of the dressing for at least 24 hours. Combine this plus tomato wedges, a lot of bacon (fried crisp, drained and crumbled) with the lettuce. Add slightly more dressing when ready to toss according to the amount of lettuce used.
Yields 1 quart.

Mrs. Mark Loveland

SALAD OIL DRESSING

Garlic Vinegar:
Pod of garlic
1 pt. white vinegar
¼ tsp. cloves

Heaping tsp. allspice
½ tsp. celery seed

Chop almost whole pod of garlic. Add garlic and remaining ingredients to vinegar. Set aside for 2 or 3 days; remove garlic. Use vinegar in the following dressing.

Dressing:
1 egg
1 tsp. salt
1 tsp. sugar
1 tsp. prepared mustard

Dash paprika
3 Tbsp. garlic vinegar
Dash pepper
1¾ cups salad oil

Beat egg well. Add all ingredients except oil. Add oil slowly and beat well.
Yields 2 cups.

Mrs. Ralph Smith

To dewax cucumbers, soak for 5 minutes in a quart of tap water containing 10 to 15 drops of liquid detergent. Then wash with 1 tablespoon of herbal or brown vinegar. Rinse in fresh tap water and dry with a towel. Do not soak in salted water.

THE M. A. AUSTIN HOME
704 West Fifth Avenue
Dr. James M. Holcomb built the original portion of this home between 1867 and 1870, then sold it to O. P. Snyder in 1870. M. A. Austin bought the home from Snyder's widow in 1888. The house was remodeled into its present style of Neo-Classical style of architecture in 1904, and it is worthy of preservation both from historical and architectural standpoints.

SWISS ASPARAGUS CASSEROLE

4 Tbsp. butter
3 Tbsp. flour
1½ cups milk
½ tsp. salt
¼ tsp. paprika
½ cup grated cheese
2 Tbsp. finely chopped celery

1 pimiento, chopped fine
2 hard-boiled eggs, chopped
1 Tbsp. grated onion
1 (14½ oz.) can white asparagus
2/3 cup bread crumbs
3 Tbsp. melted butter

Melt butter; add salt, paprika and flour. Blend until smooth. Gradually stir in milk until sauce is thick, then cheese until melted. Add celery, pimiento, eggs and onion. Drain asparagus and cut into short lengths. In a 2 quart casserole make layers of sauce and asparagus until all is used. Toss bread crumbs with the 3 tablespoons melted butter and sprinkle on top. Bake uncovered at 375° for 20 minutes, or until top is browned. This dish can be prepared early in the day, but wait until cooking to top with bread crumbs.
Serves 8.

Mrs. Edward M. Brown

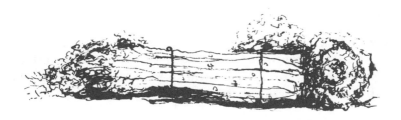

SCALLOPED ASPARAGUS AND ARTICHOKES

1 (14½ oz.) can green asparagus, drained
1 (14 oz.) can artichoke hearts, drained, halved, juice reserved
2 (4 oz.) cans mushrooms, drained
4 Tbsp. butter

4 Tbsp. flour
1½ cups milk
½ cup artichoke juice
Salt and pepper to taste
8 oz. grated sharp cheese

Cut asparagus in half lengthwise. Place asparagus, artichokes, and mushrooms into layers in a 1½ quart casserole. Melt butter and blend in flour. Slowly add milk and artichoke juice, stirring to make a thick cream sauce. Add salt, pepper, and half of grated cheese to the sauce. Pour over the vegetables. Top with remaining cheese. Bake uncovered at 350° for 25 minutes.
Serves 6.

Mrs. Armistead C. Freeman

ASPARAGUS CASSEROLE

2 (14½ oz.) cans green
asparagus
1 small onion
½ pt. whipping cream

2 Tbsp. fresh parsley, cut
fine
1½ cups cracker crumbs
Paprika

Drain asparagus and set aside. Finely grate onion into the cream and add parsley. Sprinkle enough paprika into the cream mixture to color it a light pink. In a buttered 1½ quart casserole, layer asparagus and cracker crumbs twice, ending with crumbs. Pour cream mixture over top. Bake uncovered at 350° for 30 minutes or until set.
Serves 4-6.

Mrs. Louis L. Ramsay

ARTICHOKE CASSEROLE

2 (10 oz.) pkgs. frozen
artichoke hearts
1 can cream of mushroom
soup, undiluted

1 pkg. Kraft Old English Cheese
Slices
4 slices bread, crust removed

Cook artichoke hearts by package directions. Drain and place in the bottom of a 1½ quart casserole. Cover with the soup, then cheese slices. Butter bread, cut it into 1 inch cubes and place on top. Bake uncovered at 350° for 30 minutes.
Serves 6.

Mrs. Charles Scarbrough

FRENCH BEAN CASSEROLE

3 (16 oz.) cans French style
green beans
2 medium onions, chopped
4 Tbsp. butter
1 cup grated sharp Cheddar cheese
1 can cream of mushroom soup,
undiluted

6 strips crisp bacon, crumbled
1 Tbsp. Accent
1 Tbsp. caraway seed
4 Tbsp. bean juice
Ritz crackers, plain or cheese
½ cup butter
Paprika

Simmer beans in own juice for 1 hour. Drain, reserving 4 tablespoons of the juice. Sauté onions in butter, then mix all ingredients together except for the crackers, butter and paprika. Put in a 2 quart casserole and top with a thick (1 inch) layer of cracker crumbs, dot with the ½ cup of butter and sprinkle with paprika. Bake at 350° for 30 minutes.
Serves 8-10.

Mrs. Richard Milwee

GREEN BEANS HORSERADISH

2 (16 oz.) cans whole green beans
1 large onion, sliced
Several bits of ham, diced
1 cup mayonnaise
2 hard-boiled eggs, chopped
1 heaping Tbsp. horseradish

1 tsp. Worcestershire sauce
¼ tsp. salt
¼ tsp. garlic salt
¼ tsp. celery salt
1½ tsp. parsley flakes
Juice of 1 lemon

Cook beans, ham and onion slowly for 1 hour in a medium saucepan. Blend mayonnaise and remaining ingredients, and set aside at room temperature. When beans are ready to serve, drain and spoon mayonnaise mixture over beans. These are excellent leftover cold or can be stuffed in tomatoes.
Serves 8.

Mrs. John Ed Anthony
Fordyce, Arkansas

GREEN BEANS SPECIAL

2 (10 oz.) pkgs. frozen
   French style green beans
4 slices crisp bacon, crumbled
3 tsp. chopped fresh parsley
4 chopped green onions,
   including tops
½ tsp. Accent

¼ tsp. salt
Freshly ground pepper
2 tsp. mayonnaise
2 tsp. sour cream
2 tsp. bacon grease
1 Tbsp. olive oil
Dash Lawry's Seasoned Salt

Cook green beans for about 6 minutes and drain. Mix in bacon, parsley, onions, Accent, salt and pepper. Toss with dressing of mayonnaise, sour cream, bacon grease, olive oil, and salt. Mix in the morning to serve in the evening. Cover with plastic wrap. Do not refrigerate before serving, as this is best served at room temperature.
Serves 6.

Mrs. Joe Crabb

MARINATED GREEN BEANS

2 (16 oz.) cans French style
   or regular green beans
4 Tbsp. brown sugar
4 Tbsp. bacon grease

2 Tbsp. prepared mustard
4 Tbsp. vinegar
4 strips crisply fried bacon

Heat beans in own liquid. When they are warm, drain and put in a 1½ quart casserole. Heat bacon grease, sugar, mustard and vinegar; pour over the beans. Crumble bacon over the top. Serve at room temperature.
Serves 6.

Mrs. Paul Lewey

GREEN BEAN FRITTATA

1 green pepper, chopped
1 small onion, chopped
Olive oil
½ cup grated Parmesan cheese
3 cloves garlic, pressed
¾ cup fine bread crumbs
3 eggs, beaten

¼ tsp. salt
⅛ tsp. pepper
Dash sage and oregano
¼ cup olive oil
¼ cup dry sherry
3 (16 oz.) cans green beans,
    well drained

Sauté green pepper and onion in a small amount of hot olive oil until soft, but not brown. Add to rest of ingredients, gently stirring in beans last. Pour into an oiled 2 quart (8x11 inch) dish. Sprinkle with additional Parmesan cheese and paprika. Bake at 325° for 40 minutes. Serve cold in squares as an appetizer, or hot with an Italian dinner.
Serves 6-8.

Mrs. John G. Lile

MEXICAN REFRIED BEANS

1 large onion, chopped
2 cloves of garlic, crushed
4 Tbsp. butter
2 (16 oz.) cans refried beans

½ cup chopped tomatoes
1 (4 oz.) can jalapeno relish
8 oz. grated sharp Cheddar
    cheese

Sauté onion and garlic in butter until soft. Stir in refried beans, add tomatoes and relish and heat thoroughly. Add cheese, stirring until melted. Serve hot. This can be used as a dip, or put into taco shells.
Serves 12.

Mrs. John MaGee
Longview, Texas

Wonderful accompaniment to a Mexican dinner!

BAR-B-QUE BEANS

1 large onion
1 medium green pepper
¾ cup brown sugar
½ cup ketchup
1 tsp. dry mustard

½ tsp. Worcestershire sauce
6 slices bacon, cut into
    1-inch strips
2 (16 oz.) cans pork and beans

Chop onion and pepper; add brown sugar, ketchup, mustard, Worcestershire sauce and bacon. Stir into beans and bake uncovered at 325° for 2 hours.
Serves 6-8.

Mrs. Richard M. Perdue

RED BEANS AND RICE

1 lb. dried red beans
½ lb. salt pork or ham hock
2 qts. water
3 cups chopped onion
1 bunch green onions with
   tops, chopped
1 cup chopped green pepper
2 large cloves garlic,
   crushed
1 cup parsley, chopped

1 Tbsp. salt
¾ tsp. red pepper
1 tsp. black pepper
¼ tsp. oregano
2 bay leaves
3-4 generous dashes
   of Tabasco
1 Tbsp. Worcestershire
   sauce

Cover beans with water and soak overnight, or 2-3 hours. Drain and cook beans in 2 quarts of water for 45 minutes. Add remaining ingredients and cook slowly for 2-3 hours, stirring occasionally. Serve over boiled rice. *Serves 4-6.*

Mrs. Lara F. Hutt, III

SPANISH BAKED LIMA BEANS

1 lb. dried lima beans
   (large or medium)
3 tsp. salt
1½ cups chopped onion
1½ cups chopped green
   pepper
1 clove garlic, minced

6 Tbsp. vegetable oil
1½ Tbsp. chili powder
1½ Tbsp. cornstarch
1½ cups cold water
1½ cups grated Cheddar
   cheese

Soak beans overnight. Drain. Cover with salted water and cook 45 minutes. Sauté onion, green pepper and garlic in oil until golden. Mix chili powder, cornstarch and water until smooth, add to sautéed vegetables and cook 3 minutes. Combine with drained beans and 1 cup grated cheese. Place in 2-quart casserole and sprinkle with remaining cheese. Bake uncovered at 350° for 30 minutes. *Serves 12.*

Mrs. John Tharp

BROCCOLI CASSEROLE WITH BACON

2 (10 oz.) pkgs. frozen
   broccoli spears
2 Tbsp. butter
1 Tbsp. flour
1½ cups milk
1½ cups grated cheese

1 tsp. salt
1 tsp. white pepper
¼ cup chopped almonds
7 slices crisp bacon
¼ cup buttered bread crumbs

Cook broccoli until just tender; drain. Place in a greased 1½ quart casserole. Melt butter in a pan, stir in flour and gradually add milk. Allow sauce to thicken and add cheese, salt and pepper. Sprinkle broccoli with almonds then pour the sauce over and top with bacon and crumbs. Bake uncovered at 350° for 15-20 minutes, or until bubbly.
Serves 6.

Mrs. Howard J. Wiechern, Jr.

BROCCOLI TIMBALES

1 (10 oz.) pkg. frozen
   chopped broccoli
2 Tbsp. butter
2 Tbsp. flour

¾ cup milk
2 eggs, beaten
½ tsp. salt
1 Tbsp. finely grated onion

Cook broccoli according to directions on package. Drain and press between paper towels to dry. Melt butter and stir in flour. Gradually add the milk and stir until thickened. Cool slightly and stir in beaten eggs. Add salt and onion; fold in broccoli. Pour into greased custard cups. Cook in a pan of hot water at 350° for 40 minutes or until firm. Remove from cups to serve. Good with Hollandaise Sauce (See Index) poured over timbales.
Serves 6.

Miss Grace Allen Rike

GARLIC SEASONED FRESH BROCCOLI

3 stalks fresh broccoli
   (about 2 lbs.)
3 cloves garlic, minced

2 Tbsp. oil
Juice of 1 lemon
1 Tbsp. butter

Cut stalks of broccoli into one inch pieces. Set aside the tops. Brown the garlic in oil in a large heavy skillet with lid. Place stalks in the oil and steam, covered, for 5 minutes. Add the broccoli tops, stir and steam, covered, for another 5 minutes. (Be sure to time precisely.) Toss with butter and lemon juice. Serve hot or chilled.
Serves 3-4.

Mrs. James Loney

PIMIENTO BROCCOLI

4 (10 oz.) pkgs. frozen
  broccoli spears or
  3 bunches fresh
1 cup chopped green onions
  with tops
¾ cup coarsely chopped pimiento

½ cup butter
4½ tsp. grated lemon rind
½ cup fresh lemon juice
1½ tsp. salt
¼ tsp. black pepper

Cook broccoli in small amount of boiling water until crisply tender. Sauté onions in the butter until soft, remove from heat and stir in pimiento, lemon rind, lemon juice, salt and pepper. Drain broccoli well. Pour sauce over broccoli in large serving dish, or pour over each individual portion. Serves 12.

Mrs. John G. Lile

Delicious served with chicken crepes.

PARTY BROCCOLI CASSEROLE

1 large onion, chopped
½ cup butter
4 (10 oz.) pkgs. broccoli spears
1 can cream of mushroom
  soup, undiluted

1½ rolls of garlic cheese
1 pkg. fresh mushrooms or
  3 (4 oz.) cans sliced
1 cup Pepperidge Farm Stuffing
  Mix

Sauté onions in butter; melt cheese in soup; wash mushrooms and slice. Combine all these. Cook broccoli according to package directions and drain. Alternate layers of broccoli and sauce in a lightly buttered 2 quart casserole. Crush stuffing slightly with a rolling pin and sprinkle over top of casserole. Bake at 300° for 25 minutes or until bubbly. Serves 12.

Mrs. Conner Morschheimer

BRUSSELS SPROUTS WITH CURRY SAUCE

2 (10 oz.) pkgs. frozen
  Brussels sprouts
2 Tbsp. butter
1 clove garlic
½ tsp. (scant) curry
  powder

½ tsp. sugar
½ cup chicken broth
1 Tbsp. cornstarch
¼ cup water
¼ cup toasted almonds

Cook Brussels sprouts according to package directions; drain. Melt butter in a saucepan and add garlic clove, curry powder and sugar. Bring to a bubble stage on low heat. Remove garlic and stir in chicken broth. Dissolve cornstarch in ¼ cup water, add to liquid and bring to a boil. Pour over Brussels sprouts; garnish with almonds. Serves 4-6.

Mrs. Ronald D. Blankenship

SWEET AND SOUR CABBAGE

1 large head of cabbage
1 tsp. salt
½ onion, chopped
1 Tbsp. butter
2½ Tbsp. sugar

½ tsp. caraway seed
1 Tbsp. flour
3 Tbsp. vinegar
¾ cup water

Shred cabbage and cook in salted water for 5 minutes; drain. Sauté onion in butter. Add remaining ingredients, including cabbage. Place in 1½ quart casserole and bake at 350° for 30 minutes.
Serves 4-6.

Mrs. Edward E. Brown

GLORIFIED CABBAGE

1 medium head of cabbage
1 green pepper, chopped
1 large onion, chopped
½ cup butter
1 can cream of mushroom soup, undiluted

½ lb. grated sharp cheese
1 (4 oz.) can of whole mushrooms
Dash Tabasco
2 tsp. Worcestershire sauce
Salt and pepper to taste

Parboil cabbage until barely tender. Remove from heat, drain and chop. Sauté green pepper and onion in butter until soft. Add cabbage, soup, cheese, mushrooms, and seasonings. Mix thoroughly. Place in a 1½ or 2 quart casserole. Bake uncovered at 350° for 30 minutes.
Serves 6-8.

Mrs. Louis L. Ramsay

A man's dish!

CARROT SOUFFLE

2 lbs. fresh carrots
½ cup butter

1 medium onion, grated
3 eggs, separated

Boil carrots in water until tender; drain and mash well. Add butter, onion and egg yolks. Beat egg whites stiff, but not dry; fold into carrot mixture. Place in soufflé dish. Bake at 350° for 30 minutes.
Serves 8.

Mrs. Howard C. Wilkins

GLAZED CARROTS

2 (10 oz.) pkgs. frozen Green
  Giant Carrots
½ cup butter, melted
2 Tbsp. brown sugar

Juice of 1 orange and
  grated rind
2 tsp. lemon juice
1 Tbsp. honey

Cook carrots 5 minutes longer than package directions and drain. Place in a 1½-quart casserole; pour butter over carrots. Sprinkle with sugar; add rest of ingredients. Bake at 325° for 30 minutes. Baste and turn often. *Serves 4.*

Mrs. Henry F. Marx

CELERY CASSEROLE

4 cups celery, sliced diagonally
  (¾ inch-1 inch long)
1 (8 oz.) can water chestnuts,
  drained and sliced
1/3 cup slivered almonds

1 (4 oz.) can chopped
  pimiento, with juice
1 can cream of chicken
  soup, undiluted

Boil celery in water for 5 minutes; drain. Mix in remaining ingredients and blend well. Place in 1½-quart casserole. Bake at 350° for 30 minutes. *Serves 4.*

Mrs. H. L. Wineland

CELERY VICTOR

Stalk celery
1 tsp. salt
¾ cup salad oil
¼ cup wine vinegar

1 tsp. salt
2 tsp. sugar
1 tsp. dry mustard

Cut leaves off celery and tie stalk together. Boil in water for 20 minutes with salt. Lift out by string and put in a deep pyrex dish. Combine olive oil, vinegar, salt, sugar and mustard. Pour over celery and marinate overnight or during the day. Slice the celery 1 inch thick and serve over a lettuce leaf. Garnish with pimientoes and anchovies. *Serves 6-8.*

Mrs. Warren C. Means

This adds that "extra touch" to your dinner party.

CORAL CAULIFLOWER

1 medium cauliflower	2 Tbsp. butter
1 cup boiling water	2 Tbsp. flour
1 tsp. salt	1 Tbsp. Worcestershire sauce
1 (4 oz.) jar pimiento	Dash Tabasco
1 cup milk	Parmesan cheese

Separate cauliflower into small florets; wash in cold water. Boil cauliflower in boiling water in ½ tsp. salt until tender but crisp, about 8 minutes. Drain and keep warm. In blender, blend the undrained pimiento, and milk until combined. In a 1 quart saucepan, over low heat, melt butter; stir in flour, then pimiento mixture. Cook constantly until thickened and bubbly. Stir in remaining ½ teaspoon salt, Worcestershire, and Tabasco. Pour sauce over cauliflower so that some of the florets show. Sprinkle with Parmesan cheese.
Serves 6.

Mrs. Ronald D. Blankenship

CAULIFLOWER AND ASPARAGUS TREAT

2 (10 oz.) pkgs. frozen cauliflower	½ soup can milk
1 (14½ oz.) can asparagus pieces	1 cup sharp grated cheese
1 can cream of mushroom	2 slices bread, cubed
soup, undiluted	

Cook cauliflower according to package directions. Drain. Drain asparagus and place with cauliflower in a buttered 1½ quart casserole. Mix soup with milk and cover vegetables. Top with cheese, then bread cubes. Bake uncovered at 350° for 20 minutes or until bubbly.
Serves 6.

Mrs. J. Gordon Reese

Put a piece of bread in the water when cooking cauliflower to avoid an unpleasant odor in your kitchen. Same goes for Brussels sprouts.

So that white vegetables (cauliflower, potatoes, etc.) stay white, cook them in lightly boiling water, and cover the pot.

CORN PUDDING

6 Tbsp. butter
2 Tbsp. sugar
2 Tbsp. flour
½ cup half-and-half cream

4 eggs, well beaten
1½ tsp. baking powder
2 (12 oz.) cans white cream corn
or 4 cups fresh, cut from cob

Heat butter with sugar in saucepan until butter is melted. Stir in flour until well blended; remove from heat. Gradually add cream, then eggs, then baking powder. Make certain dry ingredients are incorporated. Combine with corn and pour into a buttered 1½ quart casserole. Bake uncovered at 350° for 45 minutes.
Serves 6-8.

Mrs. Conner Morschheimer

CORN AND SOUR CREAM

2 Tbsp. chopped onions
2 Tbsp. butter
2 Tbsp. flour
½ tsp. salt
1 cup sour cream

2 (12 oz.) cans whole
kernel corn
½ lb. bacon, crisply fried
and drained
1 Tbsp. fresh parsley, chopped

Cook onion in butter until soft; blend in flour and salt. Gradually add sour cream, stirring constantly. Drain corn, add to sour cream mixture and heat thoroughly. Fold in ½ cup crumbled bacon and turn into a serving dish. Top with remaining bacon (crumbled) and parsley.
Serves 4-6.

Mrs. Paul F. Jones

Quick and tasty family dish!

SOUTHERN FRIED CORN

8 tender ears of corn
2 Tbsp. sugar
1 Tbsp. salt
1 Tbsp. flour

1 tsp. black pepper
½ cup cold water or
part milk
2 Tbsp. bacon grease

Cut corn from cob. (Cut top grain, then scrape cob with knife.) Combine sugar, salt, flour and pepper and add to corn, mixing well. Add water and milk. Melt butter in skillet over medium to low heat. Add corn mixture, cooking slowly until creamy, (about 30 minutes). Stir continuously. Remove from heat; serve immediately.
Serves 6-8.

Mrs. Lula Brown
Cateress

ELEGANT SCALLOPED CORN

1 (17 oz.) can cream corn
1 cup cracker crumbs
½ cup diced celery
½ cup diced onion
¾ cup Cheddar cheese,
  cut in small cubes

1 tsp. salt
2 eggs, well beaten
1 cup milk
2 Tbsp. melted butter
Parsley
Paprika

Combine corn, cracker crumbs, celery, onion, cheese and salt. Add eggs and stir in milk and butter. Pour into a buttered 2 quart casserole. Garnish with parsley and sprinkle with paprika. Bake at 350° for 50 minutes. *Serves 8.*

BAKED EGGPLANT

1 medium eggplant
1 medium onion
½ cup cracker crumbs
1 Tbsp. sugar
1 Tbsp. butter, melted

2 eggs, beaten
1/3 cup milk
Salt and pepper to taste
2 slices bacon

Pare and cube eggplant. Cut onion into small pieces. Boil together in salted water until tender; drain and mash. Add rest of ingredients, except bacon, mix well and turn into a buttered 1½ quart casserole. Bake at 350° for 30 minutes until firm. Top with bacon, return to oven and bake until bacon is browned.
Serves 4-6.

Mrs. Gibson Anderson

EGGPLANT CASSEROLE

1 medium eggplant
1 medium onion, chopped
2 stalks of celery, chopped
¼ cup butter
1 (8 oz.) can tomato wedges
1 egg

¼ tsp. garlic salt
½ tsp. salt
1½ cups cornbread crumbs
¾ cup grated Parmesan
  or Romano cheese

Pare and cube eggplant. Cook in unsalted water until tender and drain 1 hour (this is very important). Sauté onion and celery in butter until soft. Drain tomato wedges and chop with eggplant. Mix all the ingredients together except cheese and pour into a buttered 1½ quart casserole. Top with cheese. Bake uncovered at 350° for 30-40 minutes until slightly browned.
Serves 8.

Mrs. Paul F. Jones

ALAN'S EGGPLANT CASSEROLE

4 cloves garlic, crushed
¼ cup olive oil
2 (6 oz.) cans tomato paste
2 (8 oz.) cans whole tomatoes
1 tsp. salt
1 tsp. pepper
1 tsp. oregano
½ cup grated Romano cheese

1 cup cracker crumbs or
    Matzo meal
2 medium eggplants, cut in
    ½ inch slices
4 eggs, beaten
1 cup olive oil
8 oz. Mozzarella cheese, sliced

Brown garlic in ¼ cup olive oil; add tomato paste, tomatoes (juice included), salt, pepper and oregano. Bring to a boil; simmer 1 hour. Meanwhile, combine cracker crumbs and Romano cheese. Dip eggplant slices in eggs then meal-cheese mixture and fry to a golden brown, over medium heat in remaining olive oil. Drain well. In a 2½ quart casserole, place a layer of sauce, layer of eggplant and Mozzarella cheese. Repeat and finish with Mozzarella on top. Bake uncovered at 350° for 20 minutes. *Serves 8-10.*

Alan Goldman

Terrific meal in itself; just add a green salad and hard rolls.

ELLA MAE'S FRIED EGGPLANT

1 medium eggplant
1 egg, beaten

1 cup cracker crumbs,
    crushed fine

Peel and slice eggplant ⅛ inch thick. Dip slices in beaten egg, then in crumbs. Fry in heavy iron skillet in 1 inch of vegetable oil. Fry one layer at a time, turning once. (This takes about 7 minutes.) Eggplant should be golden brown.
Serves 4-6.

Mrs. Armistead C. Freeman

DIANE'S HOMINY

2 (16 oz.) cans white
    hominy, drained
1 cup grated sharp
    Cheddar cheese
1 Tbsp. grated onion

1 (8 oz.) carton sour cream
1 (4 oz.) can green chilies,
    seeded, rinsed, chopped
Buttered bread crumbs

Combine all ingredients. Place in 1½ quart casserole. Top with bread crumbs. Bake at 350° for 40 minutes.
Serves 6.

Mrs. Harry Bodenhamer
Fort Walton Beach, Florida

153

MACARONI CASSEROLE

2 (8 oz.) pkgs. elbow macaroni
2 cans cream of mushroom
   soup, undiluted
1½ lbs. sharp cheese, grated
½ cup butter
2 large green peppers, chopped

2 large onions, chopped
2 (4 oz.) jars pimiento, chopped
2 (8 oz.) cans water chestnuts,
   drained and sliced
2 (4 oz.) cans button mushrooms,
   drained

Cook and drain macaroni. Stir soup and cheese (reserve some for topping) into warm macaroni. Sauté onions and peppers in butter. Add sautéed vegetables, along with remaining ingredients, to macaroni mixture. Place in 1 large or 2 small casseroles, sprinkle with remaining cheese and bake, uncovered, at 350° for 30 minutes or until bubbly.
Serves 12-16.

Mrs. Clifford A. Davies

Wonderful buffet dish for a crowd!

MACARONI AND CHEESE

1 (8 oz.) pkg. elbow macaroni
3 Tbsp. butter
3 Tbsp. flour
2 cups milk

½ tsp. salt
Pepper to taste
2 cups grated sharp cheese
6-8 salted tomato slices

Cook macaroni according to package directions; drain, and place in a buttered 1½ quart casserole. Melt butter, stir in flour and blend well. Gradually add milk and cook over medium heat until thick. Add salt, pepper and 1½ cups cheese, stirring to melt cheese. Gently mix sauce with macaroni, arrange tomato slices on top (pushing each edge into macaroni). Sprinkle with remaining ½ cup cheese. Bake uncovered at 350° for 30 minutes.
Serves 6.

Mrs. Monte Bayless
Columbia, Tennessee

CURRIED NOODLES

2 (8 oz.) pkgs. medium noodles
½ cup butter
1/3 cup flour
1 Tbsp. curry powder
1 Tbsp. salt

¼ tsp. pepper
6 cups milk
1 (8 oz.) carton sour cream
½ cup chutney, chopped

Cook noodles in boiling water and drain. In a saucepan, melt butter; stir in flour, curry powder, salt and pepper until smooth. Gradually stir in milk; stir constantly until boiling. Remove from heat; stir in sour cream and chutney. Add noodles and mix together well. Turn into a greased 3-quart casserole. Bake uncovered at 350° for 30-45 minutes or until bubbly.
Serves 12-14.

Mrs. Robert Nixon

CARAWAY MUSHROOMS IN SOUR CREAM

1 lb. fresh mushrooms
¼ cup butter
½ cup chopped onion
2 tsp. caraway seeds
2 tsp. lemon juice
¼ cup flour

1 tsp. salt
⅛ tsp. white pepper
¾ cup milk
1 cup sour cream
2 Tbsp. sherry

Rinse, pat dry, and slice mushrooms. In a large skillet melt butter, add mushrooms, onions and caraway seeds; sprinkle with lemon juice. Sauté for 3-5 minutes. Blend in flour, salt and pepper. Stir in milk, and cook for 1 minute. Add sour cream, heating only until hot, and stir in sherry. Serve over toast triangles, or in baked pastry shells for a buffet.
Serves 6.

STUFFED FRESH MUSHROOMS

1 lb. large mushrooms
1 qt. water
1 tsp. salt
1 Tbsp. lemon juice
¼ cup butter

3-4 chopped green onions
 tops and all
¾ cup beef bouillon
1 cup Pepperidge Farm
 Seasoned Crumbs

Wash and core mushrooms, reserving stems. Bring water, salt and lemon juice to boil; add cored mushroom caps. Boil for 2 minutes. Drain. Sauté onions and mushroom stems in butter until tender. Add bouillon and seasoned crumbs. Fill mushroom caps, place in shallow baking pan and bake at 350° for 15-20 minutes.
Serves 10.

Mrs. Celia Mae Mason
Cateress

Serve around beef tender; garnish with parsley.

Here's a guide for substituting canned for fresh mushrooms:
   1 (6 or 8 oz.) can=1 lb. fresh
   1 (3 or 4 oz.) can=½ lb. fresh
If recipe calls for fresh mushrooms by measure instead of by weight, here's your guide:
   1 qt. (or 20 to 24 medium mushroom caps), substitute 1 (6 oz.) can
   1 pt. (or 10 to 12 medium mushroom caps), substitute 1 (3 to 4 oz.) can

---

MUSHROOM CASSEROLE

¼ cup butter
1 lb. fresh mushrooms, chopped
1 small onion, chopped
1 medium green pepper, chopped
1 can cream of mushroom
   soup, undiluted
1 (8 oz.) jar mayonnaise

6 slices bread
¼ cup butter
1½ cups grated Cheddar
   cheese, divided into thirds
2 eggs
1 soup can of milk
Buttered bread crumbs

Melt ¼ cup butter in a large skillet. Add mushrooms and cook gently for 2 minutes; add onion and green pepper. Sauté for 3 minutes, remove from heat; stir in soup and mayonnaise.

Spread bread slices with ¼ cup butter and cut in 1 inch squares. In a 9-inch baking dish, layer half of bread squares, half of mushroom mixture and 1/3 of cheese. Repeat. Beat eggs, add milk and pour over top of casserole. Refrigerate for 1 hour. Top casserole with buttered bread crumbs and remaining 1/3 of cheese. Bake uncovered at 325° for 1 hour.
Serves 6-8.

Mrs. Curt Richardson
Ann Arbor, Michigan

ONIONS AU GRATIN

2 large onions
1 beef bouillon cube
¾ cup boiling water
¼ tsp. thyme
½ tsp. salt

⅛ tsp. pepper
1 Tbsp. butter
½ cup fresh bread crumbs
2 Tbsp. melted butter
¼ cup sharp cheese, grated

Peel and slice onions into 4-5 thick slices. Arrange overlapping onions in a baking dish. Dissolve bouillon cube in the boiling water, add thyme to this; pour over the onions. Sprinkle with salt and pepper and dot with one tablespoon of butter. Cover and bake at 400° for 20 minutes. Toss bread crumbs in melted butter, add cheese. Sprinkle over the onions and bake, uncovered 10 minutes until crumbs are browned.
Serves 4.

Mrs. Clarence Roberts, III

ONION PIE

3 Tbsp. butter
2 cups sliced onions
½ cup grated Swiss cheese
4 eggs

2 cups half-and-half cream
1 tsp. nutmeg
½ tsp. salt
9 inch unbaked pie shell

Preheat oven to 400°. Sauté onions in butter, stirring until they are limp. Sprinkle onions in pie shell; cover with grated cheese. Beat eggs; stir in cream and seasonings. Strain into pie shell. Bake on lowest rack of oven for 15 minutes. Reduce oven temperature to 325°. Bake for another 30 minutes or until a knife inserted 1 inch from the edge comes out clean. Top should be lightly browned.
Serves 6.

Mrs. Robert H. Holmes

MORRIS' CHARCOAL-BROILED ONIONS

1 onion per person
Butter

Salt and pepper to taste

Place unpeeled onions, root-end down, in a pan. Cover and cook in a 350° oven until they begin to feel soft when gently squeezed. (This step can be done ahead.) Put directly on a charcoal grill and cook or smoke for about 20 minutes. Use tongs to handle onions so the juice won't be lost. To serve, remove blackened skin from onions. Cut in half and butter generously. Add salt and pepper to taste. A very surprising flavor—delicious with steak!

Mrs. Morris J. Keesee, Jr.
Clarksdale, Mississippi

OKRA, CORN, AND TOMATO MELANGE

4 strips bacon, fried crisp
4 Tbsp. bacon drippings
1 onion, chopped fine
1 pt. okra, cut into ¼ inch rings
4 ears corn, cut from cob

3 large peeled and diced tomatoes
1 small green pepper, chopped
1 tsp. sugar
Salt and pepper to taste
Dash Tabasco

Fry bacon until crisp, drain and reserve 4 tablespoons of drippings. Stir onion and okra into drippings, add corn and cook for 10 minutes, stirring constantly. Add tomatoes, green pepper and seasonings. Cover and simmer until done (about 25 minutes) stirring occasionally. Correct seasonings, pour into serving dish and sprinkle with crumbled bacon.
Serves 6.

Mrs. H. L. Wineland

FRESH SHELLED PEAS

1 pint of shelled
  black-eyed peas
2½ cups boiling water
4-4½ Tbsp. bacon drippings

1 pod hot dried
  red pepper
2 tsp. salt
Pinch sugar

Add peas to boiling water. Stir in other ingredients. Cook covered over low heat for 2 hours, stirring occasionally. Add water, if needed. This recipe can be used for any shelled peas, except English peas.
Serves 3-4.

Mrs. Armistead C. Freeman

> *When cooking canned vegetables, such as peas, beans, etc. place lettuce leaf in pan while cooking to get a fresh vegetable taste.*

BUTTER PEAS CASSEROLE

1 (16 oz.) pkg. frozen
  butter peas
1 (8½ oz.) can artichoke
  hearts, drained
2 Tbsp. butter

1 tsp. salt
⅛ tsp. pepper
Paprika
1 cup canned French
  fried onions

Cook peas by package directions. Drain off most of liquid, but leave enough so casserole won't dry out. Place artichoke hearts in a 1½ quart casserole or 8x8 inch baking dish. Pour in peas; dot with butter and sprinkle on seasonings. Top with onions and bake uncovered at 350° for 20-30 minutes or until hot and bubbly.
Serves 6-8.

Mrs. Stewart Sanders

GREEN PEAS AND BROCCOLI CASSEROLE

2 (10 oz.) pkgs. frozen
  chopped broccoli
2 eggs, beaten
1 can cream of mushroom
  soup, undiluted
1 cup mayonnaise
1 tsp. salt

½ tsp. pepper
1 cup grated sharp
  Cheddar cheese
1 medium onion, chopped
1 (17 oz.) can Le Sueur
  Peas, drained
½ cup Ritz cracker crumbs

Cook broccoli by package directions; drain. Beat eggs; mix together with everything except broccoli, peas and crumbs. Butter a 2-quart casserole. Alternate layers of broccoli, peas and sauce. Make 2 layers of each. Top with cracker crumbs and bake at 350° for 30 minutes.
Serves 6-8.

Mrs. Morris J. Keesee, Jr.
Clarksdale, Mississippi

158

MASHED POTATO CASSEROLE

8-10 boiling potatoes
1 (8 oz.) pkg. cream
  cheese, softened
2 eggs, beaten slightly
2 Tbsp. all-purpose flour

2 Tbsp. minced parsley
2 Tbsp. minced chives
Salt and pepper to taste
1 (3½ oz.) can French
  fried onions

Peel and boil potatoes until tender; drain and put in large bowl of electric mixer. Beat until smooth; add cream cheese and beat again. Blend in eggs, flour, parsley, chives and seasonings. Turn into a buttered casserole and spread slightly crushed onions on top. Bake uncovered at 325° for 25-30 minutes.
Serves 8.

Mrs. Conner Morschheimer

This casserole may be prepared ahead. Refrigerate until baking time—the onions added just before placing them in oven.

POTATO PIE

2 (9-inch) unbaked pie shells
1 lb. cottage cheese
2 cups mashed potatoes
½ cup sour cream
2 eggs

2 tsp. salt
⅛ tsp. cayenne pepper
½ cup chopped green onions
4 Tbsp. grated Parmesan cheese

Put the cottage cheese through a food mill or blender to make it smooth. Beat in potatoes, then sour cream, eggs, salt and cayenne. Stir in green onions. Spoon into pie shells and sprinkle with grated cheese. Bake at 425° for 50 minutes or until golden brown. Allow to set a few minutes before serving.
Serves 12.

Mrs. R. Teryl Brooks, Jr.

ROQUEFORT POTATOES

6 large baking potatoes
½ cup half-and-half cream
½ cup butter

1 small wedge Roquefort cheese
1 tsp. white pepper
2 tsp. salt

Bake potatoes in a 400° oven for 1 hour or until done. While hot, halve potatoes and scoop out pulp. With mixer, cream pulp and remaining ingredients together; return to shells. Bake at 350° for about 25 minutes or until hot. These can be made ahead and frozen until ready for use.
Serves 6.

Mrs. Robert Ellzey
El Dorado, Arkansas

PEARL'S PARTY STUFFED POTATOES

6 large baking potatoes
½ cup butter, softened
1 (8 oz.) carton sour cream
1 pkg. bacon-onion dip mix

1 cup grated Cheddar cheese
1 tsp. salt
¼ tsp. white pepper
Paprika

Bake potatoes in a 400° oven until tender, about 1 hour. Cut in half, lengthwise. Scoop out pulp, reserving shells. Mix pulp with butter, sour cream, dip mix, cheese, salt and pepper. Spoon back into shells, sprinkle tops with paprika. Bake at 350° for 25 minutes.
Serves 6.

Mrs. Gerald Triplett

POTATOES WITH MUSHROOMS AND CHEESE

4-5 potatoes, peeled
  and thinly sliced
1 tsp. salt
½ tsp. pepper
1 clove garlic
½ cup butter
1 lb. mushrooms, sliced
  thin

1 cup grated Swiss cheese
Small bunch parsley, chopped
1 medium onion, finely
  chopped
1 pt. whipping cream
Extra grated Swiss cheese
Butter

Season potatoes with salt and pepper. Rub a 2-quart oblong baking dish with the garlic then butter it well. Make layers of potatoes and mushrooms until all are used, ending with potatoes. Sprinkle each layer with cheese, parsley and onions. Pour cream over top. Sprinkle on the extra Swiss cheese and dot with butter. Bake covered with foil at 375° for 1 hour and 30 minutes.
Serves 8-10.

Mrs. Dick Falk
Jonesboro, Arkansas

POTATO PANCAKES

2 medium white potatoes
1 egg
1 small onion, grated
Salt and pepper to taste

¼ tsp. baking powder
2 Tbsp. bread crumbs
3-4 Tbsp. flour
Sugar (optional)

Grate potatoes into cold water. Let soak while combining egg, onion, salt, pepper, baking powder, bread crumbs and flour. Drain potatoes and add egg mixture. Drop batter by tablespoons into ½ inch of hot shortening. Fry over moderate heat until crisp on both sides. Remove and drain well. Sprinkle with sugar if desired.
Serves 5-6.

Mrs. E. W. Freeman, III

HASH BROWN POTATO CASSEROLE

1 (32 oz.) pkg. shredded
   frozen potatoes
½ cup melted butter
1 can cream of chicken
   soup, undiluted
12 oz. grated American cheese

1 (8 oz.) carton sour cream
1 tsp. salt
½ small onion, chopped
2 cups crushed cornflakes
½ cup melted butter

Place thawed potatoes in a 9x13 inch baking dish. Mix together next 6 ingredients and pour over potatoes. Top with crushed cornflakes and drizzle melted butter over all. Bake uncovered at 350° for 45 minutes. Serves 12.

Mrs. Sidney Mann

SWISS POTATO CASSEROLE

6 lbs. potatoes
2 (4 oz.) jars chopped pimientos
1 cup salad olives, chopped
2 bunches of green onions,
   chopped

12 slices Swiss cheese
1¼ cups mayonnaise
Salt and pepper to taste

Cook potatoes until done; peel and cut in chunks. Add pimientoes, olives, green onions, 8 slices of cheese (cut in cubes) and mayonnaise. Season with salt and pepper. Place in oblong 2-quart casserole. Top with remaining 4 slices of cheese. Bake uncovered at 350° for 30 minutes or until bubbly. Serves 12.

Mrs. C. D. Allison, Jr.

POTATOES IN ORANGE SHELLS

12 oranges, halved
8 sweet potatoes
2 cups white sugar
2 tsp. salt
½ cup brown sugar

2 tsp. grated orange peel
¼ cup orange juice
1/3 cup butter
½ tsp. nutmeg
2 Tbsp. vanilla

Scoop out orange halves, reserving pulp. (A grapefruit spoon is great.) Bake sweet potatoes until tender, peel and cream while still warm. Add rest of ingredients, including pulp; mix well. Stuff orange shells with mixture. Place in a *lightly* buttered pan and bake at 325° for 25-30 minutes. Picket edges of orange shells for a special occasion. Serves 24.

Mrs. Paul B. Young

SWEET POTATO CASSEROLE

8 sweet potatoes
6 Tbsp. butter
2 eggs, beaten
4 Tbsp. sherry
½ tsp. nutmeg

Salt and pepper to taste
½ cup chopped pecans
2 Tbsp. butter, melted
½ cup chopped pecans
Marshmallows

Peel, boil and mash sweet potatoes. Add butter, eggs and sherry. Whip the potatoes until fluffy. Add seasonings and fold in pecans. Place in a rectangular casserole, pour butter over top and sprinkle with pecans. Bake at 350° for 15 minutes or until hot. Top generously with marshmallows and broil until tops are brown.
Serves 8-10.

Mrs. Charles Brazil
Paragould, Arkansas

BROWN RICE

1 medium onion, chopped
½ cup chopped green pepper
2 Tbsp. bacon grease
1 cup raw long grain rice

1 can consommé, undiluted
1 can chicken broth, undiluted
1 Tbsp. Worcestershire sauce
¾ tsp. salt

Sauté onion, green pepper and rice in bacon grease until the rice is golden and the vegetables are soft. Stir often to prevent sticking. Add consommé, chicken broth, Worcestershire and salt. Place in a covered 1½-quart casserole and bake at 350° for 1 hour or until rice is done and liquid is absorbed. Add ¾ teaspoon cumin to the rice mixture for a different flavor.
Serves 6.

Mrs. Joe Crabb

CHEESE RICE

2 cups cooked white rice
1½ cups milk
1/3 cup cooking oil
1 cup chopped green pepper

6-8 Tbsp. dried parsley
  flakes
8 oz. grated American cheese
Dash garlic salt

Cook the rice and mix in milk and oil. Add the green pepper, parsley flakes, cheese and garlic salt. Place in a greased 1½-quart casserole. Bake uncovered at 350° for 1 hour.
Serves 6-8.

Mrs. Simpson Bush

Cooked rice freezes well. It can be stored in refrigerator for a week or in the freezer in tightly sealed glass container for as long as 3 months.

RUTH'S RICE

1½ cups raw rice
3 Tbsp. olive oil
½ cup chopped onion
½ cup chopped celery
¼ cup chopped parsley
1 chopped clove of garlic

2 cups chicken broth
1 cup dry white wine
½ tsp. Accent
⅛ tsp. thyme
⅛ tsp. rosemary
Salt and pepper to taste

Sauté rice, onion, celery, parsley and garlic in oil for 5 minutes. Stir constantly. Add broth, wine and seasonings. Bring to boil; then place in a 1½-quart casserole. Cover and bake at 375° for 30 minutes. Stir gently and cook for another 10 minutes until rice is tender. (Will hold in warm oven for 1 hour.)
Serves 6.

Mrs. Joe Campbell
Mena, Arkansas

RICE AND ARTICHOKE CASSEROLE

¾ cup butter
7 green onions and
    tops, chopped
2 (4 oz.) cans sliced mushrooms,
    drained
4 tsp. dry mustard

1 (16 oz.) can artichoke
    hearts, coarsely chopped
2½ cups cooked rice
Dash Tabasco
Salt and pepper to taste
½ cup dry sauterne

Sauté onions in butter, add other ingredients. Place in 1½-quart casserole. Bake at 350° for 20 minutes or until hot.
Serves 6.

Mrs. H. S. Gregory
New Orleans, Louisiana

SPANISH RICE

¼ cup bacon grease
½ cup chopped onion
½ cup chopped green pepper
2 cups minute rice

2 cups hot water
2 (8 oz.) cans tomato sauce
Salt and pepper to taste
1 chopped jalapeno pepper

Sauté onion, green pepper and rice in grease until golden brown, stirring constantly. Add hot water, tomato sauce, salt, pepper and jalapeno pepper. Bring to boil and simmer for 5 minutes.
Serves 6-8.

Mrs. Charlie F. Pope

A "quickie" to serve with Mexican food.

CONFETTI RICE RING

2 cups cooked rice
1 beef bouillon cube
Dash ginger
1½ lbs. small fresh shrimp,
   cooked and drained
1 (7½ oz.) can crabmeat,
   flaked
1 cup chopped celery
½ onion, chopped
1½ cups chopped green pepper

2 cups small fresh mushrooms
¾ cup butter
2 cans cream of mushroom
   soup, undiluted
½ tsp. red pepper
Dash garlic powder
½ cup chopped fresh parsley
1 (8 oz.) can pimiento strips
1 (17 oz.) can Le Sueur English
   Peas, optional

Stir bouillon cube and ginger into warm rice, add shrimp and crabmeat. Sauté celery, green pepper, onion and mushrooms in butter until tender. Add to rice mixture along with the soup, pepper, garlic powder, parsley and pimiento. Gently stir in peas. Pack into a 2-quart ring mold and bake at 350° for 20 minutes. Remove from oven and allow to stand for 10 minutes. Unmold on a tray and garnish with broccoli or asparagus spears. Serves 6-8.

Mrs. Lula Brown
Cateress

WILD RICE AND SAUSAGE

1 lb. Jimmy Dean Sausage
1 cup chopped celery
1 large onion, chopped
1 medium green pepper,
   chopped
1 clove garlic, minced
1 can cream of mushroom
   soup, undiluted
1 can cream of chicken
   soup, undiluted

1 (6 oz.) pkg. plain and wild
   rice mixture
3 cups chicken broth
1 (8 oz.) can sliced mushrooms,
   drained
1 (5 oz.) can water chestnuts,
   drained and sliced
Pinch thyme
1 pkg. chopped almonds,
   optional

Brown sausage lightly; remove from skillet. Drain off most of grease and sauté onions, celery, green pepper and garlic in remainder for 5 minutes. Blend all ingredients, except almonds. Place in a 2-quart casserole and top with almonds if desired. Bake at 350° for 1 hour and 30 minutes. Serves 12.

Mrs. John A. Moore, Jr.

WILD RICE CASSEROLE

8 oz. wild rice
1 cup chopped celery
1 cup chopped onion
½ cup butter

8 oz. mild Cheddar cheese
1 (8 oz.) can of mushrooms
1 cup half-and-half cream

Boil rice according to directions on package. Sauté celery and onion in butter. Mix with rice. Add grated cheese and mushrooms. Place in a buttered 1½-quart casserole and pour cream over the mixture. Bake uncovered at 350° for 30 minutes or until set.
Serves 8.

Mrs. John MaGee
Longview, Texas

LEMON SPINACH

2 (10 oz.) pkgs. chopped
  spinach
1 tsp. sugar
1 (8 oz.) pkg. cream cheese
¼ cup butter

Rind of 1 lemon, grated
¼ cup butter
Crushed Pepperidge Farm
  Seasoned Crumbs

Cook spinach according to package directions, but add 1 teaspoon sugar to the water. Drain well. While spinach is still warm, blend in cheese, butter and rind. Place in a buttered 1½-quart casserole. Melt remaining ¼ cup butter; stir in crumbs and sprinkle on top of casserole. Bake uncovered at 350° for 30 minutes.
Serves 4-6.

Mrs. Louis L. Ramsay

SPINACH CASSEROLE

3 (10 oz.) pkgs. frozen
  chopped spinach
1 medium onion, chopped fine
½ cup oleo
Salt and pepper to taste

2 Tbsp. Worcestershire sauce
1 can cream of mushroom
  soup, undiluted
Buttered bread crumbs
Parmesan cheese

Cook spinach by package directions; drain well. Sauté onion in oleo; add spinach and season. Mix together Worcestershire sauce and soup; combine with spinach. Place in 1½-quart casserole. Sprinkle top with buttered crumbs and cheese. Bake uncovered at 350° for 30 minutes.
Serves 8-10.

Mrs. Jettie Driver
Osceola, Arkansas

165

SPINACH CHEESE PIE

4 frozen patty shells
1 (10 oz.) pkg. frozen chopped
  spinach
6 eggs
1 (3 oz.) pkg. cream cheese,
  softened
½ cup shredded sharp
  Cheddar cheese

2 Tbsp. chopped green onions
1 Tbsp. snipped parsley
½ tsp. salt
Dash pepper
2 Tbsp. grated Parmesan
  cheese

Thaw patty shells in refrigerator for 2 hours. Roll out on lightly floured surface to fit a 10-inch pie plate, sealing the dough edges together. Let rest 5 minutes. Place in the pie plate and flute edges.

Cook spinach by package directions; drain well. Combine eggs, cream cheese and Cheddar cheese. Beat until well combined. Stir in spinach, green onions, parsley, salt and pepper. Turn into prepared shell; top with Parmesan cheese. Bake at 425° for 15 minutes or until edges of filling are set. Remove from oven and let set for 10 minutes. Pie may be topped with tomato slices and more Parmesan cheese and returned to oven for about 5 minutes.
Serves 8.

Mrs. Jack Gentle

SPINACH RING

4 (10 oz.) pkgs. frozen chopped
  spinach, thawed and drained
1 cup medium white sauce
2 Tbsp. prepared mustard
2 Tbsp. Roquefort or blue
  cheese, crumbled

1 tsp. grated onion
Salt and pepper to taste
1 cup bread crumbs
3 eggs, separated

Combine first 6 ingredients. Stir in bread crumbs and beaten egg yolks. Whip egg whites until stiff but not dry. Fold into spinach mixture. Pour into a greased 2-quart ring mold. Set in a pan of hot water. Bake covered at 350° for 25-30 minutes. Turn out on a platter and garnish with parsley.
Serves 8-10.

Mrs. Alfine Jones (Hortense)
Cateress

SPINACH SQUARES

1 (10 oz.) pkg. frozen chopped spinach	½ cup Parmesan cheese
2 eggs	1 Tbsp. flour
1 (8 oz.) carton sour cream	2 Tbsp. butter
1 Tbsp. grated onion	1 tsp. salt
	⅛ tsp. pepper

Cook spinach as directed on package; drain well. Beat eggs and add to spinach. Blend in other ingredients. Place in a 9x9 inch baking dish. Bake uncovered at 350° for 25-30 minutes. Cut in squares to serve.
Serves 4.

Mrs. Jerome Shainberg

OYSTERS ROCKEFELLER EN CASSEROLE

2 (10 oz.) pkgs. frozen chopped spinach, thawed and drained	1 oz. anchovy paste
2 stalks of celery	2 Tbsp. Worcestershire sauce
1 bunch of green onions tops and all (6 or 7)	½ tsp. salt
½ head iceberg lettuce	¼ tsp. black pepper
1 bunch parsley	¼ tsp. Tabasco
½ tsp. anise seeds	Dash cayenne pepper
½ cup butter	½ cup grated Parmesan cheese
2 Tbsp. Herb-Saint Liqueur (about 1 oz.)	½ cup dry bread crumbs
	1 pt. oysters, drained
	Additional cheese and crumbs

Grind all the greens in a blender or very fine attachment of grinder, along with the anise seeds. Then sauté the greens in butter in a large skillet until the moisture has evaporated from them and the butter is absorbed. Season with Herb-Saint, anchovy paste, Worcestershire, salt, both peppers and Tabasco. Blend in the ½ cup grated Parmesan cheese and ½ cup dry bread crumbs. Pick over the oysters and drain on paper towels.

Butter a 2-quart casserole dish; begin with a layer of spinach mixture, then sprinkle with a layer of additional dry bread crumbs then layer half of the oysters, then spinach, crumbs and Parmesan cheese. Bake at 350° for 30-35 minutes until the oysters are cooked.
Serves 8.

Mrs. John G. Lile

This was served at the 1975 Charity Ball Royal Supper.

BAKED ACORN SQUASH

Green acorn squash
1/3 cup butter

2/3 cup brown sugar
1 Tbsp. rum

Cut green acorn squash in half. (Allow ½ per person.) Remove seeds and place cut side down in a pan with ½-inch water in bottom. Bake at 350° for 45 minutes or until tender. Turn cut side up and place 1 tablespoon brown sugar hard sauce in center.

To make sauce: Cream butter and add sugar, mixing well. Add rum a few drops at a time.

Mrs. Clarence Roberts, III

SYDNEY'S SQUASH

3 lbs. yellow squash
1 large onion
4 Tbsp. butter
1 cup whipping cream
8 oz. American cheese, cubed

2 Tbsp. cornstarch
½ tsp. salt
¼ tsp. pepper
2 (4½ oz.) cans shrimp
20 Ritz crackers, crushed

Wash and cut up squash and onions. Boil together in salted water until tender. *Drain very well* and set aside. In a saucepan, combine butter and cream. Stir constantly over low heat. Add cheese, cornstarch, salt and pepper; allow sauce to thicken. Place squash and onions in a 2-quart baking dish. Mix in drained shrimp and cheese sauce; sprinkle with cracker crumbs. Bake uncovered at 350° for 20-30 minutes or until hot. *Serves 10.*

Mrs. M. J. Probst

YELLOW SQUASH AND DEVILED HAM

14 yellow squash
1 tsp. salt
1 large onion, chopped
1 stalk celery, chopped
½ green pepper, chopped
¼ cup butter
½ tsp. dried parsley flakes

2 eggs, beaten
1 tsp. garlic salt
1 tsp. Accent
1 (4½ oz.) can deviled ham
Pepperidge Farm Seasoned
  Crumbs
Butter

Boil squash in salted water until tender. Drain and mash. Sauté onion, celery and pepper in butter. Add sautéed vegetables to squash along with parsley, eggs, salt, Accent and deviled ham. Put in a lightly buttered 2 quart casserole and top with crumbs. Dot with butter. Bake uncovered at 350° for 20 minutes or until bubbly.
Serves 6-8.

Mrs. Ronald D. Blankenship

SQUASH ROCKEFELLER

6-8 medium yellow squash
3 Tbsp. butter
⅛ tsp. garlic powder
1 (10 oz.) pkg. frozen chopped
    spinach, thawed and drained
1 bunch green onions, chopped
2 tsp. minced parsley

1/3 cup butter
1 tsp. Worcestershire sauce
3 dashes Tabasco
Salt to taste
¾ cup bread crumbs
2 Tbsp. butter
Parmesan cheese

Cut up squash; melt butter in a saucepan along with garlic powder. Add squash, cover pan and steam until squash are tender. Place in bottom of a 9-inch baking dish. Sauté thawed spinach, onions, and parsley in butter. Season with Worcestershire, Tabasco and salt. Pour mixture over squash. Melt 2 tablespoons of butter in saucepan; stir in bread crumbs. Top casserole with crumbs and sprinkle with cheese. Bake uncovered at 450° for 15 minutes or until brown.
Serves 6.

Mrs. Howard J. Wiechern, Jr.

SQUASH CASSEROLE

1 cup milk
1 cup soft bread crumbs
1½ cups cooked squash
1 egg beaten
1 cup grated Cheddar cheese

2 Tbsp. parsley
2 Tbsp. pimiento
1 Tbsp. chopped onion
3 Tbsp. melted butter
Salt and pepper to taste

Scald milk and add the bread crumbs. Stir in the squash, beaten egg, and cheese. Mix in the rest of the ingredients. Place in a buttered 1½-quart casserole. Bake uncovered at 350° for 1 hour.
Serves 6.

Mrs. James E. Cross

SQUASH AND ONIONS

4 cups sliced yellow squash
    (about ½ inch thick)
3 Tbsp. bacon grease

1 large onion, diced
1 cup milk
Salt and pepper to taste

Cook squash over medium heat in a small amount of water until soft. Drain completely and set aside. Melt bacon grease in a heavy iron skillet; sauté onion until done, but not brown. Add squash. Blend in milk and seasonings, stirring constantly. Cook over low heat until thickened. While cooking, mash squash with back of spoon to completely blend. (Should be more creamy than lumpy.) Spoon into a dish and serve immediately.
Serves 4.

Mrs. Armistead C. Freeman

FRESH TURNIP—TENDER—MUSTARD GREENS

1 large bunch of greens (about 2 lbs.—can be mixed)
1/4 lb. salt pork or 1 ham hock

2 1/2 cups boiling water
2 tsp. salt
1 tsp. pepper
Pinch sugar

Remove stems and discolored leaves of greens. Wash in several changes of water; add a little salt to last change. Drain.

Cook meat for 10 minutes in boiling water in Dutch oven. Add seasonings and greens. Cook slowly for 45 minutes-1 hour or until tender. Check seasonings.
Serves 6.

STUFFED TOMATOES—HOT WITH VEGETABLES

1 (10 oz.) pkg. frozen mixed vegetables
5 large tomatoes
Salt
3 Tbsp. butter
1/4 cup bread crumbs

1 tsp. flour
1/2 tsp. prepared mustard
1/2 tsp. Worcestershire sauce
2/3 cup milk
8 oz. sharp Cheddar cheese

Cook mixed vegetables as directed and drain well. Cut out stem ends from tomatoes. Cut each tomato in half, scoop out pulp being careful not to cut through. Lightly sprinkle inside with salt; set aside. Melt butter in medium saucepan and remove from heat. Remove 2 tablespoons of butter, mix with bread crumbs and set aside. Into remaining butter in pan, stir flour, mustard, and Worcestershire until smooth. Gradually stir in milk; bring to boil, stirring constantly. Reduce heat and simmer 1 minute. Remove from heat. Add cheese, stirring until melted. Stir in vegetables. Spoon mixture into tomato halves and top with buttered bread crumbs. Place in lightly greased pan and bake uncovered at 350° for 25 minutes.
Serves 10.

Mrs. Dean Copeland
Atlanta, Georgia

MUSHROOM STUFFED TOMATOES

8 ripe, but firm tomatoes
½ cup butter
1½ lbs. fresh mushrooms, sliced
1 (8 oz.) carton sour cream
1 Tbsp. plus 1 tsp. flour
3 oz. Roquefort cheese

¼ tsp. fines herbs
1 tsp. chopped fresh parsley
2 Tbsp. sherry
Salt and pepper to taste
Sesame seeds, toasted
Paprika

Cut a slice from the top of the tomatoes and carefully scoop out the soft part. Set upside down to drain. In a skillet, melt butter and sauté mushrooms until all the moisture has evaporated. Mix sour cream and flour. Blend in mushrooms over low heat; cook until thick and bubbly. Stir in cheese, herbs, parsley, sherry, salt and pepper. Cool the mixture. Stuff the tomatoes loosely with mushroom mixture; place in the bottom of a 2 quart oblong dish and add a little water in the bottom of the dish. Sprinkle top of tomatoes with sesame seeds and dust with paprika. Bake uncovered at 375° for 15 minutes.
Serves 8.

Mrs. Glenn A. Railsback, III

BAKED TOMATOES CREOLE

6 Tbsp. butter
½ cup finely chopped green
    onions, including tops
¼ cup finely chopped green pepper
¼ cup finely chopped celery
1½ tsp. finely chopped garlic
1 Tbsp. finely chopped parsley

¼ cup bread crumbs
½ tsp. salt
Black pepper, freshly ground
Pinch of thyme
Dash of Tabasco
8 medium-size ripe,
    but firm, tomatoes

In a heavy skillet, heat 4 tablespoons of the butter. When foam subsides, add onions, green peppers, celery and garlic. Cook until vegetables are soft (about 5 minutes), stirring often. Remove pan from heat; add parsley, bread crumbs and seasonings.

Wash tomatoes and cut a thin slice from both ends so that tomatoes stand upright. Sprinkle with salt and pepper; place in a buttered baking dish. Spoon the onion mixture on the top of each tomato, cut the remaining 2 tablespoons of butter into bits and scatter over the tops. Bake at 350° for 15 minutes. Top tomatoes with your favorite cheese sauce if it fits your menu.
Serves 8.

Mrs. R. Teryl Brooks, Jr.

VEGETABLE PIE

1 lb. fresh mushrooms, sliced
1 onion, sliced
2 zucchini or yellow
  squash, sliced
1 green pepper, sliced
3-4 Tbsp. butter
1 tsp. salt

¼ tsp. pepper
Dash garlic salt
1 tomato, sliced
1 (10-inch) pie shell, unbaked
1 cup mayonnaise
1 cup grated Mozzarella
  cheese

Sauté vegetables in butter until crisp, but not soft. Drain well and add seasonings. Place tomato slices in bottom of pie shell; add vegetables. Pour mayonnaise-cheese mixture over vegetables. Bake uncovered at 350° for 1 hour.
Serves 6.

Mrs. H. A. Taylor, Jr.

CREOLE ZUCCHINI

2 slices bacon, cut into
  1-inch strips
1 small onion, chopped
1 small green pepper, chopped
1 tsp. sugar
½ tsp. salt

½ tsp. pepper
½ tsp. Worcestershire
  sauce
1 (8 oz.) can tomato sauce
1 lb. cooked zucchini
  squash

Fry bacon; drain, crumble and reserve grease. Sauté onion and pepper in grease until soft. Add remaining ingredients except zucchini and bacon. Cook 15 minutes, stirring occasionally. Add zucchini and bacon; mix well. Serve immediately.
Serves 6.

Mrs. Joe Campbell
Mena, Arkansas

ZUCCHINI AND CORN CASSEROLE

¼ cup butter
4 cups sliced zucchini
1 (12 oz.) can white shoe
  peg corn
½ cup chopped onion
½ cup chopped green pepper

1 tsp. salt
1 tsp. dill weed
1 tsp. oregano
8 oz. grated Mozzarella
  cheese

Melt butter in skillet; add zucchini, corn, onion, and green pepper. Add seasonings. Cover and cook until vegetables are tender. Sprinkle in cheese. Place in 1½-quart casserole. Bake at 300° for 20 minutes, or until cheese melts.
Serves 6.

Mrs. W. H. Fox

THE C. H. TRIPLETT HOME
404 Oak Street
An excellent example of Queen Anne-Victorian architecture, this house was built by C. H. Triplett, Sr., whose family came to Arkansas in 1847. The year of construction, 1886, and the owner's initials, "CHT," are in the highly ornamented gable facing the northeast. This is one of the city's historical and architectural treasures.

COQUILLES ST. JACQUES

1½ lbs. scallops
1½ cups dry white wine
1 tsp. salt
6 peppercorns
3 sprigs parsley
1 bay leaf
¼ tsp. thyme
4 Tbsp. chopped green onions
½ cup water
½ lb. fresh mushrooms,
   chopped

5 Tbsp. butter, used
   separately
¼ cup flour
¾ cup milk
3 egg yolks
½ cup whipping cream
1 tsp. lemon juice
Cayenne pepper
½ cup grated Swiss cheese
Butter bits

Combine first 9 ingredients and poach scallops 5 minutes. Strain liquid, return to pan and boil rapidly until liquid is reduced to 1 cup. Pick scallops out from herbs, cut in bite size pieces and set aside. Sauté mushrooms in 2 tablespoons butter about 5 minutes. Drain and set aside. Melt 3 tablespoons butter, add flour and blend. Add milk gradually, stirring constantly until mixture is thick and smooth. Add 1 cup of reduced cooking liquid and cook, stirring for 1 minute. Beat egg yolks with cream. Slowly beat in hot sauce. Return sauce to pan and cook, stirring, about 2 minutes, until slightly thickened. Remove sauce from heat and add lemon juice and cayenne. You may make this dish ahead to this point and refrigerate sauce, scallops and mushrooms separately. Before serving, let them come to room temperature and heat sauce in double boiler. Remove 1 cup of sauce and set aside. Add scallops and mushrooms to remaining sauce and heat. Spoon into scallop shells or individual ramekins. Mask scallops with the extra sauce. Sprinkle with cheese and butter bits. Broil 8 inches from heat about 3 minutes, until lightly browned and bubbly. This is a wonderful first course to an elegant dinner. Or, serve for lunch with a green salad and French bread.
Serves 8.

Mrs. R. Teryl Brooks, Jr.

SOLE WITH HOLLANDAISE

1 pkg. frozen sole
   fillets, thawed
1 cup dry vermouth

Salt and white pepper
1 cup Hollandaise sauce
(See Index)

Pour vermouth into 9-inch iron skillet. When simmering, add sole fillets and poach until white and flaky, turning once. Drain and place on serving plates. Salt and pepper each one and spoon 1/3 cup Hollandaise over each serving.
Serves 3.

Mrs. Robert Nixon

SEAFOOD AND MUSHROOMS IN WINE SAUCE

1 can crabmeat
½ - ¾ lb. shrimp, cleaned
   and cooked
¼ lb. fresh mushrooms
4 Tbsp. butter, used
   separately
2 Tbsp. flour

½ cup milk
½ cup white wine
½ tsp. dry mustard
1 tsp. salt
¼ tsp. pepper
4-5 drops Tabasco sauce
¾ cup bread crumbs

Pick any shell pieces from crabmeat; cut shrimp into bite size pieces; combine the two and set aside. Sauté mushrooms in 2 tablespoons butter about 5 minutes. Set aside. Melt 2 tablespoons butter, add flour, then milk; add wine, mustard, salt, pepper and hot sauce. Cook 2-3 minutes. Add crabmeat, shrimp and mushrooms. Place in buttered casserole or 4 individual, buttered shells. Sprinkle with bread crumbs and bake at 350° for 25-30 minutes.
Serves 4.

Mrs. Ben Quinn, Jr.

FISH FILLETS WITH MUSHROOMS AND WHITE WINE SAUCE

3 lbs. fish fillets
  (bass suggested)
1 (10 oz.) pkg. frozen, chopped
  spinach
1 (10 oz.) pkg. frozen, chopped
  broccoli
Lemon-pepper marinade
¼ cup butter

2 Tbsp. butter
¼ cup flour
1 can cream of mushroom soup
½ cup sherry
1 (4 oz.) can mushrooms
Salt, pepper, and cayenne
Parmesan cheese
Sliced almonds

Mix cooked, drained spinach and broccoli together. To prepare fish, sprinkle with lemon-pepper marinade and dot with ¼ cup butter, then bake at 350° for about 7 minutes, or until fish is not quite done. Save the juices. Place fish on top of spinach-broccoli mixture that has been spread in a buttered, shallow baking dish. In a 10-inch skillet, reduce fish stock until no water remains. Add 2 tablespoons butter, melt and add ¼ cup flour; cook, stirring, over moderate heat for 3 minutes. Add soup, stirring until thoroughly mixed, then add sherry. If necessary, thin with cream. Add mushrooms and season to taste with salt, pepper and cayenne. Cook until sauce is consistency of thick white sauce. Pour over fish and sprinkle liberally with Parmesan cheese. Top with sliced almonds. Bake at 400° for 10 minutes, until bubbly and lightly browned.
Serves 8.

Dr. Sam C. Harris
F. T. Cash

SEAFOOD NEWBURG

2 (6 oz.) frozen lobster
  tails, cooked
2 cups cooked shrimp
2 cans crabmeat, drained
1 cup butter or margarine
1 cup flour

1½ cups milk
1½ cups whipping cream
½ cup dry sherry
1 tsp. mustard
2 Tbsp. lemon juice
Salt

Melt butter, add flour and cook, stirring, 2-3 minutes. Add milk and cream and stir until smooth; add sherry, mustard, lemon juice and salt to taste. Add lobster (cut in bite size pieces), shrimp and crabmeat. Correct seasoning with salt. Pour into buttered casserole and bake at 300° for 30 minutes.
Serves 12.

Mrs. Cortez Washington
Cateress

CREPES WITH SHRIMP AND MUSHROOMS

Make 16 crepes (See Index).

Mushroom Duxelles:

*3 cups finely chopped
fresh mushrooms
4 Tbsp. butter
4 Tbsp. finely chopped
green onions*

*1 tsp. finely chopped
fresh parsley
1 tsp. chopped chives
Salt
Freshly ground pepper*

Squeeze mushrooms in a towel to extract juice. In a heavy skillet, melt butter and sauté onions 1-2 minutes; add mushrooms and cook 10-15 minutes, stirring often, until all moisture has evaporated. Transfer to bowl, add parsley and chives. Season with salt and pepper and mix well.

Velouté Sauce:

*6 Tbsp. butter
½ cup flour
2½ cups hot chicken stock
2 egg yolks*

*¾ cup whipping cream
1 tsp. salt
¼ tsp. white pepper
1 tsp. lemon juice*

In heavy saucepan, melt butter, stir in flour and cook, stirring constantly, over low heat 1 minute. Beat in hot stock with wire whisk and bring to boil, stirring constantly. Boil 1 minute, remove from heat. Whisk together egg yolks and cream until well blended. Add ½ cup hot sauce, *2 tablespoons at a time,* whisking constantly. Pour back into remaining hot sauce and whisk until smooth and creamy. Bring just to boiling point and cook slowly 10 seconds. Remove, add remaining ingredients. Sauce will be *very thick.*

Filling and Topping:

*1 cup cooked, diced shrimp
1 tsp. chopped fresh
parsley or tarragon
Lemon juice
Salt and white pepper*

*½ - ¾ cup whipping cream
1 cup grated imported
Swiss cheese
4 Tbsp. butter*

Preheat oven to 375°. Combine shrimp, parsley, duxelles and ½ cup Velouté sauce. Mixture should be just thick enough to hold its shape in a spoon. Add more velouté sauce if necessary. Season to taste with lemon juice, salt and pepper. Spoon 2 tablespoons filling on each crepe and roll up. Thin remaining sauce with cream until it flows heavily off a spoon. Butter a large baking dish and spread a film of sauce on bottom. Arrange crepes in dish. Mask with rest of sauce and sprinkle cheese on top. Dot with butter. Bake in upper third of oven 15-20 minutes until brown and bubbly. Serve at once.
Serves 8.

Mrs. R. Teryl Brooks, Jr.

ESCARGOTS A LA BOURGUIGNONNE

3 dozen snails and shells
1¼ cups soft butter
2 Tbsp. finely chopped
  green onions
3 cloves garlic, crushed

1 Tbsp. chopped parsley
1 tsp. salt
Dash pepper
¾ cup dry white wine
Bread crumbs

Mix butter with next 5 ingredients and cream together with a fork until well-blended. Put a little butter mixture in each shell and put in escargot pans. Put a snail in each shell and fill with remaining butter mixture. Put 2 tablespoons dry white wine in the bottom of each dish. Sprinkle tops of shells with very fine bread crumbs. Bake at 450° until they are sizzling hot and crumbs are brown. Serve immediately, in the pans, with French bread to soak in the garlic butter. Refrigerate any leftover butter and use for garlic bread.
Serves 6.

These are a perfect first course. Or serve them with a salad and white wine for a late supper. Also good with champagne!

FILET OF SOLE DUGLERE

1 lb. filet of sole
4 Tbsp. finely chopped onion
3 Tbsp. butter
2 Tbsp. flour
½ cup dry white wine
¼ cup water
½ cup whipping cream

3 large fresh tomatoes,
  skinned and chopped
⅛ tsp. each: tarragon,
  dill weed, marjoram
1 tsp. minced parsley
Dried bread crumbs
Grated Parmesan cheese

Remove all excess moisture from sole with paper towels. Place in flat, buttered, "oven to table" baking dish. Put in refrigerator while making sauce. Sauté onion in butter. Stir in flour, then wine and water. Bring to a boil, stirring constantly. Remove from heat; add cream slowly. Simmer 4-5 minutes more. Add chopped tomatoes, herbs and parsley and simmer a minute more. Pour sauce over sole, sprinkle with bread crumbs and cheese and bake at 350° for 15-20 minutes.

Mrs. Thomas F. Stobaugh

STUFFED FISH FILLETS
WITH WATERCRESS SAUCE

2 cups Pepperidge Farm
  Herb Stuffing Mix
1 (16 oz.) pkg. frozen fish
  fillets, thawed (flounder,
  turbot or whiting)
½ tsp. salt

Salad oil
1/3 cup butter
1 medium onion, thinly sliced
1 small garlic clove
1 bunch watercress, chopped
¼ cup white table wine

Prepare stuffing mix according to package directions. Set aside. Sprinkle fillets with salt. Oil a 12 x 8 inch baking dish. Cut fillets into 8 serving pieces; arrange half of fillets in dish. Top them with stuffing. Place remaining fillets on top. Brush with salad oil and bake at 350° for 45 minutes until fish flakes easily when tested with fork. While fish are baking, melt butter in a 1 quart saucepan and cook onion and garlic about 10 minutes. Discard garlic, stir in watercress and wine; cook until watercress is tender, about 3 minutes. With spatula, lift fish to warm platter. Pour sauce over.
Serves 4.

Mrs. Richard Milwee

FROG LEGS

Frog legs
Milk
Crushed garlic
Salt and pepper

Flour
Butter
B and B Liqueur

Separate frog leg joints with knife. Soak in milk for 2 hours. Drain. Rub with garlic and generously salt and pepper. Dust lightly with flour. Sauté in butter until light golden brown. Add a little water, cover and steam until fork tender. Add B and B, light with a match to burn off alcohol and steam until time to serve.

Mrs. R. Chester List

CAJUN SHRIMP

3 lbs. unpeeled shrimp
2 qts. water
2 onions, quartered
1 lemon, quartered
6 bay leaves

1 Tbsp. red pepper
1 (1½ oz.) box garlic pods
Few cloves
Plenty of salt

To water add onions, lemon and spices which have been tied loosely in cheesecloth, and salt. Bring to a boil, add shrimp and cook until they turn pink. This is a great all-purpose recipe for boiling shrimp.

Mrs. Mark A. Shelton, III

CREPES CREVETTE

12 crepes (See Index)	2 Tbsp. butter
4 egg yolks	2 (10 oz.) pkgs., frozen,
1/3 cup lemon juice	shelled shrimp, thawed
1 cup butter	1 (10 oz.) pkg. chopped
1 cup minced onion	spinach, cooked, drained

To make sauce, combine egg yolks and lemon juice in double boiler over hot water. Add ½ cup butter; stir until melted; add other ½ cup butter; stir until sauce is thick. To prepare filling, sauté onion in butter. Add chopped shrimp. Add spinach and ½ cup sauce. Spoon filling on each crepe and roll up. Place in baking dish and cover with sauce. Broil until brown and bubbly.
Serves 6.

Mrs. Alfine Jones (Hortense)
Cateress

SOLE OR FLOUNDER WITH SHRIMP SAUCE

1 lb. sole or flounder fillets	Shrimp or lobster meat,
1 Tbsp. sherry	chopped
1 Tbsp. flour	Butter
1 can cream of shrimp soup	Parmesan cheese

Mix sherry, flour and soup; pour over fish. Add shrimp or lobster, dot with butter and lightly coat with cheese. Bake uncovered at 375° for 20-30 minutes.
Serves 3-4.

Mrs. Frank Surface
Jacksonville, Florida

BROILED POMPANO WITH CHIVES

2 medium pompano,	3 Tbsp. fresh lemon juice
tenderloined	½ tsp. salt
Salt and pepper	2 Tbsp. chives (fresh
1 cup butter, melted	or freeze dried)
1 Tbsp. finely minced parsley	Red pepper to taste

Preheat broiler and broiler pan for 10 minutes. Remove pan, and butter rack. Sprinkle fish with salt and pepper. Place fish on rack, skin side down. Broil 3½ - 4 inches from heat for 6-7 minutes. Watch carefully and do not overcook. It is done when it flakes easily. Combine butter, parsley, lemon juice, salt, chives and red pepper and have ready to pour over pompano on warmed plates as soon as it is ready.

If you are lucky enough to have pompano, this is a wonderful way to enhance, rather than mask, its delicious flavor.

SHRIMP IN THE SHELLS

5 lbs. shrimp
5 qts. water
1 box McCormack Shrimp
and Crab Boil

½ bottle crushed red pepper
½ cup salt
½ cup butter

To water add crab boil, red pepper and salt; boil 5 minutes. Add shrimp and simmer 15 minutes. Pour off half the water and add butter. Can be done an hour or so ahead and reheated. Drain and serve hot (peel your own style) with cold beer.
Serves 6.

Mrs. Don Stone
Daphne, Alabama

SHRIMP JAMBALAYA

1 cup sliced celery
2 cups diced green pepper
2 medium onions,
thinly sliced
4 Tbsp. butter or
margarine, divided
1-2 cloves garlic, minced
1 lb. boiled ham, in
¾ in. cubes

2 lbs. peeled shrimp
1½ tsp. salt
Pepper to taste
¼ tsp. liquid red
pepper sauce
½ tsp. chili powder
1 tsp. sugar
2 (1 lb.) cans whole tomatoes
3 cups hot cooked rice

Cook celery, green pepper and onions in half the butter until tender, but not brown. Add garlic and ham and cook 5 minutes. Add remaining butter, shrimp, salt, pepper, pepper sauce, chili powder and sugar. Cook, tossing with fork, until shrimp are pink. Add tomatoes; heat. Stir in rice.
Serves 8.

Mrs. John E. Caruthers, Sr.

SHRIMP REMOULADE

½ cup chopped white onions
¾ cup oil
¼ cup tarragon vinegar
½ cup creole mustard
2 tsp. paprika
¾ tsp. cayenne pepper
2 tsp. salt

2 medium cloves garlic,
pressed
½ cup chopped green
onions and chives
5 cups shredded lettuce
2 lbs. shrimp, boiled and
peeled

In a blender, place first eight ingredients. Blend 5-6 seconds, turn off, stir, blend another 5-6 seconds. Add green onions, blend for 2 seconds. *Do not blend longer or you will have purée.* Chill overnight. Arrange beds of lettuce on salad plates, top with shrimp and cover with with chilled sauce.

Walker Lewis

SHRIMP MOSCA

2 lbs. large shrimp
  in shells
1 cup olive oil
8 large cloves garlic, whole
1 Tbsp. rosemary

¼ tsp. oregano
4 bay leaves
1 tsp. salt
½ tsp. fresh black pepper
½ cup sauterne

Put first 8 ingredients in large, heavy skillet and sauté over medium heat 15-20 minutes, stirring occasionally, until shrimp are slightly brown. Add sauterne and cook about 10 minutes more, until wine evaporates. Serve in soup bowls with French bread for dipping.
Serves 4.

Mrs. Bill O'Neal

BARBECUED SHRIMP

1 lb. jumbo shrimp in shells
  (with or without heads)
1½ cups melted butter
2 cloves garlic, minced
Dash Tabasco sauce

Paprika
Salt and pepper
1 lemon, sliced
1 Tbsp. chili sauce
1 cup white wine

Wash shrimp. Combine other ingredients, stir in shrimp and marinate *at least* 1 hour. Broil on barbeque grill until shrimp begin to curl, turning at least once. Serve in soup bowls with remaining marinade. We eat shells, heads, tails and all!
Serves 4.

Mrs. Eugene Harris

SHRIMP, MANALE STYLE

2 lbs. large shrimp,
  in the shell
1 cup butter
1 cup olive oil, or
  vegetable oil
8 cloves garlic, crushed
4 whole bay leaves
4 tsp. fines herbs

1 (6 oz.) bottle Louisiana
  Hot Sauce
1 Tbsp. Worcestershire sauce
2 tsp. salt
1 tsp. freshly ground
  black pepper
Juice of 2 lemons

Melt butter in large, heavy saucepan, add oil, mix. Add following ingredients, heat thoroughly, set aside for flavors to blend. When ready to cook, add shrimp, bring to a boil, lower heat and simmer about 20 minutes. Stir frequently. Serve in soup bowls with the sauce, with French bread for dipping and icy cold beer. Peel your own or eat shells too!
Serves 4.

SHRIMP STUFFED WITH CRABMEAT

1 lb. raw fresh jumbo shrimp
1 egg, beaten
¼ cup milk
½ cup bread crumbs
½ tsp. paprika
1 lb. fresh crabmeat
1 tsp. Worcestershire sauce
1 tsp. prepared mustard

2 Tbsp. mayonnaise
2 slices bread, cubed
  (crusts removed)
Salt and pepper to taste
1 medium onion, minced
½ green pepper, minced
1 cup butter

Peel shrimp, leaving tail shell on. Split down back butterfly fashion. Dip shrimp into mixture of egg and milk, then into mixture of bread crumbs and paprika. Combine crabmeat, Worcestershire, mustard, mayonnaise, bread, salt and pepper. Sauté onion and green pepper in ½ cup butter and add to crabmeat. Firmly stuff shrimp. Place in greased pan. Baste with ½ cup butter. Bake at 400° for 15 minutes or until brown. To serve as appetizer, use large rather than jumbo shrimp and half the stuffing ingredients.
Serves 4.

Mrs. Mallory Reeves
Selma, Alabama

SHRIMP DELICIOUS

1 lb. medium or large shrimp,
  shelled and deveined
1 Tbsp. flour
2 Tbsp. butter
2 cups whipping cream

1 Tbsp. ketchup
1 Tbsp. Worcestershire sauce
Cayenne pepper
2 Tbsp. sherry

Boil shrimp 3 minutes *only*. Brown flour in butter until very brown. Allow to cool and add cream. Stir until well-blended and creamy. Add ketchup, Worcestershire and pepper. Add shrimp and sherry. Heat just until hot. Serve over cooked rice.
Serves 4.

Mrs. John D. Tharp

SHRIMP AND MUSHROOM SHELLS

2 lbs. shrimp, cooked
   and peeled
4 Tbsp. butter
4 Tbsp. flour
1 egg yolk, slightly beaten
1 cup chicken broth
1 tsp. salt
⅛ - ¼ tsp. cayenne pepper

1 Tbsp. lemon juice
3 Tbsp. dry sherry
½ cup grated sharp
   Cheddar cheese
½ lb. fresh mushrooms
¼ cup butter
Fine bread crumbs

Melt butter, add flour and cook a few minutes, stirring constantly. With a wire whisk, stir in combined egg yolk and broth. Add salt and cayenne and cook until very thick. Slowly add lemon juice, sherry and cheese. Add shrimp, then mushrooms that have been sautéed in butter. Simmer 5 minutes. Put in 4 buttered sea shells or ramekins and cover with bread crumbs. (Or make 8 if using as appetizer.) Bake at 350° for about 20 minutes.
Serves 4.

Mrs. Jim Price
Jackson, Tennessee

SHRIMP CURRY

5 lbs. cooked shrimp,
   small ones are better
¾ cup butter
1¼ cups minced onions
1 cup less 1 Tbsp. flour
8 tsp. curry powder
3¼ tsp. salt

½ tsp. powdered ginger
1¼ tsp. sugar
3¼ cups chicken broth
5 cups milk
Garlic
Worcestershire sauce
Tabasco sauce

Condiments:
Salted peanuts, chopped
Pineapple chunks
Chutney

Avocado slices
Grated fresh coconut

Melt butter and sauté onion; blend in flour. Remove from heat and add curry powder, salt, ginger and sugar. Return to heat and slowly add broth and milk. Season to taste with garlic, Worcestershire and Tabasco. Add shrimp and heat thoroughly. Serve with rice and condiments.
Serves 10.

Mrs. Robert Ellzey
El Dorado, Arkansas

SHRIMP MARINIERE

2 lbs. boiled, peeled shrimp
½ cup butter
1½ cups chopped green
    onions (with tops)
6 Tbsp. flour

3 cups hot chicken broth
½ tsp. salt (or to taste)
¼ - ½ tsp. cayenne pepper
2/3 cup dry white wine

Melt butter and sauté onions until tender. Blend in flour and cook 5 minutes, stirring constantly. Stir in broth using wire whisk. Add salt, pepper and wine and cook until thickened somewhat; add shrimp and cook until piping hot. Serve on rimmed dinner plates; do not put anything on plate as sauce is thin.
Serves 4.

Mrs. J. Wayne Buckley

SHRIMP A LA JACQUES

2 lbs. cooked shrimp
1 cup medium white sauce
5 egg yolks
1 jigger white wine

Garlic butter
1 pkg. Gouda cheese,
    grated

Cut shrimp in bite size pieces and put in individual baking shells. Add a little of the hot white sauce to egg yolks, then add yolks to remaining white sauce, stirring constantly with wire whisk. Add wine, stirring. Pour over shrimp in shells. Add generous pat of garlic butter to each and top with grated cheese. Brown under broiler and serve hot. Garnish with lemon wedges.
Serves 6.

Mrs. John Crenshaw

SHRIMP MORNAY

Sauce:
1 (6 oz.) roll garlic cheese
1 can cream of shrimp soup
1 cup medium white sauce

1 (4 oz.) can mushrooms
1 (10 oz.) pkg. precooked
    frozen shrimp, thawed

For each serving:
1 Holland rusk
1 slice boiled ham

3 stalks frozen broccoli,
    cooked tender-crisp

Mix cheese, soup and white sauce; heat slowly until cheese melts. Add drained mushrooms and shrimp. Sauce will make 6 servings. On each individual mornay dish, stack next 3 ingredients in order given and cover with sauce. Bake at 350° until bubbly.

Mrs. C. D. Allison, Jr.

SALLY'S SHRIMP

½ cup butter
3 lbs. shrimp, peeled
6 cloves garlic, crushed
1 tsp. salt

¼ cup chopped fresh parsley
2 Tbsp. lemon juice
2 Tbsp. grated lemon peel
Fresh peppers, optional

Melt butter, add other ingredients and cook in a flat pan at 400° for 5 minutes. Turn shrimp and cook 10 minutes more. (Fresh banana peppers or other hot peppers, chopped can be added when in season.)

Mrs. M. Stanley Cook, Jr.

BATTER FOR FRIED SHRIMP OR ONION RINGS

1 cup flour
½ tsp. salt
2/3 cup water

2 Tbsp. oil
1 egg white, beaten stiff

Sift dry ingredients, add water and oil, beat until smooth. Fold in egg white just before frying. Coat fan-tail shrimp or onion rings and fry in deep fat until brown.

Mrs. Rufus A. Martin

CRABMEAT AU GRATIN

1 lb. can (fresh or frozen)
   crabmeat, drained
1 small green pepper,
   chopped fine
2 Tbsp. butter
2 Tbsp. flour

2 cups half and half cream
Pinch of nutmeg
Salt and pepper to taste
1 tsp. chopped pimiento
2 cups grated sharp cheese
Toast points

Sauté green pepper in butter. Stir in flour and cook a few minutes. Mix in cream, then crabmeat and seasonings. Cook slowly until it thickens, then add pimiento. Put in buttered casserole and cover with cheese. Bake at 400° for 15-20 minutes until it is hot and cheese melted. Serve on toast points.
Serves 4.

Mrs. Jack Gentle

AUNT MILDRED'S DEVILED CRAB

2 Tbsp. butter
3 Tbsp. flour
1 cup Swanson Chicken Broth
1/3 cup cream
¼ tsp. salt
Dash red pepper
2 egg yolks

Accent
½ lb. fresh mushrooms,
  sautéed in butter
2 Tbsp. parsley
2 cans crabmeat,
  drained well
Buttered bread crumbs

Melt butter, add flour and stir a few minutes. Add broth. Slowly add cream and cook until thickened. Add salt and red pepper; add egg yolks and Accent and stir until thick. Add mushrooms, parsley and crabmeat and pile in lightly buttered shells or ramekins. Bake at 350° until bubbly, then cover with bread crumbs and bake until browned.
Serves 4.

Mrs. James S. Rogers

CRABMEAT PLATONIC

8 Tbsp. butter
8 Tbsp. flour
2 egg yolks, slightly beaten
2 cups chicken broth
1-2 tsp. salt
¼ - ½ tsp. cayenne pepper

2 Tbsp. lemon juice
6 Tbsp. dry sherry
1 lb. crabmeat (lump
  crabmeat, if available)
½ cup fine bread crumbs

Melt butter, add flour and cook a few minutes. Combine egg yolks and chicken broth and add slowly, stirring with a wire whisk. Add salt and cayenne and cook until very thick. Slowly add lemon juice and sherry and allow to become very thick again. Drain crabmeat thoroughly. (Drain in colander and then on paper towels and gently pat it to remove all extra moisture.) Stir into sauce. Put in buttered sea shells or ramekins and lightly cover top with bread crumbs. Bake on cookie sheet at 350° for 30 minutes.
Serves 4-6. (8 as appetizer)

Mrs. J. Wayne Buckley

SWISS CRABMEAT

½ cup butter
½ bunch chopped green onions
½ bunch chopped parsley
  (remove all stems)
2 Tbsp. flour
1 (16 oz.) can evaporated
  milk

½ lb. Swiss cheese, grated
Worcestershire sauce to taste
Cayenne pepper to taste
Salt to taste
1 lb. crabmeat, drained
¼ cup sherry
Pastry shells

Melt butter and sauté onions and parsley. Add flour and cook over low heat for 5 minutes. Add milk slowly, stirring with wire whisk. Add cheese and cook until melted. Add seasonings, then crabmeat and sherry; cook until hot. Serve in pastry shells.
Serves 8.

Mrs. Don Ballard
Houston, Texas

CRAB AND RICE IN SEA SHELLS

1 cup cooked rice
1 (6½ oz.) can crabmeat,
  drained and flaked
5 hard cooked eggs, chopped
1½ cup mayonnaise
½ tsp. salt
¼ tsp. cayenne pepper
Dash black pepper

⅛ tsp. crushed tarragon
1 Tbsp. minced parsley
2 tsp. finely chopped onion
1 (5.33 oz.) can evaporated milk
Pimiento (optional)
Water chestnuts (optional)
½ cup grated, processed
  Cheddar cheese

Combine first 3 ingredients. Blend together all remaining ingredients except cheese. Mix into first mixture until well-blended. Fill 8 buttered sea shells or ramekins. Sprinkle with cheese. Bake at 350° for 20 minutes, or until hot and cheese is melted.
Serves 8.

Mrs. John E. Caruthers, Sr.

OYSTERS AND ARTICHOKES

Sauce:
½ cup butter	3 cups chicken broth
½ cup flour	½ cup sherry
1 1/3 cups green onions, finely chopped	¼ cup parsley, chopped fine
2 large cloves garlic, crushed	2 pinches each: thyme, oregano and marjoram
	Salt and red pepper
8 artichokes	Thin lemon slices
4 jars oysters	Parsley

Make a brown roux by stirring butter and flour over low heat. Add onions and garlic and cook over very low heat until soft. Add broth and sherry slowly, stirring with wire whisk. Add parsley, herbs, salt and red pepper to taste. Cook very slowly about 15 minutes. This can be done a day or more ahead and reheated at serving time.

Cook artichokes. Separate leaves from bottoms and discard fuzzy part. Chop bottoms into large pieces and place in 8 ramekins. Bake oysters a few minutes to remove excess liquid. Divide oysters between ramekins. Pour sauce over oysters and top each with lemon slice and sprinkle of parsley. Bake at 350° till bubbly; serve on plate surrounded by tender artichoke leaves for dipping.
Serves 8.

Mrs. R. Teryl Brooks, Jr.
Mrs. J. Wayne Buckley

OYSTERS A LA JUSTINE

Sauce from recipe for Oysters and Artichokes	Salt and pepper
	Oil
3 jars oysters	8 thin slices lemon
2 cups corn meal	Finely chopped parsley

Make 1 recipe of sauce from Oysters and Artichokes (above). Just before frying, roll oysters in meal seasoned with salt and pepper and fry them in *hot* oil in iron skillet. Do not crowd them! Drain well on paper towels. Fill 8 ramekins with hot oysters. Pour piping hot sauce over them. Place lemon slice on top and sprinkle with parsley. Serve with French bread and white wine for a delicious first course.
Serves 8.

This method is a wonderful basic recipe for Fried Oysters!

KING'S ARMS' OYSTERS

1 qt. oysters
½ cup butter
¾ cup flour
1 Tbsp. paprika
1 tsp. salt
½ tsp. black pepper
¼ cup finely chopped onion

¼ cup finely chopped
   green pepper
½ tsp. minced garlic
2 tsp. lemon juice
1 Tbsp. Worcestershire sauce
2 Tbsp. cracker crumbs

Pick over oysters for shells. Heat in oyster liquor (mixed with water to make 1½ cups). Melt butter, add flour and cook 5 minutes, stirring. Add paprika, salt and pepper and cook slowly, stirring constantly, until dark brown. (Be careful not to burn by cooking too fast.) Add vegetables and cook slowly 5 minutes. Remove from heat, add lemon juice, Worcestershire sauce, oysters with liquid and blend. Put in buttered 1½-quart casserole, sprinkle with crumbs and bake at 400° for 30 minutes.

Mrs. John G. Lile

OYSTERS BOURGUIGNONNE

2 jars oysters
4 Tbsp. dry white wine
½ cup butter
3 cloves garlic, crushed
2 green onions, finely chopped

½ tsp. salt
Dash red pepper
½ Tbsp. chopped parsley
½ cup bread crumbs

Drain oysters well. Place in 4 ramekins. Put 1 tablespoon wine in each ramekin. Mix softened butter, garlic, onions, salt, red pepper and parsley with fork. Put on top of oysters. Sprinkle bread crumbs on top. Bake at 375° for 15 minutes, until brown and bubbly.
Serves 4.

Mrs. J. Wayne Buckley

SCALLOPED OYSTERS

1 pt. oysters
2 cups cracker crumbs
   (made from saltines)

½ cup butter
Salt and pepper to taste
2 cups milk

Wash oysters and drain in colander. In a 2-quart, round, buttered casserole, layer cracker crumbs, then oysters, then butter pats. Continue layers until dish is filled. Salt and pepper oyster layers. Pour milk over this. Bake at 350° for 45 minutes, until set.
Serves 6.

Mrs. M. J. Keesee
Helena, Arkansas

OYSTERS BIENVILLE

4 doz. oysters
  (and half shells)
3 ribs celery, chopped fine
2 medium onions, chopped fine
3-4 garlic cloves, crushed
½ cup butter
1 cup flour
1 qt. milk
2 Tbsp. chervil
¼ cup chopped parsley

1 lb. cooked shrimp, chopped
1 (4 oz.) can mushrooms,
  chopped
3-4 jiggers dry white wine
Salt to taste
White pepper to taste
Rock salt
Paprika
Bread crumbs

Sauté celery, onions and garlic in butter until golden brown. Add flour and cook a few minutes, stirring. Slowly add milk and cook over moderate heat until thick. Add chervil, parsley, shrimp, mushrooms, wine, salt and pepper. Place oysters on oiled shells on beds of rock salt. Put about 1 tablespoon sauce on each oyster. Sprinkle with paprika. Cook at 350°-400° for 10 minutes or until oysters are hot. If you like, sprinkle bread crumbs on oysters after baking and place under broiler to brown lightly.
Serves 8.

Dr. Sam C. Harris

OYSTERS RIO

¼ cup butter
1 cup chopped green onions
  (include tops)
½ lb. fresh mushrooms,
  chopped fine
1 tsp. salt
½ tsp. black pepper

¼ cup dry sherry
Juice from 1 lemon
2 cloves garlic, crushed
⅛ tsp. cayenne pepper
4 oz. tomato sauce
2 jars oysters
Bread crumbs

Melt butter. Sauté onions and mushrooms with salt, black pepper, sherry, lemon juice, crushed garlic and cayenne pepper until most of moisture is absorbed. Add tomato sauce and simmer until thick. Drain oysters in colander and then on paper towels. Put in 4 buttered ramekins. Cover with thin layer of bread crumbs. Divide sauce between ramekins. Bake at 350° for 20 minutes.
Serves 4.

Mrs. J. Wayne Buckley

OYSTERS BIENVILLE A LA SHREVEPORT

1 doz. oysters
(and half shells)
1 bunch green onions, chopped
1 Tbsp. butter
1 Tbsp. flour
½ cup chicken broth
¾ cup chopped mushrooms,
sautéed in 2 Tbsp. butter

½ cup cooked shrimp, chopped
1 egg yolk
1/3 cup dry white wine
Salt and pepper
Rock salt
Grated Parmesan cheese,
bread crumbs and
paprika mixed

Sauté onions in butter until tender. Add flour and stir until brown. Add broth, mushrooms and shrimp. Beat egg yolk with wine and slowly add to sauce beating rapidly. Season to taste. Cook for 10 minutes over low heat, stirring constantly. Cool. (Sauce can be made ahead of time and refrigerated.) Place rock salt on pizza tin or 2 pie plates. Put oysters on oiled half shells and place on salt. Bake oysters at 350° for 6-8 minutes, until *partially* done. Remove from oven and pour off excess oyster liquor. Pour sauce over each oyster, top with cheese mixture. Place back in oven to brown for about 12 minutes. Recipe doubles or triples easily.
Serves 2.

Mrs. Harry Metcalf

193

OYSTERS ERNIE

24 select oysters
Salt and pepper
Flour
Butter
2 Tbsp. melted butter
¼ cup fresh lemon juice

1 cup A-1 sauce
2 Tbsp. Worcestershire sauce
2 jiggers sherry
2 Tbsp. flour
3 Tbsp. water

Salt and pepper oysters; dredge in flour. Grill on lightly buttered grill or heavy skillet until brown and crispy on both sides. Sprinkle oysters with butter while grilling. Place melted butter, lemon juice, A-1, Worcestershire and sherry in a saucepan over a low fire and heat thoroughly. Blend flour into water and stir into sauce after it is hot. Add more A-1 if sauce is too thin or sherry if sauce is too thick. Place freshly grilled oysters on serving plates and dress with heated sauce. This sauce can be saved, strained, reheated and used again.
Serves 4 as appetizer.

Mrs. Edward E. Brown

SALMON TIMBALES

1 (16 oz.) can red salmon
½ cup whipping cream
½ tsp. salt
⅛ tsp. pepper
¼ cup chopped green onion

1 Tbsp. parsley
½ tsp. lemon juice
4 eggs, separated
Hollandaise Sauce
  (See Index)

Preheat oven to 400°. Drain salmon, remove bones and skin. Flake and mash with fork. Add cream, salt, pepper, onions, parsley and lemon juice. Beat egg yolks well and add to salmon mixture. Beat egg whites until they form soft peaks and carefully fold into mixture. Grease 6 (4 oz.) ramekins or 4 (6 oz.) ramekins and pour in salmon mixture. Place in pan with 2 inch sides; pour in 1 inch of boiling water. Bake small ramekins 15-20 minutes or large ones 25-30 minutes, until knife inserted in center comes out clean. Unmold timbales, arrange on platter and top with Hollandaise sauce. Surround with parslied potato balls, if you like. This also make a nice luncheon plate with asparagus spears and a fresh fruit salad.
Serves 4-6.

Mrs. R. Teryl Brooks, Jr.

THE ROTH - ROSENZWEIG HOUSE
717 West Second Avenue
On August 4, 1894, Louis L. Roth let a contract to W. S. Helton to build this Queen Anne style house with its round shingled cupola and Tuscan-type columns. The house was sold to William Rosenzweig on September 5, 1910; and in 1970 to Ben Pearson, who then restored it.

STEAK DIANE

4 sirloin steaks (½ inch thick,
   4 inches in diameter)
Salt and pepper

2 Tbsp. butter
½ cup good cognac, warmed

Sauce:
4 Tbsp. melted butter
4 Tbsp. chopped green onions
   (include tops)
2 Tbsp. finely chopped parsley

2 Tbsp. A-1 sauce
4 Tbsp. good sherry or
   Madeira
2 Tbsp. Worcestershire sauce

Combine sauce ingredients and heat gently for 30-45 seconds.

Melt 1 tablespoon butter in a carefully controlled skillet. Season the steaks with salt and pepper. Cook 2 steaks at a time, 1½ minutes on each side. Pour half the sauce over the steaks; cook until bubbly. Prepare remaining steaks in the same way.

Add the warmed cognac, light it and spoon the mixture over the steaks. Serve immediately.
Serves 4.

Dr. James T. Rhyne

CHINESE PEPPER STEAK

1½ lbs. sirloin steak, 1 inch thick
¼ cup fat or vegetable oil
1 clove garlic, crushed
1 tsp. salt
1 tsp. ground ginger
½ tsp. pepper
3 large green peppers, seeded
   and sliced
2 large onions, thinly sliced

1/3 cup soy sauce
½ tsp. sugar
½ cup beef bouillon
1 (6 oz.) can water chestnuts,
   drained and sliced
1 Tbsp. cornstarch
¼ cup water
4 green onions, cut in 1 inch pieces
Hot cooked rice

Freeze steak for 1 hour (it's easier to slice). When ready to cook, cut into ⅛ inch wide strips. Heat fat or oil in skillet; add garlic, salt, ginger and pepper. Sauté until garlic is golden. Add steak slices; brown lightly for 2 minutes; remove meat. Add green peppers and sliced onions; cook for 3 minutes. Return beef to pan; add soy sauce, sugar, bouillon, water chestnuts, cornstarch dissolved in water, and green onions. Simmer about 2 minutes or until sauce thickens. Serve over hot rice.
Serves 6-8.

Ben Cumnock
Conway, Arkansas

PEPPERED STEAK WITH BRANDY SAUCE

2 Tbsp. peppercorns
2 (2½ lb.) steaks, ¾-1 inch thick
  (such as sirloin or porterhouse)
Salt
2 Tbsp. butter (divided)
1 Tbsp. oil

2 Tbsp. minced shallots or
  green onions
½ cup stock or beef bouillon
1/3 cup cognac
3-4 Tbsp. softened butter

Place the peppercorns in a mixing bowl and crush them roughly with a pestle or place them on a board and crush them with a pressing, rolling movement, using the bottom of a pan.

Dry the steaks on paper towels. Rub and press the crushed peppercorns into both sides of the meat with your fingers and the palms of your hands. Cover with waxed paper. Let stand for at least 30 minutes (2 to 3 hours would be better).

Put 1 tablespoon of butter and oil in skillet and place over moderately high heat until the butter foams. Sauté steak on each side for 3-4 minutes; regulate heat so that the fat is always very hot but is not burning. The steak should be medium rare. Remove to a hot platter and keep warm while making the sauce.

Pour fat out of the skillet. Add 1 tablespoon of butter and onions and cook slowly for a minute. Pour in bouillon or stock and boil over high heat, scraping up browned particles. Add cognac and boil rapidly for a minute or two. Take off heat; swirl in 3-4 tablespoons of softened butter, ½ tablespoon at a time. Pour over steak and serve.
Serves 4-6.

Dr. Ray E. Colclasure

FLANK STEAK-TERIYAKI BARBEQUE

¾ cup oil
¼ cup soy sauce
¼ cup honey
2 Tbsp. vinegar

2 Tbsp. chopped green onion
1 large clove of garlic
1½ tsp. ginger
1 flank steak (1½ lbs.), not scored

Combine first seven ingredients; add steak and marinate at least 4 hours. Drain. (Marinade may be saved for future use.)

Barbeque meat over hot coals, basting with marinade. Turn one time. Five minutes on each side will cook the steak medium.

To serve, cut crosswise to grain.
Serves 4.

Mrs. Joe Campbell
Mena, Arkansas

THE WINDSOR RECIPE:
TOURNEDOS OF BEEF QUEEN OF SHEBA

12 slices peeled eggplant
(½ inch thick)
Seasoned flour
3-4 Tbsp. butter
12 slices prosciutto ham
(paper-thin)
12 (3-4 oz.) slices beef
tenderloin

Salt and pepper
Butter for sautéing beef
24 cooked fresh jumbo
asparagus tips
Hollandaise sauce

Dredge eggplant slices in flour and brown on both sides in 3-4 tablespoons butter. Warm ham. Salt and pepper beef slices; dust the beef slices with flour and sauté in butter to desired doneness.

Wine Sauce:
1 Tbsp. butter
2 Tbsp. finely chopped
shallots

¾ cup rich brown broth
1/3 cup Burgundy wine

Lightly sauté the shallots in butter. Stir in the broth and wine. Let sauce bubble for 2 minutes.

Sautéed Mushrooms:
2 Tbsp. butter
12 mushroom caps

2 Tbsp. dry white wine
2 drops lemon juice

Lightly brown the tops of the mushroom caps in the butter. Turn the caps, sprinkle with white wine combined with lemon juice and cook for 1 minute.

Arrange the eggplant on a *warmed* serving platter. Cover each with a slice of ham and a slice of beef. Dress with wine sauce and mushrooms.

Garnish platter with asparagus, 12 on each side, arranged in pyramids and topped with Hollandaise sauce. (See Index)
Serves 6.

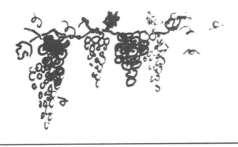

> ### MEATS
> One pound of cooked meat equals 3 cups of diced meat.
> A five pound chicken equals 4 cups diced, cooked chicken.
> Use 1 teaspoon salt to season 1 pound meat.

BEEF PARMIGIANA

1½ - 2 lbs. beef round steak
   (½ - ¾ inch thick)
3 Tbsp. flour
½ tsp. salt
⅛ tsp. pepper
3/8 cup fine dry bread crumbs
1/3 cup grated Parmesan cheese
½ tsp. basil leaves
1 egg, slightly beaten

1 Tbsp. water
3 Tbsp. cooking oil
1 (15 oz.) can tomato sauce
1 clove garlic, crushed
1 Tbsp. sugar
½ tsp. leaf oregano
4 slices Mozzarella cheese,
   (1 oz. each)

Cut steaks into 6 serving-size pieces. Mix flour, salt, pepper; dredge meat, pound with meat mallet. Combine bread crumbs, Parmesan cheese and basil leaves. Dip meat in egg-water mixture, then dredge in crumb mixture, coating evenly. Brown in oil. Remove and place in a 13½x9x2 inch baking dish.

Combine tomato sauce, garlic, sugar and oregano; pour over meat. Cover tightly with foil and cook in 350° oven, 1 hour and 10 minutes or until tender. Place cheese slices on each piece of meat and sprinkle with additional oregano if desired. Bake additional 3-5 minutes until cheese melts. Serve pan sauce with meat.
Serves 6.

Mrs. Richard Milwee

Seasoned flour: Flour mixed with seasonings in the proportions of ¼ cup flour to ¾ teaspoon salt, plus ¼ teaspoon each of pepper and paprika.

BAKED SWISS STEAK

Round steak (1½-2 inch thick)
Meat tenderizer
Worcestershire sauce
Ketchup

Green pepper rings,
   (1 whole pepper)
Onion rings (1 large onion)
3 bacon slices, uncooked

Sprinkle meat on both sides with tenderizer, piercing with a fork. Place steak in a 3 quart rectangular baking dish. Heavily sprinkle meat with Worcestershire sauce, then spread thickly with ketchup. Evenly distribute the pepper and onion rings; top with sliced bacon.

Cover the dish tightly and bake at 250° for 4 hours. About 45 minutes before the meat is done, remove cover and let brown.

The gravy will be generous and delicious. If you desire thicker gravy, remove meat and blend in a small amount of flour.
Serves 6-8.

Mrs. John Bohnert

PARSLEY STEAK ROLLS

1 large round steak	Salt and pepper to taste
1 (4 oz.) can mushrooms, drained	Dry parsley flakes
1 onion, finely chopped	1 tsp. cornstarch
3 tsp. Parmesan cheese	1 (10½ oz.) can beef broth

Place mushrooms, finely chopped onions, cheese, salt, pepper and parsley flakes on round steak. Roll into large roll. Secure with toothpicks or heavy string. Or, you may cut steak into individual serving sizes, season, then roll and secure.

Brown in hot fat on all sides. Stir cornstarch into small amount of broth. Add to remaining broth. Pour over steak rolls. Cover. Cook at 350° for 1 hour.
Serves 5-6.

Mrs. Joe Crabb

VITE CARBONNADE de BOEUF

2½ lbs. thin round steak	2 Tbsp. vinegar
Flour	2 Tbsp. tomato paste
Cooking oil	2 carrots, thinly sliced
2 cans onion soup (or several	1 Tbsp. sugar
onions and bouillon or	½ tsp. thyme
consommé in that amount)	½ tsp. parsley
1 cup beer	½ tsp. dried basil

Flour round steak which you have cut into thin strips (as for stroganoff). Using a large frying pan, brown meat in scant amount of oil. Remove meat from skillet, add 2 cans onion soup (or brown several thinly sliced onions, and add bouillon or consommé in that amount). Then add beer, vinegar, tomato paste, carrots, and sugar, plus ½ teaspoon each of thyme, parsley and dried basil. Simmer for a few minutes.

Place meat in a casserole, pour sauce over, cover and bake 325° for about 1½ hours. Good served over rice or noodles. (This sounds fancy, but it is as good for a family dish as it is for company.)
Serves 4-6.

Mrs. John G. Lile

Bouquet garni: Special herbs, usually including parsley, thyme, and bay leaf, either tied in a bunch or put in a small cheesecloth bag.

DEVILED STEAK STRIPS

1½ lbs. round steak
3 Tbsp. shortening
½ cup flour
¼ cup onion, chopped
1 clove garlic, minced
1½ cups water

1 Tbsp. vinegar
1 tsp. prepared mustard
½ cup tomato sauce
1 tsp. horseradish
¾ tsp. salt
¼ tsp. pepper

Trim excess fat from meat. Cut meat into thin 2 inch strips. Coat with flour. In skillet, brown meat, onion and garlic in melted shortening. Stir in 1 cup of the water, the tomato sauce, vinegar, horseradish, mustard, salt and pepper. Cover and simmer for 1 hour or until meat is tender, stirring occasionally. Stir in the remaining ½ cup water, scraping browned bits from bottom of pan; heat through. Serve over noodles or rice. *Serves 5-6.*

Mrs. Sam F. Cheesman

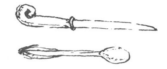

When a roast is put into the oven, set a small foil pan partly filled with flour beside it; when the flour has browned, it's ready for flavorful brown gravy making.

EYE OF RIB ROAST

Eye of rib roast
  (6-7 lbs.)
Garlic salt

Onion salt
Lawry's Seasoning Salt
Lemon pepper

Season roast to taste with garlic salt, onion salt, seasoning salt and lemon pepper. First thing in the morning place roast in a pan and put it into the oven. Turn oven to 500°. Turn off in 1 hour. Leave in the oven all day without opening the door.

Thirty minutes before serving turn oven on to 350°. With this timing the roast comes out medium rare. Adjust time for first cooking for rare or well done.

Sauce:
1 (8 oz.) carton sour cream
4 Tbsp. horseradish
2 Tbsp. tarragon vinegar

1 tsp. salt
4 Tbsp. chopped chives

Mix ingredients for sauce together and serve with roast.

Mrs. William L. Reid

BEEF WELLINGTON

3½ to 4 lb. whole filet of beef   Ham-Mushroom Duxelles (below)
Salt and pepper   Beaten egg
Pastry   Sesame seeds

Place beef on rack in shallow baking pan. Sprinkle with salt and pepper. Bake at 425° about 25 minutes; let stand until cool. Trim off all fat. Make a pie crust. (See Index) Roll pastry to rectangle large enough to wrap around beef, leaving about 3 inches longer than filet and 12 to 13 inches wide. Press cool Ham-Mushroom Duxelles into pastry, leaving an inch uncovered on all edges. Place beef on pastry, moisten pastry edges; enclose beef, pressing edges firmly together. Place roll, seam side down, on shallow baking pan. Cut decorations from pastry trimmings and place on top. Brush pastry with beaten egg (beaten with one tablespoon water) and sprinkle with sesame seeds. Bake at 400° for 30 to 35 minutes until browned. Let stand 15 to 20 minutes before slicing.

Ham-Mushroom Duxelles:
1 lb. fresh mushrooms,   2 tsp. flour
  finely chopped   Dash of pepper
¼ cup chopped green onions,   ¼ cup beef broth
  tops and all   2 Tbsp. fresh parsley
¼ cup butter   ½ cup finely chopped
½ tsp. salt   or ground ham
½ tsp. marjoram

Sauté mushrooms and onion in butter until liquid evaporates. Stir in salt, marjoram, flour, pepper and broth. Stirring constantly, cook until mixture comes to a boil and thickens. Remove from heat and stir in parsley and ham. Cool.
Serves 8.

1975 Charity Ball Royal Supper

Suggested amount of wine for cooking:		
Beef	¼ cup per lb.	Red table wine or rosé
Lamb or veal	¼ cup per lb.	White table wine or rosé
Gravy for roasts	2 Tbsp. per cup	Red or white table wine or sherry
Ham, baked	2 cups	Port, muscatel or rosé
Duck	¼ cup per lb.	Red table wine

MARINATED ROAST

5 lbs. eye of round or
  sirloin tip roast
1 clove garlic, cut in
  8 slivers

1 tsp. salt
½ tsp. pepper
1 tsp. dried thyme

Marinade:
½ cup Italian dressing
1 cup red wine

1 bay leaf, crumbled

Sauce:
2 Tbsp. flour
1 cup red wine

¼ tsp. salt
Dash pepper

The day before cooking, make 8 slits, 1-inch deep, across top of roast; insert a sliver of garlic into each. Rub entire surface of meat with seasonings. Place in a plastic bag and cover with combined marinade ingredients; refrigerate overnight.

Next day, preheat oven to 450°. Place roast in shallow, open roasting pan. Insert meat thermometer into thickest part. Roast 25 minutes; pour marinade over and roast 25 minutes longer or until thermometer registers 140° for rare or 160° for medium. Remove to a platter and keep warm. Let stand 15 minutes for easier carving.

Pour fat from roasting pan; reserve 2 tablespoons of drippings in pan. Stir in flour to make a smooth paste. Add remaining ingredients; bring to a boil, stirring well. Simmer until thickened. Slice meat thinly and diagonally. Serve with sauce.
Serves 8-10.

Mrs. Cortez Washington
Cateress

RUMP ROAST OF BEEF

Rump roast (3-4 lbs.)
Salt and pepper
Paprika

Kitchen Bouquet
Garlic powder

In heavy roaster on top of stove, sear roast (no grease) on all sides until very brown. Brush on lots of Kitchen Bouquet. Salt, pepper and paprika to taste. Use at least 1 teaspoon salt per pound of meat—don't spare pepper and paprika. Lightly sprinkle garlic powder over roast.

Add 2 cups water to pan. Cover securely and cook in 325° oven for 1 hour per pound of meat. Add peeled, quartered potatoes for last hour of cooking. Do not cheat on cooking time. Makes a well done roast.

Mrs. James F. Clark, Jr.

POT ROAST
(TWO-DAY-METHOD)

3-4 lb. eye of round or	1 pkg. Lipton's Onion Soup
3-4 lb. brisket	Mix
Suet	½ cup water

Sear roast on all sides in small amount of hot beef fat, rendered from a piece of suet. Use a heavy iron pot (Dutch oven). After searing turn down heat to simmer and add soup mix (dry) and about ½ cup water. Cover pot with close fitting lid (important) and simmer for 2 to 3 hours until meat is tender. When done remove from heat. Remove meat from pot, wrap in foil, cool and refrigerate. Reserve liquid from pot in jar or other container and refrigerate (overnight a good idea).

Next day: Slice meat about ¼ inch thick. Arrange in an oven proof dish, slices overlapping. Remove solidified fat from reserved liquid and pour the latter over the sliced meat. Cover the baking dish lightly with foil and reheat in 300° oven for one hour. Serve with rice or potatoes.

New potatoes previously boiled may be added to the sliced meat casserole (peeled, of course) before baking in oven. The meat can be served reheated again and again, getting better each time.

Mrs. E. W. Freeman, III

BEEF AND GREEN ONIONS

8 oz. beef, cut in strips	1½ tsp. soy sauce
4 oz. green onions, sliced	Sesame oil
4 Tbsp. cooking oil	
Marinade:	
1½ Tbsp. soy sauce	½ tsp. sugar
1 Tbsp. sherry	⅛ tsp. pepper
1 Tbsp. cornstarch	

Combine marinade ingredients; add beef strips for at least 20 minutes.

Heat the wok; add 1 tablespoon of oil and sliced green onions. Cook, stirring rapidly, for 1 minute. Remove onions from wok and wipe it with a paper towel.

Reheat wok; add 3 tablespoons of oil, then the meat. Cook for 1-2 minutes, then add green onions, soy sauce and 1 or 2 drops of sesame oil. Serve immediately. May be served over rice.
Serves 2-3.

Mrs. James S. Rogers

FIESTA BEEF KABOBS

Marinade:
½ envelope dry onion soup mix
  (slightly less than ¼ cup)
2 Tbsp. sugar
½ cup water
½ cup ketchup

¼ cup vinegar
¼ cup salad oil
1 Tbsp. prepared mustard
¼ tsp. salt
Dash hot pepper sauce

Meat:
1½ lbs. beef chuck or sirloin tip,
  cut into 1 inch cubes

Instant unseasoned meat
  tenderizer

Vegetables:
1 green pepper, cut into pieces
1 red pepper, cut into pieces
Onion, quartered

Tomato
Mushrooms

In saucepan, combine marinade ingredients; bring to boil. Reduce heat and simmer 20 minutes. Cool completely. Add meat, toss to coat. Refrigerate overnight or let stand at room temperature 2 or 3 hours.

Drain meat, reserving the marinade. Use meat tenderizer according to package directions.

Thread skewers, alternating meat and vegetables. Cook over medium coals, brushing with marinade 2 or 3 times. Heat remaining marinade; pass.
Serves 4.

Mrs. Howard J. Wiechern, Jr.

To keep peppers and mushrooms from splitting when skewering, dip in very hot water for a minute.

BEEF AND NOODLES

2½ lbs. chuck roast
  (cut into stew size pieces)
Flour to coat meat
¼ cup margarine
2 Tbsp. vinegar
1 cup beer
2 cans onion soup

¼ cup tomato sauce
2 or 3 celery leaves
Dash parsley flakes
2 or 3 bay leaves
¼ tsp. thyme
1 tsp. sugar
Cooked noodles

Coat meat with flour and brown in margarine. Take meat out and add other ingredients. Bring to a boil. Return meat, cover and bake at 350° for 2 hours. Serve over cooked noodles.
Serves 4.

Mrs. Jack Gasche

BENGAL CURRY AND PINEAPPLE RICE

Curry:

¼ cup shortening
4 lbs. chuck, cut into 1 inch cubes
1 cup sliced onion
2 Tbsp. curry powder
2 tsp. salt
¼ tsp. pepper
¼ tsp. cloves
¼ cup slivered crystallized ginger

2 Tbsp. chopped fresh mint leaves
(or 1 tsp. dried mint leaves)
¼ cup unsifted all-purpose flour
3 (10½ oz.) cans beef bouillon,
undiluted
1 cup canned flaked coconut
¼ cup lime juice
1 cup half-and-half cream

The day before the party, make the curry. In hot shortening, in large Dutch oven, sauté beef cubes, turning until browned all over—about 20 minutes. Remove the beef cubes as they brown. Add 2 tablespoons drippings and sauté onion, curry powder, salt, pepper, cloves, ginger and mint about 5 minutes.

Remove from heat, add flour, stirring until well combined. Gradually stir in bouillon. Return beef to Dutch oven—bring to boiling. Reduce heat; simmer, covered, 1½ hours or until beef is tender. Remove from heat, let cool; refrigerate, covered, overnight.

About 40 minutes before serving, let curry stand at room temperature 15 minutes. Prepare curry accompaniments (chopped cashew nuts, chopped unpared cucumber, prepared chutney or preserved kumquats). Put each into a small serving bowl. Over medium heat, gently reheat curry, stirring occasionally—about 20 minutes. Stir in coconut, lime juice and cream—heat gently about 5 minutes. Turn into chafing dish. Serve along with pineapple rice surrounded by curry accompaniments.

Pineapple Rice:

2½ cups raw, long-grained
white rice
2½ tsp. salt

2½ Tbsp. butter
1 (8½ oz.) can crushed
pineapple, drained

The day before the party, cook the rice. In 3-quart heavy saucepan, combine rice with 1 quart cold water and the salt. Over high heat, bring just to boiling, stirring several times with a fork. Reduce heat; simmer covered 12 to 14 minutes or until liquid is absorbed and rice is tender. If necessary, drain rice. Refrigerate covered overnight.

About 40 minutes before serving, preheat oven to 300°. Turn rice into a 15½ by 10½ by 1 inch pan; fluff it up with a fork. Sprinkle with ¼ cup water. Heat, covered with foil, 30 minutes, stirring several times with a fork. Add butter and pineapple; toss with a fork to mix well.
Serves 8.

Ralph Mitchell
New Orleans, Louisiana

BEEF RAGOUT

3 Tbsp. butter
2 lbs. stewing beef,
  cut into bite-sized pieces
12 small white onions, peeled
6 carrots, peeled and
  cut into 1 inch pieces
½-1 lb. fresh mushrooms
1 clove garlic, crushed

1 (6 oz.) can tomato paste
¼ cup chopped parsley
2 Tbsp. flour
Salt and freshly ground pepper
1 bay leaf, crumbled
Rosemary, basil, oregano
2 cups red wine
1 cup sour cream

Heat butter in a heavy skillet and brown meat. Remove to casserole. Brown onions, carrots, and mushrooms in same skillet. Add garlic, tomato paste, parsley, and flour, blending until smooth. Season with salt, pepper, bay leaf, and a pinch each of rosemary, basil, and oregano. Combine with meat in casserole. Add wine to within 1 inch of top of meat mixture. Cover and bake 1½-2 hours in a 350° oven, or until tender. Add a dollop of sour cream per serving as a garnish.
Serves 6.

Mrs. Robert Nixon

MAGIC BEEF STEW

2 lbs. cubed stew beef
2 onions, sliced
2 stalks celery, chunked
6 medium carrots
3 potatoes, quartered
2 tsp. salt
¼ tsp. pepper

2 Tbsp. tapioca
  (not tapioca pudding)
1 Tbsp. sugar
Bay leaf
Dash of garlic powder
1-2 Tbsp. Worcestershire sauce
½ cup tomato or V-8 juice

Put meat into a 2½-3 quart casserole. Arrange vegetables on top. Put in the remaining ingredients, except the juice, sprinkling over top fairly evenly. Pour juice over all.

Cover tightly with aluminum foil; tie string around foil and pull foil up over it to keep the string from burning. Cook at 250° for 5 hours or at 300° for 4 hours. *Do not peek* while it cooks.
Serves 6-8.

Mrs. J. Marshall Vaught
Mt. Dora, Florida

When simmering a ragout, stew, or any dish with a sauce that must be cooked slowly and for quite a long time, place the cover on your pot upside down, and put some water in the hollow. Keep adding water when necessary, and your sauce or liquid won't evaporate.

BEEF STEW

1½ lbs. stew meat
Salt and pepper to taste
1 medium onion, chopped
1 (4 oz.) can sliced mushrooms
1 (16 oz.) can peeled tomatoes
1 (1 ⅝ oz.) pkg. Lawry's Stew
  Seasoning
½ cup red wine (optional)
2-3 Tbsp. chopped parsley

¼ tsp. ground allspice
1 bay leaf
3 carrots, chopped in large
  pieces
1 cup quartered potatoes
1 can whole green beans
2 heaping Tbsp. flour
  dissolved in water

Brown meat in oil; salt and pepper to taste. Add onions, mushrooms; sauté until tender. Add stew seasoning, tomatoes and enough water to just cover meat and tomatoes. Optional wine may be added here. Break up tomatoes into smaller pieces, then add parsley and spices. Cover and bring to a boil. Reduce heat and simmer 1½ hours. Add carrots and potatoes, simmer until tender (about 30 minutes.) Add green beans and heat through. Dissolve flour in water and stir into mixture; adjust seasonings and simmer 15 more minutes.
Serves 4-5.

Mrs. Robert H. Holmes

EASY BURGUNDY BEEF

2½ lbs. stew meat
  (tenderized)
1 (10 oz.) can cream of
  mushroom soup
1 (8 oz.) pkg. fresh mushrooms
  sliced
2 large onions, chopped

1 pkg. dry onion soup mix
¾ cup Burgundy wine
Pepper to taste
Dash Accent
Dash cayenne
¼ tsp. garlic salt

Place meat in roasting pan and pour rest of ingredients over. Cover and bake at 325° for 3 hours. Do not uncover or check during cooking. Meat will be very tender and gravy delicious. Thicken gravy with cornstarch if desired. Serve over rice or noodles.
Serves 6-8.

Mrs. Harry A. Metcalf

BRISKET WITH SAUERKRAUT AND TOMATOES

3-4 lb. brisket
Salt and pepper to taste

1 (1 lb.) can sauerkraut
1 (1 lb.) can tomatoes

Place the brisket in a roaster. Season with salt and pepper. Pour the sauerkraut and the tomatoes over top of brisket. Bake, covered, at 350° until the meat is fork-tender, 2-3 hours.

Mrs. David Shapiro

NEW ORLEANS BOILED BEEF DINNER—COLD

4 lbs. beef brisket
3 med. onions (stuck
  with cloves)
1 carrot, chopped coarsely

12 peppercorns
2 tsp. salt
1 Tbsp. dried dill weed

Put beef into a large heavy pot and just cover with cold water. Bring to a boil, *reduce heat.* (Beef must never be in rapidly boiling water—barest simmer.) Scum will form on the surface; remove with spoon. Add rest of above ingredients, cover with tight fitting lid and allow meat to simmer gently for 4 hours. When done, let cool in its broth, covered; refrigerate. Do not remove from broth until ready to slice.

Accompaniments:
3 cucumbers
Salt
Sour cream
2 cups shelled English peas
1 tsp. sugar
1 cup light olive oil
¼ cup tarragon vinegar

1 tsp. salt
Fresh mayonnaise
1 lb. whole green beans
2 dashes cayenne pepper
¼ tsp. dry mustard
4 heaping Tbsp. drained capers
2 bunches watercress

Peel and slice cucumbers very thin. Spread out on platter, salt generously and drain 2-3 hours. Place in a colander and wash off salt. Put into a bowl, stir in a couple of dollops sour cream (just enough to coat) and refrigerate.

In a little water, cook peas with sugar and a dash of salt. When tender, drain, place in bowl and cool. Make a vinaigrette sauce by thoroughly mixing olive oil, vinegar and 1 teaspoon salt; pour ½ over peas. Allow to marinate for 2 hours. Pour off vinaigrette, reserve it, then mix the peas with enough fresh mayonnaise to just coat. Refrigerate.

Cook green beans in salted water to cover until tender, about 20 minutes. Cool, pour other ½ of vinaigrette over them and marinate 2 hours. Again, pour off vinaigrette, reserve and lightly coat beans with mayonnaise. For the sauce—you should have at least 1 cup of reserved vinaigrette. (If not, add enough vinegar and oil to make so.) Add cayenne pepper, dry mustard and capers. Mix well.

To serve: Slice the beef thin, arrange it in overlapping layers on a platter. About 10 minutes before serving, spoon half the sauce over beef; serve remaining sauce separately. Cut the stems off watercress and entirely cover a large platter. Make small mounds (individual servings) of the peas, beans and cucumbers.
Serves 4.

Ralph Mitchell
New Orleans, Louisiana

NEW ENGLAND BOILED DINNER

3-4 lbs. corned beef brisket
¼ tsp. oregano
¼ tsp. rosemary
1 bay leaf
1 tsp. dill seed
3 whole cloves
2 cloves garlic
1 medium onion, quartered

2 stalks celery, cut in half
4 carrots, peeled and halved
1 small head of cabbage,
   quartered
12 whole, small new potatoes,
   or 6 red potatoes, peeled and
   halved

In a large pot cover corned beef with water. Add next 8 ingredients, bring to a boil, reduce heat, cover and simmer about 2½ hours, or until tender. When meat is tender, remove, place on a platter and cover with foil to keep warm.

Strain the broth into a deep bowl and return strained broth to pot. Bring broth to boil and add carrots. Cook ten minutes and add potatoes. Cook ten minutes and add cabbage. Cook 12 to 15 minutes more.

While cabbage is cooking, slice meat and arrange on platter. Surround with vegetables and serve with a mustard horseradish sauce.
Serves 6.

Mrs. R. Teryl Brooks, Jr.

CORNED BEEF AND CABBAGE CASSEROLE

1 small head cabbage,
   quartered and cored
1 (12 oz.) can corned beef
4 green onions and tops, chopped
1 Tbsp. bacon drippings
3 Tbsp. butter

3 Tbsp. flour
1½ cups milk
Salt and pepper to taste
Bread crumbs
Butter for top

Boil cabbage in salted water (1 teaspoon salt) about 20 minutes. Drain. Heat bacon drippings in a skillet. Add corned beef and onions. Cook 10 minutes, breaking up meat and mixing well.

In a heavy sauce pan, melt the butter, add flour and blend. Add milk, salt and pepper and cook until thickened, stirring constantly.

In a greased 1½ quart casserole layer cabbage, corned beef and sauce. Repeat. Sprinkle with bread crumbs and dot with butter. Bake at 400° for 30 minutes.
Serves 6.

Mrs. R. Teryl Brooks
Hammond, Louisiana

Add fruit salad and cornbread—you're ready to eat in 45 minutes.

STUFFED GREEN PEPPERS

8 green peppers
1 cup finely chopped onions
2 Tbsp. cooking oil
1 lb. ground chuck or round
1 lb. can tomatoes
1½ cups water
¾ cup raw long-grain rice

1 heaping Tbsp. chili powder
1 tsp. salt
Dash of pepper
1 tsp. brown sugar
½ tsp. Worcestershire sauce
Fine dry bread crumbs

Sauté onions in oil; add ground meat and brown well. Add tomatoes, water, rice, chili powder, salt, pepper, brown sugar and Worcestershire sauce. Cover and simmer 30-40 minutes, until liquid is absorbed.

Remove tops and seeds from the peppers; parboil for 5 minutes. Drain.

Stuff the peppers with the onion-meat mixture. Stand peppers upright in greased baking dish; add small amount of water. Top each pepper with bread crumbs, if desired. Cover and bake in 350° oven for 1 hour.
Serves 8.

Mrs. Jack Gentle

GROUND BEEF STROGANOFF

¼ cup oleo or butter
2 Tbsp. flour
½ medium onion, minced
1 clove garlic, minced
1 lb. ground chuck
2 tsp. salt
¼ tsp. pepper

1(4 oz.) can sliced mushrooms
1 (10¾ oz.) can cream of chicken
  soup
¼ tsp. paprika
1 tsp. Kitchen Bouquet
1 (6 oz.) can sliced water chestnuts
1 cup sour cream

Melt butter and stir in flour. Add onion, garlic, meat and cook until meat is done. Add salt, pepper, mushrooms, soup, paprika, Kitchen Bouquet and water chestnuts to meat mixture. Cook 45 minutes.

Add sour cream and cook about 15 more minutes. *Do not boil.* Serve over rice or noodles.
Serves 4-5.

Mrs. R. M. Brunet
Corinth, Mississippi

Meatballs can be browned on a cookie sheet in a 350° oven.

212

HAMBURGER CHEESE CASSEROLE

2 lbs. ground round steak
1 tsp. garlic salt
2 tsp. salt
2 tsp. sugar
Pepper to taste
4 (8 oz.) cans tomato sauce

1 (8 oz.) pkg. cream cheese
1 pt. sour cream
5 green onions, tops and all, thinly sliced
1 (12 oz.) pkg. medium-size noodles
2 cups grated Cheddar cheese

Brown the ground round and pour off grease. Add garlic salt, salt, sugar and pepper. Cook until well blended and add tomato sauce. Simmer for 15 minutes.

Soften the cream cheese and mix with the sour cream and sliced onions.

Cook noodles as directed on package and drain.

In a buttered 4-quart casserole layer ingredients in this order: noodles, meat sauce, cheese mixture, grated cheese. Repeat layers. Bake at 350° for 30 minutes. *(Make this 24 hours ahead.)*
Serves 8.

Mrs. Howard Wright
Houston, Texas

GOOD HAMBURGER CASSEROLE

1 lb. ground meat
1 onion, chopped
1 green pepper, chopped
2 Tbsp. butter or oil
2 cups cooked, drained noodles
1 (4 oz.) can mushrooms, drained
1 tsp. Worcestershire sauce

1 (10¾ oz.) can tomato soup
1 cup water
½ tsp. salt
½ tsp. paprika
1 (1½ oz.) container Parmesan cheese

Brown beef, onion, pepper in oil. Cook noodles. Mix together the mushrooms, Worcestershire sauce, soup, water, salt, paprika and Parmesan cheese.

Grease a 1½-2 quart casserole. Make layers of ingredients in this order: noodles, meat mixture, mushroom soup mixture. Continue to alternate layers.

Cook, uncovered, at 350° about 30-45 minutes, or until bubbly hot.
Serves 5-6.

Mrs. Charles Slater

HAMBURGER PIE

2 cups Bisquick
2/3 cup milk
1 Tbsp. butter
1 cup chopped onion
½ cup chopped green pepper
1 lb. ground beef
1 tsp. salt
¼ tsp. black pepper

½ tsp Accent
2 Tbsp. flour
2 pinches tarragon leaves
5 dashes soy sauce
1 cup sour cream
2 eggs, slightly beaten
Paprika

Combine Bisquick and milk. Stir until mixture holds together. Turn out on floured board; knead 10 times. Roll out as for pie crust and place in a 9-inch pie plate.

Melt butter and add onions, green pepper and ground beef. Sauté until vegetables are soft and meat has browned. Drain well. Stir in salt, pepper, Accent, flour, tarragon and soy sauce. Place in crust. Combine sour cream and eggs. Place evenly over meat mixture. Sprinkle with paprika. Bake uncovered at 375° for 30 minutes.
Serves 6.

Mrs. John E. Caruthers, Sr.

CHINESE HAMBURGER CASSEROLE

1 lb. ground beef
2 medium onions, chopped
1 (10¾ oz.) can cream of
    mushroom soup
1 (10¾ oz.) can cream of
    chicken soup

1½ soup cans water
1 cup chopped celery
¼ cup (scant) soy sauce (less
    if you want less Chinese flavor)
½ cup raw rice
1 (3 oz.) can chow mein noodles

Cook meat and onions together in a large skillet. Add all other ingredients except chow mein noodles and mix well. Pour into a greased 2½ quart casserole and bake, covered, at 350° for 30 minutes. Uncover and bake 30 minutes more. Cover top with chow mein noodles and bake 15 minutes more.
Serves 8.

Mrs. J. Gordon Reese

BEEF 'n' BISCUIT CASSEROLE

1¼ lbs. ground beef
½ cup chopped onion
¼ cup diced green chilies
   or green pepper
1 (8 oz.) can tomato sauce
2 tsp. chili powder
½ tsp. garlic salt

1 (8 oz.) can refrigerated
   buttermilk or country-style
   biscuits
1½ cups shredded Monterey
   Jack or Cheddar cheese
½ cup sour cream
1 egg, slightly beaten

Brown ground beef, onion and chilies in large frying pan; drain. Stir in tomato sauce, chili powder and garlic salt. Simmer while preparing dough.

Separate biscuit dough into 10 biscuits; pull each apart into two layers. Press 10 biscuit layers over bottom of ungreased 8 or 9 inch square baking pan.

Combine ½ cup cheese (reserve remaining cheese for topping), sour cream and egg; mix well. Remove meat mixture from heat; stir in sour cream mixture; spoon over dough. Arrange remaining biscuit layers on top; sprinkle with remaining cheese. Bake at 375° for 25-30 minutes or until biscuits are deep golden brown.
Serves 4-5.

Mrs. Joe K. Breashears

SWEET AND SOUR CABBAGE ROLLS

1 large head cabbage
3 onions
5 stalks celery
2 (10¾ oz.) cans tomato soup
2 soup cans water
2-3 Tbsp. lemon juice

½ cup brown sugar, or to taste
Salt and pepper
2 lbs. ground chuck
2 eggs, slightly beaten
2 slices bread

Cut the core out of the cabbage and steam to soften leaves. Chop celery and 2 of the onions. Sauté in oil. Add soup, water, lemon juice, brown sugar, salt, pepper; bring to a boil and simmer slowly 30 minutes. Thoroughly mix ground meat, eggs, 1 onion (finely chopped) and bread that has been soaked in water and squeezed nearly dry.

Place meat mixture equally in each cabbage leaf and roll up. Chop any unused cabbage leaves and place in a large, shallow pan (it should be 2½-3 inches deep because there will be a lot of liquid). Top with cabbage rolls and sauce. Bake, covered, 275° for 3 hours.
Serves 8.

Mrs. Kenneth Baim

BAVARIAN MEATBALLS

Meatballs:

1 lb. ground beef	*1 Tbsp. ketchup*
½ cup chopped onion	*1 tsp. salt*
¼ cup dry bread crumbs	*¼ tsp. pepper*
1 egg, slightly beaten	*¼ cup water*
2 tsp. horseradish	*3 Tbsp. bacon drippings*

Mix first 9 ingredients. Form into balls 1¼ inches in diameter and brown on all sides in bacon drippings. Drain.

2 raw medium potatoes, grated	*¼ cup Rhine wine*
	2 tsp. brown sugar
2 apples, peeled and quartered	*½ tsp. salt*
	⅛ tsp. pepper
2 cups sauerkraut	*⅛ tsp. caraway seed*
1 onion, sliced	

Grease casserole with bacon drippings. Layer first 4 ingredients in casserole. Mix remaining ingredients; pour over. Top with meatballs. Cover and bake at 350° for 1 hour.
Serves 4.

SHEPHERD'S PIE

1 lb. ground beef	*Salt and pepper*
½ tsp. garlic powder	*1 (1 lb.) can whole tomatoes*
½ tsp. onion powder or finely chopped onion	*2 cups cooked instant mashed potatoes*
2 tsp. chili powder	*Grated cheese, optional*

Brown meat; add seasonings and tomatoes. Cook until tomatoes are mixed in well. Cook potatoes by package directions. Place meat mixture in casserole, top with potatoes and sprinkle with cheese. Bake at 350° until brown.

Julie Tanner

A child's do-it-yourself favorite!

TORTILLA BELLENO

12 tortillas
Hot cooking oil

Grated Cheddar cheese

Filling:
2 Tbsp. cooking oil
1 lb. ground beef
½ cup chopped onion
1 clove garlic, minced
1 cup chopped ripe olives
1 cup drained canned tomatoes
½ cup chopped raisins

½ tsp. chili powder
1 tsp. ground cinnamon
⅛ tsp. ground cloves
1 tsp. sugar
1 tsp. salt
2 Tbsp. vinegar

Lightly brown the ground meat, onion, and garlic in oil. Add other ingredients and simmer 20 minutes.

Sauce:
1 Tbsp. cooking oil
¼ cup chopped onion
1 clove garlic, minced
2 (8 oz.) cans tomato sauce
¼ cup chopped green pepper
1 tsp. chili powder

¼ cup chopped celery
¼ tsp. oregano
⅛ tsp. thyme
½ cup condensed
  beef bouillon

Sauté the onion and garlic in oil until transparent. Add remaining ingredients. Simmer 20 minutes.

To assemble, dip each tortilla in hot oil long enough to soften it, remove from oil and put some filling on it. Roll up and place in a greased shallow baking dish, 10x15x2 inches. When all tortillas are filled and rolled, pour half of sauce over them and sprinkle with grated Cheddar cheese. Bake at 350° for 20 minutes. Serve with remaining sauce.
Serves 4.

TACO MEAT LOAF

1½ lbs. ground beef
1 cup crushed corn chips
1/3 cup taco sauce

1 Tbsp. taco seasoning mix
1 egg, beaten
1 cup shredded cheese

Mix all ingredients. Bake in a loaf pan which has been lined with foil if desired. Cook at 350° about 1 hour. Take out, drain off fat and put in oven for a minute or two longer.
Serves 6.

Mrs. Joe K. Breashears

217

MRS. WILL MALLEY'S HOT TAMALE PIE

1 large hen or 2 lbs. veal or
   2 lbs. beef
4 cloves garlic
6 medium onions
½-¾ cup shortening

1 (1 oz.) bottle chili powder
2 heaping Tbsp. comino seed
3 (1 lb.) cans tomatoes, strained
Salt and pepper to taste
Tomato sauce, if desired

Stew hen until tender, remove from bones and cube; or cube veal or beef and simmer in water to cover until tender. Reserve stock. Grind meat with onions and garlic. Sauté in hot shortening; add remaining ingredients and simmer until thickened.

Mush for pie:
1½ - 2 cups vegetable oil
6 cups corn meal

Reserved stock with enough
water to make 3-4 cups

Heat vegetable oil. Mix meal with stock and add to oil. Stir until thoroughly mixed. Put half of mush into a greased 13x9x2 pan; add meat mixture, then remainder of mush.

Steam in a roaster with a rack for 1 hour.
Serves 10.

Mrs. E. T. Phillips

MEXICAN CASSEROLE DINNER

2 cloves garlic, chopped
1 large onion, chopped
2 Tbsp. butter or oil
2 lbs. ground round steak
2 tsp. chili powder
2 tsp. oregano
2 tsp. ground cumin

2 tsp. salt
2 tsp. MSG
4 Tbsp. sugar
2 (8 oz.) cans tomato sauce
2 (6 oz.) cans tomato paste
5½ tomato sauce cans of water
2 (13 oz.) bags corn chips

Sauté onions and garlic in the butter or oil. Add meat and brown quickly until it loses all its red color. Add all other ingredients except corn chips and simmer for 1 hour.

Serve over corn chips with any of the following garnishes:

2 green onions, sliced
1 head lettuce, chopped
¾ cup sliced olives
2 (4 oz.) cans taco sauce

2 avocadoes, chopped
1 lb. Cheddar cheese, shredded
2 pods jalapeno pepper, chopped

Serves 8-10.

Mrs. W. O. Pearcy, Jr.

TWO-ALARM CHILI

4 lbs. lean ground beef
1 (15 oz.) can tomato sauce
  with tidbits
2 (8 oz.) cans tomato sauce
8 cups water
1 onion, chopped
1 (3 oz.) bottle chili powder
2 Tbsp. ground cumin

1 tsp. oregano
2 tsp. paprika
¼-½ tsp. cayenne pepper
2 Tbsp. salt
2 (15 oz.) cans dark red
  kidney beans
¼ cup masa flour or 2 Tbsp. flour
  plsu 2 Tbsp. cornmeal

Brown the meat. Drain. Add the rest of the ingredients except the mesa flour or its substitute. Simmer about 1½ hours.

Mix the mesa flour with enough water to make a thin paste. Add slowly to the chili, stirring constantly. Simmer 15 minutes more.

This is better if made a day ahead.
Makes 5 quarts.

Donald W. Stone

LASAGNA

10 oz. lasagna noodles

1 lb. sliced Mozzarella cheese

Meat Sauce:
1 lb. hot sausage
4 cloves garlic, minced
1 Tbsp. basil

1½ tsp. salt
1 (1 lb.) can tomatoes
2 (6 oz.) cans tomato paste

Brown the meat slowly; spoon off excess grease. Add remaining meat sauce ingredients and cook slowly, uncovered, 30 minutes, stirring occasionally.

Cheese Filling:
3 cups cottage cheese
½ cup Parmesan cheese
2 Tbsp. parsley flakes

2 beaten eggs
2 tsp. salt
¼ tsp. pepper

Combine all ingredients for cheese filling.

Boil noodles at least 20 minutes in salted water. Drain.

To assemble, layer ingredients in a greased rectangular 3-quart oven-proof casserole in this order: noodles, cheese filling, Mozzarella slices, then meat sauce. Bake at 375° for 30 minutes. Let stand 10 minutes before cutting to serve.
Serves 6.

Mrs. Jerry McClain
Houston, Texas

219

ITALIAN LASAGNA

1 lb. lasagna noodles
12 oz. (or more) Mozzarella cheese
1 lb. cottage cheese

3 Tbsp. grated Parmesan
  cheese
2 Tbsp. chopped parsley

Meat Sauce:
1 lb. ground chuck
½ lb. Polish sausage
  or pepperoni, sliced
2 Tbsp. olive oil
½ cup chopped onion
½ cup finely diced celery
2 cloves garlic, crushed
1 (16 oz.) can tomatoes, drained
1 (10 oz.) can tomato purée

1 (16 oz.) can tomato sauce
1 (4 oz.) can mushrooms, drained
½ (10½ oz.) can beef consommé
1/3 cup red wine
1 tsp. soy sauce
¼ tsp. Italian seasoning
⅛ tsp. pepper
1 Tbsp. sugar
1 tsp. garlic salt

Brown the meats in olive oil for 10 minutes, then add onions, celery and garlic. Cover and steam for 5 minutes, then add tomatoes, tomato purée, tomato sauce, mushrooms, consommé, wine, soy sauce and seasonings. Simmer for 30 minutes.

Cook lasagna noodles according to package directions. Drain.

Grease a 13 x 9-inch pan and an 8 x 8-inch pan. Put in layer of noodles, then meat sauce, then Mozzarella cheese, then cottage cheese, then noodles again and continue these layers until there are 3 or more of each. Top with Parmesan and parsley. Bake at 375° for 1 hour.
Serves 8-12.

Mrs. Charles Beavers
Little Rock, Arkansas

TALLORINE

½ lb. whole almonds
1 Tbsp. butter
1 lb. lean ground beef
1 onion, chopped
1 green pepper, chopped
1 (4 oz.) can mushrooms and liquid

Salt and pepper
1 (10¾ oz.) can tomato soup
1 (16 oz.) can whole kernel corn
½ lb. cheese, grated
1 tsp. Worcestershire sauce
1 (10 oz.) pkg. medium noodles

Sauté almonds in butter and remove from pan. Add beef, onion, green pepper to the butter and brown them.

Cook noodles according to package directions and drain.

Mix all ingredients and place in buttered casserole. Set dish in pan of water and bake, uncovered, at 350° for 30-45 minutes.
Serves 10.

Mrs. Simpson Bush

CANNELLONI

1 (12 count) pkg. manicotti	Grated Parmesan cheese

Filling:

2 Tbsp. olive oil	1 lb. ground round steak
¼ cup finely chopped onions	2 Tbsp. heavy cream
1 tsp. finely chopped garlic	5 Tbsp. grated Parmesan cheese
1 (10 oz.) pkg. frozen chopped	2 eggs, lightly beaten
spinach (defrosted and squeezed	½ tsp. dried oregano
completely dry)	Salt and pepper
2 Tbsp. butter	

Sauté onions and garlic in olive oil until soft but not brown. Add spinach and cook 3 or 4 minutes until moisture has boiled away, stirring constantly. Transfer to large mixing bowl. Brown the meat in the butter; add to spinach mixture. Add remaining ingredients.

Tomato Sauce:

4 Tbsp. olive oil	6 Tbsp. tomato paste
1 cup finely chopped onions	2 tsp. basil
4 cups Italian plum tomatoes,	2 tsp. sugar
coarsely chopped but not drained	Salt and pepper

Sauté onions in oil until soft. Add other ingredients and simmer, partially covered for 40 minutes.

Besciamella:

6 Tbsp. butter	1 cup heavy cream
6 Tbsp. flour	1 tsp. salt
1 cup half and half	¼ tsp. white pepper

Melt butter, add flour and cook, stirring, until starchy smell is gone. Pour in half and half and cream all at once. Add salt and pepper. Cook over low heat until smooth and thick, stirring constantly with a whisk.

Cook manicotti until tender but not soft. Drain on paper towels. Fill each tube with meat filling.

Pour a thin film of Tomato Sauce on the bottom of a buttered 10 x 14 baking dish. Lay the stuffed manicotti side by side on top of the Tomato Sauce in 1 layer. Pour the Besciamella over them and spoon the rest of the Tomato Sauce on top. Sprinkle top with grated Parmesan, dot with butter.

Bake at 375° about 20 minutes or until sauce is bubbling. Slide under broiler for 30 seconds to brown if necessary.
Serves 6-8.

Mrs. M. Maury Goodloe

STUFFED MANICOTTI

10 manicotti shells
Cooking oil
1 (4 oz.) can chopped
    mushrooms

1 (15½ oz.) jar of spaghetti sauce
    with mushrooms or homemade
    equivalent
Mozzarella cheese

Meat Stuffing:
1 onion, chopped
2-3 Tbsp. cooking oil
1 lb. ground beef
½ (10 oz.) pkg. frozen chopped
    spinach, cooked and drained

4 Tbsp. cottage cheese
1 egg, beaten
1 Tbsp. sour cream
Salt and pepper

Brown the onion in a skillet in cooking oil. Add meat and cook until all red color is gone. Remove from heat and add all other stuffing ingredients. Mix well.

Tomato-herb Sauce:
1 (1 qt. 14 oz.) can tomato juice
3 bay leaves
1 tsp. fennel seed

½ tsp. thyme
½ tsp. rosemary leaves
About 3 cloves garlic

Combine the sauce ingredients and cook slowly about ½ day (until it thickens). Strain.

Cook the manicotti according to package directions (put a few drops of cooking oil in water to keep it from sticking). Drain. Try making your own manicotti! (See Index)

Stuff the manicotti shells with the meat mixture. Place stuffed manicotti in a greased baking dish and cover them with the chopped mushrooms and spaghetti sauce. Put a piece of Mozzarella cheese on each manicotti, then pour Tomato-herb sauce over all. Bake, uncovered, at 325° for about 30 minutes.
Serves 4-6.

Mrs. H. Moody Caruthers

REAL ITALIAN MEATBALLS

Meatballs:
1½ lbs. ground beef	1 cup chopped celery
½ lb. ground pork	½ cup chopped parsley
1¼ cups bread crumbs	4 eggs, slightly beaten
1 cup Romano cheese	Salt and pepper to taste
4 cloves garlic, minced	Deep fat for frying

Combine all meatball ingredients and work them together with your hands. Roll into balls and fry in deep fat.

Sauce:
1 medium onion	2 (6 oz.) cans tomato paste
2 Tbsp. oleo	2 (8 oz.) cans tomato sauce

Cook the onions in oleo until golden brown. Add tomato sauce and tomato paste. Put in large pot.

Add meatballs to the sauce. Add enough water to the sauce to keep it from getting too thick, and continue doing this all during the cooking time. Add salt and pepper to taste to the meatballs and sauce and cook 1½-2 hours over low heat.

Serve over cooked spaghetti.
Serves 6-8.

Women of St. Joseph's Roman Catholic Church

EASY CHEESY SPAGHETTI

1 lb. ground beef	½ lb. medium Cheddar cheese,
1 onion, chopped	grated, plus enough
1 green pepper, chopped	for the topping
1 clove garlic, minced	1 tsp. salt
1 (10¾ oz.) can	½ tsp. pepper
cream of mushroom soup	Dash of MSG
1 (10¾ oz.) can tomato soup	½ lb. thin spaghetti
1 soup can of water	

Brown the ground beef with onion, green pepper and garlic. Add the soups and 1 soup can of water. Let simmer for 1 hour. Add the cheese, salt, pepper and MSG and stir until the cheese is melted.

Cook spaghetti according to package directions. Drain well and add to meat mixture. Put into a greased 1½-2 quart casserole and top with more cheese. Bake at 350° until very hot and bubbly.
Serves 4-6.

Mrs. John G. Lile

SPAGHETTI

¼ inch thick piece of
   salt pork, chopped
¼ cup olive oil
2 lbs. ground beef
1 medium onion, chopped fine
3 cloves garlic, pressed
1½ cups red wine (claret)
½ cup parsley flakes
1 tsp. sweet basil
1 tsp. salt
¼ tsp. red pepper

¼ tsp. black pepper
1 (14 oz.) can chicken broth
2 (10 oz.) cans tomato purée
½ tomato purée
   can of water
1 whole carrot, peeled
1 whole rib of celery
1 (12 oz.) pkg. thin spaghetti
2-4 Tbsp. oleo per layer
Grated Italian cheese
   (Parmesan or Romano)

Brown salt pork in olive oil. Add meat and brown along with onions. Add garlic. Pour in wine and let cook down until nearly evaporated. Add spices and seasoning, then tomato purée, water, and chicken broth. Mix well and add carrot and celery. Cover and simmer for 2-3 hours. Remove carrot and celery.

Prepare package of spaghetti according to package directions. (A small amount of oil added to the water will keep it from sticking.) Drain and rinse in cold water.

In a large casserole (3 quart) put layer of spaghetti, dot with 4 tablespoons oleo, then put on a layer of sauce. Sprinkle with cheese. Then repeat layers. When you get to the top, pierce through all layers with a fork to make sure sauce mixes. Cover with more grated cheese.

This is better made early in the day; leave the casserole out of the refrigerator so the spaghetti will absorb the sauce. Heat in 300° oven for 30 minutes or until hot all the way through.
Serves 8.

Mrs. J. William Sanders

Valpolicella is a red wine that is delicious with Italian food. Also try Verdicchio (white) and Degesta (desert).

Mrs. Robert Cloar
Fort Smith, Arkansas

CROWN OF PORK

Crown of pork (16-18 ribs)
1 cup apple cider
Salt and pepper

Wild and white rice
Crab apples
Parsley or watercress

Speak sweetly to your butcher and have him shape your pork ribs into a crown, allowing two ribs per person.

Preheat oven to 325°. Place crown in shallow roasting pan, insert meat thermometer into center of a meaty part of one of the chops. Roast the pork until thermometer reaches 185° (about 3 hours), basting from time to time with cider and pan juices. Season with salt and pepper.

To serve—place crown on platter, fill center with cooked wild and white rice, piling high; surround roast with crab apples and parsley or watercress.
Serves 8-9.

Mrs. R. Teryl Brooks, Jr.

This is wonderful with our Plum Sauce.(See Index)

PORK ROAST

3 lb. pork butt roast
2 (12 oz.) bottles beer
1 sliced onion
6 whole cloves
1 bay leaf
1 (3 inch) cinnamon stick

½ tsp. celery seed
½ cup brown sugar
1 Tbsp. flour
½ tsp. dry mustard
2 Tbsp. currant jelly
Salt

Place the roast in a large kettle and add the beer, reserving 2 tablespoons for the glaze. Add enough water to cover the meat; add the onion, cloves, bay leaf, cinnamon stick and celery seed. Cover kettle tightly and simmer 1½ hours, or until roast is tender and the juice is clear when the roast is pierced.

Remove roast from liquid, peel off the rind and put into shallow roasting pan. Combine brown sugar, flour, dry mustard, jelly and reserved beer to make glaze. Salt the roast, then spread glaze on it.

Bake at 350° for 20-30 minutes, basting once or twice, until heated and browned.
Serves 4-6.

Mrs. William C. Bridgforth

Peach halves filled with chutney make a delicious accompaniment to roast pork.

ROAST PORK AND POTATOES

1 5 lb. pork loin, center cut
1 cut clove garlic
1 tsp. salt
6 medium large, thinly sliced
    potatoes
2 Tbsp. snipped parsley

1 cup chopped onions
1 Tbsp. seasoned salt
    (or plain)
Pepper
¼ cup boiling water
3 Tbsp. melted butter

Take pork out of refrigerator an hour in advance. Preheat oven to 425°. Rub meat with garlic and salt. Place roast, fat side up, on rack in shallow open pan. Roast pork 1 hour at 425°. Reduce heat to 400°. Remove pork from pan and pour off all fat.

In pan, toss potatoes with onion, parsley, salt, and pepper; pour in boiling water; lay pork on top; then brush potatoes with butter. Roast all about one hour at 400°.
Serves 6-7.

Mrs. Robert Nixon

PARMESAN BREADED PORK CHOPS

8 pork chops
1 cup seasoned bread crumbs
3 Tbsp. Parmesan cheese
Salt and pepper

1 egg
2 Tbsp. milk
½ Tbsp. butter or oleo

Combine bread crumbs, Parmesan cheese, salt, and pepper. Beat egg and milk in flat dish. Dip chops in crumbs, then egg mixture, then again in crumbs.

Melt oleo in baking dish and place chops in dish. Bake at 325° for 1 hour, turning after first 30 minutes. If chops are thick or not too brown, cook longer. (To use with 4 chops, reduce crumbs to 2/3 cup.)
Serves 4-8.

Mrs. J. William Sanders

MARINATED PORK CHOPS

½ cup soy sauce
½ cup Wishbone Italian Dressing

8-10 thin pork chops

Combine the soy sauce and Italian salad dressing. Marinate the pork chops in the mixture for several hours. Cook on a charcoal grill until done.

Mrs. Jerry McClain
Houston, Texas

PICATTA SLICES OF PORK TENDERLOIN

4 boned pork chops, 1 inch thick
1 whole egg, beaten
½ tsp. dry mustard
½ cup cream
½ cup bread crumbs

¼ cup Parmesan cheese
4 slices Gruyere cheese
¼ cup consommé
¼ cup white wine
Slivered, toasted almonds

Combine egg, mustard and cream. In separate bowl mix bread crumbs and Parmesan cheese. Dip chops in egg mixture, then crumb mix and sauté in butter until brown on both sides.

Five minutes before chops are done, place Gruyére cheese slice on each chop. After chops are removed from skillet, add consommé and wine to pan drippings.

Place chops on cooked rice, cover with wine sauce and garnish with slivered, toasted almonds.
Serves 4.

Mrs. Jack P. Smith

SUB GUM (CHOW MEIN)

¼ cup butter
2 cups lean pork, cut in strips
1 cup chopped onion
2 cups sliced celery
1 tsp. salt

Pepper
1½ cups hot water
1 (16 oz.) can mixed Chinese
   vegetables
Hot cooked noodles

Melt the butter, add the pork strips and brown quickly. Add the chopped onion and cook 5 minutes or less. Add sliced celery, salt, pepper and hot water. Cover and cook 5 minutes. Add the Chinese vegetables, mix and heat to boiling point.

Sauce:
2 Tbsp. cold water
2 Tbsp. cornstarch
2 tsp. soy sauce

1 tsp. sugar
1 tsp. bottled Chinese
   brown gravy sauce

Thoroughly mix the sauce ingredients. Lightly stir the sauce into the meat-vegetable combination and cook for 1 minute. Serve immediately over noodles.
Serves 4.

Mrs. Raymond A. Irwin, Jr.

CASSOULET

2 lbs. Great Northern beans
Salt and freshly ground pepper
1 onion
2 cloves
7 to 10 garlic cloves
1 bay leaf
1 pig's foot, split
1 (3 1/3 lb.) leg of lamb
    or half leg

3 lbs. loin or shoulder of pork
2 cups red wine
8 to 10 French saucisson or
    Italian sausages
1½ tsp. crumbled thyme
2 Tbsp. tomato paste
A few thin strips of salt pork
Dry bread crumbs

Cover beans well with water and soak overnight. Add salt, onion (stuck with cloves), 3-4 garlic cloves, bay leaf and pig's foot. Bring to a boil, skimming off any scum on the surface. Simmer until the beans are just tender. Be careful not to overcook. While the beans are cooking, salt and pepper lamb and pork. Place meats in a roasting pan. Cook at 325° for 1½ hours. Baste occasionally with 1½ cups of the red wine.

Cool and chill the meats in the pan in which they were cooked. Cut into 2 inch cubes. (Meat will be rare.) Reserve. Skim off the fat from juices and reserve the juices. Poach the sausage, covered in water, for 5 minutes. Cut into ½ inch slices. (Saucisson is much better and more authentic.) Blend 4-6 garlic cloves, thyme and 1 teaspoon pepper. Remove pig's foot from beans and cut away skin and meat from the bones. Drain beans, reserving liquid; discard bay leaf, onion and garlic.

Using a large earthenware or enamel iron baking dish, layer beans, garlic mixture, diced meats, meat and skin from pig's foot and sausages. Continue with layers until all ingredients are used finishing with a layer of beans. Combine remaining ½ cup wine, tomato paste, reserved pan juices and bean liquid. Pour enough mixture over cassoulet to reach almost to top layer of beans.

Top the cassoulet with salt pork and cover lightly with foil. Bake at 350° for 1 hour. Remove foil, sprinkle with bread crumbs and bake 1 hour more—or until liquid is absorbed, top is glazed, and crumbs are brown. (If liquid is absorbed too quickly during first hour or so, add more.) Serves 10-12.

Mrs. Martin G. Gilbert

This world-famous French stew is troublesome and expensive, but well worth it!

Have the butcher remove the fat kernel from a leg of lamb for a less mutton-y taste.

SAUSAGE AND MUSHROOM TARTLETS

1 lb. mushrooms, sliced
¼ cup butter
½ lb. kielbasa (Polish sausage)
1 cup heavy cream
1 Tbsp. butter

1 Tbsp. flour
1 Tbsp. lemon juice
½ tsp. salt
Pepper to taste
6 tartlets

In a large heavy skillet sauté 1 pound mushrooms, sliced, in ¼ cup butter over moderately high heat for 3 to 4 minutes. Add ½ pound poached fresh kielbasa or cooked sausage, cut into small pieces. Stir in 1 cup heavy cream and simmer the mixture, stirring occasionally, for 5 minutes.

Make a beurre manié consisting of 1 tablespoon each of butter, softened, and flour kneaded together and add it to the cream mixture in bits, stirring. Add lemon juice, salt and pepper to taste and simmer the mixture for about 5 minutes.

Spoon it into the tartlet shells and reheat the tartlets in a moderate oven (350°) until they are hot. Sprinkle them with chopped chives.

Tartlets:
Make a pastry dough for a double crust and roll it out ⅛ inch thick on a floured board. Have ready 6 tartlet tins at least 1 inch deep. Cut out 6 rounds from the pastry, each 1 inch larger than the tins; press the rounds firmly into the tins and cut off the excess dough with a floured rolling pin. Prick the bottom of the shells with a fork and chill them for 1 hour.

Line the shells with wax paper, fill the paper with raw rice and bake the pastry in a hot oven (400°) for 10 minutes. Carefully remove the rice and paper and bake the shells for 8 to 10 minutes more, or until they are lightly colored. Let them cool on a rack. This makes 14 tarts in regular size muffin tins.
Serves 6.

Mrs. Martin G. Gilbert

SWEET AND SOUR SAUSAGE

1 lb. can sliced peaches
1½ cups sugar
1 tsp. curry powder

Minced onion
1 (12 oz.) bottle chili sauce
1½ lbs. link sausage

Cook down peaches, sugar, curry powder and onion; add chili sauce. Brown sausage cut in bite-size pieces and add to mixture.
Serves 4-6.

Mrs. Wayne A. Stone

This is good for brunch and is a good hors d'oeuvre.

SAUSAGE MOSTOCCIALI (MACARONI)

1 lb. sausage (mild or hot)
1 large onion, chopped
1 medium bell pepper, chopped
1 (2 lb.) can tomatoes,
   mashed (undrained)
1 (6 oz.) can tomato paste or
   1 (8 oz.) can of tomato sauce

1-2 cups water
Salt and pepper
¼ tsp. oregano
½ tsp. celery seeds
12 oz. pkg. large elbow macaroni
4-6 oz. sliced American cheese

Crumble sausage and brown with onion and pepper; drain. Add tomatoes, tomato paste (or sauce), water, salt, pepper, oregano and celery seeds; simmer about 45 minutes, covered.

Cook macaroni according to package directions, drain, wash in cold water and drain again.

In a greased 2½ quart casserole, place a layer of noodles, then sauce, then cheese; continue layers, ending with cheese. Heat in 300° oven for 30 minutes.
Serves 6-8.

Mrs. Simmons Verlenden

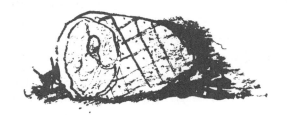

HAM ROLLS

1 cup sour cream, divided
1 cup sieved cottage cheese
1 beaten egg
¼ cup finely chopped onion
½ cup cooked chopped spinach
   (drain well)

½ tsp. dry mustard
¼ tsp. salt
8 slices cooked ham
1 (10¾ oz.) can cream of
   mushroom soup

Combine ¾ cup sour cream, cottage cheese, egg, onion, spinach, dry mustard and salt. Put about 2 tablespoons of the mixture on each slice of ham and roll up the slice.

Put into a shallow oven-proof dish and cover with mixture of cream of mushroom soup and ¼ cup sour cream. Bake at 350° for 20-30 minutes.
Serves 4.

Mrs. James Grantham
Vance, Mississippi

Good for brunch or lunch.

GINGERED HAM SLICE

1 fully cooked center cut
  ham slice, 1 inch thick
½ cup gingerale
½ cup orange juice
¼ cup brown sugar

1 Tbsp. salad oil
1½ tsp. wine vinegar
1 tsp. dry mustard
¼ tsp. ground ginger
⅛ tsp. ground cloves

Slash fat edge of ham. Pour remaining ingredients over ham in shallow dish after combining them thoroughly.

Refrigerate overnight or let stand at room temperature 2 hours. Spoon marinade over ham several times.

Brown over coals of a charcoal fire about 15 minutes on each side, brushing frequently with marinade.

Mrs. Jack Gasche
Dallas, Texas

BAR-B-QUED RIBS

½ cup butter
¾ cup ketchup
½ cup brown sugar
3 Tbsp. lemon juice
1 Tbsp. Dijon mustard

2 tsp. Heinz 57 Steak Sauce
2 tsp. hot pepper sauce
2 tsp. Worcestershire sauce
4 lbs. ribs, salted lightly
  (spare or short ribs)

Melt butter and stir in ketchup, brown sugar, lemon juice, mustard, steak sauce, hot pepper sauce and Worcestershire sauce.

Put ribs on rack in a roaster and spread them with some of the sauce. Bake at 325° for 30 minutes. Baste. Continue baking, adding sauce every 15 minutes, for about 2 hours, or until tender.
Serves 4.

Mrs. George B. Talbot

LAMB SHANKS

4 lamb shanks
¾ cup bourbon

¾ cup strong coffee
1 envelope dry onion soup mix

Place the lamb shanks in a transparent cooking bag. Mix all the other ingredients and pour into the bag. Seal the bag and punch several holes in its top side. Place on a heavy cookie sheet and cook in a 375° oven not more than five hours.
Serves 4.

Mrs. Richard S. Barnett, Jr.

LEG OF LAMB, BONED AND STUFFED

6 lb. leg of lamb
Salt and pepper
Stuffing
4 Tbsp. fat or butter

1 large carrot
1 large onion
3-4 unpeeled garlic cloves
1 cup canned beef bouillon

Stuffing:
½ cup minced onions,
   cooked in butter
¼ lb. fresh mushrooms,
   cooked in butter
¾ cup minced lean boiled ham
¼ cup finely minced fresh
   pork fat or ham fat

½ tsp. salt
¼ tsp. pepper
¼ tsp. ground rosemary
¼ tsp. sage
¼ tsp. thyme
¼ cup minced parsley

Mix all stuffing ingredients in a bowl until well blended.

The leg bone may be taken from inside the meat without making an outside incision; the meat is then sewn or skewered at the large end. Or cut it open and debone. Lay the boned meat skinside down. Season lightly with salt and pepper. Spread the stuffing over the meat and into the pockets left by the bones. Then roll the meat into a cylinder shape to enclose the stuffing completely. Sew or skewer if necessary, then tie loops of string around it at 1-inch intervals. (Alternative: Get the butcher to bone and stuff it for you.)

Preheat the oven to 450°. Brush the prepared lamb with melted fat, place it on a rack in a roasting pan and set it in upper 1/3 of oven. Turn and baste every 5 minutes for 15 to 20 minutes to brown on all sides.

Reset the oven for 350°; insert meat thermometer into fleshiest part of lamb. Place the carrot, onion and garlic in the bottom of the pan. Set in middle section of oven and roast until thermometer reads 160°-165° (allow 30 minutes per pound or 2 hours as a 6-pound roast will weigh 4 pounds after boning). You can baste it once or twice, but this is not necessary.

Discard strings and skewers, season with salt and pepper, and place roast on a hot platter. It should rest at room temperature for 20 minutes before carving. Garnish with parsley and serve with pan gravy or mint jelly.

Pan gravy: Spoon fat off of pan drippings and pour in 1 cup of beef bouillon. Boil rapidly, scraping up roasting juices and mashing vegetables into stock. Taste for seasoning and correct. Strain into hot sauce boat. *Be sure to serve this on warmed plates, as lamb fat congeals when cool.* Serves 8-10.

Mrs. John Crenshaw

LEG OF LAMB WITH MINT SAUCE

MEATS

6 lb. leg of lamb
1 Tbsp. melted butter
1 Tbsp. oil
1 Tbsp. salt
1 cup water
½ cup sugar

½ tsp. ground black pepper
1 scant cup white vinegar
1 tsp. Worcestershire sauce
2 Tbsp. strained bottled
  mint sauce

Wipe lamb with damp paper towel. Dry with paper towel. Combine butter and oil and brush mixture over the meat. Preheat oven to 450°. Place lamb in a roasting pan which has sides for holding sauce. Roast lamb for about 20 to 25 minutes, turning often, until meat is brown on all sides.

Remove pan from oven and reduce to 325°. Place a meat thermometer in thickest part. Sprinkle the salt in the side of the pan. Add water and stir. Sprinkle sugar and pepper over the meat. Pour vinegar over the meat. Baste. Return to oven and roast about 1½ hours, or until thermometer reaches 160°, basting often during the cooking.

When lamb is done, remove from pan and place on platter. Cover lightly with foil to keep warm. Skim all fat from the liquid. Add the Worcestershire and mint sauce. Reheat and serve with lamb. Sauce will be very thin and a rich dark brown.
Serves 8.

Mrs. R. Teryl Brooks, Jr.

VEAL BOCCONCINI NINO

3 eggs
Salt and pepper to taste
1 Tbsp. chopped parsley
2 Tbsp. Parmesan cheese
4 slices eggplant
½ cup flour

Vegetable oil for frying
2 slices fresh tomato
2 slices pounded veal
2 slices Italian prosciutto ham
2 slices Mozzarella cheese

Prepare a bowl of egg batter by beating eggs then adding salt, pepper, parsley and Parmesan cheese. Mix well.

Peel and slice eggplant about ¼ inch thick. Dip eggplant into flour first, then into egg batter. Fry in vegetable oil until golden brown. Drain on paper towels.

Next fry the tomato, veal and ham in the vegetable oil, after dipping in flour and batter. Drain.

Layer in a casserole so that eggplant is on bottom and top. When ready to serve, put a slice of Mozzarella cheese on top and bake in the oven at 350° until cheese melts.
Serves 2.

THE CHEZ PAUL RECIPE: COTE de VEAU ORLOFF

6 rib veal chops (6 oz. each)   3 Tbsp. butter
Seasoned flour   Freshly grated Parmesan cheese

Dredge the veal chops with seasoned flour. Cook them in butter over medium heat until brown on both sides.

Purée of Mushroom:
1 lb. fresh mushrooms   ¼ cup butter
2 shallots

Finely chop the mushrooms and shallots. Sauté them in butter for 1 minute. Squeeze them almost dry in cheesecloth and continue cooking until all liquid evaporates.

Soubise Sauce:
1 medium onion, finely chopped   2 cups milk
6 Tbsp. butter   Salt
2 Tbsp. flour   Pepper

Slowly cook onion in butter until it is tender but not brown. Blend in the flour and cook 2 minutes. Add the milk gradually and cook to a smooth sauce, stirring constantly. Season with salt and pepper and continue cooking for 20 minutes.

Cover each chop with Purée of Mushrooms and Soubise Sauce combined. Sprinkle with Parmesan cheese and brown under broiler.
Serves 6.

To tenderize veal, pour lemon juice over cutlet and let stand ½ hour.

VEAL CHOPS BRAISED IN WINE

4 veal chops or steaks   4 green onions, chopped
  (½ to ¾ lb. each)   1 cup dry white wine
Salt and pepper   ½ cup chicken broth
2 Tbsp. butter   2 Tbsp. butter
2 Tbsp. olive oil   ¼ cup chopped parsley

Salt and pepper the chops generously. Heat olive oil and butter and brown chops on both sides over medium-high heat. Add chopped onions, wine and broth. Cover and cook over low heat for 1 hour.

Remove chops. Swirl 2 tablespoons butter into sauce with a wire whisk and pour over each chop. Sprinkle parsley on top.
Serves 4.

Mrs. J. Wayne Buckley

QUICKIE ITALIAN VEAL

4 frozen veal cutlets
Flour
Salt
Pepper

Oil or butter for frying
1 (8 oz.) can tomato sauce
½ tsp. oregano
4 slices Mozzarella cheese

Dip frozen veal cutlets into flour seasoned with salt and pepper. Brown in hot oil or butter on both sides; remove to paper towels to drain. Pour off excess grease; pour tomato sauce into pan to heat. Add oregano; place veal cutlets in heated sauce. Cover and simmer very slowly for 10 minutes. Place slice of cheese on each cutlet; cover again to let cheese melt. Serve over rice or noodles.
Serves 4.

Mrs. Larry Jones

VEAL PARMIGIANA

1½ lbs. boneless veal, cut
    into pieces
1/3 cup olive oil
½ lb. fresh mushrooms
1 clove garlic

2/3 cup sherry
½ tsp. salt
⅛ tsp. pepper
½ - 1 tsp. rosemary
1 cup grated Parmesan cheese

Brown meat in oil. Transfer meat to a greased 1-quart casserole. Cook mushrooms and garlic in remaining oil in skillet about 5 minutes. Discard garlic and pour mushrooms over meat. Put wine and seasonings in same skillet, heat to boiling and pour over casserole. Sprinkle with cheese and bake, covered, in a 350° oven for 45 minutes.
Serves 4.

Mrs. Larry Jones

BREADED VEAL CUTLETS

1½ lbs. veal cutlets
Salt
Ground pepper
2 eggs, beaten lightly
    with 2 Tbsp. water

Flour
1 cup bread crumbs
3 Tbsp. butter
3 Tbsp. oil

If the cutlets are not tenderized, they need to be pounded as thin as possible. Salt and pepper the cutlets and pat flour on both sides. Dip in egg, then in crumbs. Heat butter and oil until water sizzles when sprinkled into it. Fry cutlets rapidly for 3-4 minutes on each side. Cutlets may be kept warm for a short time in 250° oven, uncovered.
Serves 4.

Mrs. Harry A. Metcalf

SAUCES

WHITE SAUCE

Type	Butter	Flour	Salt	Milk
Thin (soups)	1 Tbsp.	1 Tbsp.	½ tsp.	1 cup
Medium (basic)	2 Tbsp.	2 Tbsp.	½ tsp.	1 cup
Thick (croquettes)	3-4 Tbsp.	3-4 Tbsp.	½ tsp.	1 cup

In a heavy saucepan, melt the butter over low heat. Blend in the flour and salt (preferably with a wire whisk) and cook slowly, stirring, until the mixture is smooth and doesn't smell starchy but isn't colored (about 2 minutes). Slowly add the milk (or half and half) and beat vigorously until the mixture is smooth. Bring to a boil and cook over medium heat for 1 minute, stirring constantly.
Yields 1 cup.

SUPER WHITE SAUCE

2 Tbsp. butter or oleo
2 Tbsp. flour
Dash of pepper
½ tsp. salt

Dash of paprika
2/3 cup milk
1/3 cup sour cream

Melt butter over low heat or in double boiler. Add flour, pepper, salt and paprika. Stir until blended smoothly. Combine milk and sour cream and slowly add to mixture, stirring to avoid lumps. Cook until thick and smooth.
Yields about 1 cup.

Mrs. John Dolby
This is delicious poured on vegetables then broiled 2-3 minutes until brown and bubbly.

GRAVY

4 Tbsp. meat drippings
3 Tbsp. flour
Seasonings

2½ cups liquid (usually water or stock)

When roasted or fried meat or poultry is done, remove from the pan and pour off all fat; don't lose any of the brown sediment. Place pan on a stove burner, measure the drippings into it, then stir in the flour until it makes a smooth brown paste. Then *slowly* add the liquid, stirring constantly and scraping the brown bits from the pan. Let the mixture boil, then add salt, pepper and any other desired seasonings. Remove from heat and serve.

HOLLANDAISE SAUCE

4 egg yolks
2 Tbsp. fresh lemon juice
1 cup butter

¼ tsp. salt (if you use unsalted
   butter)
Dash black pepper

Beat egg yolks in top of a double boiler. Stir in lemon juice. Cook very slowly over low heat, never letting water in bottom of pan come to a boil. Add butter, a small amount at a time, stirring constantly with a wire whisk. Add salt and pepper; continue cooking until mixture has thickened. *Yields 1 cup.*

Mrs. Royce O. Johnson, Jr.

BEARNAISE SAUCE

¼ cup wine vinegar
½ cup dry white wine or vermouth
1 Tbsp. minced shallots or
   scallions
½ tsp. dried tarragon

¼ tsp. salt
⅛ tsp. pepper
3 egg yolks
¾-1 cup butter divided into
   6 equal parts

Boil vinegar, wine and herbs and seasonings (including shallots or scallions) in small saucepan until it is reduced to 2 tablespoons. Let this cool, then proceed with the same method used for Hollandaise Sauce above, using the vinegar mixture in place of the lemon juice. *Yields 1 cup.*

Mrs. M. J. Probst

BLENDER HOLLANDAISE SAUCE

3 egg yolks
1 Tbsp. lemon juice

Dash of cayenne pepper
½ cup melted butter

Put egg yolks, lemon juice and cayenne into a blender; cover. Quickly turn blender on and off. Heat the melted butter bubbling hot. Turn the blender on high and slowly pour the butter through the opening in the top. Blend until the sauce is thick and fluffy, about 30 seconds. Do not double recipe. *Yields 2/3 cup.*

Mrs. Jack Gasche
Dallas, Texas

PLUM SAUCE

1 (18 oz.) jar plum jelly
1 bunch green onions, chopped

3 tsp. prepared mustard
1 Tbsp. raisins

Mix all ingredients and heat. This is delicious with duck or pork roast.

Mrs. Jess Reeves

MADEIRA MUSHROOM SAUCE

4 Tbsp. flour	1 lb. fresh mushrooms
4 Tbsp. cooking oil	½ cup butter
2 onions, finely chopped	1 tsp. salt
4 cups beef stock	½ tsp. pepper
(or canned bouillon)	2 green onions, finely chopped,
3 Tbsp. tomato sauce	tops and all
Pinch of thyme	2/3 cup Madeira or dry sherry
Salt	1 tsp. chopped parsley

Cook flour in oil over low to medium heat, stirring constantly, until very brown. Add onions and cook over very low heat until soft, stirring constantly. Add hot stock, slowly, stirring until smooth with a wire whisk. Add tomato sauce and thyme and stir until thickened. Simmer until sauce is reduced to 2 cups. Taste for seasoning; add the salt now if needed. This can be done several days ahead.

Clean and dry the mushrooms and slice thinly. Melt butter in a large saucepan; add mushrooms, salt and pepper and cook until mushrooms are golden brown. Add green onions, wine and 2 cups of the above brown sauce. Simmer 5-10 minutes. Add parsley.

Serve over steak (or other beef) or poultry. It looks better if served over the meat on the plate rather than passed.
Serves 6-8.

Mrs. J. Wayne Buckley

Served at 1975 Charity Ball Royal Supper.

MUSHROOM SAUCE

½ cup butter	1 (10½ oz.) can beef consommé
¼ tsp. seasoned salt	1 lb. fresh mushrooms
3 Tbsp. flour	

Melt the butter; add the salt and flour and cook slowly until the flour doesn't smell starchy. Slowly add the consommé, then the mushrooms.

This is good over beef tenderloin.

Mrs. C. S. McNew, III

Here is a surefire remedy for curdled or separated sauce:
Place 1 teaspoon lemon juice and 1 teaspoon sauce in mixing bowl. Beat with wire whip until sauce smooths into a cream. Then beat in the rest of the sauce, half a tablespoon at a time, beating until each addition has creamed into the sauce before adding more.

SEASONED BUTTER

2 cups butter or oleo
¼ cup snipped chives, fresh or
    freeze-dried

1½ tsp. grated lemon peel
2 Tbsp. lemon juice
½ tsp. freshly ground black pepper

In a small mixing bowl cream the butter. Add other ingredients and mix thoroughly. Store in refrigerator in tightly covered container until needed.

Dr. George B. Talbot

This is good added to vegetables, spread on toast for a hot sandwich, English muffins for a brunch, or French bread. This also may be melted for a dip for shrimp, lobster and artichokes.

LEG OF LAMB SAUCE

1 cup ketchup
1 cup vinegar
Salt
Pepper

½ cup sugar
1 Tbsp. horseradish
2 bay leaves
1 cup chopped celery

Mix ingredients and heat to blend. Use sauce to baste a leg of lamb while it is cooking. (This is also good for basting other cuts of lamb.)

Mrs. Andrew C. Payne

HORSERADISH SAUCE

3 Tbsp. horseradish
1 tsp. grated onion or onion juice

½ tsp. lemon juice
1 cup mayonnaise

Thoroughly combine all ingredients. Refrigerate. This is good with roast beef, brisket or fondue. It is also good with cold cauliflower.

Mrs. Henry F. Trotter, Jr.

SPECIAL MUSTARD

1 cup dry mustard
1 cup cider vinegar

1 cup sugar
2 egg yolks

In top of double boiler mix mustard and vinegar and let stand 2 hours. Beat in the sugar and egg yolks and cook over simmering water, stirring occasionally, one hour. Cool and refrigerate. This is a very hot sauce that will keep for weeks. Wonderful with cold cuts.

Mrs. Paul Greenberg

HOT SAUCE FOR HAM

1 (18 oz.) jar apple jelly
1 (10 oz.) jar pineapple preserves

¾ cup prepared horseradish
3 Tbsp. dry mustard

Mix all ingredients and stir well. Store in refrigerator.

Georgia McCutchen Bailey
Blytheville, Arkansas

CRANBERRY-BURGUNDY HAM GLAZE

1 (16 oz.) can whole cranberry sauce
1 cup brown sugar

½ cup Burgundy
2 tsp. prepared mustard

In saucepan combine all ingredients. Simmer, uncovered, 5 minutes. During last 30 minutes of baking time for ham spoon half of glaze over it. Pass remaining sauce. Makes enough for 10-14 pound ham.

Mrs. Clendine Washington
Cateress

MARINADE FOR MEATS

1½ cups vegetable oil
¾ cup soy sauce
¼ cup Worcestershire sauce
2 Tbsp. dry mustard
2¼ tsp. salt
1/3 cup fresh lemon juice

1 Tbsp. coarsely ground black pepper
½ cup wine vinegar
1½ tsp. dried parsley flakes
2 garlic cloves, crushed

Combine all ingredients. Use to marinate beef, pork or lamb. Brush the meat with marinade every 20 minutes while it is cooking. If the meat is soaked before cooking, the marinade can then be drained off and used again.
Yields 3½ cups.

Mrs. Jack Crandall
Santa Monica, California

PINE BLUFF STEAK SAUCE

1 cup butter
1 large clove garlic, crushed

1/3 cup Worcestershire sauce
Juice of 1 lemon

Melt the butter. Add the garlic, then Worcestershire and lemon juice. Mix well and serve hot over steak.

MARINADE SAUCE FOR BEEF TENDERLOIN

2 pkgs. Good Seasons Onion
   Salad Dressing Mix
6 Tbsp. sherry
2 Tbsp. soy sauce

4 Tbsp. fresh lemon juice
1 heaping Tbsp. M.B.T. beef base
1 cup cooking oil

Mix all ingredients. Pour over beef tenderloin and let stand at least 8 hours; turn meat several times while marinating. Baste meat with sauce while broiling or baking it. Drippings can be used for gravy.

Mrs. Celia Mae Mason
Cateress

QUICK BARBEQUE SAUCE

1 cup ketchup
1/3 cup Worcestershire sauce
1 tsp. chili powder

Dash of salt
½ cup water
2 dashes of Tabasco

Combine all ingredients in a saucepan. Heat to boiling and remove. Yields about 1¾ cups.

Mrs. J. Gordon Reese

CUMBERLAND SAUCE

1 (12 oz.) jar currant jelly
¼ - ½ cup red wine
Grated rind of 1 orange
½ tsp. ground ginger

½ tsp. Dijon mustard
1 Tbsp. lemon juice
Arrowroot
½ cup dried currants

In saucepan melt jelly; add wine, orange rind, ginger, mustard and lemon juice. Thicken with arrowroot mixed with a little wine. Add currants. Excellent with duck.

Variation for Beef Wellington:
Beef drippings (or bacon grease)
2-3 Tbsp. flour

1 (10½ oz.) can beef consommé
Cumberland Sauce

Stir flour into drippings from first cooking of beef (or bacon drippings). Stir in consommé, then Cumberland Sauce. Serve over Beef Wellington.

Mrs. Alfine Jones (Hortense)
Cateress

REMOULADE SAUCE

Group 1:
¾ tsp. salt
2 tsp. dry mustard
½ tsp. paprika

Small clove garlic, mashed
2 hard boiled egg yolks, sieved
6 Tbsp. olive oil

Group 2:
2 Tbsp. wine vinegar
1 Tbsp. horseradish
1 Tbsp. chopped parsley

2 Tbsp. finely diced onion
1 celery heart, diced

Combine all ingredients in Group 1, saving the olive oil until last. Add olive oil gradually and beat to make a smooth paste. Stir all ingredients in Group 2 into the first mixture and blend thoroughly. Serve over shrimp. *Serves 4 as a first course.*

Mrs. Frank O'Shanick

CREOLE TARTAR SAUCE

1 cup mayonnaise (preferably
  homemade with olive oil)
1 Tbsp. Creole mustard
¼ cup minced green onions,
  including tops

2 Tbsp. minced parsley
1 tsp. lemon juice
Dash of Tabasco
Salt to taste

Combine all ingredients and blend well. Serve with seafood.
Makes about 1½ cups.

Mrs. R. Teryl Brooks, Jr.

VINAIGRETTE SAUCE

1-2 Tbsp. wine vinegar
⅛ tsp. salt
¼ tsp. dry mustard

6 Tbsp. olive oil
Dash black pepper

Place all ingredients in a screw top jar and shake for 30 seconds. May add part or all of the following as desired: parsley, chives, tarragon and capers. *Yields ½ cup.*

Mrs. R. Teryl Brooks, Jr.

THE ELMS
Altheimer, Arkansas
The Elms was built by Doctor and Mrs. Samuel Jordan Jones in 1866 and is now occupied by the great grandson and his wife, Mr. and Mrs. Richard S. Barnett, Jr. It utilizes a "raised" style of construction in having an above-ground or "English" basement, typical of the finer homes built in the flood plain areas during the early eighteenth century. This home has recently been placed on the National Register of Historic Places by the United States Department of Interior.

BARBECUED CHICKEN

6 chicken halves
Salt and pepper
3 cups cider vinegar
4 Tbsp. margarine
1½ Tbsp. red pepper
1½ Tbsp. black pepper

¾ Tbsp. powdered garlic
9 Tbsp. Worcestershire sauce
3 Tbsp. shortening
1½ Tbsp. chili powder
2 dashes of Tabasco
2 tsp. salt

Lightly salt and pepper chicken halves. Combine remaining ingredients in a saucepan and bring to a boil, turn down to simmer for 10 minutes or more. This sauce will keep indefinitely when poured in a jar and refrigerated.

Put chicken in a 350° oven or on an enclosed barbecue grill. Baste the chicken with sauce every 15 minutes and turn every 30 minutes. Do not place chicken directly over coals. Cook 2½-3 hours. Soaked hickory, sassafras, or other woods may be added to coals for flavor during cooking. Serves 6.

Mr. Frank Gilbert
Prescott, Arkansas

OVEN BARBECUED CHICKEN

3 medium sized fryers,
  cut in half
Salt and pepper
¾ cup butter
1 Tbsp. vinegar

1 (10 oz.) bottle A-1 Sauce
1 tsp. sugar
1 Tbsp. Worcestershire sauce
1 A-1 bottle of water
2 Tbsp. ketchup

Sprinkle salt and pepper over chicken. Arrange halves in roasting pan, skin side down. Put butter in chunks over the chicken. Place in 350° oven and cook uncovered for 30 minutes.

Combine remaining ingredients in a saucepan and heat. Turn the chicken and pour the warm barbecue sauce over it. Return to oven and cook uncovered until tender and well browned—about 30 minutes. Serves 6.

Mrs. Rufus A. Martin

OVEN-FRIED CHICKEN AND BISCUITS

¼ cup shortening
¼ cup butter
1 chicken, cut for
   frying
1 cup flour
2 tsp. salt
¼ tsp. pepper

2 tsp. paprika
1 (1 lb. 14 oz.) can cling peach
   halves
Whole cloves
Biscuits—canned or homemade
2 Tbsp. flour
1½ cups hot milk

Place shortening and butter in 13x9 inch pan and set in 425° oven to melt. In a paper bag mix the flour, salt, pepper and paprika. Shake a few pieces of chicken at a time in the bag and coat thoroughly. Place chicken, skin side down, in hot shortening. Bake 45 minutes and turn. Push chicken to one end of pan. On the other end, place uncooked biscuits in a single layer. Do not drain off shortening. Drain peach halves, stick each with a whole clove and place on top of chicken. Bake another 15 minutes.

To make gravy: Remove chicken, biscuits and peaches to serving platter. Add 2 tablespoons of flour to pan drippings and bring to a boil. Add milk and boil 1 minute.
Serves 4.

Mrs. Stanley McNulty, Jr.

RULES FOR FRYING CHICKEN

1. Cut up chicken. Chickens pre-cut lose a great deal of flavor and moistness.
2. Buy small chickens. Larger ones just do not have the flavor of the smaller.
3. After cutting up the chickens, be certain to remove outside skin. They fry crisper when skin is removed.
4. Always place dark meat in center of skillet because these pieces take a little longer to cook.
5. Never salt and pepper chicken before frying, but generously season immediately after removing pieces from skillet.
6. Chicken should be allowed to drain on paper towels at least one minute before being placed on a serving platter.

Mrs. Louis Morschheimer
Parkdale, Arkansas

FRIED CHICKEN AND CREAM GRAVY

Read the *Rules for Frying Chicken* and apply throughout this recipe. In medium size bowl combine 1 egg and 1 tablespoon water, per chicken. Beat slightly. Place pieces of chicken in egg mixture to sit while you are heating skillet. Use just enough oil (*always* cooking oil) so that when chicken is placed in skillet, oil does not come up over halfway on the pieces. Make certain oil is *very hot* before frying. (A good test is to drop a little of the egg mixture in skillet to see if it sizzles.)

Put a generous amount of flour into a brown paper bag. Place chicken pieces in sack and shake vigorously. (Hold top securely or you'll have a mess!) Starting with dark pieces, place them in the middle of skillet. Then place the rest of chicken to outside. Allow pieces to brown at least 1 minute, turn and brown on other side. (Use tongs to turn—do not pierce with a fork.) Place lid on skillet and reduce heat to medium. Let chicken cook 10 minutes on one side, turn and cook 10 minutes more. Remove lid and turn heat on high again. Cook about 1 more minute. Remove chicken and drain.

Cream Gravy:

2 Tbsp. oil from fried chicken	1½ cups milk
2 Tbsp. butter	½ cup whipping cream
5 Tbsp. flour	2 Tbsp. butter
Salt and pepper	Paprika
	Red pepper

Pour off all but 2 tablespoons of oil from the chicken, keeping the brown crispy bits in the skillet. Add butter and stir over medium high heat. Add about 5 tablespoons flour. (This varies, depending on how thick or thin you prefer gravy.) Stir and reduce heat. Continue to stir at least 3 minutes. Add salt and pepper. Pour in milk and cream. Reduce heat again and let gravy bubble 2-3 minutes. Add remaining 2 tablespoons butter and a generous amount of paprika. Stir well and remove from heat.

If gravy is too thick, add more milk and cream; if too thin, put flour in a glass with a small amount of milk and stir vigorously before adding to gravy. (This avoids lumps.) Sprinkle red pepper over gravy if desired.

Mrs. Louis Morschheimer
Parkdale, Arkansas

Ladies who have fried chicken for years tested this method and rated it Platonic.

When straining grease after frying chicken—put napkin on top of coffee can with rubber band and pour grease through.

CAJUN FRIED CHICKEN

2 small fryers, cut up
Salt and freshly ground pepper
Cayenne pepper

½ tsp. minced garlic
Vegetable oil
Flour for dredging

Several hours before frying chicken, wash pieces and shake off excess water. Sprinkle each piece generously with salt, pepper, cayenne, and garlic. Place chicken in a single layer on a platter, cover with plastic wrap. Refrigerate until ready to fry.

Heat 4 or 5 inches of oil in deep fryer to 375°. Dredge chicken in flour and fry 2-4 pieces at a time until brown. Do not crowd frying basket. (Large pieces should take 12-15 minutes, smaller ones 9-10 minutes.) As each batch is completed, drain thoroughly and place on large platter lined with several layers of paper towels. Place in preheated 200° oven to keep warm until all the chicken is fried. This chicken is also great cold.

OVEN FRIED CHICKEN

¾ cup butter
1 clove garlic, minced
2 tsp. salt
⅛ tsp. pepper

2 cups dry breadcrumbs
¾ cup Parmesan cheese
¼ cup minced parsley
1 fryer, cut up

Melt butter with garlic in it. Combine salt, pepper, crumbs, cheese and parsley. Dip chicken pieces in butter, then in crumbs. Lay in shallow baking pan. Do not overlap! Do not turn! Bake, uncovered, at 350° for 1 hour.
Serves 4.

Mrs. Jasper Pyeatt
Searcy, Arkansas

SESAME SEED CHICKEN

1 fryer, cut up
1½ cups milk
1 egg, beaten
½ cup flour
1 tsp. salt

2 Tbsp. sesame seeds
1/3 cup oil
1 can cream of mushroom soup
1 (3 oz.) can mushrooms
½ cup sliced stuffed olives

Combine milk, egg, flour, salt and sesame seeds. Salt and pepper chicken and dip in batter. Brown in hot oil. Place in baking dish and cover with soup, undrained mushrooms and olives. Bake in slow oven for about 30 minutes or more. Add some milk to sauce if necessary. Serve over hot rice.
Serves 4.

Mrs. C. D. Allison, Jr.

SADIE'S DEEP DISH CHICKEN POT PIE

2 cups cubed, cooked chicken
½ cup celery, chopped fine
¼ cup onion, chopped fine
4 Tbsp. butter

4 Tbsp. flour
2 cups chicken stock
Salt and pepper

Sauté celery and onion in butter until tender. Add flour and mix well. Gradually add stock, stirring and cook slowly until medium thick. Season to taste and set aside to cool.

Pastry:
3 cups flour
1½ tsp. salt

6 heaping Tbsp. shortening

Mix until dough looks like coarse meal. Sprinkle with ice water (10-12 teaspoons) until dough sticks together. Roll into ball and divide into two parts. On floured board, roll 1 part of dough to ¼ inch thick. Line a 2-quart round baking dish with pastry, allowing it to extend a little over the sides. Add chicken and sauce. Roll other part of dough and place over top of baking dish. Handle pastry carefully to avoid holes. Trim any excess crust around edge of dish. Moisten edges of crust with ice water and stick together. Make several slashes in top crust to allow steam to escape while cooking. Bake at 350° for 1 hour.

Mrs. Sadie Mae Brown

GOOD AND EASY CHICKEN PIE

3 whole chicken breasts
1 tsp. celery salt
1 tsp. tarragon
2 Tbsp. lemon juice

2 cans cream of chicken soup
Salt and pepper
Pillsbury Crescent Dinner Rolls

Simmer chicken breasts about 1 hour in a covered pan with celery salt, tarragon, lemon juice and about 1½ cups water. When tender, drain (reserving broth) and remove skin and bone from meat. Chop into large pieces. In 11x7 inch baking dish, pour soup and thin with ½ cup of the broth. Season with salt and pepper; stir in chicken pieces. Top with roll dough (unrolled, but not separated). Dough need not meet exactly in center or on sides. Bake at 375° until crust is brown and filling is bubbling (about 20-30 minutes).
Serves 6.

Mrs. Sam Boellner
Little Rock, Arkansas

To season chicken when boiling, add to the water any combination of the following: celery stalks with leaves, quartered onions, parsley, bay leaf, celery seeds, Accent, plenty of salt and pepper.

CHICKEN AND DUMPLINGS

1 large fryer
1 onion, quartered
1 stalk celery
1 Tbsp. salt

½ tsp. pepper
1 Tbsp. butter
1 can chicken broth,
 if needed

Boil fryer in water to cover (about 2 quarts) with onion, celery, salt, pepper and butter. Remove fryer when very tender; strain and reserve broth. Remove skin and take meat off bones. Cut meat into large pieces. When ready to serve, cook dumplings in broth, add chicken and heat thoroughly. If there is not enough broth, add can of chicken broth.

Thin Dumplings:
2 cups flour
½ tsp. salt

½ cup butter
Cold water

Mix and roll out as pastry. Cut in strips. Bring reserved broth to a boil. Stretch each strip as you place in broth. Cook uncovered until done, about 10 minutes.

Mrs. Harold Seabrook

Thick Dumplings:
2 cups flour
½ tsp. soda
½ tsp. baking powder
½ tsp. salt

1 cup buttermilk
1 Tbsp. oil or melted
 shortening

Sift together flour, soda, baking powder and salt. Add buttermilk and oil. Stir until well mixed, adding more flour if necessary to make a stiff dough. Turn out on floured board and knead until dough is workable. Roll to a thin dough, cut in strips, and drop in boiling broth. Cook about 20 minutes.

Mrs. Jack Gentle

FRENCH CHICKEN

1 fryer, cut up
Salt and pepper

1 bottle Kraft French Dressing
1 pkg. dry onion soup

Salt and pepper chicken and put in roasting pan. Cover with dressing, sprinkle soup over top and refrigerate overnight. Bake covered 2 hours, at 300°, basting often.
Serves 4.

Mrs. Simon Joseph

This is such an easy, family supper for a busy day!

250

BROILED CHICKEN

8 chicken quarters   Salt
Juice of 2 lemons   ¾ cup butter, melted

Squeeze lemon over chicken and salt each quarter liberally on each side.
Preheat broiler and place chicken on the rack of the broiling pan, skin side
down. Pour half the butter over chicken and broil 6 or 7 inches from the
flame for 20 minutes. Turn, pour remaining butter over, and broil 20
minutes more. Pour pan juices over chicken before serving.
Serves 8.

CHICKEN THOMAS JEFFERSON

8 broiled chicken quarters   16 bacon curls
16 sautéed chicken livers   2 recipes of Madeira
16 small, grilled   Mushroom Sauce
   sausage links   Watercress or parsley

Broil chicken using the Broiled Chicken recipe. On each warmed dinner
plate, place a chicken quarter and garnish with 2 sautéed chicken livers
(See Index), 2 grilled sausage links and 2 bacon curls. Pour Madeira
Mushroom Sauce (See Index) over all. Decorate with a large bouquet of
watercress or fresh parsley.
Serves 8.

For a variation: Substitute tomato quarters, sautéed lightly in olive oil, and
cooked frozen artichoke hearts for the chicken livers, sausage and bacon;
or use french fried onion rings and oven brown potatoes (cut the size of
new potatoes). Pour sauce over all.

POPPY SEED CHICKEN

12 chicken breasts   Salt and pepper
   boiled and boned   35-40 Ritz Crackers, crumbled
2 cans cream of chicken soup   2 Tbsp. poppy seeds
1½ pts. sour cream   6 Tbsp. butter, melted
¼ cup sherry

In 2 (2-quart) casserole dishes or 1 large baking dish, put layer of coarsely
chopped chicken. Mix soup, sour cream and sherry and season to taste
with salt and pepper. Pour over chicken. Top with cracker crumbs mixed
with poppy seeds. Pour melted butter over crumbs. Bake at 350° for 30
minutes. Can make a day ahead.
Serves 12.

Mrs. Ed McCorkle
Arkadelphia, Arkansas

CHICKEN BROCCOLI CASSEROLE

2 cups cooked chicken
  breast, cut up
2 pkgs. frozen broccoli spears
2 cans cream of chicken soup
1 cup mayonnaise

¼ tsp. curry powder
2 Tbsp. lemon juice
1 cup sharp Cheddar cheese
Cracker crumbs

Cook broccoli and place in casserole; cover with chicken. Mix next 5 ingredients and pour over chicken. Top with cracker crumbs. Bake at 350° for 30-40 minutes.

Mrs. Douglas E. Behm
Ft. Walton Beach, Florida

CHICKEN WITH SPINACH NOODLES

2 or 3 fryers, boiled
  (reserve broth)
2 cups chopped celery
2 cups chopped onion
2 cups chopped green pepper
1 pkg. Spinach Noodles

1 can cream of mushroom soup
1 lb. grated processed
  American cheese
1 can sliced mushrooms
2 cans water chestnuts
Salt and pepper

Cook vegetables in some of the chicken broth until tender. When vegetables are done, use remaining broth and cook noodles until tender. (Add a can of broth if necessary). Noodles should have absorbed most of the broth. Add soup and stir in cheese until it is melted. Add mushrooms with juice, water chestnuts, vegetables and chicken (cut in fairly large pieces). Mix well; salt and pepper to taste. Put in 3 buttered casseroles and bake at 350° until bubbly. This is better if made the day before it is to be baked and served.

Mrs. Robert Turley

HICKORY SMOKED TURKEY

Turkey
Salt and pepper
Seasoned Salt

3 small hickory sticks
½ cup Worcestershire sauce
½ cup butter

Season turkey inside and out with salt and pepper. Sprinkle until red with Seasoned Salt. Place in disposable open pan and put on grill when coals are very hot. Cover only with lid of grill. Soak hickory sticks in water at least 1 hour. Put these on fire after turkey has cooked an hour. Baste turkey with Worcestershire sauce and butter combined, about 3 times during cooking. Roast 14 pound turkey for 3 hours and 30 minutes.

Mrs. Martin G. Gilbert

CHICKEN SPAGHETTI

1 (4-5 lb.) hen
4 chicken breasts
2 cups chopped celery
1 cup chopped onion
1 scant cup chopped
  green pepper
4 cups tomatoes, chopped
2 (8 oz.) cans tomato sauce
1 (4 oz.) can mushrooms

1 Tbsp. chili powder
Tabasco to taste
4 Tbsp. Worcestershire sauce
Salt and pepper to taste
2 cups reserved chicken broth
1 pkg. spaghetti
4 cups grated, sharp
  Cheddar cheese
1 can pitted black olives

Boil hen and breasts in salted water. When tender, remove bones and chop meat. Save 2 cups broth. Cover bottom of skillet with oil and brown onions, green pepper and celery. Remove from skillet and put into a heavy roaster or Dutch oven along with chicken, tomatoes, tomato sauce, mushrooms, chili powder, Tabasco, Worcestershire, salt and pepper. Simmer ½ hour.

To reserved broth add enough water to equal 4 quarts; boil spaghetti and drain. Combine chicken mixture, spaghetti, cheese and olives in a Dutch oven or large casserole. Bake at 250° for 1 hour. This is better made a day ahead and refrigerated until ready to bake. Freezes well. *Serves 12.*

Mrs. James Stobaugh

CHICKEN RAVIOLI

1 (4-5 lb.) hen or 3 fryers
1 onion, quartered
2 ribs celery
Bay leaf
Salt and pepper
2 large onions, chopped
4-5 stalks celery, chopped
½ green pepper, chopped

6 Tbsp. bacon drippings
1 (12 oz.) pkg. noodles
1 (5 oz.) pkg. noodles
1 (4 oz.) can mushrooms
1 (2 oz.) jar pimientos
Cheese
1 can chicken broth (optional)

Boil chicken with onion, celery, bay leaf, salt and pepper until tender. Debone chicken, leaving in large pieces. Strain stock and save. Sauté onions, celery and green pepper in bacon drippings. Cook noodles in broth as directed on package. Leave noodles in broth. Drain off some broth only if there is a great deal of liquid. Add chicken, sautéed vegetables, mushrooms and pimiento to noodles. Put into large casserole. Cover with foil. Heat 30-40 minutes at 350°. About 10 minutes before end of cooking time, remove foil and top with grated cheese. (If this looks dry as it cooks, add more broth, either fresh or canned.) *Serves 15-18.*

Mrs. Dodi Harrelson
Jonesboro, Arkansas

CHICKEN ENCHILADA CASSEROLE

1 fryer, boiled and de-boned
2 cups chicken broth
1 large onion, chopped
1 garlic clove
½ cup celery, chopped

1 can celery soup
2 jalapeno peppers
Salt and pepper to taste
1 pkg. (15) tortillas
1 lb. grated Cheddar cheese

Skim fat off broth. Sauté onion, celery and garlic in fat. Add broth, soup, chicken and peppers to onion and heat. Correct seasoning. In buttered casserole, arrange layers of tortillas, chicken sauce, cheese, ending with cheese on top. Bake at 350° for 35 minutes or until it bubbles.
Serves 8.

Mrs. Fred Coleman

CHICKEN OSSO BUCO

12 chicken thighs
½ cup flour
1 tsp. salt
¼ tsp. pepper
¼ cup butter or margarine
1 cup chopped onion
1 cup sliced carrots
½ cup chopped celery

1 clove garlic, minced
1 cup dry white wine
1 (8 oz.) can tomato sauce
1 tsp. dried leaf basil
1 tsp. dried leaf thyme
Hot cooked rice,
  preferably saffron

Coat chicken thighs with mixture of flour, salt and pepper. Melt butter in large skillet. Add chicken and brown on both sides; remove. Sauté onion in pan drippings until tender. Add carrots, celery, garlic, wine, tomato sauce, basil and thyme, mixing well. Return thighs to skillet, cover and simmer one hour. Serve chicken and sauce over rice.
Serves 6.

Mrs. Richard Milwee

CHICKEN CROQUETTES

2 cups diced cooked chicken	2 eggs, lightly beaten
½ small onion, finely chopped	½ tsp. salt
	¼ tsp. black pepper
8 oz. fresh mushrooms, diced very fine	¼ tsp. red pepper
	1 Tbsp. dry sherry
4 Tbsp. butter	1 egg beaten
½ tsp. salt	4 Tbsp. milk
½ tsp. fresh pepper	1 Tbsp. salad oil
1 Tbsp. dry sherry	½ tsp. salt
4 Tbsp. butter	Flour
4 Tbsp. flour	Fine bread crumbs
1 cup milk, scalded	Deep fat for frying

Sauté onions and mushrooms in butter with salt, pepper, and sherry until moisture is absorbed. Set aside. Melt 4 tablespoons butter in saucepan, add flour and cook, stirring constantly over medium low heat until roux begins to turn golden. Gradually add hot milk, stirring with wire whisk; add 2 eggs and cook until very thick. Season with salt, pepper and sherry. Add chicken and mushrooms and cook, stirring constantly, until mixture cleans sides of pan. Correct seasoning with salt; cool in refrigerator.

Shape croquettes into cones. Beat egg, milk, salad oil and salt. Dip croquettes in flour, then egg mixture, drain and roll in bread crumbs. Fry in deep, hot fat until golden brown. Serve with Velouté Sauce.
Serves 4.

Velouté Sauce:

4 Tbsp. butter	½ tsp. salt
4 Tbsp. flour	¼ tsp. red pepper
2 cups hot chicken broth	

Melt butter, add flour and cook slowly, stirring constantly for about 5 minutes. Gradually add chicken broth, stirring constantly with wire whisk. Simmer, stirring constantly, until thick as heavy cream. Add salt and red pepper. This sauce can be made ahead and heated just before serving over croquettes.
Serves 4.

Mrs. J. Wayne Buckley

Elegant enough for luncheon or dinner party.

PAELLA VALENCIA

¼ cup oil
2 (9 inch long) pepperoni
  sticks, sliced thickly
8 boned chicken breast halves
1 large onion, chopped
1 garlic clove, minced
2 cans minced clams,
  drained (reserve juice)
1½ lbs. shelled and deveined
  shrimp (fresh or frozen)
2 cups long-grain rice
1 tsp. freshly ground black
  pepper

2 tsp. salt
10-15 pieces of saffron (or
  about ¼ tsp. powdered
  saffron)
2 small jars sliced pimientos
  (well drained)
4 cups liquid (including the
  reserved clam broth)
2 tsp. instant chicken
  bouillon granules
½ tsp. Accent
Garnish of clam shells, pimiento,
black olives, asparagus, peas, etc.

In a large skillet or paella pan, heat oil until smoky hot and brown the pepperoni slices. Remove pepperoni with slotted spoon, drain, and reserve. Add the chicken breasts and brown in the same oil; then set aside. Add the chopped onion and garlic and sauté until translucent; then remove. Stir in the drained, minced clams and shrimp and cook until shrimp are almost done. Set aside. In remaining oil (adding a tiny bit more if necessary), add the rice, black pepper, salt, and saffron, and brown slightly; then stir in onion, 4 cups of liquid, the chicken granules, and the Accent. Cover pan tightly and cook about 10 minutes; then uncover and add the reserved pepperoni, chicken breasts and seafood. It can be prepared ahead to this point. May have to add a little more liquid at this time.

Cook, uncovered in 400° oven another 20-30 minutes, or until rice is done. The more traditional way, if you have a paella pan, is to cook uncovered in the oven the whole cooking time. Serve at once after garnishing attractively with whatever garnishes you have chosen, but especially with shells if possible. If you can obtain the brand of canned clams with clams in the shells, arrange them around the top of the paella pan before the last baking time. Wonderful preceded by gazpacho, and served with hard, crusty bread and butter, and lots of Sangria!
Serves 8.

Mrs. John G. Lile

This takes time to prepare but it is not at all hard and is well worth the trouble!

CHICKEN WITH ORANGES

2½ lb. chicken,
   cut into quarters
1 Tbsp. butter
4 carrots, very
   thinly sliced
4 ribs celery, very
   thinly sliced

Salt
Freshly ground pepper
¼ cup chopped parsley
   (or chopped dill)
3 navel oranges
Extra orange juice

Clean chicken. In a heavy casserole with a tight fitting cover, melt the butter over very low heat. Arrange the slices of carrots and celery on the bottom, arrange pieces of chicken on top, seasoning everything with a little salt and a generous amount of pepper as you go. Sprinkle with the parsley or dill also. Grate the rind of one of the oranges and scatter it over the chicken.

Carefully peel all the white pith (over a bowl to catch all the juice) from the oranges. Cut out the orange sections between the membranes with a sharp knife and reserve. Pour whatever orange juice has collected in the bowl over the chicken. Cook, tightly covered, over a low heat for 40-45 minutes. Add orange sections and cook, covered, another 5-10 minutes. (Add a bit of additional orange juice during cooking if necessary.)
Serves 4.

Mrs. Paul B. Young

SWEET 'N SOUR CHICKEN

1 (8 oz.) can pineapple chunks
2 lbs. chicken breasts
2 Tbsp. butter
½ cup chicken bouillon
2 large carrots, sliced
¼ cup firmly packed brown sugar
2 Tbsp. cornstarch

¼ cup vinegar
2 Tbsp. soy sauce
1 medium onion, sliced
   and separated into rings
½ green pepper cut in strips
1 (8 oz.) can water chestnuts,
   thinly sliced

Drain pineapple, reserving juice. Set aside. Bone chicken breasts and cut meat into slivers. Sauté in butter until no longer pink. Add bouillon and carrots. Cover and cook until carrots are tender. Combine reserved pineapple juice, brown sugar, cornstarch, vinegar, and soy sauce. Add to chicken and carrots and cook until mixture thickens. Just before serving, add pineapple, onion, green pepper, and water chestnuts. Cook just until heated. Serve over hot rice.
Serves 4-6.

Mrs. C. D. Allison, Jr.

CHICKEN FILLED CREPES

Makes 16 small crepes. (See Index)

Chicken Sauce:
¾ cup flour, unsifted
2/3 cup sherry
1 (14 oz.) can condensed
*   chicken broth*
2 cups half and half cream

½ tsp. salt
⅛ tsp. pepper
Later: ½ cup grated
*   Swiss cheese*

With a wire whisk, blend flour with sherry. Stir in chicken broth, cream, salt and pepper. Over medium heat, bring to a boil, stirring constantly. Reduce heat and simmer 2 minutes. Set aside.

Chicken Filling:
¼ cup real butter
¾ lb. mushrooms, chopped
*   or 1 (6 oz.) can, drained*
*   and chopped*
½ cup chopped green onions

2½ cups diced, cooked
*   chicken*
½ cup sherry
½ tsp. salt
Dash pepper

In large skillet, melt butter and sauté mushrooms and onions until golden brown (about 10 minutes). Add chicken, sherry, salt and pepper. Cook over high heat, stirring constantly, until no liquid remains. Remove from heat and stir in half the sauce; blend well. Can set aside.

Place about ¼ cup filling on each crepe. Roll up and arrange seam side down, in buttered, 3-quart shallow baking dish. Pour rest of sauce over crepes; sprinkle with the Swiss cheese. Bake at 350° for 25 minutes or until cheese is bubbly.
Serves 8.

Mrs. John G. Lile

LONDON CHICKEN

6 chicken breasts
Salt
½ cup butter
½ lb. fresh mushrooms
*   (or more)*

6 Tbsp. flour
2 cups milk
Pinch of thyme
Pinch poultry seasoning
½ cup white wine

Salt chicken and brown in butter; remove to flat, glass baking dish. Brown mushrooms in same butter and remove to baking dish. To make London Sauce, add more butter if necessary to make about 6 tablespoons in same skillet. Add flour and cook until bubbly. Add milk and cook until thick. Season with thyme and poultry seasoning. Add wine and salt to taste. Cook for a few minutes. Pour sauce over chicken and bake, covered, at 350° for 1 hour 30 minutes. (This may be prepared the day before and baked just before serving.)

Mrs. Wayne Waller

CHICKEN ANDALUSIA

4 large, boned chicken
breasts (halves)
Salt and pepper
Flour
6 Tbsp. melted butter

1 cup chopped green onions
2 chopped tomatoes (squeeze
out extra juice)
½ green pepper, chopped
½ cup half and half cream

Salt and pepper chicken, dredge in flour, brown in melted butter and
remove from skillet. Add onions, tomatoes and green pepper; sauté until
tender. Blend in cream. Return chicken to skillet and simmer in sauce 10
minutes. (The chicken is done when you prick with a fork and juice runs
clear.) Serve with saffron rice.
Serves 4.

Mrs. Don Lewis
Jackson, Tennessee

ROLLED CHICKEN WASHINGTON

1 (3 oz.) can broiled chopped
mushrooms, drained
2 Tbsp. butter or margarine
2 Tbsp. all-purpose flour
½ cup half and half cream
¼ tsp. salt
Dash cayenne pepper

1¼ cups shredded sharp
Cheddar cheese
6 or 7 small, boned, whole
chicken breasts
All-purpose flour
2 slightly beaten eggs
¾ cup fine dry bread crumbs

Cheese filling: Cook mushrooms in butter, about 5 minutes. Blend in flour;
stir in cream. Add salt and cayenne. Cook and stir until very thick. Stir in
cheese. Cook over very low heat, stirring constantly, until cheese is melted.
Turn mixture into pie plate and cover. Chill *thoroughly* about 1 hour. Cut
into 6 or 7 equal portions; shape into short sticks.

Cutlets: Remove skin from chicken. Place each piece of chicken, boned
side up, between 2 pieces of Saran Wrap. (Overlap meat where split.)
Working out from center, pound with wooden mallet to form cutlets not
quite ¼ inch thick. (Or ask your butcher to flatten chicken breasts for you.)
Peel off Saran. Sprinkle meat with salt.

Place a cheese stick on each cutlet. Tucking in the sides, roll the cutlets as
for jellyroll. Press to seal well. Dust chicken rolls with flour, dip in egg,
then roll in bread crumbs. Cover and chill thoroughly, at least 1 hour. (Or
fix ahead and chill overnight.) About an hour before serving time, fry rolls
in deep, hot fat (375°) for 5 minutes or until crisp and golden brown. Drain
on paper towels. Place rolls in a shallow baking dish and bake in slow
oven (325°) about 30-45 minutes. Serve on warm platter.
Serves 6-7.

Mrs. Paul Lewey

CRAB STUFFED CHICKEN BREASTS

6 whole, boned chicken
  breasts
½ cup chopped onion
½ cup chopped celery
3 Tbsp. butter
3 Tbsp. dry white wine
1 (7½ oz.) can crabmeat,
  drained and flaked

½ cup herb seasoned
  stuffing mix
Salt and pepper
2 Tbsp. flour
½ tsp. paprika
2 Tbsp. butter, melted

Cook onion and celery in butter until tender. Remove form heat and add wine, crabmeat and stuffing mix. Sprinkle each breast with salt and pepper. Divide stuffing among breasts and roll and secure with toothpicks. Coat each breast with flour mixed with paprika. Place in baking dish and drizzle with butter. Bake uncovered at 375° for 1 hour. Serve with White Wine Sauce with Mushrooms.
Serves 6.

Mrs. Clifford A. Davies

White Wine Sauce with Mushrooms:
½ lb. fresh mushrooms,
  washed and chopped
4 Tbsp. butter
Salt
5 Tbsp. butter

5 Tbsp. flour
1½ cups chicken broth
½ cup dry white wine
½ cup whipping cream
Salt and red pepper

Sauté mushrooms in butter until liquid is absorbed. Salt to taste. In saucepan, melt butter, add flour and cook over low heat for a few minutes, stirring constantly. Add broth slowly, stirring constantly with wire whisk. Add wine and cook until thick, stirring. Add mushrooms; stir thoroughly. Add cream; stir until hot. Season to taste with salt and red pepper.

CHICKEN BREASTS IN SOUR CREAM GRAVY

10 boned chicken breast
  halves
Salt and pepper
Paprika
½ cup butter or margarine

1 can cream of mushroom soup
1 (8 oz.) carton sour cream
1 can onion rings
  (Durkees O and D)

Salt and pepper chicken and sprinkle with lots of paprika. Top with butter patties and bake at 350° for 1 hour. Remove chicken and make gravy in drippings with the mushroom soup and sour cream. Top with onion rings and bake 20 minutes more.
Serves 8-10.

Mrs. Jim Shuffield
Little Rock, Arkansas

CHICKEN ROYAL

4 whole chicken breasts	Dash pepper
¼ cup flour	1 recipe Pepperidge Farm
½ tsp. salt	Herb Stuffing Mix
¼ tsp. paprika	½ cup butter, melted

Remove bone from breast. Combine flour and seasonings in paper bag. Add chicken and shake. Fill cavity of each chicken breast with 1 large tablespoon of stuffing. Hold stuffing in by skewering with toothpicks. (Fold *sides* together and skewer; fold each *end* over and skewer *tightly*.) Dip chicken in melted butter and place in baking dish. Drizzle remaining butter over top. Bake at 325° for 45 minutes; turn, bake an additional 45 minutes or until tender. Sprinkle with chopped parsley and serve with Sour Cream Mushroom Sauce.

Sour Cream Mushroom Sauce:

½ lb. fresh mushrooms	½ cup whipping cream
¼ cup minced onions	½ cup sour cream
2 Tbsp. butter	½ tsp. salt
2 Tbsp. flour	¼ tsp. pepper

About 15 minutes before time to serve, cook mushrooms and onions lightly in butter until tender but not brown. Cover and cook 10 minutes over low heat. Push mushrooms to one side and stir in flour. Add whipping cream, sour cream and seasonings. Heat slowly almost to boiling point, stirring constantly. Put in sauce bowl and serve with chicken breasts. *Serves 4.*

Mrs. Jim Price
Jackson, Tennessee

CHICKEN BREASTS SUPREME

8 fryer breasts	2 cloves garlic, minced
2 (8 oz.) cartons sour cream	4 scant tsp. salt
¼ cup lemon juice	½ tsp. pepper
4 tsp. Worcestershire sauce	1¾ cups dry breadcrumbs
4 tsp. celery salt (optional)	½ cup margarine
2 tsp. paprika	½ cup shortening

Combine sour cream with lemon juice, Worcestershire, celery salt, paprika, garlic, salt and pepper. Add chicken, coating each piece well. Cover with *plastic wrap* and let stand in refrigerator overnight. Remove chicken and roll in crumbs, coating evenly. Arrange in single layer in baking pan. Melt butter and shortening and spoon half this mixture over chicken. Bake at 350°, or 325° in glass, uncovered for 45 min. Spoon remaining shortening mixture over chicken. Bake 15-20 minutes longer. *Serves 8.*

Miss Frances McGaughy

CHICKEN BREAST BRAZILIA

4 boneless, whole chicken
  breasts (6-7 oz. each)
1 (14 oz.) can hearts of palm
Melted butter

Salt and white pepper
Hollandaise sauce
Chopped chives

Salt inside of chicken breasts and wrap each one around stalk of palm heart. Attach with a toothpick. Place seam down in a buttered pan and cover breasts generously with melted butter. Season with salt and white pepper. Bake at 400° for 30 minutes. Run under broiler to brown, if desired. Top with Hollandaise sauce and sprinkle with chopped chives. Superb!
Serves 4.

CHICKEN COSMOPOLITAN

2 lbs. chicken breasts
  (or 4 pieces)
Flour, salt and pepper
¼ cup shortening or oil
1 can cream of mushroom
  or cream of celery soup

1 1/3 cups water
1 (10 oz.) pkg. frozen broccoli
  (spears or chopped)
1 cup grated Cheddar
  cheese

Combine flour, salt and pepper. Roll chicken in seasoned flour. Sauté in fat, browning on all sides. Remove chicken. Combine soup and water with drippings in skillet, blending well. Return chicken to skillet. Cover and simmer until tender, about 45 minutes. Cook broccoli as directed on package. Drain and arrange in greased, shallow baking dish. Remove bones from chicken if desired and place on broccoli. Cover with gravy and sprinkle with cheese. Broil to melt cheese.
Serves 4.

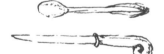

Mrs. Larry Jones

CHICKEN IN WINE

1 fryer, cut up
  (or chicken breasts)
Salt, pepper and flour
Olive oil

½ cup white wine
½ cup sliced stuffed olives
1 tsp. oregano
¼ cup water

Salt, pepper and flour chicken. Fry (in covered skillet) in olive oil. Pour off oil and add remaining ingredients. Simmer over low heat about 10 minutes and allow to set, covered, about 10 minutes.
Serves 3-4.

Mrs. Leonard Dunn

CHICKEN VERMOUTH

¼ cup butter
1 fryer, quartered
Salt

½ lemon
4 Tbsp. chopped parsley
¼ cup dry Vermouth

Place oven rack 6 inches below broiler. Put butter in pan just large enough to hold chicken pieces without crowding, and place under broiler to melt. Put chicken in butter, turning to coat all sides. Brown chicken under broiler, turning once. Salt each side as it is browned. Pour off all but 4 tablespoons of butter and drippings. Sprinkle lemon juice and parsley over chicken, cover pan loosely with foil and bake at 325° for 1 hour.

Remove chicken from pan and pour off all but 3 tablespoons liquid. Place pan over medium burner and add Vermouth. Stir quickly, scraping browned bits from pan and mixing thoroughly as wine heats. Pour this over chicken and serve.
Serves 4.

Mrs. Robert Nixon

CHICKEN CELESTINE

1 fryer, cut up
  (or just chicken breasts)
Salt, pepper and flour
1/3 cup butter
½ lb. small mushrooms
2 large, peeled
  tomatoes, diced

1 cup dry white wine
2 Tbsp. consommé
2 Tbsp. sherry
Cayenne pepper to taste
2 Tbsp. parsley
Chives and garlic to taste

Salt, pepper and lightly flour chicken pieces. Brown quickly in butter. Add mushrooms and tomatoes. Cook 10 minutes. Add wine, consommé and sherry. Bring to gentle boil. Add cayenne pepper, cover, and cook until tender. Remove chicken. Skim grease off top of pan drippings and add parsley, chives and garlic; simmer until reduced by half. Serve over chicken.
Serves 4.

Mrs. Robin M. Rousseau
Little Rock, Arkansas

COQ AU VIN

2 small chickens, cut up
Seasoned flour
½ cup butter
3 Tbsp. cognac
1 cup bouillon
1 doz. small onions
1 doz. small mushrooms

1 jar Belgian carrots
1 cup Burgundy wine
1 bay leaf
1/3 tsp. thyme
¼ tsp. marjoram
Garlic salt

Flour chicken; brown in butter; add cognac and flame. Add remaining ingredients. Cover and cook slowly 2 hours. Looks beautiful piled on large silver tray. Serve with new potatoes.
Serves 6-8.

Mrs. Frank Surface
Jacksonville, Florida

SKILLET COQ AU VIN

½ cup all-purpose flour
1 tsp. salt
¼ tsp. pepper
1 (3-3½ lb.) broiler-fryer
  cut up
6 slices bacon
6 small onions
½ lb. fresh mushrooms
½ tsp. dried thyme leaves

1 bay leaf
2 large sprigs parsley
4 carrots, halved
1 tsp. instant chicken
  bouillon (or 2 cubes)
1 cup hot water
1 cup Red Burgundy
1 clove garlic, crushed
½ tsp. salt

Mix flour, 1 teaspoon salt and pepper; coat chicken. Fry bacon in large skillet until crisp; remove bacon, drain. Brown chicken in bacon fat over medium heat. Remove chicken. Cook and stir onions and mushrooms in skillet until tender, about 5 minutes. Drain off fat. Tie thyme leaves, bay leaf and parsley in cheesecloth. Crumble bacon; stir bacon, herbs in cheese cloth and remaining ingredients into skillet. Add reserved chicken and cover. Simmer until done, about 1 hour. Remove cheese cloth. Spoon off fat. Serve in individual bowls and garnish with parsley.
Serves 4-6.

Mrs. Walter M. Simpson

264

PICNIC CORNISH HENS

8 (10-12 oz.) Cornish hens
Salt and pepper
½ cup Dijon Mustard
2/3 cup white bread crumbs

3 Tbsp. minced shallots
½ cup butter
White wine

Rub each bird with salt, pepper and 1 tablespoon of the mustard. Sprinkle with bread crumbs. Place in square of foil and fold to center. Add 1 teaspoon shallots (or green onions), 1 tablespoon butter and 3 tablespoons white wine to each package. Fold over the foil tightly and bake at 400° for 45 minutes. Open foil, baste hens, and bake about 15 minutes more, until browned. Reseal and carry to picnic in foil. Good cold too! (If you are serving at home, remove from foil, stuff cavity with fresh parsley and serve juices separately.)
Serves 8.

Mrs. Frank Surface
Jacksonville, Florida

CHICKEN MADEIRA

2 (2 lb.) roasting chickens
   or 4 Rock Cornish hens
½ cup butter
1 Tbsp. salt
½ tsp. white pepper

½ cup Madeira
2 cups tiny crisp croutons
½ cup grated Parmesan
Lemon peel, cut in thin
   strips (no white)

Rub chicken inside and out with butter, salt and pepper. Place in shallow pan and roast at 375° for 20 minutes. Then baste with wine and continue roasting for 30 minutes or until done, basting frequently. Remove from oven; cut in half (removing back bone); and, if using chickens, cut in quarters. Place on top of croutons sprinkled with cheese on serving tray. Add lemon peel to pan juices and stir constantly over high heat to reduce to a slightly thicker consistency. Pour over chicken.
Serves 8.

Mrs. Marc Oudin

CORNISH HENS

Cornish hens, split in half
Ingredients for each half:
Salt, pepper, and paprika
2 Tbsp. olive oil
¼ tsp. thyme

¼ tsp. poultry seasoning
2 Tbsp. chopped parsley
2 tsp. Worcestershire sauce
2 Tbsp. dry white wine

Season hens with salt, pepper and paprika. Place each half on square of heavy foil. Pour olive oil over bird and grease well. Place skin side down and fill cavity with other ingredients mixed together. Fold foil around bird to keep in juices. Bake at 300° for 1 hour. Just before serving, open foil, turn bird skin side up and raise oven heat to brown (about 20 minutes). Serve with pan juices. (Serve 2 halves per person for more hearty servings.)

Mrs. A. G. Bedell
Little Rock, Arkansas

ALAN'S CHINESE CORNISH HENS

4 Cornish hens
1 Tbsp. szechuan
   peppercorns
4 scallions, chopped
4 slices fresh ginger root

4 garlic buds
2 Tbsp. cornstarch
½ cup soy sauce
1 tsp. Five Spice Powder
1 qt. peanut oil

Crush peppercorns, scallions, ginger root and garlic together and mix well. Rub this mixture over birds, inside and out. Cover with plastic and marinate at least overnight. Place birds in steamer and steam for 1½ hours or until tender. Remove from steamer and allow to dry at least 6 hours. Mix next three ingredients and rub over dry birds. Allow this mixture to dry on birds. Heat peanut oil and deep fry each bird separately until golden brown.

6 Tbsp. peanut oil
½ lb. peeled shrimp
2 Tbsp. pale dry sherry

½ pkg. frozen peas
2 cups cooked rice
Parsley

Heat 2 tablespoons oil in frying pan and cook shrimp 1½ minutes (until pink). Add sherry and cook 1 minute. Remove shrimp. Heat 2 tablespoons more oil and add peas. Cook 30 seconds and add peas to shrimp. Heat 2 tablespoons more oil and add rice. Stir until heated through. Then add peas and shrimp to rice. Split the breast bone of each hen with sharp scissors or knife and open up bird. Mound rice mixture in cavity of each bird. Arrange on silver tray and garnish with parsley.
Serves 4.

Alan Goldman

This takes planning ahead and is well worth it!

CORNISH HENS WITH ORANGE SAUCE

4-6 Cornish hens
Salt and pepper
1 lemon, not peeled
½ cup butter, melted
½ tsp. nutmeg

1 Tbsp. grated orange peel
¾ cup orange juice
¼ cup dry white wine
(or chicken broth)
Orange sauce

Thaw hens, rinse and dry with paper towels. Sprinkle the cavities with salt and pepper. Cut lemon in 4-6 wedges and place a wedge in each cavity, squeezing to release juice. Tie legs and place in shallow pan. Combine butter and nutmeg; pour over hens. Roast at 350° for 15 minutes. Combine orange peel with juice and wine and pour over hens. Continue roasting 45 minutes longer, basting frequently with pan juices until hens are browned. Remove from pan and keep warm while preparing sauce.

Orange Sauce: (3½ cups)
2 cups liquid drippings
(add orange juice and/or
wine, if necessary)
½ Tbsp. cornstarch
2 Tbsp. cold water
1 bay leaf
1 cup seedless grapes

1 orange, sliced
(not peeled)
2 Tbsp. Grand Marnier
(or brandy)
Salt and pepper
Orange wedges
Parsley

Pour 2 cups drippings into saucepan using as much brown glaze as possible. Add cornstarch blended with water, then bay leaf. Bring to a boil over medium heat, stirring constantly. Boil 1-2 minutes. Add grapes and orange slices and gently simmer 5 minutes. Remove bay leaf; add brandy and correct seasoning with salt and pepper. Spoon some sauce over each hen and serve remaining sauce separately. Garnish with orange wedges and parsley. Serve with white and wild rice.
Serves 4-6.

Mrs. Robert H. Holmes

Moist, delicious and beautiful!

CHICKEN LIVERS WALTON

1 lb. chicken livers, sautéed
(See Index)
¼ cup butter
1 large bunch green
onions, chopped

½ cup A-1 Sauce
½ cup dry sherry
4 slices toast
8 slices crisp bacon

Sauté chicken livers. Melt butter and sauté onions until soft. Add A-1 and sherry and simmer slowly for a few minutes. Place livers on toast on individual plates. Pour sauce over livers and garnish with crisp bacon.
Serves 4.

SAUTEED CHICKEN LIVERS

1 lb. chicken livers
Salt and ground pepper
Flour

2 Tbsp. butter
1 Tbsp. oil

Season livers and coat with flour. Heat butter and oil until it crackles; add livers and sauté (medium high heat) 2 minutes on each side or longer if you prefer them well done.

Variations: To butter and oil, add few drops Worcestershire sauce, 2 teaspoons lemon juice, and 1 small clove garlic, minced. Or, to butter and oil, add 1 tablespoon onion juice and 2 tsp. lemon juice and, after frying livers, add ¼ pound sautéed, fresh mushrooms. Or, serve on toast points garnished with toasted almonds.
Serves 4.

Mrs. Harry A. Metcalf

CHICKEN LIVERS ATHENS

1 lb. sautéed chicken livers

Sauce:
1 bunch green onions,
  chopped, with tops
2 Tbsp. butter
2 Tbsp. olive oil
2 Tbsp. flour
1 (28 oz.) can tomatoes
  chopped, with juice

2 Tbsp. beef flavored
  instant bouillon
2 cloves garlic, crushed
1 tsp. salt
1 tsp. basil
½ tsp. pepper

Sauté green onions in butter and olive oil until tender. Add flour and cook over low heat for a few minutes, stirring constantly. Add tomatoes and blend well. Add (dry) bouillon, garlic, salt, basil, and pepper. Set aside. (Sauté chicken livers while frying eggplant.)

Eggplant Base:
1 eggplant, peeled and
  sliced ¼ inch thick
2 quarts water
2 Tbsp. salt

2 cups cornmeal
1 Tbsp. salt
Oil for frying

Soak eggplant in salt water for 20 minutes or more. Dredge in cornmeal that has been seasoned with the 1 tablespoon salt. Fry in oil about 1 inch deep until brown. This will take a few minutes as you can only fry 2-3 pieces in a skillet at a time. Drain on paper towels. Place 2-3 slices eggplant on each plate. Put chicken livers on top of them. Pour heated sauce over them.
Serves 4.

Mrs. J. Wayne Buckley

THE BELL TOWER AT
THE UNIVERSITY OF ARKANSAS AT PINE BLUFF

The bell tower, a gift from the school's alumni, is in the center of the quadrangle at the University of Arkansas at Pine Bluff. The college was first known as Branch Normal of the Arkansas Industrial University at Fayetteville and later, in 1927, as Arkansas Agricultural, Mechanical and Normal College. It was first located at West Second Avenue and Oak Street and in 1880, was moved to a twenty acre tract between West Second and Fourth Avenues, bordering on Plum Street on the east. The college moved to the present campus on December 15, 1929, and merged with the University of Arkansas in 1972.

DELICIOUS CHARCOALED DOVE

Dove breasts
Soy sauce
Olive oil

Bacon
½ cup butter
¼-½ cup lemon juice

Make a mixture of 1 part soy sauce to 1 part olive oil (the amount depending on the number of dove breasts you wish to prepare) and marinate breasts for 1 hour. Wrap a strip of bacon around each breast and place on barbeque grill over low fire about 10-15 minutes on each side until bacon is crisp.

Melt butter and add lemon juice. Place cooked breasts in this and place pan on grill on lowest fire (just to keep warm).

Vernon T. Tarver
Fayetteville, Arkansas

This can also be used for wild duck breasts. Marinate for 4-5 hours, wrap in bacon and grill for 5-8 minutes per side. Sprinkle lightly with lemon juice and serve.

H. Watt Gregory, Jr.
Little Rock, Arkansas

BASTED DOVES

10 to 12 doves
Salt, pepper
4 Tbsp. butter, divided

½ cup water
¼ cup sherry

Salt and pepper the cleaned doves. Melt about 2 tablespoons of butter in an oven-proof skillet. Put doves into skillet, breast-side down; sear. Turn and sear on other side.

Add about 2 more tablespoons of butter and the water. Cover and bake at 325° about 1 hour or more (until tender), basting 3 or 4 times. Add sherry the final 30 minutes.
Serves 3-4.

Mrs. Morris Keesee, Jr.
Clarksdale, Mississippi

Birds should not be kept in freezer longer than eight or nine months.

DOVE CASSEROLE (OR QUAIL)

6 doves (or quail)	1 (8 oz.) carton of sour cream
Butter or oleo	
1 (10¾ oz.) can cream of	
mushroom soup	

Brown the birds in butter; reserve drippings. Place birds in greased casserole. Mix remaining ingredients with the drippings and pour over browned birds. Cook, covered, at 350° for 1 hour and 15 minutes. *Serves 2.*

Mrs. Frank Surface
Jacksonville, Florida

QUAIL PONTALBA

6 (4 oz.) oven-ready quail	1½ cups dry white wine
1 tsp. salt	3 oranges
½ tsp. ground black pepper	2 tsp. cornstarch
½ cup flour	½ cup Curacao or other
2 Tbsp. butter	orange liqueur
¼ cup vegetable oil	½ cup coarsely chopped walnuts

Pat quail completely dry, inside and out. Season cavities and skin with salt and pepper. Truss birds neatly; roll in flour, shaking off excess. Melt butter and oil over moderate heat in heavy 12 inch skillet. When foam subsides, brown birds evenly and carefully on all sides. As they brown, remove to a plate.

Pour wine into remaining fat, bring to a boil; stir well, scraping brown particles from bottom and sides. Return quail and any accumulated liquid to skillet; baste. Reduce heat to low, cover tightly, simmer for 30 minutes.

Using small sharp knife, remove peel from oranges without cutting into bitter white pith underneath. Cut peel into strips 1½ inches by ¼ inch; drop in boiling water for 1 to 2 minutes. Drain peel well and spread on paper towels. Cut all pith and membranes from 2 oranges (save third orange for another use); section the two oranges and drain on paper plates.

Transfer quail to heated platter; keep warm. Mix cornstarch and liqueur. Stirring constantly with a wire whisk, add to liquid in skillet; cook until sauce is thickened and smooth. Stir in orange peel, orange sections and walnuts; cook only to heat through. Taste sauce for seasoning, ladle over quail and serve immediately.
Serves 6.

Dr. Sam C. Harris

Entrée, 1976 Charity Ball Royal Supper

QUAIL WITH MUSHROOMS

6 quail
Lemon
Salt
Pepper
1 heaping Tbsp. butter
1 tsp. chopped parsley

1 tsp. chopped onion
1 Tbsp. flour
1 (4 oz.) can mushrooms
  with liquid
1 cup sherry
Dash Tabasco sauce

Rub each quail with the cut side of a lemon and season birds inside and out with salt and pepper. Melt the butter in a skillet and brown the quail. Remove and set aside.

Make a sauce by sautéing the parsley and onion in the pan drippings until brown. Add flour and brown. Add the mushrooms and their liquid. Add sherry, ½ teaspoon salt, ½ teaspoon pepper and Tabasco. Add quail, breast-side down, and simmer ½ hour, or until tender.
Serves 3-4.

Mrs. Thomas F. Stobaugh

STUFFED QUAIL

12 quail
Pork pan sausage (enough to
  stuff the birds)
Bacon

Flour
Salt and pepper
½ cup oleo
3 cups red wine, divided

Slightly brown the sausage, then drain off the grease. Stuff the quail with sausage, wrap bacon around the breast and roll in flour seasoned with salt and pepper.

In a large skillet, melt oleo; place quail breast down in skillet long enough for bacon to brown. Place the browned quail in a baking dish, breast up. Add enough seasoned flour to the drippings for gravy; then add 2 cups of red wine and enough water to make a thin gravy. Pour over the quail.

Bake, uncovered, at 350° for 45 minutes. Baste, cover with foil, cook for 1 hour and 15 minutes. Add the remaining cup of wine the last 15 minutes.
Serves 6.

Hawkeye Hunting Club
Center, Texas

DUCK AND WILD RICE CASSEROLE

2 medium ducks (3 cups
   cubed meat)
3 stalks celery
1 onion, halved
Salt
Pepper
½ cup oleo
½ cup chopped onion

¼ cup flour
4 oz. sliced mushrooms
1½ cups half and half cream
1 Tbsp. chopped parsley
1 (6 oz.) pkgs. seasoned wild
   and long-grain rice
Slivered almonds

Boil ducks for 1 hour (or until tender) in water to cover, with celery, onion halves, salt and pepper; remove and cube meat. Reserve broth. Cook the rice according to the package directions.

Melt oleo; sauté onion; stir in the flour. Drain mushrooms, reserving broth; add mushrooms to the onion mixture. Add enough duck broth to the mushroom broth to make 1½ cups of liquid; stir this into the onion mixture.

Omitting almonds, add remaining ingredients plus 1½ teaspoons salt and ¼ teaspoon pepper. Put into greased 2-quart casserole. Sprinkle almonds on top.

Bake covered, at 350° for 15-20 minutes. Uncover and bake for 5-10 more minutes, or until very hot. (If the casserole has been refrigerated it will take longer to heat.) If you don't have ducks, try substituting chicken—it's still good!
Serves 6.

Mrs. Thomas F. Stobaugh

This recipe is so delicious that its fame is widespread. Certainly no collection of Pine Bluff's favorite recipes would be complete without it.

HOT DUCKS

2 ducks
2 cups water
1 Tbsp. vinegar
1 clove garlic

Crushed red pepper
1 cup chopped onion
1 cup chopped celery
Salt to taste

Combine all ingredients except the ducks. Simmer the ducks in the mixture until they are very tender; remove. Boil down remaining juices and vegetables and use as sauce on wild rice to accompany ducks.
Serves 4.

Mrs. W. H. Fox

ROAST DUCK

Duck	Black pepper
2 celery tops	Chili powder
½ onion	Bacon
2 garlic cloves	2 Tbsp. chopped onion
Peppercorns	½ cup butter
½ tsp. salt	About 1/3 cup flour
Potato	2 tsp. ketchup
Celery	

Cover duck with water in a large cooker. Add celery tops, garlic cloves, onion, peppercorns and salt. Cover and simmer on top of the stove for 1½ hours. Remove duck and place in roaster. Reserve broth. In breast cavity, put a piece of potato and celery. Split skin of breast lengthwise. Sprinkle generously with black pepper and chili powder. Place strip of bacon the length of the duck. Add chopped onion to top of duck.

In large skillet melt butter; make paste with flour and stir until lightly browned. Add duck broth to make thin gravy, stirring until smooth. Pour gravy around duck, cover roaster and cook at 350° for 30 minutes, then baste. Cook until tender, 2-3 hours, basting often. The last 30 minutes, add ketchup to breast of duck and cook uncovered.
Serves 2.

Mrs. Frank Gilbert
Prescott, Arkansas

EASY AND DELICIOUS DUCK

1 duck	¾ of a (10½ oz.) can cream
½ cup cooking sherry	of mushroom soup
½ envelope dry onion soup mix	Seasoning salt

Place the duck on a large piece of heavy-duty aluminum foil. Combine the sherry, onion soup mix and mushroom soup; pour over the duck; sprinkle to taste with seasoning salt. Close foil, making a tent 2 inches above the duck breast. Place in a baking pan, preferably on a rack. Do not cover. Bake at 350° about 2 hours. It is best not to open the tent during the baking time unless you need to test for tenderness. The stock makes excellent gravy.

Do not cook more than one duck in a tent. If ducks are smaller than a mallard, reduce the ingredients proportionally.
Serves 2.

J. W. Bellamy

WILD DUCKS

Wild ducks (cleaned)
Adolph's Meat Tenderizer
Salt and pepper
Garlic powder
Apples, quartered
Onions, quartered
Celery stalks

Bacon
Lemon slices
Consommé, undiluted
Flour
2 bay leaves
1 cup Burgundy or sherry
1 cup whipping cream

Sprinkle ducks with tenderizer, refrigerate overnight. Rub whole birds inside and out with salt, pepper and garlic powder. Stuff breast cavities with apple, onion and celery; place ducks in large roaster and strip with bacon. Add lemon slices. Pour consommé into roaster (do not pour over ducks) to cover half the birds. Roast, covered, at 300°-325° for 3-3½ hours or until barely tender. Do not overcook; add more consommé if needed. (It may take 7 to 8 cans, depending on number of ducks.) Drizzle any moisture which collects in top of roaster over ducks.

Remove ducks; halve. Discard bacon, vegetables and lemon slices. Add additional consomme, if necessary (depending on amount of gravy desired) and thicken with a small amount of flour. Add bay leaves. Add duck halves, breast side down and baste with wine. Simmer on top of stove about 1 hour; continue to baste frequently. Turn off heat; just before serving, stir cream into gravy. Remove bay leaves. The meat should be juicy, fork tender and falling away from the bone.

Mrs. Joe E. Cook

Even tastier the next day!

DUCKS IN ORANGE AND WINE SAUCE

2 ducks
2 (6 oz.) cans frozen orange juice,
   diluted according to directions

Butter
¾ to 1 cup sherry
Seasoning salt

Salt ducks with seasoning salt. Put ducks into deep pan; add orange juice. This should produce enough liquid to almost cover ducks. If ducks are not fat, add ½ cup butter. Cook uncovered at a fast boil until ducks are barely tender. Add sherry and continue cooking. Reduce heat as the sauce begins to thicken and cook down. Turn ducks frequently. Take duck from sauce, cut in half and garnish with fresh orange slices that have been dipped into the sauce. Serve with wild rice.
Serves 4.

Mrs. Robert Rowland

WILD DUCK OREGANO

1 wild duck
Salt and pepper
4 tsp. oregano

½ cup butter
2 cups water

Split duck down back and open out in pan; sprinkle with salt, pepper and oregano. Add the butter and water to pan; cover and bake at 325° about 2 hours. Uncover and brown the last few minutes. Duck is done when meat will pull loose from the bone.
Serves 2.

Walter Trulock, Jr.

CHARCOALED MARINATED DUCK BREASTS

Duck breasts
½ cup red wine vinegar
1 cup vegetable oil
½ tsp. salt
½ tsp. meat tenderizer

¼ tsp. thyme
½ tsp. tarragon
¼ tsp. pepper
2 bay leaves
Bacon

Combine all ingredients except duck breasts and bacon. Marinate duck breasts for at least 24 hours, turning several times. Wrap each breast with bacon and secure with toothpicks. Grill briefly over hot coals until bacon is done.

Mrs. John G. Lile

FAVORITE BAKED DUCK

2 wild ducks
Salt and pepper
1 apple, quartered
1 onion, quartered

2 stalks celery, sliced large
Bacon
1 cup hot water

Salt and pepper cavity of breast; stuff with apple, onion, celery. Wrap with bacon and place in a heavy Dutch oven. Add hot water, cover with tight fitting lid and bake at 350° for at least 2½ hours or until fork tender. Baste frequently.

Mrs. Dick Falk
Jonesboro, Arkansas

BUFFET WILD DUCK

5 wild ducks, cleaned and dried   1 cup Burgundy
3 red apples, cored and quartered   ½ cup water

Stuff ducks with apples. Place in a large roasting pan. Pour Burgundy and water over ducks. Cover pan with lid or foil and bake in 325° oven for 2 hours or until very tender. Pour off the juice and chill ducks until they are very cold (meat slices more easily). Place ducks on carving board and remove all meat from the bones. Slice meat into slivers, cover and store in refrigerator. (This can be done a day ahead.)

Sauce (prepare 2 or 3 hours before serving):
1 cup butter, melted   1 Tbsp. Worcestershire sauce
1/3 cup lemon juice   1½ tsp. prepared mustard
¼ cup chopped parsley   Salt
¼ cup chopped green onions   Pepper
    (tops and all)

Heat butter in a heavy saucepan, stirring in half the lemon juice, until very hot but not boiling. Taste sauce, which should be tart but not sour, adding more lemon juice if needed. Add the parsley, Worcestershire sauce, onions and mustard and stir well.

Put ¼ of the duck in serving casserole. Season with salt and pepper, drizzle with lemon butter sauce and continue until all duck and sauce are used. Cover with lid or foil and let stand unrefrigerated for 30-60 minutes. Place covered casserole in 325° oven for 1 hour. Increase sauce by half if ducks are large mallards.
Serves 10.

Mrs. Robert Deal

DUCKS WITH MUSHROOMS AND WINE

3 wild ducks   Flour
1 cup oleo or butter, divided   1 cup chicken broth
1 cup sliced mushrooms   ¼ cup white wine
½ cup diced onions   3 Tbsp. cognac

Debone the ducks, keeping the breast and legs intact; brown in ½ cup oleo or butter. Remove duck; sauté onions and mushrooms until limp; remove. Add remaining ½ cup of butter and enough flour to thicken. Add broth, wine and cognac; stir until smooth. Add duck, onions and mushrooms to sauce and simmer for 2 hours.
Serves 6.

Mrs. Murray Claycomb
Warren, Arkansas

VENISON IN A SLOW-COOKER

4 lb. venison roast
Salt
2 Tbsp. flour
Vegetable oil for browning
2 cloves garlic, minced
1 large onion, sliced

2 Tbsp. brown sugar
1 Tbsp. Worcestershire sauce
1 tsp. dry mustard
¼ cup vinegar or lemon juice
1 (16 oz.) can tomatoes

Marinade:
½ cup vinegar
2 cloves garlic, minced

2 Tbsp. salt
Cold water to cover roast

Combine the marinade ingredients. Allow the roast to stand overnight in the marinade.

Remove the roast and pat it dry. Season with salt, roll in flour and brown in heated oil in skillet. Place in slow cooker appliance. Add remaining ingredients and cover. Cook on high for 2 hours, then turn to low for 8-10 hours.
Serves 8.

Mrs. Mark A. Shelton, III

VENISON STEAKS

Venison steaks sliced ½ inch thick
  (loin or ham cut)
Unseasoned meat tenderizer
Flour

Milk
¼ cup (approximately) oil or
  bacon drippings
Salt

Remove all tissue from the venison. Cut into very small pieces (about the diameter of a cup or even as small as a silver dollar). Sprinkle each steak with tenderizer, pierce with a fork, dip into flour, then milk, then flour again. Fry in iron skillet in oil or drippings until brown. Do not overcook, as they will become tough. Salt after cooking.

Mrs. Jack Hollingsworth

279

VENISONBURGERS

2 lbs. venison, ground	Dash of Tabasco
2 cloves garlic, finely chopped	Butter
1 Tbsp. freshly chopped chives	Oil
2 tsp. salt	Bourbon (optional)
1 tsp. freshly ground black pepper	Red wine

Blend well the venison, garlic, chives, salt, pepper and Tabasco. Form into patties and sauté in half butter and half oil until nicely browned on both sides and still quite rare in the center. Flame with bourbon if desired. Remove to a hot platter and rinse pan with red wine. Pour over the venisonburgers. Serve with baked potatoes and crisp fried onion rings. *Serves 4.*

Mrs. Thomas C. Railsback

These are also delicious served on hamburger buns that have been spread with garlic butter and toasted.

VENISON CHILI

4 large onions, thinly sliced or finely chopped	1 tsp. coriander
	½ tsp. ground cumin
2 cloves garlic, finely chopped	Dash of Tabasco
2 Tbsp. vegetable oil or olive oil	1 cup beer
2 lbs. venison, ground	½ cup tomato paste
2 Tbsp. chili powder	1½ tsp. salt

Sauté the onions and garlic in oil until they are limp and golden. Add the ground venison, stirring until browned. Add the rest of the ingredients and blend. Reduce the heat and simmer for 45 minutes to 1 hour. Taste for seasoning and correct. Add more beer if the mixture gets too dry. Cook until it is well thickened and rich in flavor.

Serve with pinto or kidney beans, and rice.
Serves 6.

Mrs. Thomas C. Railsback

This makes a tasty sauce for frankfurters. Place grilled franks in hot toasted buns and top each frank with a teaspoonful of chili and then a spoonful of chopped raw onion.

THE PINE BLUFF CIVIC CENTER
The Pine Bluff Civic Center, dedicated in ceremonies in 1968, was designed by Edward Durrell Stone. It contains the City Hall, police department headquarters, the central fire station, the public library, and the Southeast Arkansas Arts and Science Center.

SCALLOPED APPLES

6 tart apples
1 cup sugar
½ tsp. nutmeg

¼ tsp. cinnamon
½ cup butter
3 cups bread crumbs

Peel and slice apples. Mix apples, sugar and spices. Melt butter and pour over bread crumbs. Place layer of apples in buttered casserole, then bread crumbs. Alternate layers, ending with crumbs on top. Bake at 350° for 45 minutes.
Serves 6.

Mrs. Charles Scarbrough

These are delicious with pork chops or ham. Can even be served with whipped cream as a dessert.

RED APPLESAUCE

1 large jar applesauce
1 (1-2 oz.) pkg. cinnamon
  red hots

Nutmeg
1 cinnamon stick

Heat applesauce. Add red hots; stir until they melt. Add nutmeg to taste. Cool. Pour applesauce back into original jar and add cinnamon stick. Keep refrigerated.

Mrs. Randy Zook
Little Rock, Arkansas

This is so good with toast for breakfast. Also makes a nice little gift.

SURLE'S HOT FRUIT

1 cup pears, canned
1 cup peaches, canned
1 cup Queen Anne cherries,
  canned
1 cup pineapple chunks,
  canned
3 oranges

½ cup white raisins
¾ cup sugar
½ tsp. salt
3 Tbsp. butter
3 Tbsp. flour
½ cup sherry

Drain all fruit, saving the juices. Slice oranges with peelings on, in rounds, and cook in water until tender. Add the sugar and salt to the drained fruit and mix. Let stand. Make sauce with butter, flour and ¾ cup of fruit juices. Cook until quite thick. Place fruit in shallow 9x14 inch dish. Pour sauce over fruit. Pour sherry over the fruit and let cool. Refrigerate overnight. Heat before serving.

Mrs. Jay Dickey, Jr.

HOT CURRIED FRUIT

1 (16 oz.) can peaches
1 (16 oz.) can pears
1 (16 oz.) can pineapple

1 Tbsp. cornstarch
2 Tbsp. brown sugar
1 tsp. curry powder

Drain fruit, saving juice. To juice add remaining ingredients, stirring until cornstarch dissolves. Cook stirring occasionally, until this begins to thicken. Add fruit and cook until thoroughly heated. Serve hot. You may substitute or add canned fruits of choice to this dish.

Mrs. Frank Milwee
Little Rock, Arkansas

BAKED BANANAS

12 bananas (not too ripe)
Juice of 1 or 2 lemons
6 Tbsp. butter

½ cup brown sugar
Cinnamon

Peel bananas and slice lengthwise. Arrange in shallow, buttered baking dish. Squeeze lemon juice over bananas and dot with butter. Sprinkle brown sugar over bananas and then a tiny bit of cinnamon. Bake at 325° for 30 minutes. May brown under broiler if desired.
Serves 12.

Mrs. Don Lewis
Jackson, Tennessee

BAKED PINEAPPLE

1 (16 oz.) can pineapple
  tidbits
1 cup grated Velveeta
  Cheese

1 cup sugar
2 Tbsp. flour
1 cup croutons
2 Tbsp. butter

Drain pineapple, reserving juice. Mix pineapple with cheese in 8x8 inch casserole. Mix sugar, flour and juice. Heat just enough to blend well. Pour over pineapple and cheese. Melt butter; toss in croutons. Place over mixture in casserole. Bake at 350° for 20-30 minutes.

Mrs. Ray McLaurin
Bastrop, Louisiana

BRANDIED CRANBERRIES

1 lb. fresh cranberries
2 cups sugar

4 Tbsp. brandy
¼ cup sugar

Place berries in a shallow pan. Sprinkle with 2 cups sugar. Bake covered at 350° for 1 hour. Remove from oven and sprinkle with brandy and remaining sugar. Refrigerate.

Mrs. Harold Blach, Jr.
Birmingham, Alabama

FIG PRESERVES

5 cups sugar
½ cup water (approximately)
1 lemon, sliced

1 stick cinnamon
5 cups figs, washed

Put sugar into a kettle, adding just enough water necessary for dissolving. Heat this to boiling. Add lemon and cinnamon. As syrup boils, drop a few figs at a time into kettle. Cook for about 20 minutes, or until fruit takes on a clear, translucent appearance, and the syrup is thick. Pour into a bowl and let preserves stand overnight. Pour into hot sterilized jars and seal. *Yields 3 pints.*

Mrs. E. Russell Lambert, Jr.

When making preserves grease the bottom of the pan to prevent sticking.

MINT JELLY

1½ cups mint leaves, packed
3¼ cups water
Green food coloring

1 box pectin
4 cups sugar
Juice of 1 lemon

Carefully pick and wash fresh mint leaves. Heat to a boil with water; cover and allow to steep for at least 10 minutes. Strain through double cheesecloth; measure 3 cups mint infusion. Add a few drops green food coloring to tint. Add pectin; bring to a boil. Add sugar and lemon juice; bring to a hard rolling boil. Boil for 1 minute, stirring constantly. Remove from heat; skim off foam with metal spoon. Pour at once into hot sterilized jars and seal. *Yields 6½ pints.*

Mrs. T. E. Townsend

HOT PEPPER JELLY

¾ cup ground bell peppers
¼ cup ground hot peppers
1½ cups cider vinegar

6½ cups sugar
Green food coloring
1 (6 oz.) bottle Certo

Combine all ingredients, except Certo, in saucepan and bring to a boil. Continue boiling for 5 minutes, take off heat and add Certo. Pour into sterilized jars and seal. (Note: Wear rubber gloves.)

Mrs. Sorrels DeWoody

Great served over cream cheese with Melba rounds. For a color change, use red bell peppers and red food coloring!

PEPPER HASH

15 green peppers
15 red peppers
15 white onions
6 hot peppers

1 qt. white vinegar
2 cups sugar
3 Tbsp. salt

Remove seeds from peppers. Grind all peppers together with onions. Combine vinegar, sugar and salt in large pot and add vegetables. Boil for 20 minutes. Place in sterilized jars; seal.

Mrs. J. William Sanders

HEYDEN RELISH

1 gal. peeled ripe tomatoes
1 gal. cabbage
1 qt. onions
12 bell peppers
6 hot peppers
1 cup salt, non-iodized
7 cups sugar
2 quarts cider vinegar

2 tsp. cinnamon, ground
2 tsp. ginger, ground
2 tsp. cloves, ground
2 tsp. dry mustard
2 tsp. tumeric
2 tsp. celery seed
1 cup flour

Cut vegetables in small pieces, then measure. Sprinkle with salt, let stand 1 hour, then drain. Add other ingredients except flour and boil 30 minutes. Make a paste of flour and water and add to relish. Cook slowly 10 minutes. Seal in hot, sterilized jars.
Yields 12 pints.

Mrs. Richard Reed, Jr.

PEAR RELISH

4 lbs. pears, chopped fine
6 medium white onions,
   chopped fine
3 cups sugar
8 green bell peppers,
   chopped fine

4 red bell peppers, chopped fine
5 hot peppers, chopped fine
3 cups vinegar
2 Tbsp. salt
1 Tbsp. celery seed
1 Tbsp. mustard seed

Combine all ingredients in large saucepan. Bring to a boil for 30-40 minutes. Stir often. Put into sterilized jars and seal at once.

Mrs. Charles Rowland

ONION RELISH

2 medium onions
Grated rind and juice of
   2 lemons
¼ cup sugar

2 Tbsp. chopped red pepper
2 Tbsp. chopped green pepper
Black pepper, freshly ground

Peel and finely chop onions. Combine with rind and juice of lemons, sugar and chopped peppers. Mix well. Chill at least 1 hour.

Mrs. Robert Nixon

Good with roast beef and Yorkshire Pudding (See Index.)

SQUASH SALAD

4-6 small squash
1/3 cup salt
1 cup purple onion, chopped
   fine
1 cup bell pepper, chopped
   fine

1 (2 oz.) jar pimiento, chopped
1¼ cups sugar
1 cup white vinegar
1 Tbsp. mustard seed

Slice squash into 1½ quarts cold water into which the salt has been added. Refrigerate overnight. Drain. Add onion, bell pepper and pimiento to squash. Boil sugar, vinegar and mustard seed. Pour over vegetables. Refrigerate covered, overnight.

Mrs. George Kyle

PICKLED SQUASH

2 lbs. squash (yellow or summer)
3 medium onions
¼ cup salt
2 cups white vinegar

2 cups sugar
1 tsp. celery seed
1 tsp. tumeric
2 tsp. mustard seed

Wash squash; slice thinly. Peel onions; slice thinly. Cover both in water and add salt. Let stand 1-2 hours. Drain. Bring vinegar and seasonings to a boil and pour over vegetables. Let stand 3-4 minutes. Put on burner and bring to boil, stirring, allowing to boil 4 minutes. Pour into hot sterilized jars and seal.

Mrs. Joe Crabb

PEACH PICKLES

6 lbs. Alberta freestone peaches (not too ripe)
3 lbs. sugar

1 pt. white vinegar
1 stick cinnamon
Few whole cloves

Peel peaches. Combine sugar, vinegar, cinnamon and cloves and bring to a boil. Add peaches and let boil until they just start to get tender. If overcooked they will fall off the seed. Place peaches in sterile jars. Pour hot syrup over peaches and seal.

Mrs. J. W. Johnston
Fulton, Kentucky

PICKLED GREEN TOMATOES

7 lbs. green tomatoes (wash, don't peel)
5 lbs. sugar
3 qts. apple cider vinegar

¼ cup salt (non-iodized)
1 pkg. pickling spice (tied in piece of cloth)
1 sack pickling lime

Soak the washed and sliced tomatoes overnight in a crock of lime water (crock should hold 2 gallons water mixed with 1 sack pickling lime). Stir lime and tomatoes a few times during the night. The next day, pour out lime water and wash tomatoes several times in sink until water is clear of lime. Let soak in clear water several hours.

Make a syrup of the sugar, vinegar, salt and pickling spice bag. Bring to boil and add drained tomatoes. Cook 1½ hours. Pour into 6 hot sterilized pint jars and seal.
Yields 6 pints.

Mrs. Richard Reed, Jr.

GREEN TOMATOES AND MUSTARD PICKLES ·

3 qts. green tomatoes, chopped
½ cup salt
1 cup flour
5 cups sugar
3 Tbsp. dry mustard
2 Tbsp. tumeric
½ gal. white vinegar
1 large head cauliflower, buds separated and split once

2 qts. white onions, finely chopped
1 doz. green bell peppers, chopped
1 doz. hot red peppers, chopped
1 large bunch celery, finely cut
12 large kosher dill pickles

Sprinkle salt over tomatoes and let stand while preparing other ingredients. In a separate pan mix flour, sugar, dry mustard, and tumeric; pour in enough vinegar to make a light paste. Cook to boiling, add balance of vinegar and bring to a rolling boil. Add cauliflower, onions, peppers, and celery and cook until tender. Add tomatoes, cook about 10 minutes, then add chopped pickles and turn off heat. Allow to set about 2 minutes. Fill hot sterilized jars and seal.
Yields 12 pints.

Mrs. Arl V. Moore

For a different and delicious treat at your next party, set this out to be spread on party rye!

BREAD AND BUTTER PICKLES

1 gal. cucumbers, finely sliced
2 green peppers, shredded
8 white onions, thinly sliced
½ cup salt

5 cups vinegar
5 cups sugar
2 Tbsp. mustard seed
1 tsp. celery seed
1½ tsp. tumeric
½ tsp. ground cloves

Pack cucumbers, peppers, onions and salt in ice for 3 hours. Drain. Combine remaining ingredients and pour over pickles. Place over low heat. Stir with wooden spoon until mixture reaches the scalding point. Do not boil. Put in sterilized jars and seal.
Yields 7 pints.

Mrs. Clyde Tracy

QUICK PICKLED BEETS

Pour off half of juice of 16 ounce jar of small whole cooked beets. Add 7 tablespoons sugar, fill rest of jar with vinegar. Shake until sugar dissolves. Refrigerate overnight. This will keep for several weeks in refrigerator.

Mrs. Armistead C. Freeman

MRS. SUVA'S KOSHER DILL PICKLES

Cucumbers
Garlic cloves
Peppers
Dill

Alum
13 cups water
1 cup apple cider vinegar
½ cup salt (non-iodized)

Pack hot sterilized jars with cucumbers, 1 clove garlic, 1 pepper, dill and ⅛ teaspoon alum. Bring water, vinegar and salt to boil and pour over cucumbers, filling jar. *Quickly* seal. Do not open for 6 weeks.

Mrs. Ben Pearson

Cucumbers used for pickles should not be gathered more than 24 hours before pickling.

Mrs. Mark Shelton

BASIC HOT CHILI SAUCE

4 large green bell peppers,
  chopped fine
1 large red bell pepper,
  chopped fine
2 large onions, chopped
  fine
2 Tbsp. Texas chili powder

1/3 cup vegetable oil
3 cups tomato purée
1 cup chicken broth
1 or 2 Tbsp. jalapeno juice
  (optional)
4 or 5 jalapeno peppers,
  chopped fine (optional)

Tenderize peppers and onions in oil, but don't let brown. When onion is clear and peppers tender, add chili powder. Stir constantly for a few minutes. Watch, as it burns quickly. Add tomato purée and chicken broth. Simmer 10 minutes. Add jalapenos, if desired. This is a basic chili sauce—can be used on eggs, meats, etc., and will freeze indefinitely. For cheese dip, add ½ the above sauce to 1-1½ pounds grated Velveeta and let melt. *Yields 1½ quarts.*

Mrs. M. Stanley Cook, Jr.

LOUISIANA SEASONING

1 (26 oz.) box salt
1½ oz. ground pepper
2 oz. ground red pepper

1 oz. garlic powder
1 oz. chili powder
1 oz. Accent

Combine ingredients well. This can be used on salads, meats, chicken, vegetables, fish—anything! Great in tomato juice or sprinkled on cream cheese as an hors d'oeuvre.

Mrs. Scoffield Round
Hammond, Louisiana

THE PINE BLUFF CONVENTION CENTER
The Pine Bluff Convention Center with its 2,000-seat auditorium and arena with a capacity of 7,800, was dedicated on June 27, 1976. This view is from the pecan grove park on the west of the complex.

APPLE SHORTCAKE

Crust:
1 cup sifted flour
6 Tbsp. shortening

¼ tsp. salt
2 Tbsp. ice water

Cut shortening into flour and salt. Add water and form into dough. Roll pie crust thin, cut into squares or circles, prick and bake at 400° for 10 to 15 minutes or until lightly browned.

Apple Mixture:
6 large Rome apples
¾ cup sugar
3 Tbsp. water

1 Tbsp. butter
¼ tsp. cinnamon

Peel and cut apples into cubes. Combine with remaining ingredients and simmer over medium heat until apples are tender. Serve hot between two squares of crust, topped with whipped cream or ice cream. *Serves 6 to 8.*

Mrs. C. D. McSwain
Prescott, Arkansas

Shortcakes also excellent filled with sweetened strawberries.

APRICOT FRIED PIES

Filling:
1 (8 oz.) pkg. dried apricots

½ cup sugar

Crust:
4 cups sifted flour
½ tsp. salt

1 cup shortening
1 cup ice water

Rinse apricots, barely cover with cold water and simmer covered, over low heat until tender. Mash and add sugar. Cool completely.

To make crust, work shortening into flour and salt until crumbly. Gradually add water, working together with fingers. Roll out on a floured board until about ⅛ inch thick. Cut into 3½ inch circles. Roll each circle again, slightly, so edges won't be thick.

Place 1 heaping teaspoon of filling on each circle. Fold circle in half, using ice water to seal edges together. *Be very careful to seal completely.* Fry over medium heat in ½ inch of melted shortening (or enough to cover pies half way). Turn often, being careful not to pierce pastry. When pies are golden brown, remove to paper towels to drain. Shake powdered sugar on all sides while hot.
Yields 36.

Mrs. William Ursery

Variations: Substitute dried apples or dried peaches for the apricots.

EASY CHARLOTTE RUSSE

24 ladyfingers, split
2 Tbsp. unflavored gelatin
2 cups milk
4 cups whipping cream
1½ cups sugar

2 tsp. vanilla
1 cup whipping cream, whipped
Powdered sugar to taste
Chocolate curls

Line a 10-inch springform pan with the ladyfingers. Mix gelatin and milk; heat until the gelatin dissolves. Whip 4 cups cream, gradually adding sugar. Fold in cooled gelatin mixture. Add vanilla. Turn into prepared pan; refrigerate until set. Unmold. Ice with whipped cream sweetened with sugar. Decorate with chocolate curls. Good served with sweetened sliced strawberries.
Serves 10-12.

Mrs. J. William Sanders

APPLE DUMPLINGS WITH SAUCE

Pastry for 2-crust pie
1 (1 lb. 14 oz.) can sliced
  pie apples
Lemon juice

1 cup sugar
¼ cup butter, in chunks
Whipping cream

Place a colander in a large pan. Pour apples into the colander; sprinkle with a little lemon juice. Add sugar and butter. Toss. Set aside. Reserve juice mixture that drips through.

Roll out crust, cut into squares 5x5 inches. Place about 2 tablespoons of apple mixture in the center of each square. Pull all corners up together; pinch tightly. Place dumplings on a cookie sheet, brush each one with a little cream. Bake for 25-30 minutes at 350° until golden brown.

Sauce:
Reserved juice mixture
Fruit juices
1 Tbsp. lemon juice

Cornstarch
Water
2 Tbsp. butter

To reserved juice mixture, add any fruit juices you may have (pineapple, pear, etc.) to make about 1 cup. Add lemon juice; boil. Mix a little cornstarch and water together to make a thin paste, add to juices. Cook until no longer starchy tasting. Remove from heat. Stir in butter. Pour over dumplings. Serve with whipped cream.

Mrs. Ruby McClinton
Pine Bluff Country Club

MARQUISE de CHOCOLAT

1 1/3 cups semisweet chocolate
pieces
1 cup unsalted butter
3 Tbsp. superfine sugar
6 eggs, separated

1 Tbsp. superfine sugar
2 Tbsp. Grand Marnier
Liqueur
Finely shaved chocolate or
crushed macaroons

Combine chocolate pieces, butter and 3 tablespoons sugar; place over low heat until chocolate melts. Beat egg yolks slightly; slowly add the chocolate mixture and beat on high speed of an electric mixer for 10 minutes. Beat egg whites until stiff; add 1 tablespoon sugar. Add stiffly beaten egg whites to the chocolate mixture; add Grand Marnier and beat on high speed another 10 minutes. Pour into a buttered 2-quart soufflé dish; refrigerate at least 12 hours. Unmold 2 hours before serving by dipping the bottom and sides of the dish in hot water; run a knife around the sides of the mold to loosen. Invert the mold onto a serving plate; smooth the surface with a knife. Decorate with shaved chocolate or crushed macaroons. Refrigerate until serving time.
Serves 12.

Mrs. James S. Rogers

Sinfully delicious!

Use your blender to make regular sugar into superfine sugar.

FRESH COCONUT BAVARIAN

1½ Tbsp. gelatin
¼ cup cold water
1 cup milk
1 cup sugar

2 cups whipping cream, whipped
2 cups grated fresh coconut
1 tsp. vanilla
⅛ tsp. salt

Soften gelatin in cold water; set aside. Scald milk, add sugar; add softened gelatin. Combine the remaining ingredients; carefully fold both mixtures together. Pour into a large ring mold; refrigerate until firm.

Sauce:
1 cup brown sugar, packed
1 cup sugar
1 Tbsp. flour

1 Tbsp. butter
1 1/3 cups milk

Combine sugars and flour; add butter and milk. Bring to a boil. Serve hot over the Bavarian. May be made well ahead and reheated.
Serves 10-12.

Mrs. Robert Smith

Served at 1974 Charity Ball Royal Supper

CHOCOLATE CHIFFON DESSERT

1 Tbsp. unflavored gelatin
1/3 cup cold water
2 (1 oz.) sqs. bitter
  chocolate
½ cup boiling water
½ cup sugar

3 egg yolks, beaten
3 egg whites
½ cup sugar
Angel food cake
Whipped cream

Soften gelatin in cold water. Melt chocolate in boiling water, add ½ cup sugar and egg yolks. Cook until thick. Cool. Beat egg whites with ½ cup sugar until stiff; fold into chocolate mixture. Remove crust from cake, tear into pieces. Layer cake and filling. Refrigerate. Serve with whipped cream. Serves 8.

Mrs. W. Hampton Hall

Can substitute 1 tablespoon cocoa plus ½ teaspoon shortening for 1 square unsweetened chocolate (1 ounce).

EASY POTS de CREME

1 (6 oz.) pkg. semisweet
  chocolate pieces
2 Tbsp. sugar
Pinch of salt
1 egg
1 tsp. vanilla

1½ tsp. dark rum or 1 tsp. instant
  coffee
¾ cup scalded milk
Whipped cream
Candied orange rind (optional)

Place first 6 ingredients in blender. Heat milk to boiling; pour into blender over other ingredients. Cover and blend one minute. Pour into pot de creme cups, demitasse cups, or sherbet glasses. Chill several hours. Top with whipped cream and decorate with candied orange rind.
Serves 4.

Mrs. John Temple

MOTHER'S BOILED CUSTARD

4 egg yolks
½ cup sugar (scant)
2 heaping Tbsp. flour

1 qt. milk, scalded
1 tsp. vanilla

Beat yolks, sugar and flour; add 1 cup of the hot milk and mix well. Add the remaining milk and stir constantly over medium heat until thickened. Refrigerate.
Serves 6-8.

Mrs. Richard Smart

FRENCH BAKED CUSTARD WITH CARAMEL

Custard:

3 eggs	1 tsp. vanilla
2 egg yolks	1 cup milk
½ cup sugar	1 cup whipping cream

Mix eggs and sugar with wire whisk only until well blended, not bubbly. Add vanilla. Scald milk and cream in a saucepan slowly. Pour in a steady trickle on the egg mixture, stirring with whisk the entire time. Pour custard through a strainer lined with cheesecloth. Put aside.

Caramel:

2 cups sugar	½ cup cold water (scant)
½ tsp. cream of tartar	

Over a slow fire, stir sugar, cream of tartar and water with a metal spoon until the sugar dissolves. Place a large bowl of cold water nearby. Allow sugar and water to boil (10 or 15 minutes) until it becomes a lovely amber color. Watch carefully because it will darken and burn quickly. Turn off heat and allow bubbles to subside. Set saucepan in the bowl of cold water to stop cooking. Immediately pour caramel into 4 individual soufflé dishes or one large one. If using large one, tilt bowl around to coat sides as well as bottom.

Pour custard over caramel. Place bowls in a shallow pan ½ filled with hot water. Place in preheated 325° oven. Individual molds should bake for 50 minutes or until silver knife comes out clean. Large mold should bake 1¼ to 1½ hours. Allow custard to cool first at room temperature. Run a knife around inside of mold. Unmold on plate, by placing plate on top of mold and reversing it very quickly. Refrigerate either in mold or on plate. Serves 4.

Mrs. Edward E. Brown

MISS BESS'S EGGNOG PUDDING DESSERT

1 Tbsp. gelatin	¼ cup bourbon whiskey
2 Tbsp. cold water	2 cups whipping cream, whipped
¼ cup milk	12 ladyfingers, split
2 eggs, separated	Chopped nuts
½ cup sugar	

Soak gelatin in cold water. Boil milk and pour over softened gelatin. Beat egg whites until very stiff. Beat egg yolks; add sugar and whiskey; beat to blend. Add softened gelatin and egg whites. Fold in half the whipped cream. Pour the pudding into a bowl lined with 6 of the ladyfingers. Top with remaining ladyfingers. Chill until set. Turn out onto serving plate, ice with remaining whipped cream and sprinkle with nuts.

Mrs. C. H. Triplett

APRICOT DESSERT CREPES

Crepes:
4 eggs
½ cup milk
½ cup water
2 Tbsp. cognac
2 Tbsp. butter, melted

1 cup flour
¾ tsp. salt
1 tsp. vanilla
2 Tbsp. sugar

Mix all ingredients in an electric blender until smooth. Allow to stand at room temperature for 30 minutes to 1 hour. Use 2 tablespoons batter for each crepe; cook in a lightly oiled 6-inch skillet until pale brown on each side. Enough batter for 20-22 crepes. These freeze well.

Filling:
4 (3 oz.) pkgs. cream cheese
1½ cups sour cream

½ cup apricot preserves

Soften cream cheese at room temperature; mix with remaining ingredients. Fill each crepe with 2-3 tablespoons of this mixture.

Sauce:
½ cup butter
½ - ¾ cup apricot brandy,
    warmed

½ cup apricot preserves

Melt butter and preserves in chafing dish. Pour in warmed brandy; ignite and allow excess alcohol to burn off. Serve warm over crepes.
Serves 10.

Mrs. Robert Ellzey
El Dorado, Arkansas

CREME BRULEE

3 cups whipping cream
6 egg yolks
1/3 cup sugar

1 tsp. vanilla
1/3 cup brown sugar, packed
Fruit (optional)

Heat cream in top of double boiler over simmering water until bubbles appear around the edge. Beat egg yolks and sugar with wire whisk until blended. Pour scalded cream over egg mixture, stirring constantly. Return mixture to top of double boiler; cook over simmering water until mixture coats the back of a spoon. (Do not overcook or the custard may curdle.) Remove from heat; stir in vanilla. Pour into 1½ quart soufflé dish; refrigerate overnight. One to three hours before serving, preheat broiler and sift brown sugar over custard; broil until sugar is melted and bubbly. Chill. This is also good served over fruit.
Serves 8-10.

Mrs. Frank Roland
Hanover, New Hampshire

CREPES au MOCHA

Crepes:

1 cup flour	1½ Tbsp. instant coffee
1½ Tbsp. sugar	2 eggs, beaten
Pinch of salt	1 1/3 cups milk
1½ Tbsp. cocoa	2 Tbsp. melted butter

Sift together flour, sugar, salt, cocoa and coffee; add eggs. Stir in the milk and melted butter until smooth. Strain through a fine sieve and let batter stand for at least 2 hours. Batter should be as thin as cream.

For each crepe, melt a bit of butter in a small skillet (6 to 8 inches in diameter) and add 2 to 3 tablespoons batter. Swirl pan to coat entire bottom; cook about 1 minute on each side. Makes about 24 crepes. Fill with the following:

Rum Cream Filling:

2 cups whipping cream	¼ cup light rum
¼ cup sugar	

Whip cream; gradually add sugar. Fold in rum. Fill each crepe and roll up. (May be done ahead, covered tightly and refrigerated.) Top with Hot Fudge Sauce (See Index).

Mrs. John G. Lile

Served at the 1975 Charity Ball Royal Supper.

FROZEN CREAM CUPS

1 (8 oz.) pkg. cream cheese	1 tsp. vanilla
1 cup sifted powdered sugar	Fresh fruit
2 cups whipping cream	

Beat softened cream cheese until smooth; blend in powdered sugar, then whipping cream and vanilla. Pour into 8 paper-lined muffin tins and freeze. Remove paper liners; spoon fresh fruit on top of each cream. *Serves 8.*

Mrs. Ronald D. Blankenship

COFFEE ANGEL CAKE

1 angel food loaf cake	2 cups whipping cream
1 small pkg. chocolate instant pudding mix	2 tsp. instant coffee

Slice cake lengthwise into 3 layers. Beat cream and pudding mix together until almost stiff; add instant coffee. Continue to beat until stiff. Spread coffee mixture between layers and on top and sides of cake.

Mrs. Simon Joseph

TIPS ON STEAMED PUDDINGS

1. Always grease mold well.
2. Never fill mold more than two-thirds full.
3. If you do not have a regular pudding mold with a clamp-on lid, you may use coffee cans, deep custard cups for individual molds, or a deep salad mold with a smooth rim. To make a lid for these containers, crimp a double layer of foil around the top as tightly as possible and secure with a string or rubber band.
4. Set mold on a rack in a deep kettle that has a tight lid.
5. Fill the kettle with boiling water up to two-thirds the height of the mold. Reduce to a low boil and maintain.
6. To test for doneness, remove mold, unclamp lid, let stand for 5 minutes and unmold. If the mold resists, cook 1 hour longer.
7. To flame puddings for a more festive touch, warm ¼ cup brandy, pour over warm pudding and flame.
8. Puddings can be made ahead, cooled after cooking, wrapped in foil and refrigerated or frozen. To serve, return the pudding to the mold and resteam 1 or 2 hours.

PLUM PUDDING

2 cups raisins
½ cup finely chopped citron
Grated rind of 1 orange
Grated rind of 1 lemon
½ cup sliced candied cherries
¼ cup chopped pitted dates
1 apple, peeled and chopped
1 cup orange marmalade
¼ cup orange juice
¼ cup brandy
3 eggs
½ cup sugar

1 cup molasses
1½ cups fine dry bread
  crumbs
¼ lb. ground suet
1 cup flour
1 tsp. salt
¼ tsp. baking soda
1 tsp. baking powder
1 tsp. cinnamon
½ tsp. allspice
½ tsp. ground cloves

Combine the first 10 ingredients; let stand overnight. Beat eggs until very light; add sugar and molasses gradually. Add bread crumbs, suet and soaked fruit mixture. Sift flour, salt, baking soda, baking powder, and spices together; stir into the pudding mixture. Turn into 2 greased 1-quart pudding molds; cover tightly and steam 8 hours (or until firm) on a rack in boiling water. Remove. Let stand 5 minutes, unmold. Serve with Hard Sauce or Brandy Hard Sauce (See Index). May be frozen after steaming and cooling; thaw and steam 1½ hours.
Serves 16.

Mrs. John G. Lile

STEAMED GINGER PUDDING

2¼ cups flour
½ tsp. salt
1 tsp. baking soda
1/3 cup shortening
½ cup sugar

3 eggs, well beaten
¾ cup milk
¾ cup dark molasses
1/3 cup chopped
    crystallized ginger

Sift flour, salt and soda together. Cream shortening and sugar until light and fluffy. Stir in eggs. Add dry ingredients alternately with milk; stir well after each addition. Add molasses and ginger. Pour into well-greased 2½ quart pudding mold; cover tightly. Place mold on rack in a deep kettle; fill to half the height of the mold with hot water. Cover; bring to a boil. Boil gently for about 2 hours, adding boiling water if necessary. Remove, uncover and allow to stand for 5 minutes. Loosen and unmold. Serve with Lemon Sauce or Peach Sauce (See Index).
Serves 8.

Mrs. John G. Lile

SOUTHERN PEACH COBBLER

¾ cup shortening
2 cups sifted flour
½ tsp. salt
1 Tbsp. sugar

Ice water
8-10 fresh peaches
¼ cup butter
½ cup sugar plus 2 Tbsp.

Cut shortening into flour, salt and 1 tablespoon sugar with pastry blender. Add just enough ice water to hold dough together. Roll out on floured board to about ⅛ inch thick. Line the sides and bottom of a 2-2½ quart baking dish with crust; flute edges of sides. Cut remaining dough into 1x1½ inch pieces; set aside.

Peel and slice peaches. Put a layer of peaches in pastry-lined baking dish. Dot with 2 tablespoons butter and ¼ cup sugar; top with one half the reserved pastry pieces. Make another layer of peaches, butter and sugar, ending with pastry pieces; sprinkle with 2 tablespoons sugar. Bake at 325° for about 1 hour, or until dough is done and slightly browned at edges and top. Great served plain, or with a pitcher of thick cream.
Serves 8-10.

Mrs. Ernest A. Hercher

PEACHES ROYALE

6 medium peaches (1½ lbs.)
1 cup sugar
1 cup water
3 Tbsp. brandy

1½ tsp. vanilla
½ cup sour cream
2 Tbsp. powdered sugar
1 Tbsp. brandy

Blanch and peel peaches; pit and cut into quarters. Combine peaches, sugar and water; bring to a boil, simmer 1 minute. Stir in 3 tablespoons brandy and vanilla. Let stand until fruit reaches room temperature, then chill. Arrange peaches on 6 dessert plates. Combine sour cream, powdered sugar and 1 tablespoon brandy; spoon over fruit.
Serves 6.

Mrs. James S. Rogers

Wonderful for company—easy enough for family.

> Leave a lemon in the brown-sugar jar, to keep the sugar soft. Keep lid on tightly, too.

RASPBERRY DELIGHT

2 (10 oz.) pkgs. frozen red
  raspberries, in syrup
1 cup water
½ cup sugar
2 tsp. lemon juice
4 Tbsp. cornstarch
¼ cup cold water

50-60 large marshmallows
1 cup milk
2 cups whipping cream
1¼ cups graham cracker crumbs
¼ cup chopped pecans
¼ cup melted butter

Heat raspberries, 1 cup water, sugar and lemon juice. Dissolve cornstarch in ¼ cup cold water; stir into raspberry mixture. Cook until thickened and clear; cool. Melt marshmallows in milk over hot water; cool. Whip cream. Fold into marshmallow mixture.

Mix crumbs, nuts and butter. Press firmly into a 9x13 inch pan. Spread marshmallow mixture over crumb mixture. Top with raspberry mixture. Refrigerate until firm.

Mrs. Glenn A. Railsback, III

MOTHER'S FAMOUS "LITTLE FELLOWS"

Pastry for 2-crust pie
¾ cup butter
2 cups sugar

1 Tbsp. flour
4-5 egg yolks
Juice and rind of 2 lemons

Line miniature muffin tins with pastry. Mix remaining ingredients; put approximately 1 teaspoon mixture into each tart. Bake at 350° for 15 minutes. Best when fresh!
Yields 60.

Mrs. James T. McFall

POACHED PEARS WITH CUSTARD SAUCE

6 pears, slightly under ripe
Water with lemon juice
4 cups water
2 cups sugar
1 Tbsp. lemon juice

1 tsp. grated lemon rind
1 cinnamon stick
3 whole cloves
Custard sauce

Peel pears, leaving stems. Drop immediately into cold water with a little lemon juice added to keep them from darkening. Boil 4 cups water, sugar, 1 tablespoon lemon juice and grated rind. Add pears, cinnamon and cloves; cover and keep syrup at rolling boil to keep pears cooking evenly. Cook 20-30 minutes until tender (easily pierced with a fork and slightly translucent). Carefully transfer pears to a shallow, flat dish; stand upright, trimming bottoms if necessary. Drizzle a little syrup over the pears, cool, cover and refrigerate several hours. At serving time, place each pear on a crystal plate; top generously with custard sauce.

Custard Sauce:
6 Tbsp. sugar
4 egg yolks
1 tsp. cornstarch

1½ cups whipping cream
2 tsp. vanilla

Gradually beat sugar into yolks and continue beating for about 3 minutes until the mixture is pale yellow, creamy and forms a ribbon. (When mixture is lifted on the beater, it will fall back into the bowl forming a slowly dissolving ribbon on the surface.) Beat in cornstarch. Heat cream just to boiling. While beating yolk mixture, add hot cream in a *very thin* stream so that yolks are *slowly* warmed. Cook over *very low* heat, stirring constantly, until thick and coats the back of a spoon. Do not allow to boil. Remove from heat, beat 1-2 minutes to cool, add vanilla. Cool, cover and refrigerate.
Serves 6.

Mrs. R. Teryl Brooks, Jr.

This is an elegant and light dessert!

FROZEN MARDI GRAS CAKE

20 ladyfingers, split
1 (6 oz.) can frozen
    orange juice, undiluted
½ gal. vanilla ice cream
1 (10 oz.) pkg. frozen
    strawberries

1 (8¼ oz.) can crushed
    pineapple, drained
12 maraschino cherries
½ cup chopped pecans
¼ cup powdered sugar
1 cup whipping cream

Line the bottom and sides of a 10-inch spring form pan with ladyfingers. Mix orange juice and half the ice cream; pack into prepared pan; freeze. Mix strawberries and pineapple; spread over ice cream layer and freeze. Chop cherries, blend with nuts and remaining ice cream. Mix and spread over fruit layer; freeze. Add sugar to cream, whip and then spread over top; freeze. About ½ hour before serving, remove from freezer and unmold. Serves 16-20.

Mrs. Stephen A. Matthews

Makes a lovely luncheon dessert.

MINCEMEAT ICE CREAM DESSERT

12 ladyfingers, split
1 (28 oz.) jar mincemeat
½ gal. vanilla ice cream,
    softened

3 Tbsp. rum
1 tsp. vanilla
1 cup whipping cream, whipped

Line the sides of a 9-inch springform pan with ladyfingers. Mix mincemeat, ice cream, rum and vanilla. Do not let get softer than necessary. Turn into prepared pan. Top with whipped cream; cover with foil and freeze. Unmold and slice. Serves 12.

Mrs. C. D. Allison, Jr.

TORTONI ICE CREAM DESSERT

1½ cups crushed macaroons
1½ cups whipping cream
½ cup powdered sugar, sifted
Pinch of salt

2 cups whipping cream
2 tsp. vanilla
Maraschino cherries
Unsalted almonds, toasted

Mix macaroons, 1½ cups cream, sugar and salt together; set aside for 1 hour. Whip 2 cups cream and vanilla until thickened but not stiff. Fold the two mixtures together; turn into 8 paper-lined muffin tins. Freeze partially; decorate with cherries and almonds and return to freezer. Serves 8.

Mrs. Robert Cloar
Fort Smith, Arkansas

FLAKY PASTRY FOR A 2-CRUST PIE

2 cups sifted flour   ¾ cup shortening
1 tsp. salt   4-5 Tbsp. ice water

Sift flour; measure. Sift flour with salt into a medium bowl. With a pastry blender, or 2 knives, using a short cutting motion, cut in shortening until mixture resembles coarse cornmeal. Quickly sprinkle ice water 1 tablespoon at a time over all pastry mixture. Toss lightly with a fork after each addition and push dampened portion to side of bowl; sprinkle only dry portion remaining. Pastry should be just moist enough to hold together, not sticky. Bake unfilled pie shell at 425° for 12-15 minutes or until lightly browned.

Mrs. Cortez Washington
Cateress

OLE TIME LIGHT AND FLAKY PIE CRUST

3 cups unsifted flour   3-4 Tbsp. ice water
1 tsp. salt   for each crust
1¼ cups shortening

Mix flour and salt. Cut in shortening until mealy. (This mixture may be kept in a covered container in the refrigerator until needed.) For each crust, take about one cup of the mixture and toss it with 3-4 tablespoons ice water. Handle as little as possible and work the dough rapidly.
Yields 3-5 crusts.

Mrs. Doris Pendleton

So convenient to have basic mixture on hand and use just enough for 1 pie each time!

VINEGAR PIE CRUST

1 tsp. white vinegar   1 tsp. salt
1 egg, beaten   1 cup plus 2 Tbsp. shortening
7 Tbsp. water   3 cups flour

Blend vinegar and beaten egg; add water and salt. Cut shortening into flour with pastry blender. Combine the two mixtures. Chill, if possible, before rolling out. Bake unfilled pie shell at 425° for 12-15 minutes.
Yields 3 (9-inch) crusts.

Mrs. Simpson Bush

You will not believe how easily this handles.

GRETA'S COCONUT PIE

1 10-inch or 2
   8-inch pie shells, baked
1 Tbsp. gelatin
¼ cup cold water
3 eggs, separated
½ cup sugar
½ tsp. salt

1 cup evaporated milk, scalded
1 tsp. vanilla
⅛ tsp. cream of tartar
¼ cup sugar
Whipped cream, sweetened
   to taste
Toasted coconut

Soften gelatin in cold water. Beat egg yolks with ½ cup sugar and salt; add to scalded milk. Cook until slightly thickened (do not overcook); add softened gelatin and vanilla. Blend. Cool until the consistency of unbeaten egg whites. Beat egg whites until frothy, add cream of tartar; beat to soft peaks, gradually adding ¼ cup sugar. Fold meringue into cooled custard mixture. Pour into baked shell; chill until set. Top with a layer of sweetened whipped cream and sprinkle with toasted coconut. *Serves 8-10.*

Mrs. James Stobaugh

Variations: Substitute fresh strawberries, slivered semisweet chocolate or freshly grated nutmeg for coconut.

> *Use pinking·shears, dipped in flour, to cut lattice strips for fruit pies.*

RICH CHESS PIE

1 8-inch unbaked pie shell
3 large eggs
1½ cups sugar
1 Tbsp. cornmeal

1 Tbsp. vinegar
½ cup butter, melted
1 Tbsp. vanilla

Beat eggs with fork until light; add sugar, cornmeal, and vinegar. Stir to mix well, but do not beat. Add cooled butter and vanilla; stir to mix well. Pour into pie shell. Bake at 350° for 60 to 65 minutes. *Serves 6.*

Mrs. C. B. Hall
Wynne, Arkansas

LEMON CHESS PIE

1 9-inch pie shell, unbaked
4 eggs, slightly beaten
2 cups sugar
½ tsp. salt

Juice of 2 lemons
Grated rind of 2 lemons
5 Tbsp. melted butter

Mix ingredients together and pour into unbaked pie shell. Bake at 350° for 45 minutes until mixture is firm and brown on top. *Serves 6-8.*

Mrs. Charles Scarbrough

CHOCOLATE MERINGUE PIE

1 9-inch pie shell, baked
1/3 cup sifted flour
1 cup sugar
¼ tsp. salt
2 (1 oz.) sqs. unsweetened
  chocolate

2 cups milk
3 egg yolks, beaten
2 Tbsp. butter
½ tsp. vanilla
3 egg whites
6 Tbsp. sugar

Mix flour, sugar and salt. Melt chocolate in milk, heating until milk is scalded. Gradually add to flour mixture. Cook over moderate heat, stirring constantly, until mixture thickens and boils. Cook 2 minutes; remove from heat. Add small amount to egg yolks; then add yolks to chocolate mixture. Cook 1 minute, stirring constantly. Add butter and vanilla; cool slightly. Pour into baked shell and cool. Beat egg whites stiff, gradually adding sugar. Cover top of pie, sealing to edges. Bake at 350° for 12-15 minutes until meringue is browned.
Serves 6-8.

Mrs. J. C. Welch

INSTANT CHOCOLATE PIE

1 8-inch pie shell, baked
1 (4½ oz.) pkg. instant
  chocolate pudding mix
1 cup milk

2 cups non dairy
  whipped topping
¼ cup chopped pecans
Chopped pecans

Prepare pudding mix according to directions, using only 1 cup milk. Blend in 1½ cups whipped topping and ¼ cup pecans. Spoon into baked pie shell. Decorate with remaining ½ cup whipped topping and additional nuts. Chill at least 1 hour.
Serves 6.

Mrs. Paul Johnston
Jonesboro, Arkansas

HOT FUDGE PIE

3 (1 oz.) sqs. bitter chocolate
½ cup margarine
1¼ cups sugar
¼ cup flour

Pinch of salt
¼ tsp. vanilla
3 large eggs
Ice cream

Melt chocolate and margarine together in the top of a double boiler; beat in sugar. Fold in flour and salt. Add vanilla. Beat eggs; fold into mixture. Turn into a greased 9-inch pie pan. Bake at 350° for 20-30 minutes. Do not overcook. Top each slice with ice cream while still warm. May be reheated.
Serves 6.

Mrs. David K. Gunti

CRANBERRY-RAISIN PIE

Pastry for 2-crust pie
1½ cups cranberries, halved
¾ cup raisins

1½ cups sugar
2 Tbsp. flour
2 Tbsp. water
¼ cup butter

Combine all ingredients except butter. Turn into unbaked pie shell; dot with butter. Top with latticed strips. Bake at 350° until bubbly and pastry is slightly browned.
Serves 6-8.

Mrs. Frank Gilbert
Prescott, Arkansas

GRANDMOTHER'S PECAN PIE

1 8-inch pie shell, unbaked
1 cup sugar
1 cup dark Karo
3 eggs, well beaten

2 Tbsp. butter
1 tsp. vanilla
Heaping cup pecans

Boil sugar and Karo until thick. Pour over eggs, beating constantly. Add butter and vanilla. Place pecans in shell; cover with egg mixture. Bake at 425° for 10 minutes; reduce heat to 350° and bake 30 minutes longer.
Serves 6-8.

Mrs. M. J. Probst

SHERRY PIE

Crust:
1 cup flour
¼ cup brown sugar

½ cup chopped pecans
½ cup butter

Mix all ingredients with pastry blender; crumble into a 9-inch pie pan. Bake at 375° for 25 to 30 minutes, stirring every 10 minutes. Remove from oven; shape mixture into a crust in pie pan, reserving a few crumbs. Let cool.

Filling:
½ cup sherry
½ lb. marshmallows

1 cup whipping cream, whipped

Melt marshmallows in sherry in top of double boiler. Cool. Fold into whipped cream. Turn into cooled crust; top with reserved crumbs.
Serves 6-8.

Mrs. Royce O. Johnson

Even better the next day!

DATE NUT PIE

1 cup vanilla wafer crumbs
1 tsp. baking powder
¼ tsp. salt
3 egg whites
1 cup sugar

1 cup chopped dates
1 cup chopped nuts
1 tsp. vanilla
1 cup whipping cream, whipped

Combine crumbs, baking powder and salt. Beat egg whites with sugar until stiff; fold into crumb mixture. Fold in dates, nuts and vanilla. Turn into a greased 9-inch pie plate. Bake at 350° for 25-30 minutes. Cool. Serve topped with whipped cream.
Serves 6-8.

Mrs. Larry Joerdan
Georgetown, South Carolina

PUMPKIN PIE

1 9-inch pie shell, unbaked
1 cup canned pumpkin
1 cup sugar
1 cup milk
½ tsp. ginger
½ tsp. cloves

½ tsp. cinnamon
½ tsp. nutmeg
1 egg, beaten
1 Tbsp. flour
¼ tsp. salt
Whipped cream (optional)

Combine ingredients. Pour into pie shell. Bake at 500° for 10 minutes. Reduce heat to 300°, bake 1 hour longer. Serve with a dollop of cream, if desired.
Serves 6-8.

Mrs. William H. Roberts

SWEET POTATO PIE

2 cups cooked, mashed
    sweet potatoes
½ cup butter, softened
2 egg yolks
1 cup brown sugar
¼ tsp. salt
½ tsp. cinnamon

½ tsp. nutmeg
½ tsp. ginger
½ cup milk
2 egg whites
¼ cup sugar
1 9-inch pie shell, unbaked

Mix the first 8 ingredients together while potatoes are still warm. Add milk. Beat egg whites until stiff, gradually adding sugar. Fold into potato mixture and pour into unbaked pie shell. Bake at 400° for 10 minutes, then lower temperature to 350° and bake until set.
Serves 6-8.

Mrs. Martin G. Gilbert

BAKED ALASKA PIE

Crust:
2 cups Baker's Angel   ¼ cup melted butter
  Flake Coconut

Mix coconut and melted butter. Press into an 8 or 9-inch pie pan. Bake at 300° about 30 to 35 minutes or until golden brown.

Filling:
8 large marshmallows   1 tsp. vanilla
1 (4 oz.) pkg. German's   2-3 pts. vanilla
  Sweet Chocolate   ice cream
¾ cup evaporated milk

Melt marshmallows and chocolate in evaporated milk over hot water. Remove from heat; add vanilla. Cool. Pack ice cream into crust, rippling with chocolate sauce. Freeze until *very* firm.

Topping:
3 egg whites   6 Tbsp. sugar
⅛ tsp. salt   2/3 cup coconut

Beat egg whites and salt until foamy. Gradually beat in sugar. Beat until meringue stands in peaks; spread over filling, sealing crust. Sprinkle meringue with coconut. Place pie on a wooden board (this is necessary), bake at 500° about 1 to 2 minutes or until brown.
Serves 6-8.

Mrs. Frank Lyon
Little Rock, Arkansas

PAPA PERDUE'S FAVORITE ANGEL PIE

Meringue Shell:
2 egg whites   ½ cup sugar
⅛ tsp. salt   ½ tsp. vanilla
⅛ tsp. cream of tartar   ½ cup chopped pecans or walnuts

Beat egg whites, salt and cream of tartar until foamy. Add sugar, 2 tablespoons at a time, and continue to beat until stiff peaks form. Fold in vanilla and nuts. Spoon into a lightly greased 8-inch pie pan; build up sides ½ inch above edge of pan. Bake at 275° for 55 minutes. Cool.

Filling:
1 (4 oz.) pkg. German's   1 tsp. vanilla
  Sweet Chocolate   1 cup whipping cream, whipped
3 Tbsp. water

Melt chocolate in water over low heat. Cool; add vanilla. Fold in whipped cream. Pile into meringue shell. Chill 2 hours.
Serves 6-8.

Miss Marie A. Ferrara

COFFEE ICE CREAM PIE

1 9-inch graham cracker
crust, baked
1 (11 oz.) jar fudge
topping

1 (3½ oz.) pkg. almonds, toasted
1-2 qts. coffee ice cream
Shaved chocolate

Spread topping over bottom of crust; sprinkle with the almonds. Pack softened ice cream over almonds and decorate with shaved chocolate; freeze.
Serves 6-8.

Mrs. Paul Lewey

PEANUT BUTTER ICE CREAM PIE

Crust:
1½ cups graham cracker crumbs
1 Tbsp. sugar

1/3 cup margarine, melted

Mix crumbs, sugar and margarine; press into a 9-inch pie pan. Chill.

Filling:
1 quart vanilla ice cream
½ cup crunchy peanut butter

¼ cup whipping cream,
whipped

Beat ice cream and peanut butter until soft. Fold in whipped cream. Turn into above crust; freeze until firm.
Serves 6-8.

Mrs. Ruby McClinton
Pine Bluff Country Club

PEPPERMINT PIE WITH RICE KRISPIES CRUST

Crust:
1 (4 oz.) bar German's Sweet
Chocolate

4 Tbsp. margarine
3 cups Rice Krispies

Break chocolate into pieces; add margarine; stir until melted. Take off fire and add Rice Krispies. Mix well and press in bottom and sides of a 10-inch pie pan. Refrigerate.

Filling:
½ gal. vanilla ice cream,
softened

¾ cup crushed peppermint
candy

Break candy into very small pieces; stir into softened ice cream. Put filling in crust and freeze until firm, 3-4 hours.
Serves 8.

Mrs. Ruby McClinton
Pine Bluff Country Club

FRESH APPLE CAKE

1½ cups vegetable oil
2 cups sugar
3 eggs
3 cups flour
1½ tsp. soda

½ tsp. salt
1 cup chopped pecans
1 tsp. vanilla
4 medium Delicious apples,
   peeled and cut in cubes

Mix oil and sugar. Add eggs one at a time and beat well. Save ¼ cup flour and mix with pecans. Mix together remaining flour, soda and salt; gradually add to sugar mixture. Add floured pecans and vanilla; fold in apples. Bake in greased and floured tube pan at 300° for 1 hour and 20 minutes. Test for doneness before removing from oven.
Serves 12-14.

Mrs. Paul Lewey

ARMENIAN CAKE

1 cup butter
2 cups brown sugar, packed
2 cups flour
1 tsp. soda

1 cup sour cream
1 egg, well-beaten
1 tsp. cinnamon
1 tsp. nutmeg

Mix first 3 ingredients together until crumbly. Place ½ of mixture in a greased 8-inch square pan. Pat down gently. Mix together soda and sour cream and add to remaining flour mixture along with egg and spices. Beat well and pour into pan. Bake at 350° for 40 minutes or until done. Top with lemon sauce or whipped cream.
Serves 9.

Mrs. Joe Campbell
Mena, Arkansas

Great for brunch or coffee.

Keep cake from sticking to pan by wrapping a towel dipped in hot water around the pan when it is removed from oven.

• • •

Sprinkle cake plate with powdered sugar to keep cake from sticking.

• • •

When rolling out sugar cookies, add a little granulated sugar to the flour on your pastry board. This keeps cookies from sticking to the board.

BANANA NUT CAKE

1 box yellow cake mix
2 eggs
1 cup milk

1/3 cup oil
1 (4¾ oz.) jar strained bananas
1 cup chopped pecans

Combine first 5 ingredients and beat until batter is smooth. Mix in nuts. Pour into 2 well-greased and floured 8-inch round cake pans. Bake at 350° for 30 to 40 minutes or until done.

Banana Icing:
¾ cup butter
1 (16 oz.) box powdered sugar
1 (4¾ oz.) jar strained bananas

1 tsp. vanilla
½ cup chopped pecans

Cream butter and sugar. Add bananas and vanilla; then add nuts. Ice cooled cake layers.
Serves 10-12.

Mrs. William A. Roberts

WORLD'S BEST CHOCOLATE CAKE

¾ cup shortening
½ cup sour cream
2 cups sugar
2 eggs
2 cups sifted flour

1 tsp. soda
½ tsp. salt
3 Tbsp. cocoa
1 cup boiling water
1 tsp. vanilla

Cream together shortening, sour cream and sugar. Add eggs one at a time, beating well after each. Sift together flour, soda, salt and cocoa 4 times. Add gradually to egg mixture, beating well. Add water and vanilla; mix well. Grease, flour and line cake pans with wax paper. Bake on bottom rack in two 9-inch cake pans at 350° for 30-35 minutes; or bake in one 9x13x2 inch pan for 40-45 minutes.

Fudge Frosting:
1½ cups sugar
¼ cup butter
1 Tbsp. light corn syrup
2 Tbsp. cocoa

7 Tbsp. milk
¼ tsp. salt
2 tsp. vanilla

Combine all the above ingredients except vanilla in sauce pan. Bring to a full, rolling boil over medium heat, stirring constantly. Boil briskly one minute. Add vanilla and beat until thick enough to spread over cake. This will ice one sheet cake; double recipe for a layer cake.
Serves 14-16.

Mrs. George Heister

313

BUCHE de NOEL (YULE LOG)

6 eggs
1 cup sugar
1 tsp. vanilla

1 cup sifted cake flour
½ cup butter, melted

Mocha Filling:
¾ cup unsalted sweet butter
¾ cup sifted powdered sugar
2 egg yolks, beaten

1 Tbsp. hot water
1 tsp. instant coffee

Chocolate Glaze:
2 (1 oz.) squares unsweetened
    chocolate
2 (1 oz.) squares semisweet
    chocolate

2 tsp. honey
4 Tbsp. butter

Combine eggs and sugar in large pan over hot, not boiling water. (Regular double boiler is too small as mixture will triple in bulk.) Beat with electric mixer for 15 minutes. Remove from heat; stir in vanilla. Sift the flour a little at a time, over the egg mixture and fold in carefully with a rubber spatula. Add cooled, melted butter and mix well. Pour into teflon (or buttered and wax paper lined) 15x10x1 inch pan. Bake at 350° for 15 minutes. Immediately turn out onto damp towel. Cool 10 minutes; lift off pan. Sprinkle top with powdered sugar. Trim crusts from edges; from 10 inch side roll up towel and warm cake as for jelly roll. Cool for 30 minutes.

To make filling, cream butter and gradually beat in sugar until smooth. Beat in egg yolks. Dissolve coffee in hot water; add to mixture. Unroll cake; spread with filling almost to edges. Roll again. Refrigerate covered for several hours.

To make glaze, melt chocolate over hot, not boiling, water. Add honey and butter, stirring until butter melts. Beat until cool and thickened, about 20-30 minutes. Place log on serving platter; slip wax paper pieces around cake to catch drip from glaze. Pour glaze evenly over cake (except ends). Slice off ends so filling shows; remove wax paper. Run tines of fork down length of log to simulate bark. Decorate with real holly. Cover and refrigerate until an hour before serving. Keeps well for a week in refrigerator. Yields one 10-inch log.

Mrs. Edward E. Brown

Cake may be filled with 1 cup whipping cream, whipped (will not keep as long.)

Mrs. Ruby McClinton
Pine Bluff Country Club

CHEESECAKE

Crust:
2½ cups graham cracker   *½ cup butter, softened*
   crumbs

Mix crumbs and butter together; pat into a greased 10-inch spring form pan.

Filling:
3 (8 oz.) pkgs. cream cheese,   *4 eggs*
   softened   *2 tsp. vanilla*
1 cup sugar

Beat cheese in mixer until creamy. Beat together eggs, sugar and vanilla; add to cheese and mix until well-blended. Pour into crust and bake at 325° for 45 minutes. Remove from oven and cool 30 minutes. Combine the following and spread on top:

2 (8 oz.) cartons sour cream   *2 tsp. vanilla*
2 Tbsp. sugar

Bake at 325° for 15 minutes. Cool and refrigerate. When completely cold, top with your favorite pie filling or the following:

Topping: (optional)
2 cans blueberries, drained   *1 Tbsp. lemon juice*
¾ cup blueberry juice   *2½ Tbsp. cornstarch*
¼ cup sugar

Mix together sugar, cornstarch and lemon juice slowly adding blueberry juice. Cook over medium heat until very thick. Add berries and cook 2 more minutes. Cool and pour over cheesecake. Refrigerate until serving time; then remove sides of pan.
Serves 16.

Mrs. Kenneth Baim

SEVEN-UP POUND CAKE

½ cup shortening   *1 (7 oz.) 7-Up*
1 cup butter   *1 tsp. almond extract*
3 cups sugar   *2 tsp. vanilla*
5 eggs   *1 tsp. lemon juice*
3 cups flour

Cream shortening, butter and sugar. Add eggs, one at a time, beating after each addition. Add flour and 7-Up alternately. Add flavorings and mix well. Bake in a greased and floured tube or Bundt pan at 325° for 1 hour and 15 minutes. Test for doneness. Cool in pan for 15 minutes before removing to serving plate.
Serves 12-14.

Mrs. Homer Eskue

AUNT LUCY'S FRESH COCONUT CAKE

1 coconut
¾ cup shortening
1 cup sugar
4 medium eggs, separated
½ tsp. vanilla
¼ cup fresh coconut

2¼ cups sifted cake flour
2¼ tsp. baking powder
½ tsp. salt
¾ cup coconut milk
½ cup sugar

Preparation of coconut: Pierce 3 holes in coconut; drain out milk and save. Heat coconut in 350° oven 30 minutes; cool. Break shell and chisel out meat. Peel off the brown skin with a potato peeler. Cut white meat in one inch pieces and grate on medium size grater or in blender.

Cream together shortening and sugar. Add well-beaten egg yolks and vanilla, beat well. Mix in grated coconut. Sift together cake flour, baking powder and salt. Add milk to coconut milk to make ¾ cup if necessary. Add dry ingredients alternately with milk. Beat egg whites until peaks are formed; gradually beat in ½ cup sugar until whites are stiff. Fold into batter. Bake in 3 greased and floured 9-inch layer pans at 350° for 25-30 minutes or until done.

Icing:
1 cup sugar
1/3 cup water
1/3 tsp. cream of tartar

2 egg whites
1½ tsp. vanilla
Fresh grated coconut

Boil first 3 ingredients in saucepan until 242° is reached on a candy thermometer. Keep pan covered first 3 minutes. Beat egg whites until very stiff. Pour hot syrup very slowly into egg whites, beating constantly. Add vanilla. Frost between layers, top and sides of cooled cake, sprinkling with as much coconut as desired.
Serves 14-16.

Mrs. Joe Holmes

QUICK AND EASY COCONUT CAKE

1 box Duncan Hines Golden
   Butter Cake Mix
2 (6 oz.) pkgs. frozen coconut

1½ cups sugar
1 (8 oz.) carton sour cream

Mix cake according to package directions; bake three layers instead of two. Mix thawed coconut with sugar and sour cream. Ice between layers, top and sides of cooled cake. Refrigerate until serving; may be made a day before.
Serves 12-14.

Mrs. Ruby McClinton
Pine Bluff Country Club

ORANGE DATE CAKE

1 cup butter
2 cups sugar
4 eggs
2 Tbsp. grated orange rind
1 tsp. soda

½ cup buttermilk
3½ cups flour
1 (8 oz.) pkg. chopped dates
1 cup chopped nuts

Glaze:
2 cups powdered sugar
1 cup orange juice

2 Tbsp. grated orange rind

Cream butter and sugar; add eggs one at a time; beat well. Add orange rind. Dissolve soda in milk. Mix ½ cup flour with dates and nuts. Add remaining flour alternately with milk to batter; mix well. Add floured dates and nuts. Pour into a well-greased tube pan. Bake at 275° for 2 hours. Test for doneness. Cool in pan for 10-15 minutes. Turn out onto cake plate; punch holes in top. Combine glaze ingredients and spoon over warm cake. Serves 12-14.

Mrs. Cecil Allison

DATE NUT LOAF CAKE

2 cups butter
2½ cups sugar
4 eggs, separated
2 tsp. lemon extract

4 cups flour
2 (8 oz.) pkgs. chopped
dates
1 lb. chopped nuts

Melt butter; add sugar and mix well. Beat egg yolks with lemon extract; add to butter mixture. Beat in 3 cups flour; mix remaining flour with dates and pecans; then add to batter. Fold in stiffly beaten egg whites. Bake in two greased and floured loaf pans at 300° for 2½ hours or until done.

Mrs. T. Walker Lewis, Jr.

CHRISTMAS LOAF

1 cup butter
2 cups sugar
6 eggs

2 cups flour, unsifted
1 lb. candied cherries
1 lb. pecans, chopped

Cream butter and sugar. Add eggs one at a time, beating well after each. Measure flour unsifted, reserve ½ cup and mix with cherries and nuts. Sift remaining flour into egg-butter mixture; beat well. Add floured cherries and nuts. Bake in a greased and floured loaf pan at 325° for 60-75 minutes or in two small loaf pans for 45-55 minutes. Test for doneness.

Mrs. Walter A. Simpson

Quick and easy—nice baked in very small loaf pans for Christmas gifts.

ORANGE SLICE CAKE

3½ cups flour
½ tsp. salt
1 cup butter
2 cups sugar
4 eggs
1 tsp. soda
½ cup buttermilk

1 lb. candied orange slices,
  cut up
1 (8 oz.) pkg. chopped dates
2 cups walnuts, chopped
1 cup coconut
1 cup orange juice
2 cups powdered sugar

Sift flour and salt together. Cream butter and sugar well. Add eggs, flour mixture, soda and buttermilk; mix well. Fold in orange slices, dates, walnuts and coconut. Bake in a greased and floured tube pan at 300° for 1¾ to 2 hours. Mix together the juice and sugar. Pour over hot cake. Cool cake in pan for 20 minutes; turn out onto cake plate. *Serves 16-20.*

Mrs. Bill Holland
Hanover, New Hampshire

Very good served during the holidays as a fruit cake.

DELMONICO NUT CAKE

½ cup butter
½ cup shortening
2 cups sugar
5 eggs, separated
1 tsp. vanilla

2 cups flour
1 tsp. soda
1 cup buttermilk
1 cup coconut
1 cup pecans or walnuts

Cream butter, shortening and sugar. Beat in egg yolks and vanilla. Add flour mixed with soda alternately with buttermilk. Fold in coconut and chopped nuts; then fold in stiffly beaten egg whites. Bake in a greased and floured Bundt pan at 350° for 50-60 minutes or until done.

Icing:
1 (8 oz.) pkg. cream cheese
¼ cup butter

¾ (1 lb.) box powdered sugar
1 cup pecans or walnuts

Allow butter and cream cheese to soften. Cream with powdered sugar and add nuts. Spread on cooled cake.
Serves 14-16.

Mrs. Mark A. Shelton, III

PLUM FUN CAKE

1½ cups flour
1 cup sugar
1 tsp. soda
1 tsp. baking powder
½ tsp. salt
½ cup cold water
½ cup chopped walnuts

1/3 cup seedless raisins
1/3 cup oil
1 Tbsp. vinegar
1 tsp. vanilla
1 egg
1 (4¾ oz.) jar baby-food strained
  plums (reserve 1 Tbsp.)

In a 9-inch square pan, combine flour, sugar, soda, baking powder and salt. Add remaining ingredients; stir vigorously until well mixed. Bake at 350° for 30-35 minutes.

Icing:
1 Tbsp. reserved plums
2 cups powdered sugar
¼ cup butter, softened

½ tsp. vanilla
Dash of salt

Combine icing ingredients; beat until icing is at a spreading consistency. If necessary, thin with a few drops of water. Frost cooled cake while still in pan.
Serves 9.

Mrs. Donald Faust

MIAMI BIRTHDAY CAKE

1 (6 oz.) pkg. semisweet
  chocolate pieces
½ cup graham cracker crumbs
1/3 cup butter, melted
½ cup nuts
2 cups flour
1 tsp. soda
1 tsp. salt

½ cup butter
1½ cups sugar
2 eggs
2 tsp. vanilla
1¼ cups buttermilk
2 cups whipping cream
2 Tbsp. sugar

Melt 1/3 cup of the chocolate chips; set aside. Combine graham cracker crumbs and melted butter; add finely chopped nuts and remaining unmelted chocolate chips. Set mixture aside. Combine flour, soda and salt. Cream ½ cup butter, gradually adding 1½ cups sugar. Add eggs one at a time, beating well after each. Blend in melted chocolate and vanilla. Add flour mixture alternately with buttermilk, beginning and ending with dry ingredients. Pour into 2 greased and floured 9-inch cake pans. Sprinkle with crumb mixture. Bake at 375° for 30-40 minutes. Cool. Whip the cream with the 2 Tbsp. sugar. Use to frost between layers, sides and top of cake. Refrigerate until ready to serve.
Serves 14-16.

Mrs. Martha Velvin

LEMON CAKE

¾ cup butter
1½ cups sugar
1 tsp. vanilla
3 eggs

3 cups sifted cake flour
3 tsp. baking powder
1¼ cups milk

Cream butter, sugar and vanilla. Add eggs one at a time, beating well after each. Sift together flour and baking powder. Add to egg mixture in four parts alternately with milk. Begin and end with flour; stir only until smooth. Bake in 3 buttered 9-inch cake pans at 350° for 20-25 minutes. Cool completely.

Lemon Filling:
1 Tbsp. grated lemon rind
½ cup lemon juice
1 1/3 cups sugar

½ cup butter
3 eggs, slightly beaten

In a sauce pan over low heat combine first 4 ingredients. Stir well; slowly pour in beaten eggs. Turn heat to medium; stir constantly until mixture is thickened. Do not boil; cover and chill.

Place one cake layer on serving plate. Spread with ½ cup of Lemon Filling. Repeat with second layer. Add third layer and frost with a mixture of the following:

1½ cups whipping cream
1/3 cup powdered sugar

Remaining Lemon Filling

Whip cream until almost stiff; add sugar and beat until stiff. Fold in remaining filling. Frost top and sides of cake. Cake will keep several days in refrigerator.
Serves 14-16.

Mrs. Howard J. Wiechern, Jr.

Makes a beautiful birthday cake.

ISLANDER'S CAKE

3 cups flour
2 cups sugar
1 tsp. soda
1 tsp. salt
1 tsp. cinnamon
3 eggs, slightly beaten

1½ cups butter flavored oil
1 (8 oz.) can crushed
    pineapple, drained
2 cups mashed bananas
1 tsp. vanilla
1 cup chopped nuts

Mix all dry ingredients in a large bowl. Make well in center and add remaining ingredients. Stir; do not beat. Bake in a greased and floured tube pan at 350° for 1 hour and 15 minutes. Test for doneness.
Serves 12-14.

Mrs. Stanley McNulty, Jr.

CHOCOLATE POUND CAKE

1 cup butter
2 cups sugar
4 eggs
3 cups cake flour
½ tsp. soda

1 tsp. salt
1 cup buttermilk
1 (4 oz.) pkg. German's Sweet
   Chocolate

Cream butter and sugar. Add eggs one at a time, beating well after each. Sift together flour, soda and salt. Add to butter mixture alternately with buttermilk. Melt chocolate and add to batter. Beat until fluffy, almost like whipped cream. Bake in a greased and floured tube pan at 300° for 1 hour and 30 minutes or until done.
Serves 12-14.

                                                   Mrs. Kenneth Baim

GEORGE WASHINGTON GINGERBREAD

2¼ cups flour
1½ tsp. ginger
1½ tsp. cinnamon
½ tsp. cloves
½ tsp. nutmeg
½ tsp. salt
2 tsp. baking powder

2 eggs
¾ cup brown sugar, packed
¾ cup molasses
¾ cup oil
½ tsp. soda
1 cup boiling water

Sift first seven ingredients together. Beat eggs; add sugar, molasses and oil; mix until creamy. Add flour mixture and cream well. Last, dissolve soda in boiling water and stir into mixture. Bake in a greased and floured 9x13x2 inch pan at 350° for 35 minutes. Cool; cut in squares and serve with Lemon Sauce (See Index).
Serves 20.

                                         Mrs. Walter M. Simpson

BITTERSWEET ICING FOR POUND CAKE

½ cup milk
3½ cups marshmallows
1 Tbsp. strong coffee

1 (12 oz.) pkg. chocolate chips
1 cup heavy cream, whipped
1 Sara Lee Pound Cake

Combine first 4 ingredients in double boiler and cook until marshmallows are melted. Cool; fold in whipped cream. Slice pound cake into 4 layers. Ice between layers, top and sides of cake. Refrigerate until serving time.
Serves 6-8.

                                       Mrs. C. Fletcher Welch, Jr.

Quick, easy and delicious!

MARBLE CAKE

1 cup butter
2 cups sugar
3 eggs
3 cups flour
2 tsp. baking powder

½ tsp. salt
1 cup milk
1½ tsp. vanilla
¾ cup chocolate syrup
¼ tsp. soda

Cream butter and sugar. Add eggs one at a time, beating well after each. Add dry ingredients, which have been sifted together, alternately with milk and vanilla. Pour 2/3 of batter into a greased and floured tube pan. Mix remaining batter with syrup and soda. Add to top of batter in tube pan; *do not mix*. Bake at 350° for 1 hour or until done. Cool 30 minutes before removing from the pan. Dust with powdered sugar.
Serves 14-16.

Mrs. Kenneth Baim

PINEAPPLE UPSIDE-DOWN CAKE

4 eggs
1 cup sugar
1 cup flour
1 tsp. baking powder
1 tsp. vanilla

¼ tsp. salt
1 cup brown sugar
½ cup butter
6-8 canned pineapple slices
Maraschino cherries

Beat eggs until frothy; add sugar and mix well. Add flour, baking powder, vanilla, and salt; beat well and set aside. In a 10-inch iron skillet, melt brown sugar and butter, stirring constantly. Arrange pineapple slices in the brown sugar mixture, putting a cherry in the center of each slice and between slices. Pour cake batter carefully over pineapple. Bake at 350° for 35 minutes or until cake tests done. Cool 15-20 minutes; turn out onto cake plate. Cut into wedges and top with whipped cream.
Serves 6-8.

Mrs. Ernest A. Hercher

POPPY SEED BUNDT CAKE

1 box yellow cake mix
4 eggs
1 cup water
½ cup oil

¼ cup poppy seeds
1 small box vanilla instant
  pudding
2 Tbsp. lemon juice

Glaze:
1 cup powdered sugar

3 Tbsp. lemon juice

Beat cake ingredients in an electric mixer until well-blended and batter is smooth. Pour into well greased 10-inch Bundt pan and bake at 350° for 40-45 minutes. Cool in pan for 10 minutes, then turn out onto serving plate. Blend sugar and lemon juice until smooth. Brush on warm cake.
Serves 12-14.

Mrs. Hubert Eisenkramer

GRAND MARNIER SPONGE CAKE

6 eggs, separated
½ tsp. cream of tartar
1 cup sugar
1 tsp. vanilla
1 cup sifted cake flour or 1 cup
    less 2 Tbsp. regular flour
1 tsp. baking powder
3 oranges

1 lemon
1 oz. Grand Marnier
1 Tbsp. sugar
1 cup whipping cream, whipped
3 Tbsp. powdered sugar
½ oz. semi-sweet chocolate
Grated rind of 1 orange

Beat egg whites with cream of tartar until peaks form. Add sugar slowly and beat until stiff. Beat yolks and vanilla until thick and pale yellow. Add 1/3 of whites to yolk mixture, mixing gently and thoroughly. Add flour and baking powder to yolk mixture; carefully fold yolk mixture into remaining whites. Grease a 9-inch spring form pan and line with wax paper. Pour batter into pan and bake at 300° for 40-50 minutes.

Squeeze oranges and lemon. Measure 7 ounces of combined strained juices; add Grand Marnier. When cake is done, turn upside down to cool, removing wax paper. Poke holes in cake and pour juice mixture over cake until all is absorbed. Sprinkle with 1 tablespoon of sugar. Refrigerate overnight. Mix whipped cream and powdered sugar and ice cake. Decorate with orange slices, shaved chocolate, and grated rind.
Serves 16.

Mrs. Robin M. Rousseau
Little Rock, Arkansas

STRAWBERRY MERINGUE CAKE

1 box yellow cake mix
4 eggs, separated
1 1/3 cup orange juice
¼ tsp. cream of tartar

1 cup sugar
1 cup whipping cream, whipped
¼ cup sugar
½ cup chopped strawberries

Blend cake mix, egg yolks and orange juice. Beat well and pour into two greased and floured 9-inch cake pans. Beat egg whites and tartar to soft peaks; gradually add 1 cup sugar and beat until stiff peaks are formed. Spoon over unbaked yellow cake mix. Bake at 350° for 35 minutes. Cool; turn out on rack and flip over to plate. Mix whipped cream, sugar and strawberries; spread between layers and on top of cake. Decorate with whole strawberries. Make and use on same day. Keep in refrigerator.
Serves 12.

Mrs. Leonard Dunn

APRICOT BARS

Crust:
½ cup butter
¼ cup sugar

1 cup flour

Filling:
1 (8 oz.) pkg. dried
 apricots
2 eggs, beaten
1 cup light brown
 sugar, packed

1/3 cup flour
½ tsp. baking powder
¼ tsp. salt
½ tsp. vanilla
½ cup chopped nuts

Blend crust ingredients until crumbly. Pack into greased 9-inch square pan. Bake at 350° for 15 minutes. In covered saucepan simmer dried apricots in water to cover for 15 minutes; drain and chop. Combine filling ingredients; beat until well mixed. Pour over crust and bake 30 minutes longer. Cool; dust with powdered sugar and cut into squares.
Yields 16 squares.

Mrs. John E. Caruthers, Sr.

BROWNIES

1 cup melted butter
2 cups sugar
4 eggs
½ cup cocoa

1½ cups flour
½ tsp. salt
3 tsp. vanilla
1½ cups chopped pecans

Mix butter and sugar; beat in eggs. Add cocoa, flour, salt and vanilla; mix well. Stir in nuts. Bake in a greased 8x11 inch pan at 325° for 30-35 minutes. Cool; then cut into squares.
Yields 20 squares.

Mrs. William A. Roberts

PATRICIA'S BLONDE BROWNIES

1 cup butter
2 cups flour
2 cups light brown
 sugar, packed
1 tsp. soda

2 eggs
2 tsp. vanilla
1 (12 oz.) pkg. semisweet
 chocolate pieces
1 cup chopped pecans

Mix well butter, flour, sugar and soda. Beat in eggs; add vanilla. Stir in chocolate chips and nuts. Bake in a well-greased 9x13x2 inch pan at 350° for 25-30 minutes. Cool and cut into squares.
Yields 24 squares.

Mrs. Joe E. Cook

TRULIE'S BROWNIE CUPCAKES

1¾ cups sugar
1 cup flour
4 eggs
1 cup butter

4 (1 oz.) squares semisweet
chocolate
1 cup chopped pecans
1 tsp. vanilla

Combine sugar, flour and eggs; blend, do not beat. Melt butter and chocolate in a saucepan; add nuts and stir. Combine two mixtures; add vanilla. Blend only to mix well. Pour into 24 paper-lined muffin tins. Bake at 325° for 25-30 minutes.
Yields 24 cupcakes.

Mrs. Ross Sanders

CHEESE SQUARES

Crust:
1 cup graham cracker
crumbs

¼ cup melted butter
½ cup chopped pecans

Filling:
1 (8 oz.) pkg. cream cheese
1 (8 oz.) carton cottage
cheese
3 eggs

1 cup sugar
1 tsp. vanilla
1 Tbsp. lemon juice

Mix ingredients for crust and press into bottom of a greased 8x11 inch pan, reserving a small amount of crumbs for topping. Cream cheeses; beat in eggs one at a time. Add sugar gradually, then flavorings. Pour over graham cracker crust. Sprinkle remaining crumbs on top. Bake at 350° for 45 minutes. Cut while warm.
Yields 24 small squares.

Mrs. Jerome Shainberg

DESSERT BARS

1 box yellow cake mix
1 cup brown sugar
½ cup butter
2 eggs

2 tsp. vanilla
1 (6 oz.) pkg. semisweet
chocolate pieces
¾ cup chopped pecans

Mix all ingredients except chocolate chips and nuts. Beat well. Pour into greased 9x13x2 inch pan. Sprinkle chocolate pieces and pecans on top. Bake at 350° for 25 minutes. These are chewy and may not look done but are. Cool and cut into bars.
Yields about 24 bars.

Mrs. Leonard Dunn

DREAM BARS

½ cup sifted cake flour
½ cup light brown sugar
½ cup butter
2 eggs, beaten
1 cup light brown sugar
1 tsp. vanilla

2 Tbsp. flour
½ tsp. baking powder
¼ tsp. salt
1½ cups coconut
1 cup pecans, ground

Mix flour, ½ cup brown sugar and butter until crumbly. Pat into 10x16 inch pan. Bake at 375° for 10 minutes. Combine eggs and 1 cup brown sugar; mix in remaining ingredients. Spread on crust and bake at 375° for 20 minutes. Cool slightly; cut into squares.
Yields 24 squares.

Mrs. Richard Taylor
Camden, Arkansas

LAYERED SURPRISES

First Layer:
½ cup oleo
½ cup shortening
½ cup granulated sugar
½ cup brown sugar
2 egg yolks

1 tsp. vanilla
2 cups sifted flour
¼ tsp. salt
1½ tsp. baking powder

Second Layer:
1 (6 oz.) pkg. semisweet
   chocolate pieces

4 Tbsp. water

Third Layer:
4 egg whites

1 cup brown sugar, packed

Cream oleo and shortening; gradually add sugars, mixing well. Add egg yolks and vanilla. Mix in dry ingredients which have been sifted together. Spread this over bottom of 9x13 inch pan. For second layer, melt chocolate pieces in water in double boiler. Stir and spread over first layer. For third layer, beat egg whites almost stiff; gradually add brown sugar, beating until stiff. Spread over chocolate layer. Bake at 325° for 25-30 minutes. Cool and cut into squares.
Yields 24 squares.

Mrs. Charles Slater

PECAN SLICES

Crust:
1 cup flour   ½ cup butter, softened

Filling:
2 eggs   2 Tbsp. flour
1½ cups brown sugar   ¼ tsp. baking powder
¾ cup coconut   ½ tsp. salt
1 cup chopped pecans   1 tsp. vanilla

Icing:
2 Tbsp. butter   3 Tbsp. orange juice
1½ cups powdered sugar   1 Tbsp. lemon juice

Blend crust ingredients until crumbly. Press into 9-inch square pan; bake at 350° for 15 minutes. Beat filling ingredients until well mixed; pour over crust and bake 20 minutes longer; cool. Beat icing ingredients until creamy and spread on top; sprinkle with a few chopped pecans for decoration. Cut into squares.
Yields 16 squares.

Mrs. W. R. Jones

LEMON BARS DELUXE

Crust:
2 cups flour   1 cup butter, softened
½ cup powdered sugar

Filling:
4 eggs, beaten   ¼ cup flour
2 cups sugar   ½ tsp. baking powder
1/3 cup lemon juice

Sift flour and powdered sugar together. Cut in butter until mixture clings together. Press into greased 9x13x2 inch pan. Bake at 350° for 25-30 minutes or until *lightly* browned.

Combine eggs, sugar and lemon juice; beat well. Sift together flour and baking powder; stir into egg mixture. Pour over baked crust. Bake at 350° for 25-30 minutes. Cool; sprinkle with powdered sugar and cut into bars.
Yields 3 dozen.

Mrs. Donald Faust

RIBBON CAKES

1 cup butter
1 tsp. vanilla
1 cup sugar
4 eggs
2 cups flour
1 tsp. salt

1½ cups sour cream
½ cup finely chopped pecans
6 Tbsp. seedless red
 raspberry jam
¼ cup apricot jam

Invert a 15½x10½x1-inch pan; grease and flour the bottom. Cream the butter with the vanilla. Gradually add the sugar, creaming until fluffy. Add the eggs, one at a time, beating well after each addition. Mix in the flour and salt. Spread 1/3 of the batter on the prepared pan. Spread evenly to ½ inch from edges of pan. Bake at 350° about 10 minutes. Remove from oven and carefully cut layer in half crosswise, forming 2 layers; remove carefully to a wire rack to cool. Repeat twice with the remaining batter, making a total of 6 thin layers. Wash, grease, and flour the pan before each baking.

Mix the sour cream and the pecans. Place one cake layer, top side up, on a cutting board. Spread evenly with about ¼ cup of the sour cream mixture. Then spread carefully and evenly with about 2 tablespoons of the raspberry jam. Then add the second cake layer and spread with ¼ cup sour cream mixture and 2 tablespoons of apricot jam. Repeat with remaining layers, leaving the top plain. Place a board on top to compress the layers; cover tightly with plastic wrap and chill overnight.

Butter Cream Icing:
½ cup butter
2 cups powdered sugar,
 unsifted

Dash salt
½ tsp. vanilla
1 Tbsp. milk

Cream butter and sugar with electric mixer. Add salt and vanilla. Add milk only if icing is too thick to spread. Trim crusty edges from cake. Ice top of cake smoothly. Cut into squares.
Yield 32 squares.

Mrs. John G. Lile

This is an exquisite tea-time delicacy, so pretty and unusual!

AGGRESSION COOKIES

1½ cups brown sugar,
   packed
1½ cups butter

3 cups quick oats
1½ tsp. soda
1½ cups flour, sifted

Cream sugar and butter; add remaining ingredients and mix thoroughly. Form dough into small balls; place on ungreased cookie sheets. Butter the bottom of a small glass, dip it in sugar and flatten cookies. Bake at 350° for 10-12 minutes. Cool for a few minutes before removing to paper towels to crispen.
Yields 7 dozen.

Mrs. Martin G. Gilbert

BUTTERSCOTCH OATIES

1 (6 oz.) pkg. butterscotch
   chips
¾ cup butter
2 Tbsp. boiling water
1 tsp. soda

2 cups quick oats
1 cup flour
¾ cup sugar
Dash of salt

Melt chips and butter in pan over low heat; remove from heat. Mix boiling water and soda; add along with remaining ingredients to chip mixture; stir well. Drop by teaspoons on ungreased cookie sheets. Bake at 350° for 10 minutes. Cookies should be very crispy.
Yields 5 dozen.

Mrs. Robert Smith

FROST N' BAKE COOKIES

1 cup butter
1 pkg. coconut almond or
   coconut pecan frosting mix

2 tsp. vanilla
1½ cups flour
¼ tsp. salt

Frosting:
1 (6 oz.) pkg. semisweet
   chocolate pieces
½ cup evaporated milk

¼ tsp. salt
1 tsp. vanilla

Cream butter, frosting mix and vanilla. Add flour and salt; mix well. Shape into one inch balls. Place 1½ inches apart on ungreased cookie sheets; flatten. For frosting, melt chocolate pieces in milk on low heat. Remove from heat; blend in salt and vanilla. Place one teaspoon of frosting on each cookie. Bake at 300° for 15-18 minutes or until lightly browned.
Yields 4½-5 dozen.

Mrs. James F. Townsend, Jr.

CINNAMON BARS

1 cup butter
1 cup sugar
1 egg, separated

2 cups flour
4 tsp. cinnamon
1 cup pecans, chopped fine

Cream butter and sugar. Add egg yolk, then flour sifted with cinnamon. Pat into an ungreased 15x10 inch pan. Pour unbeaten egg white over surface; drain off excess. Sprinkle nuts over top, pressing down lightly. Bake at 325° for 25-30 minutes. Cut into bars while hot. These freeze well. *Yields 3 dozen.*

Mrs. F. Wilson Bynum, Jr.

FORGOTTEN COOKIES

2 egg whites
Pinch of salt
¾ cup sugar
1 tsp. vanilla

1 (6 oz.) pkg. semisweet
chocolate pieces
1 cup chopped pecans

Beat egg whites and salt; add sugar gradually, beating until stiff. Fold in remaining ingredients; stir well. Drop by teaspoons on foil covered cookie sheet. Place in 350° oven and turn oven off. Leave cookies in oven overnight. *Do not open door.*
Yields 3-4 dozen.

Mrs. M. Stanley Cook, Jr.

FRUITCAKE BONBONS

1 (6 oz.) can frozen orange
    juice concentrate, thawed
½ cup molasses
3 cups raisins
2 cups mixed candied
    fruits and peels
½ cup butter
2/3 cup sugar

3 eggs
1¼ cups sifted flour
⅛ tsp. soda
1 tsp. cinnamon
½ tsp. nutmeg
¼ tsp. allspice
¼ tsp. ground cloves
½ cup chopped nuts

Combine orange juice, molasses and raisins; cook over medium heat, stirring occasionally, until mixture comes to a boil. Reduce heat and simmer 5 minutes; remove from heat. Reserve ½ cup of fruit for garnish; stir remainder into orange juice mixture. Cream together butter and sugar; beat in eggs, one at at time. Sift together flour, soda and spices; add to butter mixture; stir well. Add orange juice mixture and nuts; mix well. Place a teaspoon of mixture into paper-lined miniature muffin tins. Top with 1 or 2 pieces of reserved fruit or half a candied cherry. Bake at 350° for 25 minutes (check to be sure they are not overcooked). Cool; prick with a fork and sprinkle with brandy or Cointreau. Store in airtight tins; these will keep well.
Yields 100.

Mrs. John G. Lile

GUMDROP COOKIES

1 cup shortening
1 cup brown sugar
1 cup granulated sugar
2 cups flour
¼ tsp. salt
1 tsp. soda
1 tsp. baking powder
2 eggs, beaten
1 cup coconut
2 cups quick oats
1 cup small gumdrops
1 tsp. vanilla

Cream shortening and sugars. Sift flour, salt, soda and baking powder together. Add to sugar mixture alternately with eggs. Add remaining ingredients. Form into walnut-sized balls; flatten slightly. Bake on greased cookie sheets at 350° for 15-20 minutes or until golden brown. Yields 4-5 dozen.

Mrs. T. C. Masters
Mena, Arkansas

SPICY MOLASSES COOKIES

1 cup butter
1 cup sugar
½ cup molasses
1 tsp. cloves
1 tsp. ginger
1 tsp. cinnamon
½ tsp. vanilla
1 egg
1 tsp. soda
3 cups flour

Cream butter and sugar. Add molasses, spices and vanilla, then egg. Stir soda into 3 tablespoons water and add to batter. Add flour and mix well. Chill overnight. Roll dough very thin; cut with cookie cutter. Bake at 350° for 10-12 minutes or until golden brown. This dough keeps for several days in refrigerator.
Yields 4-5 dozen.

Mrs. Martin G. Gilbert

THUMBPRINT COOKIES

1 cup oleo
1 tsp. almond extract
1 tsp. vanilla
½ cup sugar, heaping
2 cups flour
½ tsp. salt
½ cup finely chopped
  pecans

Icing:
1 cup powdered sugar
2 Tbsp. cocoa
2 Tbsp. hot water
1 tsp. vanilla

Cream the first four ingredients well; gradually mix in flour and salt. Stir in pecans. Roll into balls; make an indentation in center of each with your thumb. Bake on ungreased cookie sheets at 400° for 10-12 minutes. Beat icing ingredients until creamy. Drop a teaspoonful into center of each cookie; let harden. These cookies freeze well.

Mrs. John Turley

JUNIOR SESAME CLUB COOKIES

¾ cup shortening	2 egg yolks, unbeaten
3 Tbsp. boiling water	2 cups flour
1 Tbsp. milk	1/3 cup sugar
1 Tbsp. fresh lemon juice	1 tsp. salt

With a fork mix first four ingredients until all the liquid is absorbed and the mixture stands up in soft peaks. Add egg yolks and beat until mixture is golden. Sift flour, sugar, and salt into bowl with egg mixture and stir rapidly with round-the-bowl strokes, making dough cling together. Knead dough and refrigerate. Working with half of dough, roll out to ¼ inch thickness between sheets of wax paper. Cut into diamond shapes, prick with a fork, and bake on a cookie sheet at 400° for 10-15 minutes. (The secret to working with this dough is keeping it cold.)

Filling:

½ cup sugar	1 egg
4 tsp. flour	¼ cup water
Juice and grated rind of 1 lemon	2 tsp. butter

Blend sugar, flour, egg, lemon rind and juice in double boiler over hot water. Stir in water and butter and cook until very thick. Cool well and put between two cookies.

Icing:

2 cups powdered sugar	1 tsp. vanilla
3 Tbsp. hot water	

Mix together icing ingredients and put a thin layer on top of each cookie. Decorate with slivered almonds.
Yields 1½ dozen.

Mrs. Alfine Jones (Hortense)
Cateress

SUGAR COOKIES

1 cup butter	4 cups flour
1 cup shortening	1 tsp. cream of tartar
1 cup powdered sugar	1 tsp. soda
1 cup granulated sugar	1 tsp. vanilla
2 eggs	

In large bowl cream butter and shortening until fluffy. Slowly add sugars, creaming thoroughly; beat in eggs. Sift together tartar, soda and flour; add to mixture along with vanilla. Chill dough for several hours. Working with ¼ of dough at a time, shape into small balls and place on greased baking sheets. Flatten with glass dipped in sugar. Bake at 350° for 8-10 minutes or until cookies are light colored with a faint brown edge.
Yields 8-10 dozen.

Mrs. Richard A. Dodds

PECAN MERINGUE DROPS

1 egg white	1 Tbsp. flour
1 cup light brown sugar	1 cup chopped pecans
¼ tsp. salt	Pecan halves

In a small bowl, beat egg white until stiff. Slowly beat in sugar, salt and flour. Stir in chopped pecans. Drop by teaspoons on greased cookie sheet. Place pecan half on each cookie. Bake at 300° for 15 minutes. *Yields 5 dozen.*

Mrs. Wilton Steed

PETER PAN COOKIES

1 cup oleo	2 eggs, beaten
½ tsp. salt	1 Tbsp. milk
1 cup peanut butter	2 cups flour
1 cup sugar	1 tsp. soda
1 cup brown sugar, packed	

Combine oleo, salt and peanut butter; mix well. Add sugars gradually and cream. Add eggs and milk; mix well. Add flour and soda. Drop from teaspoon on greased cookie sheet. Press top lightly with a fork to flatten slightly. Bake at 325° for 15-20 minutes. *Yields 5 dozen.*

Mrs. Mark A. Shelton, III

POTATO CHIP COOKIES

1 cup butter	½ cup crushed potato chips
½ cup sugar	½ cup chopped pecans
1 tsp. vanilla	2 cups sifted flour

Cream butter, sugar and vanilla. Add potato chips and pecans. Stir in flour. Form into balls. Put on ungreased cookie sheet; grease bottom of glass, dip it in sugar and use to flatten cookies. Bake at 350° for 10-15 minutes. *Yields 3½ dozen.*

Mrs. Lynne Stout
Lufkin, Texas

MOTHER'S SPRITZ COOKIES

1 cup sugar	2 cups flour
1 cup butter	1 tsp. almond flavoring
1 egg, beaten	

Cream butter and sugar. Blend in beaten egg. Add sifted flour and flavoring; mix well. Put dough through a cookie press. Bake at 400° for 10-15 minutes. *Yields 6 dozen.*

Mrs. James T. McFall

OLD-FASHIONED CUSTARD ICE CREAM

8 eggs, beaten
2 qts. milk
3 heaping cups sugar

2 tsp. vanilla
1 cup whipping cream

Cook first 3 ingredients in the top of a double boiler just until they coat the back of a spoon. (Do not overcook.) Strain mixture into freezer can; cool. Add vanilla and cream; freeze according to freezer directions.

Mrs. John D. Tharp

COFFEE ICE CREAM

2 Tbsp. instant coffee
1½ cups boiling water
2 (14 oz.) cans sweetened, condensed milk

3 cups half-and-half cream
3 cups milk
1 Tbsp. vanilla

Dissolve coffee in boiling water. Mix all ingredients and freeze according to ice cream freezer directions. Wonderful served with Coffee Walnut Sauce (See Index).

Mrs. Thomas F. Stobaugh

APRICOT ICE CREAM

1 (1 lb. 14 oz.) can peeled apricots
Juice of 3 lemons
Juice of 3 oranges
½ - 1 cup sugar

Pinch of salt
4 cups whipping cream
3 egg whites, beaten until stiff

Drain apricots, reserve juice. Purée apricots. Mix apricots, reserved juice, lemon juice, orange juice, sugar and salt. Pour into freezer can. Freeze slightly. Add cream and egg whites; freeze until firm.

Mrs. Harold Seabrook

EASY HOMEMADE FRUIT ICE CREAM

2 (14 oz.) cans sweetened, condensed milk
1 (13 oz.) can Pet Milk

3 cups frozen fruit
Half-and-half cream

Combine both milks, add fruit. Pour into freezer can, fill ¾ full with half-and-half. Freeze until firm.

Dick Falk
Jonesboro, Arkansas

LEMON-ORANGE ICE CREAM

Juice of 12 oranges
Juice of 12 lemons
2 cups sugar

1 (13 oz.) can Pet Milk
Half-and-half cream

Combine juices and sugar; mix well and refrigerate overnight. Add milk to juice mixture, pour into freezer can. Fill freezer can ¾ full with cream; freeze.

Dick Falk
Jonesboro, Arkansas

CREAMY PEACH ICE CREAM

4 cups peaches, mashed
3½ cups sugar
Juice of 2 lemons

2 cups whipping cream
Half-and-half cream

Mix peaches, sugar, lemon juice. Turn into ice cream freezer can. Mix in whipping cream. Fill can ¾ full with half-and-half.

Mrs. William B. Benton
Helena, Arkansas

Variation: For fresh strawberry ice cream, substitute strawberries for peaches, omit lemon juice and decrease sugar.

PEACH ICE CREAM

3 egg whites
2 cups sugar
2/3 cup water

1 qt. sweetened mashed peaches
2 cups whipping cream
Milk

Beat whites until stiff. Boil sugar and water until it forms a thread; pour over egg whites. Fold in peaches and unwhipped cream. Pour into freezer can, fill can ¾ full with milk; freeze.

Mrs. Leonard Dunn

This is heavenly!

BASIC HARD SAUCE

½ cup butter   Pinch of salt
2 cups sifted powdered sugar   1 tsp. vanilla

Cream all ingredients together until light and fluffy. Chill.
Yields 1 cup.

Mrs. John G. Lile

Variation: For Brandy Hard Sauce, beat in 2 or more tablespoons brandy and omit vanilla.

OLD-FASHIONED LEMON SAUCE

½ cup butter   1 egg, well beaten
1 cup sugar   3 Tbsp. lemon juice
¼ cup water   Grated rind of 1 lemon

Combine all ingredients. Cook over medium heat, stirring constantly until boiling. Serve warm. May be refrigerated and reheated.
Yields 1 1/3 cups.

Mrs. John G. Lile

Wonderful over Steamed Ginger Pudding (See Index).

PEACH SAUCE

1 (1 lb.) can cling peach   1 egg yolk
  slices   2 Tbsp. honey
1 cup whipping cream   ¼ tsp. almond extract

Drain peaches *well,* cut into pieces. Whip cream until slightly thickened, beat in egg yolk. Drizzle in honey, continue beating until thick and creamy. Fold in peaches and extract. Chill. Stir well before serving.
Yields 1 quart.

Mrs. John G. Lile

To be served over Steamed Ginger Pudding (See Index).

AUNT MILDRED'S SHERRY SAUCE

½ cup butter   ¼ cup whipping cream
1½ cups powdered sugar   2 Tbsp. sherry

Combine butter, sugar and cream in top of a double boiler until well-blended; add sherry. Serve warm over any plain cake.
Yields 2 cups.

Mrs. James S. Rogers

CHOCOLATE-PEPPERMINT SAUCE

1 (4 oz.) bar German's Sweet
    Chocolate
4-5 sticks (thin, 4-6 inch)
    peppermint candy, crushed

3 Tbsp. water
2 Tbsp. half-and-half cream
Chopped pecans (optional)

Melt chocolate, peppermint and water over very low heat or in double boiler. Remove from heat and add the cream. Add pecans if desired. Serve over vanilla ice cream.
Yields ¾ cup.

Mrs. Frank Surface
Jacksonville, Florida

COFFEE WALNUT SAUCE

1 Tbsp. instant coffee
½ cup water
1½ tsp. cornstarch
½ cup honey

1 Tbsp. brandy
1 tsp. grated orange rind
½ cup chopped walnuts

Combine coffee, water and cornstarch; add honey, brandy and grated orange rind. Cook over medium heat, stirring constantly until the sauce comes to a boil. Reduce heat, simmer 1 minute. Add walnuts. Cool and refrigerate.
Yields 1 cup.

Mrs. James Stobaugh

HOT FUDGE SAUCE

1 cup butter (no substitute)
4½ cups powdered sugar
1 1/3 cups evaporated milk

4 (1 oz.) sqs. unsweetened
    chocolate

Melt butter in double boiler. Add sugar and milk and stir until dissolved. Add chocolate and melt, stirring until smooth. Continue to cook over hot water for 30 minutes *without stirring.* Remove from heat; stir until creamy smooth. May be refrigerated and reheated over boiling water.
Yields 5 cups.

Mrs. John G. Lile

BUTTER CRUNCH CANDY

1 cup butter
1 cup sugar
2 Tbsp. water
1 Tbsp. light corn syrup

1 cup finely chopped pecans
4 (1 oz.) squares semi-sweet
chocolate

In a 2-quart saucepan over low heat, melt butter. Remove from heat; stir in sugar until well blended. Return to heat, stirring until mixture bubbles. Add water and corn syrup. Stirring frequently, cook until mixture reaches 290° on candy thermometer (about 15-20 minutes). Remove from heat; stir in pecans. Pour onto lightly greased marble or cookie sheet. Spread to ¼ inch thickness. When cooled, loosen from sheet with spatula. Melt 2 squares of chocolate over hot water; remove from water; stir well. Spread evenly over crunch; set aside until chocolate is firm. Turn candy over; spread with remaining melted chocolate. When firm, break into pieces. Store in tightly covered container in cool place.

Mrs. Edward M. Brown

DIVINITY

2 cups sugar
½ cup water
½ cup light corn syrup
Pinch of salt

2 egg whites
1 tsp. vanilla
1 cup chopped pecans, toasted
½ cup crystallized cherries

Cook sugar, water, syrup and salt until it forms a very hard ball (250°) in cold water. Beat egg whites stiff. *Slowly* pour half of syrup over egg whites, continuing to beat. Cook remaining syrup to hard crack (280°) stage. Slowly add to egg white mixture, along with vanilla, beating until mixture holds its shape when dropped from a spoon. Add toasted pecans and cherries (if desired). Drop onto wax paper. Store in tins when cool.

Mrs. Sloan Cummins

ROCKY ROAD FUDGE

1 (12 oz.) pkg. semisweet
chocolate pieces
1 (14 oz.) can sweetened
condensed milk

6 oz. miniature
marshmallows
½ cup chopped pecans

In top of double boiler, melt chocolate pieces. Remove from heat; add milk, marshmallows and nuts. Stir to mix; marshmallows will be only partially melted. Put in buttered pan; cool, refrigerate, and cut in squares.

Mrs. Robert H. Holmes

BUTTERMILK FUDGE

1 cup buttermilk
1 tsp. soda
4 Tbsp. light corn syrup
2 cups sugar

¼ tsp. salt
¼ cup butter
1 tsp. vanilla
1 cup pecans

Mix buttermilk and soda; set aside for 20 minutes. Mix buttermilk with syrup, sugar and salt; bring to a boil. Add butter; let boil until it forms a soft ball when dropped in cool water. Remove from heat; add vanilla. Cool 30 minutes. Beat until creamy; add pecans and pour in greased pan.

Mrs. Joe Crabb

BURNT CARAMEL FUDGE

2 cups sugar
1/3 cup light corn syrup
¾ cup half and half cream
Pinch salt

½ cup sugar
¼ cup butter
1 tsp. vanilla
2 cups toasted pecans

Bring first four ingredients to a boil in large saucepan. At the same time put ½ cup sugar in heavy skillet to caramelize. Shake skillet to mix sugar to prevent burning. When mixture gets golden brown, pour into first mixture that is boiling. Cook until this reaches a soft ball (240°) stage. Remove from fire ; add butter and vanilla. Let set a minute; then beat until candy holds shape when dropped from a spoon. Add broken pecans. Drop on wax paper; store in tins.

Mrs. Sloan Cummins

CHOCOLATE PEANUT BUTTER CANDY

1½ cups peanut butter
1 (16 oz.) box powdered sugar
1 cup oleo

6 Tbsp. melted paraffin
3 (8 oz.) plain Hersheys

Mix peanut butter, sugar and oleo with mixer; heat in double boiler. Add 3 tablespoons melted paraffin. Stir and remove from heat. Melt Hersheys over water; add 3 tablespoons melted paraffin. Pour half of chocolate into 10-inch glass dish; let harden. Pour cooled peanut butter mixture over; let harden. Add remaining chocolate and refrigerate. Cut into squares.

Marc Oudin, Jr.

MILLIONAIRES

1 (14 oz.) pkg. Kraft caramels
2 Tbsp. evaporated milk
1 cup pecans

1 (6 oz.) pkg. semisweet
  chocolate pieces
¼ block paraffin

Melt caramels and milk in double boiler. Add pecans; mix well. Drop on cookie sheet; cool until set. Melt chocolate pieces and paraffin in double boiler. Dip candies in chocolate, recool.

Mrs. Charles Chadick

SPICED NUTS

1 cup sugar
1 tsp. salt
4 Tbsp. water

½ tsp. cinnamon
2 cups toasted pecan
  halves

Mix and cook sugar, salt, water and cinnamon until it spins a thread when dropped from a spoon (about 242°-244°). Remove from heat; add pecan halves while they are still warm. Toss with fork until nuts are coated. Pour out quickly and separate. Cool and store in tins. These freeze well; thaw to room temperature before using.

Mrs. Sloan Cummins

PEANUT BRITTLE

2 cups raw peanuts
1 cup sugar

1 cup light corn syrup
1½ tsp. soda

Cook peanuts, sugar and syrup to hard crack stage. Add soda and stir briskly; pour into buttered pan but don't spread. Put in cool place until hard; break into pieces. Store in tightly covered tin.

Mrs. Poole Wagoner
Mena, Arkansas

JIFFY PRALINES

1 (3¾ oz.) box butterscotch
  pudding
½ cup brown sugar
1 cup sugar

½ cup evaporated milk
1 Tbsp. butter
1½ cups pecans, broken

Mix first 5 ingredients in a saucepan until boiling, stirring constantly. Cook over low heat to soft ball stage. Add pecans and beat until almost stiff. Spoon onto wax paper.
Makes 14-16.

Mrs. Clarence Roberts, III

METRIC CONVERSION TABLE

Each table of the metric system contains a definite unit. The meter (M.) is the unit of length, the liter (L.) of volume, and the gram (Gm.) of weight. Measurements are made in multiples of 10 or divided by 10.

1 liter (L.)	1000 milliliters (ml.)	
1 meter (M.)	1000 millimeters (mm.)	
1 gram (Gm.)	1000 milligrams (mg.)	
1 Gm.	1 ml.	1 cc (cubic centimeters)
20 drops	1 ml.	
5 ml.	1 teaspoonful	
10 ml.	1 dessert spoonful	
15 ml.	1 tablespoonful	
30 ml.	2 tablespoonfuls	1 fluid ounce
240 ml.	1 cup	8 fluid ounces
480 ml.	1 pint	16 fluid ounces
960 ml.	1 quart	32 fluid ounces
30 Gm.	1 ounce	
454 Gm.	1 pound	
1 kilogram (kg.) (1000 Gm.)		
1 meter (M.)		
1 inch		

COMMON MEASURES

Measure	Equivalent	Measure	Equivalent
1 Tbsp.	3 tsp.	1 cup	½ pint, liquid
2 Tbsp.	1 liquid ounce	2 cups	1 pint
4 Tbsp.	¼ cup	4 cups	1 quart
5 Tbsp. plus 1 tsp.	1/3 cup	2 pints	1 quart
		4 quarts	1 gallon
8 Tbsp.	½ cup	8 quarts	1 peck
12 Tbsp.	¾ cup	4 pecks	1 bushel
16 Tbsp.	1 cup	16 ounces	1 pound
1 cup	8 ounces, liquid		

EQUIVALENTS

5-ounce can almonds	1 cup slivered, toasted
2 bouillon cubes	1 teaspoon beef extract
2 slices bread	1 cup soft bread crumbs
5 slices bread	1 cup fine dry crumbs
¼ pound cheese	1 cup freshly grated cheese
20 square crackers	1 cup cracker crumbs
½ cup whipping cream	1 cup whipped
1 clove fresh garlic	¾ teaspoon garlic salt
1 clove fresh garlic	⅛ teaspoon garlic powder
8-ounce package noodles	3½ cups cooked
13-ounce can evaporated milk	1 2/3 cups
1 pound molasses, honey, sorghum	about 1½ cups
4-ounce can mushrooms	½ pound fresh
2 teaspoons minced onion	1 teaspoon onion salt
3-ounce can pecans	1 cup
1 pound confectioner's sugar	4 cups unsifted
1 cup uncooked long-grained white rice	4 cups cooked

FRESH VEGETABLES

2½ pounds asparagus	4 servings
1½ pounds green beans	4 cups cooked
2½ pounds green lima beans	5 cups cooked
2 pounds broccoli	4 servings
1¼ pounds Brussels sprouts	4 servings
1 pound cabbage	4 cups shredded
1 large carrot	1 cup grated raw carrot
4 medium ears corn	1 cup cut from cob
2-3 pounds peas (crowder, etc.)	2½ cups shelled; 4 servings
3 pounds green peas	4 servings
2 pounds spinach	4 servings
2 pounds yellow squash	4 servings
4 medium or 1 pound tomatoes	2½ cups cooked
2 pounds turnips	6 medium; 4 servings

INDEX

A

ACCOMPANIMENTS, 281-290

APPETIZERS, 7-26

C

D

THE JUNIOR LEAGUE OF PINE BLUFF, INC.

P. O. BOX 1693 • Pine Bluff, AR 71613

Please send me _____ copies of **Southern Accent** at .... $16.95 ea. $ _____
Plus postage and handling at .... $2.50 ea. $ _____
                                                                                    Total $ _____

Name _____

Address _____

City _____ State _____ Zip _____

Method of Payment: Check ☐   Money order ☐   Visa ☐   Master Card ☐
                                                    ☐☐☐☐ ☐☐☐☐ ☐☐☐☐

Expiration Date _____   Signature _____

*Make checks payable to **Southern Accent**.*
24 hour answering machine available: 501-535-5027
Prices subject to change without notification.

THE JUNIOR LEAGUE OF PINE BLUFF, INC.

P. O. BOX 1693 • Pine Bluff, AR 71613

Please send me _____ copies of **Southern Accent** at .... $16.95 ea. $ _____
Plus postage and handling at .... $2.50 ea. $ _____
                                                                                    Total $ _____

Name _____

Address _____

City _____ State _____ Zip _____

Method of Payment: Check ☐   Money order ☐   Visa ☐   Master Card ☐
                                                    ☐☐☐☐ ☐☐☐☐ ☐☐☐☐

Expiration Date _____   Signature _____

*Make checks payable to **Southern Accent**.*
24 hour answering machine available: 501-535-5027
Prices subject to change without notification.

THE JUNIOR LEAGUE OF PINE BLUFF, INC.

P. O. BOX 1693 • Pine Bluff, AR 71613

Please send me _____ copies of **Southern Accent** at .... $16.95 ea. $ _____
Plus postage and handling at .... $2.50 ea. $ _____
                                                                                    Total $ _____

Name _____

Address _____

City _____ State _____ Zip _____

Method of Payment: Check ☐   Money order ☐   Visa ☐   Master Card ☐
                                                    ☐☐☐☐ ☐☐☐☐ ☐☐☐☐

Expiration Date _____   Signature _____

*Make checks payable to **Southern Accent**.*
24 hour answering machine available: 501-535-5027
Prices subject to change without notification.

Names and addresses of bookstores, gift shops, etc. in your area would be appreciated.

_____

_____

_____

_____

_____

_____

_____

Names and addresses of bookstores, gift shops, etc. in your area would be appreciated.

_____

_____

_____

_____

_____

_____

_____

_____

Names and addresses of bookstores, gift shops, etc. in your area would be appreciated.

_____

_____

_____

_____

_____

_____

_____

_____